Also by Catherine Keller

From a Broken Web:
Separation, Sexism, and Self

Apocalypse Now and Then

Catherine Keller

A Feminist

Guide to

the End of

the World

Apocalypse Now and Then

Beacon Press
Boston

Beacon Press
25 Beacon Street
Boston, Massachusetts 02108-2892

Beacon Press books are published under the auspices of
the Unitarian Universalist Association of Congregations.

Grateful acknowledgment is made for permission to quote from the following:

"They say she is veiled," from *The Queen of Wands*, by Judy Grahn, copyright 1982. Reprinted by permission of The Crossing Press.

"Beginners," from *Candles in Babylon* by Denise Levertov, copyright 1982 by Denise Levertov. Reprinted by permission of New Directions Publishing Corp.

Sister Outsider, by Audre Lorde, copyright 1984. Reprinted by permission of The Crossing Press.

"In this Motherless Geography," by Elaine Orr. Reprinted by permission of Elaine Orr.

"IT'S THE END OF THE WORLD AS WE KNOW IT (And I Feel Fine)" by William Berry, Peter Buck, Michael Mills, and Michael Stipe. © 1989 Night Garden Music (BMI). All Rights Administered by Warner-Tamerlane Publishing Corp., BMI. All Rights Reserved. Used by Permission. WARNER BROS. PUBLICATIONS U.S. INC., Miami, FL 33014.

"Natural Resources," from *The Fact of a Doorframe: Poems Selected and New, 1950–1984* by Adrienne Rich, copyright 1984 by Adrienne Rich. Copyright 1975, 1978 by W. W. Norton & Company, Inc. Reprinted by permission of the author and W. W. Norton & Company, Inc.

"Turning," from *Time's Power: Poems 1985–1988* by Adrienne Rich, copyright 1989 by Adrienne Rich. Reprinted by permission of the author and W. W. Norton & Company, Inc.

"Now I Become Myself," from *Collected Poems 1930–1993* by May Sarton, copyright 1993, 1988, 1984, 1980, 1974 by May Sarton. Reprinted by permission of W. W. Norton & Company, Inc.

01 00 99 98 97 96   8 7 6 5 4 3 2 1

Text design by Elizabeth Elsas
Composition by Wilsted & Taylor

Library of Congress Cataloging-in-Publication Data

Keller, Catherine, 1953–
    Apocalypse now and then : a feminist guide to the end of the world / Catherine Keller
       p. cm.
    Includes bibliographical references (p.   ) and index.
    ISBN 0-8070-6778-4
       1. End of the world.   2. Millennialism.   3. Apocalyptic literature.
    4. Civilization, Modern–20th century.   5. Feminist theory.   I. Title.
    BL501.K45   1996
    291.2′3–dc20   96-13478

For John B. Cobb, Jr.,

guide to a world without end

Contents

Preface

A guide to the end of the world? Who would want to go *there*?

It is the contention of this book that you don't have to. We are already there, *in apocalypse*–in its narrative, its aftermath, its compulsion, its hope. So how approach "The End"? A growing (still, at millennium's end) pile of books warns of ecological, economic, or (once again) thermonuclear Armageddon if we do not, against all odds, change our civilizational ways. They influence the present text, but it does not number among them. Nor does it contribute to the rapidly expanding corpus of studies of the (also rapidly proliferating) millennialist and apocalyptic movements of the day, which grasp hold of The End as a great opportunity for their own new beginnings and whose apocalyptic codes are certainly worth investigating as symptoms of the approaching millennial moment: Solar Temple suicides, the Waco conflagration and its anniversaries, the politics of routine Christian fundamentalism, skinheads singing "The Iron Guard of Europe / Has risen from the grave. / They march along as one now. / A New Order they must save."

Secular doomsaying as well as sociological analysis of religious movements tend to place "apocalypse" at a distance from our sense of self, except inasmuch as the material or cultural dangers its adherents pose begin to impinge; then they may instill a sense of threat, and perhaps of guilt, if we do not respond with adequate activism. But I will not examine the construct of apocalypse primarily as an outside force. Neither will I psychoanalyze it. Apocalypse as I wish to "reveal" it constitutes a multidimensional, culture-pervading spectrum of ideological assumptions, group identities, subjective responses, and–perhaps most interesting of all–historical habits.

If apocalypse cannot be situated *within* most people's belief systems, neither does it lie *outside* of our subjectivities: it metabolizes both within us and outside of ourselves. I don't even believe we *can* step outside of it if we want to.

But this is not necessarily "the end of the world" ...

Bear in mind that "it"–apocalypse–did not originally denote cataclysm or end. The Greek word *apokalypsis* means to unveil, to disclose, to reveal: so the title of the last book of the New Testament is traditionally translated as "The Revelation of John." Of course that little book does, as did other Jewish and Christian specimens of its genre, present a vision of the imminent fiery destruction of the known cosmos, political and natural. Out of this purgation would come a radical renewal of the world and salvation for the faithful few–those true to the revelation, of which John's Apocalypse is the culmination.

While I am also not a biblical scholar, I do intimately engage that ancient text and its violently oppositional, occasionally beautiful, always vivid phantasmagoria. In sight of the fragmented, contradictory, and insistent effects of John's Apocalypse on Western history, rereading its tale as part of our own has seemed irresistible. No doubt I am also in its thrall. But the point is then to make our way *within* the topography of apocalypse, within its, within *our* (because whoever reads here, of whatever background, is willy-nilly and to some degree a part of it) two millennia of broken narratives and dauntless hopes.

Certain questions, their tone urgent yet oddly teasing, instigate this exploration. To what extent, for instance, does "the apocalypse script" function as a self-fulfilling prophecy? When and where does our history as a whole–do our own individual and cultural stories in particular–reenact apocalyptic strategies of transformative dissociation: a desire for justice braced with righteous moral dualism; an investiture with sacred meaning of the simple opposition of good and evil, of we and they, of now and then, of male and female?

Furthermore, what would make this book a "feminist" guide? That very term now conjures its own fragmented history of imminent utopias, chimerical unities, and "the end" of patriarchy. But then perhaps feminism is in its own apocalypse.

Would such a claim allow us to scurry off to join those who have been declaring "the end" of feminism more or less since its birth? Only if I were to agree to the bad translation of "apocalypse" as literal "end" could the answer be affirmative. Women's movements, Euroamerican feminism in particular, have prophesied numerous ends and ages behind and before. Julia Kristeva, reflecting on "women's time," early suggested that the immediate future of feminism requires a "de-dramatization of the 'fight to the death' between rival groups and thus between the sexes."[1] Such a de-dramatization, if it does not imply a failure of nerve for needed confrontation, characterizes the spirit of the present work. Even my proclivity in this book to defer sex/gender analysis belongs to the operative strategy: I have wanted to let the feminist construction of gender refract through the lens of apocalypse as one "configural zone" among others—like time and place, community and spirit—rhetorically intersecting and transfiguring them, gaining at once support and relativity from their proximity.

Apocalypse, then, provides a kind of kaleidoscope for cultural self-consideration. This book is offered, nonetheless, as a work of theology, my discipline after all. I won't even make what Derrida called in a different context a "discrete graphic intervention" and join the convention, however tempting, of renaming it "the*a*logy." This project is far too immersed in the effects of a theological assumption, still redolent of senescent patriarchal potencies, upon us all. (And I would not presuppose or systematize a divine femininity, any more than I would exclude its/her self-revelation.) Does this mean I presuppose a "logos of God"? Here I can only suggest that the distinctions of believer and unbeliever, of sacred and secular, of religious and rational, while they serve important polemical purposes, symptomatize the binary habit. So the reader will also find me deferring analysis regarding the discourse of "the spirit," let alone of "God."

Deferral, of course, is the stuff of eschatology—a clumsy nineteenth-century term from systematic theology meaning "teachings about end things" and referring to the larger doctrinal category of which apocalypse is an instance. *Eschatos* originally means either a spatial or a temporal end, or edge. This work, for all its refractions of an already composite gaze, does *take place* within such a spiritual boundary, an edgy and porous one, to be sure, political and self-questioning—a horizon that always recedes again into a "not yet" that "already is," or is nothing at all. That horizon does inscribe hope across the ambiguous density of our relationships. But this book would counter any constructions of hope which would pilot us, in rage or rapture, beyond the complex ground of the present.

"Hope," wrote Lux Xun, a Chinese dissident philosopher of the early twentieth century, "can be neither affirmed nor denied. Hope is like a path in the countryside: originally there was no path—yet, as people are walking all the time in the same spot, a way appears."

Presumably the author of Apocalypse had no difficulty finishing the Book. I did, however, and *this* work, its own end repeatedly deferred, knows a debt to so many that its own boundaries melt, its authorship fragments, its gender blurs. A dense horizon of relations surrounds it, and none who stand there are anonymous to me. But some must be named—never blamed—for their indelible contribution to this *final* draft.

For the weightiest readings, endless thanks to Mary DeShazer and Ben Ramsey. Carol Adams and Rita Nakashima Brock offered invaluable and timely interventions. Charles Strozier, author of a companion *Apocalypse*, accompanied my apocalyptic walk, and Virginia Burrus and Glen Mazis read with indelible care. For significant contributions to what was authored and to the life of its author, I am grateful to Karen McCarthy Brown, Sharon Betcher, Peter Ochs, Heather Murray Elkins, Bill Elkins, and Peter Madsen. Thanks to Steve Young, who labored multiphasically on the manuscript, to Lee Chiaramonte and Suzanne Seger, for the final midwifery, and to my sensitive Beacon editor, Susan Worst, as well as excellent copy editor, Chris Kochansky. *Gracias* to the Salvadorans, especially Marta Benevides, who have permitted me to recycle certain dis/closive moments as story. I remain glad for the polyphonic context of Drew University, both supportive of this long reflective process and distracting from it. And for Jason Starr, who touches this book's end with the sparkle of beginning.

Morristown, New Jersey
January 24, 1996

1. Opening

Dis / closing "The End"

> They say she is veiled
> and a mystery. That is
> one way of looking.
> Another
> is that she is where
> she has always been,
> exactly in place
> and it is we,
> we who are mystified,
> we who are veiled
> and without faces.
>
> *Judy Grahn, "They say she is veiled"*

> It's the end of the world as we know it
> and I feel fine.
>
> *REM, (song title)*

1

Apo-kalypso: to unveil; thus to reveal, to disclose. Prebiblically the term connotes the marital stripping of the veiled virgin. In the biblical text of John's Apocalypse, the title of which is also translated as "The Revelation of John," the moment of truth blinks with cosmic excitement. The revealing gaze is male. At the end, after all the fire and blood, the virgin New Jerusalem descends from heaven, "prepared as a bride adorned for her husband" (Rev. 21:2). John then seals the book shut in a burst of magical curses on anyone who would dare to alter it.

Why reopen such a text? It is my suspicion that we stand—we of the West, Christian or not—even now in an unfinished history of apocalyptic finalities. If this most influential text of disclosure is at the same time the ultimate Western text of closure, we live, arguably, among its effects. For those dwelling in the dregs of modernity, preoccupied by the shutdown of sustainable ecologies, viable communities, and historical hopes, a "coming again" to "The End" may, paradoxically, dis/close an opening.

It has seemed to me, in the light of a generational experience of nuclear threat, ecological deterioration, proliferating "hot" wars abroad and chilling social backlash at home, that as a theologian at least I could offer a meditation on the end of the world. Or more specifically, upon little-considered connections between the ancient text purportedly prophesying the end of the world and my own anxieties about the multiple, converging means of realizing that end. Perhaps, I have wondered, it is not mere coincidence that the last book of the holy book of the Western world envisions a cataclysmic end, given that the West seems in its modernity hell-bent on producing some literal form of that end. Odd, I thought, that Western modernity has espoused an optimistic millennialism of progress while busily facilitating the most demented of ecological or nuclear dooms. I became curious about the nature of the link between the multiple readings of a divinely authored denouement and what one might dub the *man*made apocalypse of the late second millennium C.E. Expectations seek, after all, to realize themselves. So the religious habit of imagining the world out of existence would not seem to be irrelevant to the material habits of world-waste running our civilization; in right-wing religious anti-environmentalism, for instance, the expectancy that Our Father will make us a shiny new world when this one breaks explicitly correlates with a willingness to dump this one. But environmentalists resort to apocalypse as well, predicting premature points of no return or declaring the imminent "end of nature."[1]

2

Here, in brief, is the canonical version. Its author, who calls himself John, composed the narrative in the form of a letter to seven churches in Asia Minor. He describes being lifted in vision into the divine throne room, whence he is then taken on a tour of end things–*ta eschata*. The events are organized around the opening of the scroll of seven seals, once the right reader, the Lamb with the mortal wound, appears. The first four correspond to the four horses of the apocalypse, each signaling global calamity. The tribulations unfold and worsen according to a pattern of sevens, and midway the text shifts to more developed allegories– "seven signs"–among them a birthing woman clothed with the sun, crowned with stars, chased into the wilderness by the red dragon; the imperial whore of Babylon, stripped, burnt, and devoured by her beastly cohorts; the final battle of Armageddon, yielding the victory of the messianic warrior, i.e., Christ's Second Coming, and his thousand-year reign. Then, after a last shakedown and the final resurrection and judgment of the dead, comes the descent of the gem-adorned New Jerusalem, the "healing of the nations," and the end of suffering and death–but for the majority condemned to burn eternally in the pit below.

3

A brief slice of current culture exposes that old narrative, still exercising its public allure. Waiting for a train in the third week of a record-breaking heat wave, I noticed a headline among the cheesier papers: "BIBLE PREDICTS WORST-EVER WEATHER–Scriptures Forecast Dark Days Before World Ends." A "leading Bible expert" then capped his "dark and deadly forecast" with a citation: "In Revelations [*sic*], it is written, '. . . there was lightning and rains and thunder and earthquakes and great hail.'"[2] So instead of nuclear war with the Soviets or with Saddam, bad weather is now God's chosen weapon of doom. Deadly heat will kill thousands, etc. Just a variation on my own ecological fears, I thought, though the *Sun* made no mention of any human responsibility for this weather from hell. Edified by the prophetic perspective on my perspiration, I thumbed through the paper, only to come upon a quite different application of the apocalypse–the pastor of the new First Church of Elvis, Presleyterian, predicting that "Elvis will make his second coming at the end of the millennium."[3] When I read a bit later (in a more up-scale paper) of an academic conference on Elvis, the eschatological language of a literary editor of Elvis short stories seemed to have no less force for being less deliberate. On sabbatical, she visited Moscow just as the Soviet Union was collapsing, and went to see a Russian Elvis impersonator per-

3

form. "His name was Elvis-Stroika," she said. "Suddenly the boundaries of the world and even of time began melting away."[4]

Popular culture offers a cornucopia of apocalypses, usually more bitter than whimsical, but endlessly varied. Let me suggest that all of these variations on the theme of Revelation constitute a kind of cultural *apocalypse script*. On screen, beyond the rich tradition of science fiction (stories of the end of the world cum utopian renewal for the chosen few survivors), *Apocalypse Now* interpreted Vietnam, and *The Terminator* and *Terminator 2: Judgment Day* presented a theology of nuclear war, complete with a second coming of Mary and Jesus figures. Movies like *The Andromeda Strain* and *Breakout* privileged deadly plagues as the means of apocalypse, as did a widely watched TV mini-series called "The Stand," an evangelical allegory about a Christ-figure holding out against a New Age–style Antichrist terrorizing the survivors from his base in Vegas. *Twelve Monkeys* mixed neo-Wellsian sci-fi with a deterministic endtime scenario. The electronic media successfully market the apocalypse script.

The script takes high cultural forms as well. The wildly successful Broadway production of Tony Kushner's *Angels in America: Millennium Approaches* and its sequel, *Perestroika*, subtly but dramatically conjure the themes of final judgment, prophecy, revelation, and the radical transition of ages, in a spirit-charged response to homophobia and the AIDS plague. Kushner thus places himself within a long tradition of dissident apocalypses: the script of ancient prophetic anti-imperialism echoes in contemporary denunciations of injustice.

Performance of the apocalypse script does not restrict itself to theatrical entertainment. It literalizes itself in history, in the self-interpretation of actors, dissident or reactionary, on the scene of crisis. But crisis is routinely available, and the true believer may interpret any crisis in such a way as to radically up the apocalyptic ante. Within the United States much apocalyptic religiosity runs toward the right. No single bit of information more strongly motivated my interest in the effects of the Book of Revelation than the discovery of its influence on U.S. policy in the 1980s. For instance, President Reagan's first Secretary of the Interior, James Watt, a devout Assembly of God fundamentalist, told a committee of the House of Representatives in response to questions about the environment, "I do not know how many generations we can count on before the

Lord returns."[5] His president was also a believing premillennialist. That is, both expected Armageddon, probably in nuclear exchange with "the evil empire," "very soon"–most likely within their own generation. (Perhaps they felt this left very little time for them to see to it that we use up the gifts the Lord had granted to us in our "dominion" over the earth.) Reagan's anticommunist and Near East policies could draw upon the inspiration of scripture, as interpreted by his fundamentalist mother and, later, by friends such as Jerry Falwell. For instance, *New York Times* columnist William Safire reported that Reagan, addressing a group of Jewish leaders, said that "Israel is the only stable democracy we can rely on as a spot where Armageddon could come."[6]

More recently we have witnessed state and antistate gun rites. Armed to the teeth, the government called the bluff on the Waco apocalypse, only to trigger its realization; and a gun cultist immersed in the millennialism of anarchist militia and hate groups memorialized Waco with an anniversary apocalypse of fire, smoke, and blood. And even now the Waco survivors wait in meek grief for the second coming of their messiah and their dead children, abhorring–as would John's own community–the active practice of violence as means to The End.

The Christian end-script has traveled widely in space as well as time. Often still it erupts with heart-rending spontaneity: Standing amidst piles of trampled corpses at the Rwandan border, a resident of Goma exclaimed, "This is the beginning of the final days. This is the apocalypse."[7] What other historic text can deliver an imaginary adequate to absolute doom?

Yet the script contains the germs of history's most vivid hope as well, cultivated in the *utopian apocalypses*, sown worldwide by a colonizing Christianity and often reaped in decolonizing discourses. For instance, in the Philippines an indigenous community called Ciudad Mystica (an allusion to the Virgin Jerusalem) prepares for the coming redemption of the islands from colonialism at the base of a sacred mountain, practicing ecologically sustainable livelihoods. In an intriguing case of gender subversion, God is addressed here as both male and female; and though the group considers itself Catholic, all its priests are women. Its iconography pairs Christ with José Rizal, the national martyr-liberator, and is centered by a vision of a woman crowned with stars–their founder, Maria Bernarda, in the persona of the woman of Revelation 12.[8]

4

The apocalyptic imaginary provides in our time—as in so many times before—a colloquial idiom spectacular enough to bring to the surface the totalizing threat which lurks just beneath mass consciousness. In postmodern parlance, it presents "the unrepresentable." But at the same time it promises to resolve it. If one only accepts the premises of its metanarrative, apocalypse transforms the object of fear into the site of hope. Therefore apocalypticism has always availed itself of a kind of sliding scale of hope: depending upon context and construction, the script allows for either a more pessimistic or a more optimistic apocalypse. The most extreme form of the former, the premillennialism popular among U.S. fundamentalists, focuses upon the tribulations which will descend before Christ comes to rule in the millennium. However, since bornagain Christians will escape these tribulations in "the rapture," the narrative is in fact absolutely optimistic for its own believers, though radically pessimistic as to human historical aspirations. When optimism predominates, we have to do with what is called chiliasm, rendered as millenarianism, millennialism, or post-millennialism, in which the anticipated doom softens into birth pangs, and a gentler sense of progress is seen to serve divine will.

Either of these visions—optimistic or pessimistic—can take sacred or secular form, though of course the progress-millennialism of modernity represents the main example of the secularization of apocalypse in its most blithely sanguine form. Not that I want to overdraw the distinction between faith and culture, theism and atheism, or religion and indifference. With multiple fundamentalisms blossoming globally in response to modernity's betrayal of its promises, the late-modern confidence in the upward March of Progress seems almost as old-fashioned in its arrogance as the theisms it sought to supersede.

Notably, even a theologian of the Nietzschean death of God, Thomas Altizer, could move to the next phase of his own dialectic only by embracing a Blakean apocalypse, "a vision which," according to Altizer, "gave us not only the first imaginative enactment of the death of God, but an apocalyptic death of God."[9] For him, new creation "occurs by way of a uniquely modern apocalyptic enactment of the death of God, an enactment calling forth a final and apocalyptic age or aeon."[10] The Christian apocalypse becomes the metaphor for the late-modern apocalypse of

Christianity, "a genesis which is a new creation, and an absolutely new creation which is the consequence of an apocalyptic ending of an old world or an old totality."[11] But rarely do we encounter on the U.S. cultural horizon such overt espousal of the spirit of the apocalypse myth *as* a myth.

5

Usually the overt uses of apocalyptic rhetoric belong to the work of conservative Christian literalists. We may designate such attempts to return to the *letter* of John's letter as instances of a *retroapocalypse.* These communities understand the text to speak immediately to our own present: when John was speaking about the tribulations, the endtime, the great whore, he meant us, now, two thousand years later. No process of interpretive mediation between contexts is required, because there is no context but the Lord's.

For instance, to take an example from the text itself: "The first angel blew his trumpet, and there came hail and fire, mixed with blood, and they were hurled to the earth; and a third of the earth was burned up, and a third of the trees were burned up, and all green grass was burned up" (Rev. 8:7). If the Bible says there will be bad weather, there will be bad weather, and we brushed above with a literalist reading of such climactic climatic conditions. Any actually accelerating violence of nature near the end of the millennium can certainly be seized upon to lend credence to the reading of the Apocalypse as directly referencing the present moment. At least fundamentalists, unlike the numb consumer mainstream, pay attention to the "signs of the times"!

Without homogenizing Christian biblicists, one may claim that all hold to what Charles Strozier has called endism, the "displacement of the self into a future scenario" in which "God will remake the world in a huge firestorm of destruction."[12] This endism, with its absolute *telos,* can be defined as retroactive in nature precisely because all that is happening and has not yet happened is referred back to a past prophetic moment. It is not that the past is referred to the future, which would imply a feedback loop or a hermeneutical circle in which the present was acknowledged as the site of interpretive production; rather, the future remains centered in the past, to which it is joined as by a line. Nor is this endism a matter of a renewal of the "original" version, for John and his intended audience, while they were certainly "endist" in Strozier's sense, seem if anything to be incapable of either literalist or linear thinking, let alone of reducing the future to a past prediction.

6

But while (incredibly) opinion polls repeatedly suggest that one fourth of the U.S. population believe the Second Coming will occur within their own generation, along with the rapture and other premillennialist trappings of the retroapocalypse, the rest (and maybe many of the one fourth, when they are not being asked the question) participate in another version of the script. This I will call the *cryptoapocalypse*. It drifts in the subliminal margins, not really inaccessible to awareness but unaccountable to it. Neither an object of consciousness nor an ideology with which the subject identifies itself, it charges itself from the indistinct zone of fascination and repulsion Julia Kristeva has designated as the "abject."[13] I am not here concerned so much with the variations of individual psychology as with the psychosocial zone in and of which all selves variously constitute themselves. But the explosive, revolting, and enthralling force of abjection—whose bond to biblical apocalypticism Kristeva herself came to recognize—may help account for the influence of the apocalypse pattern even among those who do not "believe" in it. (We will return to the "abject" a bit later.)

Both the cryptic and the retrograde apocalypses belong to the larger complex. Indeed, they function as interdependent dynamics in what can only be described as a civilizational habit. Like other habits, this one can be addictive or merely repetitive, self-destructive or dangerous to others. It may be more or less conscious. As to scary weather, those in the state of unacknowledged apocalypticism will simply not perceive any possible connection between an old text and the current reality, but they may be inclined to *expect* the burning of the rainforests, for instance. And they may feel some mix of foreboding and inevitability about "the environment," enabling their own numbed complicity in the economic system that is causing the end of the world for so many Amazonian species, and threatening it for innumerable ethnic minorities.

It is this pervasive cryptoapocalypse in which I think we all take part, rather than the obvious external force of fundamentalism, that has motivated the present project. The movement of reactionary religion into positions of mainstream political power evoked in me a typical liberal apocalypticism—that is, I readily demonized the conservative demonizers, endowing them with a terrifying and totalizing power. As I came slowly to grips with my own performances of the apocalypse script, and therefore with its social width, I could then also perceive its historical depth: while the cryptoapocalypse was hardly a possibility in, say, medieval Europe, when apocalyptic images remained in the cultural foreground (indeed on the bas reliefs of every cathedral), it operates at the very core of five hundred years of modernity. Columbus himself will function as the hinge figure in the present project's narrative. Only through these perambulations in time could I perceive the political and the spiritual need for a radically ambiguous and respectfully nuanced approach to the apocalyptic imaginary.

7

By beginning with the foregoing collage of incongruous current apocalypses, I do not mean to promise an archetypal typology of an eternal pattern, or a metanarrative of apocalypse as the essential subtext of Western history. I will not pursue the sociology or psychology of fundamentalism, that quintessential consumer of apocalypse. I will not even offer up patriarchy as the "true cause" of apocalypse—one would have to explain why most patriarchies do not turn apocalyptic. Yet the very incommensurability of these different phenomena hints at the tenacity, the width, and the versatility of the cultural performance of apocalypse. And there is a certain consistency. Whatever their position on the theopolitical spectrum, each of the groups described in the examples above constructs its constituency as actual or potential victims of some sinister power. Each of these groups situates itself within some cultural Babylon of domination, and therefore anticipates the end of that hegemony—of that "world."

Though such apocalyptic representations often take public form, they signal something like what James Scott calls a hidden transcript.[14] Analyzing "the impact of domination on public discourse," Scott shows that there are two different kinds of "subordinate discourse": the "public transcript" of humility and acceptance of subordination in the presence of a dominant, and the "hidden transcript," or that "discourse that takes place 'offstage,' beyond direct observation by powerholders." Not accidentally, his first key example of subordinate discourse comes from a slave narrative of the antebellum U.S. South, in which a black cook named Aggy reacts to the master beating her daughter in the kitchen (*after* he leaves the room) with a classic apocalyptic prophecy: "Thar's a day acoming! White folks blood is arunnin on the ground like a ribber, an de dead's heaped up dat high. . . . Oh Lor! roll on de chariots, an gib the black people rest and peace."[15] Thus did an oral tradition among African Americans internalize the apocalypse narrative of doom for the dominators and hope for the oppressed as its own hidden transcript.

The Book of Revelation, I would suggest, counts in Bible-based cultures as the master script of the hidden transcript. So it will be worth noting that the book itself, with its darkly cryptogrammatic symbolism, already functioned in its own historical *Sitz-im-Leben* and "rhetorical setting" as a countercultural code for dissent. The long story of its outbreaks from secrecy into public forecasting and open defiance–sometimes so stereotyped as to be rendered harmless, sometimes explosive in revelatory ways–will contribute much of the fibre of the present text. Such hiddenness intersects oddly with the cryptic character of the apocalypse pattern when it is unconscious; then it does not need to hide for its own survival, but still carries something of the taint and the mystique of a necessary secrecy. But I presume that within the history of late modernity, power and resistance–as well as public and private discourse–configure themselves in shifting, self-reversing, and unpredictable ways. Cause for alarm and for hope!

I will not re-present the Apocalypse as the canonical text of subversion, though it has certainly served the social revolutions of the West. But I will present its operative ambiguity, capable of both revolution and reaction, and often of combustions of the two. For while it has certainly been a favored tale of underdogs, it also sits enthroned as the culmination of the biblical canon. That is, it is the end piece of the holy book of the newly Christianized Roman Empire. I want to decode the mixed signals this narrative continues to emit from its potent shadows at the edge of canon and culture: even when it serves the crusading master scripts of public Christendom, it tends to hide in those margins.

8

So I am more interested in how these explicit yet secretive apocalypticisms symptomatize a wider matrix of unconscious tendencies, an *apocalypse habit.* That habit manifests itself as the performance of an apocalypse script, which is in most cases written out as a text, disseminated through a complex history of interpretations of that text, and acted out in multifarious secular and subliminal practices. But it would be misleading to grip too firmly to any metaphor or to the fact of the text: before such a text, and massively published through it, one can discern a broader, vaguer *apocalypse pattern.* Let me try to summarize its traits:

This pattern, always adjacent to suffering, rests upon an either/or morality: a proclivity to think and feel in polarities of "good" versus "evil"; to identify with the good and to purge the evil from oneself and one's world once and for all, demanding undivided unity before "the enemy"; to feel that the good is getting victimized by the evil, which is diabolically overpowering; to expect some cataclysmic showdown in which, despite tremendous collateral damage (the destruction of the world as we know it), good must triumph in the near future with the help of some transcendent power and live forever after in a fundamentally new world. Because the pure and permanent state of the desired identity and its community can never be achieved, such scripts are characterized by an explosive futurism. Most often within this pattern, the extremes of innocence and of vice are coded as impersonally feminine, while the active agencies of good and of evil are figured as masculine heroes and their enemies.

All of the above signs of the pattern do not necessarily appear together (for instance, among apocalypse-prone environmentalists there is no assurance of a new creation), and these elements, loosely disseminated through our cultural anxieties, may work with more or less dualism or determinism. I am talking about a habituated and reactive tendency, collectively instilled and readily acted out in individual bursts of self-righteous certainty: we may "do an apocalypse" in our most intimate relations as well as in our most visionary politics.

Let me confess up front that I find the apocalypse pattern neither good nor evil, sometimes very good and sometimes very evil. Resistance to either/or logic in assessing the habit of apocalypse belongs to the present strategy for healing from the habit. For, whatever the anti-imperialist merits of the original metaphors may be, I consider the habit *as a habit* destructive, and perhaps first of all self-destructive.

What about other cultures? If such an apocalypse pattern in fact pervades Western narrative and metanarrative, it may seem so universal as

11

to be trivial, perhaps characterizing some generic structure of narrative itself. But one need only compare it to the myths of indigenous and Asian cultures, or even to Western prebiblical hero myths. Outside of some biblical influence (anthropological "contamination"), it is hard to find stories of single centers of power and virtue dualistically arrayed against the demonic. Think, by contrast, of the amorality of the Olympians and their human heroes, or of the transmoral shape-shifting of Winnebago tricksters. And while other civilizations evince varieties of world cataclysms—of the death and rebirth of cultures and universes such as the myriad world-ends and beginnings of Hinduism, of sequences of ages progressing or downgrading—a dualistic time scheme is so rare outside of missionary influence or Western anthropological projection as to be an exception. While these contrasts extend beyond the responsibility of the present book, they would help bring into focus the distinctness of the apocalypse pattern. But I will limit excavation to sites where direct effects of the apocalypse script can still be reconstructed.

I have wondered whether Revelation voices a darkly lucid and quite valid intuition into "the spiral of violence,"[16] or whether Western civilization has been acting out a self-fulfilling prophecy. And I have come to believe that inasmuch as either or both are true, it behooves us to make conscious the importance of that prophecy, to attend to the multiple facets and functions of that prophecy, to expose its uses in all their contradictions. With the following exegesis both of the Apocalypse and of its effects, I mean to offer a space for such attention, for making public its hidden transcript. (Not that I could "out" all its secrets—many open themselves only to communities which exclude me.) But I will argue that with good historical reason, progressive politics—and even the feminist movement, so antidualistic in its philosophical self-dispositions— has enacted its own apocalypticism. Now that the private tales of women have so massively re-narrated public history, however, we as and for women require self-knowing alternatives to the apocalyptic binarism of much of the feminist metanarrative.

9

We the denizens of Western postmodernity of many possible classes, races, or genders cannot extricate ourselves from apocalypse. We are *in* apocalypse: we are in it as a script that we enact habitually when we find ourselves at an edge, and we are in it as the recipients of the history of social and environmental effects of that script. In other words, apocalypse is both a state of affairs and an interpretation of that state of affairs, which latter is at times compelling because this vision and habit has been predicting and/or shaping such a state of affairs all along. I find I have no choice but to use the term therefore with a systematic ambiguity: sometimes to focus on the script by which reality is being managed, imagined, and narrated, sometimes to stress the blunt horror of the end of a world—genocide, ecocide, some cultural or local omnicide—and sometimes then to stress also the wild hope for a world to come.

Since "world" is always already a term of interpretation and appropriation, a boundary of the knowable as known from a particular perspective, such ambiguity is not surprising. Indeed, for one school of European poststructuralists represented in a volume entitled *Looking Back on the End of the World*, "world" is a totalizing concept, whose "end" is a matter of philosophical good riddance.[17] However, I would have to count their enthusiasm for their own end-of-the-world script as itself a symptom of the peculiarly postmodern apocalypse. For them the end has already come. In Baudrillard's words, "we have already passed it unawares and now find ourselves in the situation of having overextended our own finalities, of having short circuited our own perspectives, and of already being in the hereafter, that is, without horizon and without hope." In the "catastrophe in slow motion," modernity ebbs into its exhaustion, its "post-."[18] The very notion of that "post-," inscribing present significance by definition upon a deferral, a beyond (that is, beyond a life-world in which we would still seem to be citizens), recapitulates inadvertently the not-yet/already of all eschatology—denuded of its utopic optimism, to be sure.

So if the term "apocalypse" indulges in the ensuing text a certain looseness of self-reference, it means to connote always both an interpretive and a material set of collective habits, always some tense coupling of hope and despair—always an end of some world and a corollary vision. But context, proportion, rhetoric, and effects will vary bewilderingly. And, I hope, *revealingly.*

We will trace effects of the apocalypse myth rippling through our history, revolutionary as well as reactionary, political as well as religious, the myth itself perhaps even prejudicing our attempts to dispel its more sinister effects. But it will not be enough merely to observe how the moral dualism "revealed" in Revelation has underwritten Western civilization, or how it ramifies in our social movements, how it pulses in motions of thought and feeling in what Jacques Derrida has delicately named "an apocalyptic tone."[19] Such deconstruction of a pattern that habituates itself readily into metanarrative—into any form of grand, telic history—will itself serve apocalyptic ends if all it does is yield more academic distance: paralyzed by irony, deactivated, we collude with the cruder endtime scenarios of our period. Whatever arcane tales and veiled hermeneutics we may enjoy, the point is after all to struggle against the more obtuse apocalypses—the massive, monstrous, self-literalizing ones like the annihilation of peoples and species. These are processes of relentless termination, bringing down no New Jerusalem. Yet warnings of social, economic, ecological, or nuclear disaster have become so numbingly normal that they do not have the desired effect on most of us, who retreat all the more frantically into private pursuits. Apocalyptic discourse, even or especially in the form of various "anti-apocalypses," has been coming *at* us, and we flee inside ourselves.

I want therefore to poke openings *into* the apocalypse pattern, to enter attentively into the gravitational pull of apocalypse. I want to invite the reader inside with me. Or, more accurately, to consider together how we might find ourselves already inside of it. What might keep us awake to the dimensions of the danger—so gruesomely literal, so massively material, that it can hardly be addressed without recourse to the phantasmagoric? How can we sustain resistance to destruction without expecting to triumph? That is, how can we acknowledge the apocalyptic dimensions of the late-modern situation in which we find ourselves entrenched without either clinging to some millennial hope of steady progress or then flipping, disappointed, back to pessimism? For within the U.S. context, there is a traditional tendency to get active, to get enraged, and then to give up, surrendering to the lull of the comforts and conveniences extracted from the tribulations of the rest of the planet. I do this too. We see ourselves (or perhaps others) as innocent victims, and hope for ultimate vindication, and are soon disillusioned with the prospects. We think that we must "save the earth." Who can carry this? In other words, to the extent that we get uncritically hooked on apocalypse—not merely the situation but the habit—we contribute to it. We wish for messianic solutions and end up doing nothing, for we get locked into a particularly apocalyptic either/or logic—if we can't save the world, then to hell with it. Either salvation or damnation.

10

Would I advocate, then, a kind of anti-apocalypse? Indeed, I have been tempted toward such clarity. But such a stance is quite literally impossible: anti-apocalypse, an apocalypse of apocalypse, turns out to be an oxymoron. Interesting, perhaps, as a strategy of rhetorical disarmament. But as a stance its terms mirror those of apocalypse. It aggressively oversimplifies its "other" in order to judge and supersede it: precisely the apocalypse habit, if in a lower and more sympathetic key.

For instance, in a recent little book neatly named *Antiapocalypse*, Lee Quinby, a feminist postmodern philosopher, identifies "apocalypse" with the urge to unify, to homogenize, to dualize. She argues soundly that even though her book "takes an antiapocalyptic stance," she is "not arguing that feminism must be 'cleansed' of its apocalypticism": "In fact, I am arguing that such a cleansing is not possible—nor is it entirely desirable. To some extent, feminism must meet apocalypse on its own ground in order to be heard. And let's face it—feminist apocalypse is rhetorically powerful and has moved women to social action."[20]

A smart approach, yet Quinby's "anti-" not surprisingly performs the very kind of homogenization she criticizes as apocalyptic. For instance, to show how pervasively apocalyptic the culture is, she uses opinion polls about religious assumptions in the general population. They show that a high percentage of respondents say they believe in the devil, or that "God created man pretty much in his present form at one time within the last ten thousand years," or that God guided evolution.[21] While I agree that the culture is drenched in apocalypse, these polls fail to make the case. The first instance only shows the width of biblical literalism in general, which might or might not take apocalyptic form; the latter two provide evidence only of *some* theological belief system, for "notions of divine origin" may or may not lead to mythologies of the end.

No doubt theological distinctions blur from a traditionally atheist viewpoint; but it is precisely such a leveling of differences which one fears in apocalypse itself. Quinby's book of course does not and need not engage the scriptural tradition itself, and goes on to perform delightful Foucaultian genealogies (for example, on eugenics and blue jeans) in honor of ordinary and ongoing life. She disarms apocalypse by stepping outside the entire religious myth system rather than tapping that text's own deconstructive energies. While I value such a strategy, I remain accountable, in my own project, to the cultural hunger for a spirituality

15

that might actually compete with apocalyptic fundamentalisms on behalf of sustainable and shared life in the present. This means at least taking the biblical text seriously—if only to read there the self-fulfilling
prophecies or the vague psychopolitical intuitions that made themselves
available to endless literalizing fantasies. By contrast, anti-apocalypse
would simply brush off any link, for instance, between ancient halluci-
nations of a world-consuming fire and present ecological deterioration
(seeing the first as a myth of divine wrath, and the latter as largely a factual consequence of human choices), but at least the brush-off would be
conscious and critical. A sharpened anti-apocalypse may remain blind
to its own apocalypse, but it clears the cultural space for the differenti-
ated theological discourse it cannot itself perform.

11

Most academic theologians, indeed most religious leaders affiliated with
oldstream denominations, simply dismiss or ignore the Book of Revelation. If only by default, one would have to list them also among the anti-
apocalypticists.

In his analysis of apocalyptic rhetoric, Stephen O'Leary has argued
for Augustine's "anti-apocalyptic eschatology." Augustine's "comic understanding of prophecy and history," by acknowledging the calamities
of every epoch without a sense of their predetermined tragic necessity,
cautions his "readers to be skeptical in evaluating apocalyptic claims."[22]
Indeed, Augustine wisely counsels a deliteralization of millennialism so
that "when we fall into a panic over present happenings as if they were
the ultimate and extreme of all things, we may not be laughed at by those
who have read of more and worse things in the history of the world."[23] In
other words, the comedy of an ultimately providential outcome supersedes the laughter of scorn at false predictions and delayed parousias.
The theological precaution of anti-apocalypse captured Christian
thought for nearly a thousand years, and its orthodoxy for good. But I will
suggest later that in its *locus classicus*, Augustine's *City of God*, as ever after, anti-apocalypse demonstrates an unacknowledged and therefore irresponsible cathexis to apocalypse.

One may also find a few Christian theological voices reading the
Apocalypse as a prophetic resource for social and ecological accountability today, who therefore differ from the fatalism, the supernaturalism, and the esoteric secrecy associated with the apocalyptic seers, and

who place the text in its own critical context and deploy it as a tool for political struggle within analogous contexts in the present. To these I attribute a *neoapocalypse*.

Liberation theology, as represented by Allan Boesak, Elisabeth Schüssler Fiorenza, and Pablo Richard, includes what must now count as an entire genre of revolutionary, full-volume commentaries on John's Apocalypse.[24] They recognize in John a precursor of their own anti-imperialist, decolonizing projects. We will examine Boesak's contribution in the next chapter; Richard's *Apocalypse: A People's Commentary* does for Latin American Christianity what Boesak did for South African.

In a related vein, Jürgen Moltmann's early *Theology of Hope* was a dramatic renewal of Christian eschatology as centered not in "end things" but in hope: "From first to last, and not merely in the epilogue, Christianity is eschatology, is hope, forward looking and forward moving, and therefore also revolutionizing and transforming the present."[25] We will note the distinction between eschatology and apocalypse shortly. Suffice it to say that the revolutionary elements of Moltmann's work brought him into serious dialogue with liberation theologians. As his Eurocentrically systematic theology has matured, it has become perhaps less prone to neglect the present in favor of the future.[26] But it has persisted in its overt embrace of an apocalyptic historicism. For Moltmann, the "theological adversary" which in the 1930s was the religious and political ideology of "blood and soil," "race and nation," has come to be "the nihilism practiced in our dealings with nature." Thus he can unambiguously deploy the rhetoric of apocalypse: "It is a crisis of life on this planet, a crisis so comprehensive and so irreversible that it can not unjustly be described as apocalyptic. It is not a temporary crisis. It is the beginning of a life and death struggle for creation on this earth." Later, in relation to Christology, he considers Christ's Parousia, the messianic return definitive of Christian apocalyptic imagery, "not a dispensable appendage to the history of Christ." On the contrary (he does not mince teleological words), "it is the goal of that history, for it is its completion."[27]

The passion partially motivating such endist rhetoric is seen in Moltmann's denunciation of the "blasphemous apocalypse" of the nuclear and ecological threats to survival, which during the eighties were so often justified as divine by appeal to the biblical text.[28] Thus he systematically interlinked the symbol of the Resurrection with that of the Parousia as the means of the apocalyptic "new creation." Against literalist notions of the end of the world and the supernatural new creation, he argues that "the eschatological new creation of this creation must surely presuppose *this whole* creation. For something new will not *take* the place of the old; it is *this same 'old'* itself which is going to be created anew."[29] Thus apocalypse allows him to trace the "cosmic meaning" of the resurrection trope, and thus to raise a formidable voice as a biblical ecologist on behalf of "the resurrection of nature."[30] Yet one must ask whether the terms of his confidence in the new creation do not once again fatally, indeed fatalistically, undermine the "struggle for creation." In his reconstruction of the doctrine of Christ's Parousia, he colludes in the eager anticipation of the end not only of unjust destruction but of finitude itself: "For the future of Christ also brings the end of becoming and the end of passing away." How would the end of the temporal evanescence of life, growth, and mortality mean anything but the end of nature?[31]

Anne Primavesi, a British ecofeminist theologian, presents perhaps the "greenest" apocalypse: "Ecology, in its practical approach, faces the present Day of Judgment, Apocalypse now, with faith in a new creation and commitment to the regeneration of life. . . . Apocalypse is not postponed until the end of time, but is a vision of *how things really are* at this moment."[32]

Such neoapocalypticists mobilize the text to preach warning and renewal rather than transcendent doom and closure. Within Christian rhetorical contexts, such a strategy works disclosingly—it *opens apocalypse*. However, its adherents tend to stand by the text and the terms of Revelation unconditionally, in the tradition of Christian apologetics, rather than holding the text accountable for its own effects. They do not link the text to its history of uses and abuses. Thus, eager to enlist the progressive energies of apocalypse across contexts, they open the obtuse ancient symbolism into contemporary solidarity.

John of Patmos used an established prophetic idiom of visionary-political Judaism to criticize the oppressive status quo of his day; he metaphorically addressed the spiral of violence as it gripped the entire known world. But his text was canonized by the very sort of imperial Roman establishment for whose overthrow he provided the symbolic *locus classicus*. Has Revelation been functioning with a strange doubleness ever since?—at once quite accurately "predicting" within the nonlinear and nonliteral discourse of ancient seerdom and later private transcripts "the way things really are" (or were going in history, and perhaps still are) and becoming canonized as a source for the crusading energy by which both the technological utopia and the greens' doom vision of modernity would eventually be fueled?

12

I cannot rest with the unambiguously progressive reading of the neo-apocalypticists, though I respect and indeed depend upon their illumination of John's political sensibility and its ecological and social uses today. To elude the double bind of an anti-apocalypse which must continuously confess its indebtedness to its opposite, and at the same time to disavow any righteous inevitability of The End, I have come to claim the space of a *counter-apocalypse.*

"Counter-" as prefix at once opposes the encounters; it knowingly performs an analog to that which it challenges. A "counter-apocalypse" recognizes itself as a kind of apocalypse; but then it will try to interrupt the habit. It suggests an *apo/calypse*: a broken, distorted text, turned to abusive purposes, only revelatory as it enters a mode of repentance for Constantinian Christendom and its colonial aftermath. If counter-apocalypse reveals anything, it does so in ironic mimesis of the portentous tones of the original—with which it dances as it wrestles. It cannot "unveil" any naked truth, though it may perhaps indulge a translucent fluttering of veils, textures neither transparent nor opaque. To whom? Not to the ogling inner eye of the passive visionary, nor to the gaze of an observer who thinks "him"self outside. Perhaps to a myriad of eyes, twinkling on either side of the veil? We will see more of them.

Counter-apocalypse dis/closes: it would avoid the closure of the world signified by a straightforward apocalypse, and it would avoid the closure of the text signified by an anti-apocalypse. As mediated through the emancipatory discourses of neoapocalypse, which reopen the book, the tradition of the Apocalypse has much to disclose. But the slash through the mystagogic terms of the canonical history of disclosure is drawn in penance for, in interruption of, the history of anti-Jewish, anti-flesh, anti-pagan, anti-female Christian truth claims. This slash, empathizing with the gashes in history opened in the bloody name of The End, is placed in mimicry of the stylus with which John was commanded by the spirit to "write!"

To criticize without merely opposing; to appreciate in irony, not deprecate in purity, our relation to tradition; to situate ourselves in a fluid relation to the text, itself alarmingly mobile between multiple contexts. If, then, counter-apocalypse echoes and parodies apocalypse in order to disarm its polarities, it also savors its intensity, its drive for justice, its courage in the face of impossible odds and losses. Dis/closure signifies a broken consciousness—that to unlock the time and space of apocalypse is to look another way, to reveal the truth told by suffering and to delight in the healing opening not unlike the clearing in the woods of Toni Morrison's novel *Beloved* where broken bodies get spirited and dance.

A counter-apocalyptic reading, in other words, has affinities with both anti-apocalyptic and neoapocalyptic versions. But in a perhaps perverse parody of fundamentalism—whose retroapocalypse it must work not to counter-demonize—it would linger with the link between past text and present history. So, regarding Revelation 8:7 once more, counter-apocalypse would engage the fiery vision of the signifying text and the significance of the contemporary view of burning forests. While it reads John as addressing his own time and not ours, it notices the text nonetheless emanating a certain uncanny applicability. So if counter-apocalypse returns with a certain ambivalent fidelity to the text, it does so only to locate the biblical burnmarks in the present—a curiosity meant to hold attention to the suffering. According to Freud, "the uncanny" emanates from the same source as the obsession to repeat, so perhaps the healing strategy will be to return to the source, to repeat it mournfully, playfully, to gently dislodge the causal links between habituated, tormented expectations and present possibilities.

13

The apocalyptic as a literary genre must be understood as a species of the larger genre of eschatology, the study of "end things"—*ta eschata*, the edge or horizon spatially or temporally. Eschatology in general is distinguished by its indignation in the face of injustice, that is, its prophetic critique of the status quo, its privilege of the future as the horizon of renewal, and its historicizing account of its time. In this, eschatology marks itself off dramatically from the pervasive agrarian narratives of cyclical death and renewal, though it echoes their rhythms. And yet it seems not to originate, strictly speaking, in the biblical tradition.

Eschatology originates in the distinctive context of perhaps the earliest recorded resistance to the imperial mythologies of an eternally hierarchical and oppressive status quo. It was the prophet Zoroaster who as early as 1500 B.C.E. challenged the inevitability of social injustice with a vision of a coming time, *Frashokereti*, the "making wonderful." In a radical transformation of the traditional divine combat myth, the high God Ahura Mazda—made higher by Zoroaster than any single previous deity—would defeat the evil Angra Mainyu and with him the unjust. The dead would be resurrected and loved ones reunited.[33] Here, first constructed on behalf of defenseless seminomads against predatory warlords (who, according to the narrative, would soon be consumed in the final fire), we have the simultaneous origination of *cosmic* and of *moral* dualism.

"Zoroastrian teachings retained their capacity in certain circumstances," according to historian of apocalypse Norman Cohn, "to inspire dissenting individuals or groups to look forward with confidence to the day when the established order would be abolished, the existing authorities exterminated, and they themselves vindicated and exalted."[34] Such "circumstances" would include the experiences of exiled Jews, remembering their formative saga of desert oppression. Adherents of Zoroastrian eschatology seem to have mingled in cities with the descendants of Hebrew herders. Perhaps preferring a narrative of the creation of the biblical sense of history out of the exodus liberation paradigm, biblical scholars have notably underplayed the Zoroastrian influence.

Though apocalyptic elements are apparent in the earliest Zoroastrian sources, "apocalyptic" as a category belongs most accurately to a specific late development of Hebrew eschatology. Martin Buber early clarified the difference. "There are two basic forms of eschatology: the prophetic, which at any given moment sees every person addressed by it as endowed ... with the power to participate by his [*sic*] decision and deeds in the preparing of Redemption; and the apocalyptic, in which the redemptive process in all its details ... has been fixed from everlasting and for whose accomplishment human beings are only used as tools. ... The first of these forms derives from Israel, the second from ancient Persia."[35]

While Buber perhaps overdraws the distinction, it still holds, influencing Paul Hanson's more recently definitive differentiation of "prophetic eschatology" and "apocalyptic eschatology" as two perspectives upon a single continuum. Prophetic eschatology "focuses on the prophetic announcement to the nation of the divine plans for Israel and the world ... which [the prophet] translates into the terms of plain history, real politics, and human instrumentality."[36] This tradition undergoes a metamorphosis during the "bleak post-exilic conditions" of the sixth to fifth century B.C.E.

> Apocalyptic eschatology we define as a religious perspective which focuses on the disclosure (usually esoteric in nature) to the elect of the cosmic vision of Yahweh's sovereignty—especially as it relates to his acting to deliver his faithful—which disclosure the visionaries have largely ceased to translate into the terms of plain history, real politics, and human instrumentality due to a pessimistic view of reality.[37]

The conditions in which these visionaries performed apocalypse "seemed unsuitable to them as a context for the envisioned restoration of Yahweh's people."[38]

Elisabeth Schüssler Fiorenza, normally thought of as a leading feminist theorist rather than as an expert on John's Apocalypse, lifts the Book of Revelation into relief upon the matrix of early Christian uses of Jewish eschatology. She argues that "the symbolic universe and world of vision in Revelation ... is a fitting response to its sociopolitical 'rhetorical situation'";[39] it seeks to inspire its listener-readers to dislodge themselves from the "imperial cult," to choose instead of assimilation "the worship and power of God," and "to stake their lives on this decision." She understands this vision to be the primary Christian vehicle for the transmission of "Jewish theology as the exodus and liberation from slavery rather than as the redemption of individual souls."[40] Having thus brought Hanson's continuum a full "revolution," she discerns in John's appropriation of the apocalyptic not a sublimation of the more political and worldly eschatology of the prophets but, on the contrary, the main source for subsequent prophetic activity among Christians. Yet, unlike the prophets and many other apocalyptic scribes, the author of the Revelation of John operates in a rhetorical setting of urban social alienation rather than of address to a royal court: "The Book of Revelation is written for those 'who hunger and thirst for justice' in a sociopolitical situation that is characterized by injustice, suffering and dehumanizing power."[41]

14.

"The abject is edged with the sublime," writes Julia Kristeva.[42]

Countering apocalypse does not permit mere anti-apocalypse; yet a

simple "anti-," judging the Book of Revelation as at best a vindictive sexist text of ressentiment and at worst a potent self-fulfilling prophecy,
would have allowed me to dispatch that text to its own burning pit. The
emergence of a counter-apocalyptic grammar has obliged me instead to
encounter the text, to enter into relationship with it. This means first of
all recognizing the prehistory of relationship in which we already stand,
facing apocalypse as text and effect, in order to make it *con/scious*–etymologically to "know with" each other, to "know with" the text itself–
and in the intimacy of this biblical knowing to expect a certain up-close,
hermeneutical mutuality. But this relation is not a matter of true love.

Rather it sets one "on edge" (at the *eschaton*) and it has colored my
own thought with the affective tonality of Kristeva's "abjection." The "abject" designates that site of simultaneous fascination and repulsion
based on proximity to something that neither maintains the distance of
an object nor attains identity with oneself as a subject. Thus I suggest of
the apocalypse pattern that while few would identify with its bizarre
claims, we had best not imagine ourselves merely outside of it, able to regard its adherents as mere objects of analysis.

Within the context of a psychoanalytic discussion of the French sur-
realist author Louis-Ferdinand Celine, Kristeva tenuously traces a
thread between abjection and apocalypticism. In Celine's phantasmagoria of nightmare and desire, Kristeva recognizes the genre: "Suffering,
horror, and their convergence on abjection seem to me more adequate
marks of the apocalyptic vision contributed by Celine's scription."[43] Indeed, she goes on to summon the historic textual origins of the style:

> The great Palestinian apocalyptic movement ... encodes a seeingness
> that, contrary to the philosophical revelation of truth, imposes through a
> poetic incantation that is often elliptic, rhythmic, and cryptogrammic the
> incompleteness and abjection of any identity, group or speech. Such a
> seeingness asserts itself as the premise of an impossible future and as a
> promise of explosion.[44]

Itself often elliptic, rhythmic, and cryptogrammic, Kristeva's writing
suggests a stylistic link with what she elsewhere names the semiotic, the
maternal marking upon discourse, the psychological vestige of a prediscursive relationship culturally suppressed, yet formative of the subject and his/her linguistic capacity. Here we may only (incompletely)
note an atmosphere emanating from the marginal interplay between her

text, Celine's, John's, and perhaps my own. I will not seek to dispel this atmosphere, though occasionally, when the counter-apocalypse breaks through, it may clear.

15

From those openings I connect abjection to a methodologically feminist ambivalence, indeed a *constructive ambivalence*. This will let me pick up my dis/ease with the text and walk.[45] Such ambivalence is not a matter of lukewarm indecision but of a rather precise contrast of affirmation and negation, resembling the Taoist logic rendered in Jung Young Lee's theology of multicultural marginality as "neither/nor *and* both/and." According to Lee, "new marginal people" refuse the traditional entrapment of the marginalized between worlds, where "they must think in terms of neither/nor"–that is, where they belong nowhere.[46] Apocalypticism in its pessimistic forms tends to the double negation–no more of this world, not yet of the next; in its optimistic millennialisms, it tends, by contrast, to a triumphalist "both/and." But to think "in simultaneous double negations and double affirmations"[47] allows the acknowledgment of outsiderness and thus of a prophetic critique while insisting on access to the center, on belonging to both the already and the not-yet.

Such constructive ambivalence acknowledges, for instance, that we can't either just take or just leave apocalypse–and perhaps *should* not even if we could. The stance here invoked has as its (epistemological) criterion neither correctness of reference nor immediacy of divine revelation–that is, neither the truth of Western objectivism nor that of a reified prophetic vision. "And yet," writes Kristeva of this dual heritage, "if *apocalypse* means, etymologically, a vision, it must be understood as the contrary of revelation of philosophical truth, as the contrary of *aletheia*."[48] The etymology of the latter, the Greek word for "truth," itself suggests an unveiling: as the "unhidden," *aletheia* refers to that which is uncovered to the cooler eye of theory. Counter-apocalypse needs at once to distinguish between these two eyes of the Western truth-gaze and to see *through* the peripheries of both. Thus we claim a certain counter-apocalyptic dis/closure–not of "the truth," but of a relational truth-telling which inscribes within its self-relation the tale of its own relativity, its irony, its bias, its hope. Thus to "relate truth" is to attend to the relations constituted and deconstituted in its telling.

To stabilize this relational ambivalence within the wider "reflective equilibrium" of which my field is capable,[49] let me suggest that such a counter-apocalyptic strategy appeals to a range of textual, historical, and constructive perspectives to be found within the forcefield of biblical faith. That "within" has always (if not always consciously) been characterized in feminist theology by a volatile and productive ambivalence, committed to some normative option within the tradition while systematically questioning the hegemonic performances of the tradition itself. I had earlier read my own ambivalence as a kind of internal prohibition against the discipline of theology itself. Now I promote it as theological methodology.

The ambivalence with which feminist theology often approaches the Bible as a whole seems at once more pointed and more poignant in relation to this particular text. Jewish feminist theologian Judith Plaskow succinctly formulates the question for women within traditional religions: "What can we claim that has not wounded us?"[50] If that woundedness seems acute for Christian feminists eyeing John's sexist Revelation, it strangely mirrors the wound of the text itself, whose messiah is "the Lamb with the marks of slaughter," reflecting the communal marks of external and internalized oppression.

Whatever our evaluation of the importance of scripture for the theological task, feminist theologians tend to maintain a fairly abstract relation to the biblical text itself. With notable exceptions—such as Rita Nakashima Brock's in-depth exploration of the Gospel of Mark as the basis of her "christology of erotic power,"[51] or Rosemary Radford Ruether's preliminary but promising midrash opening *Sexism and God-Talk*[52]— feminist theology tends to leave biblical interpretation to feminist exegetical and historical scholars. In this we resemble "malestream" theologians: mining the bible for occasional examples, which are then used to justify abstractions which are posited as "biblical." This way one does not risk the interdisciplinary infractions which might be incurred by a more sustained encounter.

16

In the present work, in fear and eros, I take those risks. While unimpressed by the patriarchal "authority of scripture," I do understand my task here as a scripturally grounded narrative engagement, indeed a form of "narrative theology." Otherwise it might still consist, to borrow

Paul Ricoeur's diagnosis of mainline theology, "[of] extracting anemic generalities from the narratives recorded in the Scriptures."[53] Ricoeur himself seeks to develop a fresh sort of narrative theology, one that takes into account the rich and troubling complexity of the biblical narratives themselves. In this attention to internal ambiguities he differs from the "Yale School," who first coined the phrase "narrative theology." Developed especially by Hans Frei and George Lindbeck, the "cultural-linguistic" approach decries the "eclipse of biblical narrative" and refuses the apologetic truth-claims of modern theological metanarratives;[54] its adherents insist instead on the particularity of communities of interpretation within a pluralist society. But to free the text from Enlightenment readings, this school defines itself as outside "the world." "It is the text," writes Lindbeck, "which absorbs the world, rather than the world which absorbs the text."[55] By "world" Lindbeck means any "presuppositional and extra-linguistic contextual factors about states of affairs in the world" which might be brought to bear on the text.[56] In other words, these absorbent heirs of neoorthodoxy mark themselves off from progressive theologies, which locate themselves within the world, borrowing quite worldly analyses of the causes of worldly suffering. In fact, the socioeconomic critique of radical theologians is directed against that very "world" of imperial Mammon and priestly patriarchy to which the biblical Jesus took exception.

In an essay on narrative theology, Paul Ricoeur questions the lamented "eclipse of biblical narrative." He suggests that *the* biblical narrative which informs our culture consists of a "grandiose but frozen one-dimensional narrative in which all the varieties of discourse are leveled off." What remains is a "flat linear account that amounts to a world-history."[57] The flattened temporality of "the history of salvation" running from Genesis to Revelation stretches time into a line progressing toward its End. This flatness (as we shall see in Chapter 3) was facilitated by an Augustinian anti-apocalypse that relied upon the vision of Revelation. On behalf of a method that would reanimate the fundamental capacity to tell stories, Ricoeur challenges the Yale School's uncritical (and, I might add, stylistically storyless) evocation of just such a master narrative, for which he borrows Ulrich Simon's trenchant critique of "the Christian pattern."[58]

Given the potent role of the apocalypse in the imprinting of the

"Christian pattern," Ricoeur's attention to how that pattern reduces the "rich interplay of temporal qualities" to a "univocally chronological schema" strengthens the case for a counter-apocalyptic reading of the Apocalypse. Not that he would direct us to restore to the text a dubious innocence, but because its temporal diversity pulses with contested meanings: "Then memory and hope would be delivered from the *visible* narrative that hides that which we may call, with Johann-Baptist Metz, the 'dangerous memories' and the challenging expectations that together constitute the unresolved dialectic of memory and of hope."[59] This dissident dialectic hidden from view by the "visible narrative" may be said to correspond to Scott's "hidden transcript."

I understand the present project to nest in a complex, twisted history of biblical narrative effects. I consider myself part of the story. With Ricoeur, and unlike the Yale School, I consider that story to be intertwined with endless other ones, and therefore intertextually absorbing but also absorbed and absorbable in them, internally contested and externally relativized. In my own occasional appeal over against the apocalyptic Parousia to "the historical Jesus" or the Nazarene of the Gospels, I may betray, however, my own textual dependency, indeed my own normative recourse to a certain weave of biblical texts. But it is not my task here to lay out a canon within the canon. The canon itself is malformed by heterosexist power elites and ethnic chauvinisms. I do admit that I am inspired by certain strands of creation-affirmative mythos, by prophetic denunciation of systemic injustice, and by the ecumenism of wisdom spirituality for a pluralist setting. John's Apocalypse draws upon the cosmological, prophetic, and wisdom teachings of the biblical tradition, but radically realigns their significatory fields. I may therefore trace the distortions within the intertextual fabric and in its extratextual effects—for instance, how does prophecy turn apocalyptic, and then apocalypse turn into a master script? How does that script, habituated in endless nontextual effects, interface with the Christian pattern? But I do not seek to expel the text from the world, or either the text or the world from myself.

Rather than constructing some nice counter-apocalyptic feminist version of the Christian pattern, I would hope to open a more troubled space, one at once disturbing and attractive, a discursive zone in which to attend to the multiple and contradictory effects of a particular biblical text. My attention is assuredly selective, directed to some extent by an aesthetic preference for that which loves the jumbled life of the earth and so supports relations of social justice and ecological mutuality. These criteria are drawn from multiple sources—but so is the text.

And always I must return to this point: that whatever liberal pluralism has shaped my vocabulary of meaning, whatever mix of communities religious, intellectual, and political give me voice, I recognize the apocalypse at their edges.

17

The text of apocalypse, then, will be read in what follows as a canonical captive to the anti-apocalyptic (and yet precisely thereby still highly apocalypticized) moves of the early imperial Christian pattern. But to liberate the apocalypse pattern to its wounded denouement is clearly not the present intention. A feminist counter-apocalypse cultivates its own liberating capacity within the interstices of apocalyptic anxiety and the margins of the text, where we might break into a rereading of our own unacknowledged dependencies upon these interlocking master scripts. Feminist theology serves thus to unlock problems far wider than gender and yet inescapably gendered: the problem of how to hold a cultural habit accountable to the text which in some sense produced it, but which neither remembers the story nor even how to tell one. But what makes such a project a matter of *feminist* theology?

The apocalypse, as text or as effect, is a quintessentially male product. Women have often laid claim to its potencies, because it provided the main Western currency for revelation or for revolution. In recent decades, multiple currencies have made themselves available to women's movements, some, like the socialist and the psychoanalytical, only dimly reminiscent of apocalypse. At present, many of us enjoy a mobility between what bell hooks articulates as center and margin.[60] And also we move between pre-modern, modern, and postmodern epochs, or *etates*, in the language of the eleventh-century apocalyptic prophet Joachim, activating the place of their overlapping.[61] Feminism early noted that these epochal differences are unimpressive next to the stability of the sex/gender paradigm. This vision has unleashed among women at once the explosiveness and the clarity of our revelation—even as we resist the dualistic habits of the andromorphic apocalypse. This "seeingness"[62] lends feminists, womanists, *mujeristas* a certain counter-apocalyptic privilege. But only if we come to terms with our own dependency upon the "hidden transcript."

Here is the paradox for feminist meditation on "the end of the world": while innumerable women have found means of private resistance and public voice in the symbols of the Apocalypse, overt or subvert, the toxic misogyny of much of its imagery cannot, as will I hope become apparent, be flushed out of the text or its tradition. At the same time, we cannot purge the history of the women's movement of its prophetic-millennialist energies without self-depletion.

On the bulletin board before me hangs a postcard in the style of a post-modern collage. It depicts a classical sculpture of three naked women connected by a veil, joyously embracing; on their pedestal is scrawled graffiti which reads "Die Zukunft ist weiblich oder gar nicht" (The future is either female or nothing). The monument is superimposed upon a seascape framed by a broken wall, suggesting war damage, overcome by the ocean reaching to an open blue horizon. In its contrast of muselike idealizations of women and sloppy graffiti, the piece parodies its own slogan; it frames the text of its feminist apocalypse as dissident street work spray-painted under a cloak of darkness, in a burst of stifled laughter.

On my desk lies *Is the Future Female?* The author, Lynn Segal, a British socialist feminist, worries about "the increasing fragmentation within the women's movement with the emergence of divisions between women and the growth of Black feminist perspectives." Examining the fractures of class and of theory, she warns of the practical disunity within feminist organizations, as well as their failure to work with a viable political movement (such as European democratic socialism). Responsible for this fragmentation, in Segal's view, is a particular style of U.S. feminism: "An *apocalyptic feminism has appeared* which portrays a Manichean struggle between female virtue and male vice, with ensuing catastrophe and doom unless 'female' morality and values prevail."[63] She answers the title's question unambiguously: "The future is not female. But feminism, a feminism seeking to transform socialism and end men's power over women, has a crucial role to play in its construction."[64] Yet in her well-reasoned anti-apocalypse, how can we miss the cryptoapocalyptic call to unity, a dread of differences, indeed an overstatement which counter-demonizes the "bad" feminism? Indeed, on what basis does she assume that women *had* been and might still be united under the banner of a thoroughly Caucasian feminism? What endism does such a myth of our own origin serve?

By now, in the dubious chronology of feminist "waves," Segal's voice sounds old-fashioned. Poststructuralism, which she counted among the fracturing theories, has taken on the mantle of anti-apocalypse. Might we perhaps nudge, shift, undulate into forms, *etates*, movements of women which will not rush like lemmings to the cliffs of the Future, will not ricochet between apocalypses?

18

To stand in some particular fragility of place and time, with one's fragments of community and materialities of gender, and to love life: that is perhaps the only real basis of action against the end of the world. Amidst our multiple modern dislocations, we may nonetheless locate ourselves as radically related—radically in both the sense of a subterranean rootedness in influences beyond our control, to which we also willy-nilly add, ourselves influencing the next moment, and in the sense of a socio-ecological politics which distinguishes between those relations which sustain a complex and differentiating web of life and those relations which destroy the sustainable basis for that life.

To theorize a counter-apocalyptic theology of relations is simply one among many possible strategies for stabilizing the unsentimental conditions of a life lived in the mutuality difference affords, a way of conceiving a sustainable, just, and lovable future by living it *already*. There is no way *there* but *here* and *now*. At the latest "end" of a history that crowds, consumes, and closes the present, the opening of the present as the only site of memory and hope grounds—without founding—the political work of dis/closure.

The spirit of that finite and vulnerable life requires our cooperation, and for this reason the task of this text remains indelibly theological—that is, its theory articulates a set of spiritual practices. Jürgen Moltmann, who early transformed theology into eschatology, has more recently turned to pneumatology—the logos of the spirit. Naming "God" the "immanent transcendence" within nature and history, he can identify "the Holy Spirit" as "the spirit of life."[65] While I hope to avoid the religious, not to say sexist, literalisms to which even such biocentric God-talk is prone (not to mention the obfuscations of any discourse of "transcendence"), I engage it for the sake of holding open a disciplined discursive space of spirit. Ultimately we may read the intertextual tension of a counter-apocalypse as yielding, through the yearnings gripping its dense historicity, to a kind of political pneumatology. Such a feminist theology does not shy away from cosmology. For the healing of *kosmos*, in its full etymological meaning of an aesthetic, social, and natural order of relations, is the endless "end" of counter-apocalypse.

For the sake of that present purpose, this book will offer six dimensions, or aspects, of reflection. Its structure will reflect in a certain sense the literary structure of the Apocalypse, which Schüssler Fiorenza has described as a "conic spiral" and compared to the radiant paintings of Sonia Delaunay.[66] The text unfolds in a kaleidoscopic pattern of sevens—seven messages to seven churches, seven seals, trumpets, bowls, signs, etc.–but really the seven is always six, as in each series the seventh contains the entire next septet, and each set of seven in some sense recapitulates and intensifies the prior disclosures. The composition thus churns up a helical movement, neither circular nor linear, but generating a forward momentum.

The first of these chapters, or aspects, will take the form of a midrash on the Book of Revelation, which, as the final text of the Text of Texts, facilitates a meditation on textuality itself. *Midrash* refers to the ancient tradition of rabbinic commentaries on scripture, in which multiple readings, developing and disputing each other, would literally surround the scriptural text on the printed page. Of the common denominator of various *midrashim*, Daniel Boyarin writes: "The interpretations found in these several works are manifold in nature, but all of them are more or less different from the commentary of the European traditions in that they do not seem to involve the privileged pairing of a signifier with a specific set of signifieds."[67] I note that his is not the facile poststructuralist dismissal of *any* correspondence of signifier with signified, of sign with a meaning beyond its language. Several contemporary Jewish thinkers have renewed the method of the midrash in conjunction with a postmodern interest in the plurivocality of text itself, especially as articulated in Derrida's perhaps crypto-Judaic notion of "intertextuality."[68] "The text is in-between; it is intertext," writes David Blumenthal in a work that literally reproduces the printed face of midrash. "The text is a fabric, woven (Latin *texere/textus*) from many threads." Interpreters are weavers who become themselves subsequent threads: an apt self-inscription for any theology of radical relation. "The text-fabric is never finished. It is a cloth with loose ends; a tissue which varies in transparency, color and text-ure. Hence, all texts are plurisignificative; they mean more than one thing."[69]

The midrash I attempt on Revelation lacks the communal coherence of a single religious perspective, even one so conversationally complex as those inscribed in traditional midrashim. Its many voices represent both my own and those of others who speak for parts of myself. But that inter-woven "self," an endless, finite, multi-tensed composite of agency and relation, is itself intertextually constituted of real relations: "real," precisely in their shifting plurisignifications, embodied within and as *material*, fragmented and far-flung ecologies of interchange. My own midrash may more resemble what one astute interpreter of texts has labeled "philonic allegory."[70] It takes liberties with the tropes of a text which it cannot change. But those metaphors become living and complex figures, contradicting their closure in the Apocalypse, taking on a parabolic life of their own, loosening their ends.

The subsequent five chapters of this work each unearth a stream of the historical effects of Revelation. They do this in order to then swing into the responsive cosmological play of counter-apocalypse. On the themes of time, place, community, gender, and spirit, these chapters move with a certain sporadic, helical chronology toward the threshold of the present.

Why these themes in particular? Indeed, why such abstract, over-extended ideas, larded with metaphysical murk? Certainly there is no predetermined necessity to this selection; these topics do not constitute a set to and from which, like Revelation itself, one may neither add nor subtract. However, I trust that the counter-apocalyptic topography to which these idea-zones point will support a certain internal movement through the text of Revelation, through its subsequent readings and his-torical explosions, and above all into the currents of a present position. I will consider these zones as configural fields of rhetoric and action. That is, text, time, space, community, gender, and spirit will con/figure each other. Thus they will provide a shifting ground against which the refig-urations and disfigurations of apocalypse may appear—toward the end of prefiguring a subjectivity, or intersubject, capable of entertaining their conceptual interaction. Capable of grounding, like lightning rods of theory, after-effects of apocalypse.

These chapters come heavily freighted with the burden of a *Wirkungsgeschichte* (a history of effects, or "effective history" in the sense of Hans-Georg Gadamer's philosophy of interpretation as hermeneutics) of the text of Revelation. As readers we stand within the hermeneutical forcefield of the text, and within our own limiting perspective. But I would not have us quite so enclosed within a "hermeneutical circle" as does Gadamer, requiring a reverential "understanding" (standing-under) of the text: feminist and other doubts break open the circle, leaving for us perhaps rather a "hermeneutical circulation." We stand within that forcefield—within its configural fields—whether we read the text or not, merely by virtue of standing within Western history, and only by claiming a certain interpretive reciprocity of the text may we break its encircling closure. Unlike Gadamer, then, I will construe the effects of the text as considerably more materialized, more concretely historical and political, than a mere intellectual history of a text. Yet counter-apocalypse requires at once affirming and breaking through something like Gadamer's "event horizon," which otherwise becomes a black hole, from which nothing can escape. Dis/closure slashes open the closed circle for the sake of a wider spiral of hermeneutical circulation, while still acknowledging the horizon, always permeable and moving, of any truth-relation.[71]

Thus, Foucault's reprise of Nietzsche's *wirkliche Historie*—"real history," sometimes also misleadingly translated "effective history"—lends further methodological support. "History becomes 'effective' to the degree that it introduces discontinuity into our very being."[72] So if we find apocalyptic threads and fuses running through our history, if we sniff out even long chains of effects, they would never add up to some sort of apocalyptic core, or continuum underlying Western civilization. The apocalypse script can only be read as one scroll of effects among others, significantly intermeshed in the complex intertextuality of biblical influences, but wild with its own contradictory meanings. Unwieldy in its eruptions and dispersions, barely recognizable in its sublimations and repressions, in its poetry and its literalism, the apocalypse script neither offers nor constitutes a constant or underlying unity of history.

Like other poststructuralists, Foucault means to provide, precisely by his historical method, an anti-apocalyptic moment oddly identical with his antihistoricism: "The historian's history finds its support outside of time and pretends to base its judgments on an *apocalyptic objectivity.*"[73] Foucault draws this inference from his own loose identification of teleology, eschatology, and apocalypse. Certainly these concepts all privilege the future, a future that thinly veils the present power drives of an embracing vision—but in very different ways. Thus Foucault unites an objectivism derived from the classical, philosophical meaning of "truth" (*aletheia*) with a nonrational authority derived from truth as revelation. Ironically, perhaps due to his formative concentration upon modernity, Foucault fails to recognize that the apocalyptic script is one of the main purveyors of discontinuity and rupture in the Western history of history. (His anti-apocalypse, like others, must distortingly—indeed, apocalyptically—homogenize apocalypse.) Yet his critique of the "suprahistorical perspective" helps to focus a counter-apocalyptic approach to time, and so also to expose the closures perpetrated as effects of apocalypse, "a history whose function is to compose the finally reduced diversity of time into a totality fully closed upon itself . . . ; a history whose perspective on all that precedes it implies the end of time."[74]

In the present work, the exploration of the configural zone of *time* picks up with a period subsequent to that of the biblical text, moving through the patristic and Augustinian readings of Revelation into a theology of time, and then counters with a kind of contemporary spirituality of timefulness. The chapter concerned with *place* offers a kind of genealogy of Christopher Columbus's self-avowed apocalypse, and a response from an indigenizing sense of place. *Community* pursues medieval and modern outbursts of apocalypse as revolt, allowing us to address postmodern anti-utopian skepticism as to the viability of any community. *Gender* faces us with the apocalypse of feminism itself—and counters with no end of feminism. Finally, the pneumatological in/conclusion allows the theological presumptions and hopes of counter-apocalypse to become visible under the aspect of *spirit*, letting a polyglossia of the multiple, delicate tongues of flame counter the glossary of roaring endtime conflagrations.

If I do not acknowledge that this work is a theological inside job, its tongues will be tied. But of course all along the way "they" (double-edged, these tongues, as we will soon recognize) inscribe their plurivocal vision in a dis/closive space. A place that can be inhabited but not enclosed. Where one may *in theory practice* alternative ways of reading, timing, placing, communing, engendering, inspiriting.

═══════════

> *Around the throne were four living creatures full of eyes before them and behind them. . . . And the four living creatures, each of them had six wings, they were full of eyes around and within.*
>
> Revelation 4:6ff

In the wilderness the woman has peeked up into the heavenly throne room for another perspective. She grimaces at these old spirits of lion, ox, eagle, and human. Long before they had appeared, edging Ezekiel's vision-vehicle with a neat rim of eyes. Now they are "full of eyes." Congested with vision. They are going in no particular direction. As she lets her veil down, they land on her book, smelling gamey. Grunting, clucking, humming arguments with each other, mewing poetry, they claw it open to The End. She sees herselves mirrored in their polyoptic gaze(s). What a postmodern monstrosity, she thinks. But up here they twinkle. She wills her feet down to the ground.

Seeing Voices

1

The apokalypsis of Jesus Christ, which God gave him to show to his servants what must soon take place; and he made it known by sending his angel to his servant John, who bore witness to the word of God . . . even to all that he saw. Blessed are those who read aloud the words of the prophecy, and blessed are those who hear, and who keep what is written therein; for the time is near. (Rev. 1:1–3)

The minds of some readers will glaze over at such formulaic pieties. But many, after two millennia, read with excitement that "the time is near." Who am I to dismiss them? I hear myself muttering that "yes, the time is near," thinking of the deepening backlash against women's rights, gays and lesbians, people of color; economic doom for the global majority; ecological ruin for the globe itself–a list that can only whimper off into an apocalyptic ellipsis. Inversely, I imagine ourselves converging upon a moment of opportunity: as our species careens to the brink, it will see, it will hear, it will turn around in time . . .

In which time? Neither the horror nor the hope of the Apocalypse speaks to me with the immediacy it demands. It does not address my time, or all times, or timelessness, but rather its own time. If meaningful parallels, indeed continuous trajectories, can be traced between its context and future ones, it was not the text of the Apocalypse which initially inspired me to seek them. But if John seems to be asserting in the above passage his authority to reveal unmediated truth, the gaps in its immediacy wink at curious readers. The Book of Revelation inscribes multiple meditations–from God, to Christ, to an angel, to "John," to his writing. Already leavened with past prophetic citations, the new text is to be read aloud, mediated from vision to scroll to oral performance. Does the text, tense with its layered Last Word, resist its own closure? Is the time of its own deconstruction–as the origin of endless Western oversimplifications–near?

That would not mean the text's destruction. On the contrary, it would permit us at least to claim this much: just in case Western history gets partly mediated to us through rhetoric inspired by this text, the common liberal habit of ignoring it counts as culpable ignorance. But how can we "hear" freshly the presences warped into its menacing promises? Its mythopoeic medium, maddeningly nonlinear even as it marches from Alpha to Omega, mocks academic analysis. So I will be tempted toward the mode to which John himself had recourse–the pneumatic. *Pneuma*– breath, wind, spirit–breezes through the tightest texts. John was "in the Spirit" when he was told to "write what you see in a book." If I surrender now and then to a kindred pneumagraphic bent, the "spirit-writing" insists on its own fallibility, and though I cannot re-present any immediate vision, I do proceed with eyes open. To "hear" this text, possibly the world's primary source of closure, I must resist my impulse to foreclose on its meaning. So I mimic the style of a midrash, that unique, rabbinic model of a layered multiplicity of interpretations. I cannot send readers *up* to the throne room with John. But I do invite them back *into* this text, this subtext of our history and pretext of our fantasies.

Reading now not like John's community, aloud and together, but silently and alone, we join the intertextuality by which this text has exerted its aggressive effects on the world. Why not accept the blessing and, in our fashion, "keep what is written?"–for still, "the time is near." Besides, what author does not bless "those who hear"?

2

I, John, your brother, who share with you in Jesus the tribulation and the kingdom and the patient endurance, was on the island called Patmos on account of the word of God and the testimony of Jesus. (Rev. 1:9)

I will let two commentators limit this reading of the Apocalypse at its political edges. As types more than as individuals, they mediate my response and contradict each other meaningfully. (Influenced by other axes, I fall short of the purity of either position.) Both witness to "the time" and announce a *kairos* (a moment of unique historic potentiality) in which a vision of earthly well-being passes judgment on the old order. Both locate evil in a global superstructure of oppression which dominates the righteous community—whose identity is equally unambiguous. For both, there is no evading the either/or—the with-us-or-against-us, the rigorous commitment—of "salvation." And for both of these interpreters the new age has begun to realize itself in the very work of the text.

Both, in other words, can be described as apocalyptic prophets. But while one of these commentators finds in John of Patmos a comrade, the other locates him among the destroyers. One addresses me from the outer matrix of my cultural formation, the other from its more intimate reaches.

The first of these exemplary commentators is Allan Boesak, who re-reads the Apocalypse as a black South African clerical leader in the midst of the struggle against apartheid. His superb commentary on Revelation, *Comfort and Protest*, serves at the same time as an exegesis of the politics of South Africa before Mandela's release. Like most liberation theologians, he finds the text "prophetic, historical, contemporary." But, he insists,

> we shall have to learn to read it differently. We shall have to do away with those sterile escape mechanisms and dead-end arguments about numbers and symbols and signs by which the real message of Revelation is so often paralyzed. We shall have to stop reading the Apocalypse as if it were meant to be a practical guide to heaven and hell.[1]

For Boesak, it is not esoteric depth but political necessity that dictates Revelation's rhetorical opacity: it functions as "underground literature" written to "make it as difficult as possible for informers to understand."[2] Boesak imagines John's community as much like his own, speaking in cryptic ciphers. For example, "Babylon" is a code name for Rome, the oppressor of early Christians. Unlike the typical white Christian commentator, who may in fact identify more readily with Rome, Boesak recognizes in John's Apocalypse a life-or-death situation. John's "intention was to comfort, encourage, inspire; by writing a book of protest to call the church to persistent faith and obedience to Messiah, the true *Kyrios*"[3]–that is, the "lord" who for early Christians encodes that power before whom all the little lords of the earth will finally cringe and collapse. Thus John's letter empowers the powerless.

Boesak locates "the key" to reading the Apocalypse as protest literature for a resistance movement in Revelation 1:9–"I who share with you . . . the tribulation and the kingdom and the patient endurance, . . ."[4]

> Those who do not know this suffering through oppression, who do not struggle together with God's people for the sake of the gospel, and who do not feel in their own bodies the meaning of oppression and the freedom and joy of fighting against it shall have grave difficulty understanding this letter from Patmos. . . . It is the struggling and suffering and hoping together with God's oppressed people that open new perspectives for the proclamation of the Word of God as found in the Apocalypse.[5]

His reading performs its politics. The time is immediate; the *kairos* or moment of dis/closure is inscribed in the "Kairos Document" that South African resistance churches composed not only against their country's apartheid, but also against all the varieties of economic, race, and gender apartheid spreading on our planet.[6] Boesak presumes that John was in exile on Patmos, a Roman prison isle. The verse we are discussing, reads only "I, John, . . . was on the island called Patmos on account of the word of God and the testimony of Jesus." As Pablo Richard puts it in his recent *Apocalypse: A People's Commentary on the Book of Revelation,* an analogous liberation commentary written for the Latin American context:

> Revelation arises in a time of persecution–and particularly amid situations of chaos, exclusion, and ongoing oppression. In such situations, Revelation enables the Christian community to rebuild its hope and its awareness. Revelation transmits a spirituality of resistance and offers guidance for organizing an alternative world.[7]

According to liberationist reading, Revelation belongs to an entire genre of resistance to colonization. It echoes earlier prophetic traditions in the light of a rising level of crisis: the threat of genocide, that is, of religious and cultural extinction as well as economic repression, was real when the text was set down. As Richard Horsely puts it, "Because the severity of the new historical situations was unprecedented in biblical traditions, it is also not surprising that the traditional 'symbolic universe' was adapted in certain respects." Accordingly, "apocalypticism was the distinctive cultural form taken by imagination in late Second Temple Jewish society."[8]

Yet some scholars question the metanarrative of the extraordinary oppression of Christians, or of John's community of Christians, under Diocletian.[9] They argue that there is no evidence of any particular persecution of John; he may have been visiting Patmos not as prisoner but simply to carry on his mission. Indeed, the theory of the liberation ethic of the ancient apocalyptic authors remains contested. Were they the Gramscian "organic intellectuals" of their people, as, for instance, New Testament scholar Oberey Hendricks would claim as part of his "guerilla exegesis" from an African American perspective?[10] They were themselves scribes, scholars; quite possibly they possessed no conscious intention to serve the interests of peasants. Jonathan Z. Smith, for instance, questions the "lachrymose theory" of "apocalypticism as growing out of a situation of general persecution and the popular recent theory that it reflects lower class interests."[11] Present agendas surely exaggerate the politics of apocalypse, importing an optimistic modern concept of "the people" as a "new subject in history" and of their resistance and struggle. But the text's subsequent history will suggest that no teary-eyed, ideological anachronism can quite account for the long trajectory of revolutionary New Jerusalems. The subaltern reading of Revelation sustains it as "hidden transcript" (and often not so hidden, as we will see) not just of Christian but of Western history.

But even granting some version of this emancipatory hermeneutic, cracks open in the surface of any revolutionary reception of John's text. Might feminists, among others, find "the key" in liberation *from* rather than liberation *by* the self-revealing warrior word?

Here enters the voice of the other ideological pole along the liberation continuum: "Since myth functions as self-fulfilling prophecy, it is especially interesting to consider the fact that christian myth promises what is popularly known as 'the end of the world.' A common source for 'information' about this impending disaster was the Book of Revelation."[12] Mary Daly thus deftly links the Christian with the nuclear apocalypse, which "has facilitated movement beyond mere passive expectation to active enactment of the envisioned horror show." How would she account for the continuity? No mystery there: "Here we see christian myth merge with the language of another sect of the religion which is Patriarchy." For a radical feminist, the apocalyptic impulse simply aggravates systemic "male-violence," idolizing a transcendence which controls, resents, and ultimately destroys life.

But in light of the liberation readings from the Southern hemisphere, does one want to dismiss Revelation as mere patriarchal mystification— and find oneself occupying a white, antirevolutionary subject-location? Moreover, does radical feminism suffer from an equally questionable purism? Indeed, what if radicalism itself proves inseparable from this text? Let us defer the apocalypse of gender until more of the story has been told. Suffice it to say for now that gender is complicated by and complicates progressive politics in ways that precede and may outlive current challenges to its identity politics. Distinguishing women's participation in the struggle from that of certain masculine models, Rigoberto Menchú suggests a Latin American spirit akin to that read by other liberationists out of the above text of John. She notes that "we don't do [these things] because we want power, but so something will be left for human beings. And this gives us the courage to be steadfast in the struggle, in spite of the danger."[15] *"Here is a call for the endurance of the saints"* (Rev. 13:10).

Is this the book of cosmic-historical revolution? The book of paranoid patriarchy? Or does it cut, like its own double-edged speech, both ways?

3

In his right hand he held seven stars, from his mouth issued a sharp two-edged sword, and his face was like the sun shining in full strength. When I saw him, I fell at his feet as though dead, but he put his right hand upon me, saying, "Fear not, I am the first and the last, and the living one; I died, and beyond I am alive for evermore.... Now write what you see, what is and what is to take place hereafter." (Rev. 1:16–19)

"Now write!" What writer has not fallen "as though dead" before such a command? An apparition "like a son of man" ("like a human being"–this is not the supernatural honorific of later Christology),[14] with dazzlingly white hair and robes, eyes "like a flame," feet like "burnished bronze," and a voice "like the sound of many waters" makes the demand. First this figure's voice is *heard*–while John was "in the Spirit," that is, in an altered state. But then when John turns "to *see the voice* that was speaking" to him, the main medium of this text–vision–opens its show.

Write what you see. Yet most biblical traditions discourage the gaze. The eyeing of heavenly realities, an immodest, idolatrous ocularity, invited occult ogling, indeed an objectifying "specularity" (Irigaray); while the hearing of the Voice denotes obedience to a severely reserved Transcendence.[15] The Hebrews emphasized time over space, and, correspondingly, hearing over vision.[16] So does the *seen voice* here begin to script a new sense of space and time?

In the meantime, the vision-voice flashes impressive attributes–he is first and last of creation, the living one, who having died can't die, who controls entrance to Death and Hades. The allusion to Jesus seems obvious. Certainly most commentators simply identify him as the glorified Christ.[17] But does that settle anything? Earlier in the chapter the same signs of temporal ultimacy, "I am the Alpha and the Omega," had been spoken by "the Lord God, who is and who was and who is to come, the Almighty." Here John cites Isaiah 44:6, an aggressively monotheizing passage: "I am the first and the last, besides me there is no other." But then why simply identify the sword-tongued apparition with the resurrected Jesus–certainly for Jewish Christians an "other," however mystically linked with the everlastingly "same" Yahweh? Within the next three centuries, Christian orthodoxy would control any hints of multiplicity by means of the trinitarian device. But first-century Christology remains fluid, visionary, and, by contrast to orthodoxy, understated.[18]

The vision, authorizing John as author, *asks* to be written down, inscribed into permanence. Prophets, including Jesus, spoke to the immediate situation and left the rest to scribes. Apocalypticism straddles the distinction between scribe and prophet. The writing down of laws and covenants was traditional, but the few precedents for a prophecy asking to be written cluster in the eschatological tradition, as in Jeremiah 30:2–3: "Write in a book all the words that I have spoken to you. For the days are surely coming. . ."[19]

Revelation 1:16 embodies the ancient Hebrew Word which goes forth from the mouth of God. Its paradigmatic form–the prototype of oral authority–is the speech by which the world was created: "Then God said

... and there was ..." But now, with a perfunctory glance back to the alpha of Genesis, John, gaze fixed on the omega, sees word harden into sword. The word of creation becomes the sword of discreation; its homologue is the stylus, the pen. With its stars and sun soon to be swept down by a dragon's tail, this periscope placed at the tail end of the canon grimly parodies the opening text of the biblios that it will write shut. Yet liberation commentators would rightly remind us that the text does not will but rather suffers an end of a world: the s/word of apocalypse is invoked as a promise of action—now, finally, divine justice will be done. Yet how deny the scope of the retaliation, which afflicts not just the violators, but also, in a literary act of tail-swallowing, the creation narrative itself? The omega devours the alpha. Did this fantasy of restorative annihilation somehow require the hardening of the oral, via the visual, into the textual? If this book can end, why not the world?[20]

We have to do (from the context of its canonization) with not just a book of victims but paradoxically with the ultimate book of the Holy Book of the world-dominating civilization of the Book. So might its preoccupation with its own writing dis/close something we—who work within the privilege of that civilization—need to know about ourselves? Current academic discourse refers in tones of awe to "the text"—a notable singular in the grammar of pluralism. The term means to defy precisely the canonized, authoritative singular of the Book of monotheism; deconstructive postmodernity pits writing, as the endlessly decanonizing "text," against the closure of "book" modeled on the prototypical *biblios.*[21] But then doesn't the trope of "the text" subliminally connote the hushed sanctity of the long Western tradition—Jewish, Christian, and Muslim—of the exegesis of holy books? Amidst the "endless proliferation of signifiers" (Derrida) does not the textocentric foundation of current antifoundationalism need to attend more honestly to its apocalyptic precedents?[22]

The Book of Revelation bristles with allusions to writing—from the opening imperative to "write," to the scroll of seven seals, John's swallowing of a small scroll, and the final warning not to add to or subtract from itself. This book that barely made it into the canon will shut it with self-preserving curses. The "political unconscious" of writing inscribes its will to power upon The End.[23] Let me suggest that a qualitative break from the rest of the Bible occurs: writing is no longer a derivative, mimetic act, a matter of mere scribal memory, but a performative power. Is it right here, in the final book of the Book of Books, that writing–a visual rather than oral medium–inscribes its primacy on the Christian mind?

Writing or reading this (or any?) book, one may ask how Western bookishness, for all its oedipal revolts against the Bible, even against its own book-ness, colludes with the closures of worlds.

4

He who conquers and who keeps my works until the end, I will give him power over the nations, and he shall rule them with a rod of iron, as when earthen pots are broken in pieces, even as I myself have received power from my Father. (Rev. 2:26f)

Far from any gospel of love, this text promises power–raw, global, political power. Those who "conquer" will "rule" with the ruthless sovereignty of "the Father." In context, the rhetoric of conquest stimulates perseverance under sociopolitical pressure, strengthening, after all, the "love and faith and service and patient endurance" (2:19) of communities tempted to assimilate to the dominant culture. Such metaphors may provide, in the language of Adela Yarbro Collins, catharsis under crisis, and they may offer comfort in moments of despair, thus mobilizing protest under persecution; nonetheless, many of us read this text from within a rhetorical situation which politically resembles that of empire more than that of empire's victims.[24] Though dissident subcultures have repeatedly resonated to its original context, the textual effects cannot be purged of imperial Christian traces; we whose class benefits from Western hegemony can hardly read "conquest" and "power of nations" as innocent metaphors.

Who, moreover, has played the "earthen pots" to John's "iron rod"? Could one find more gendered pictographs?[25] Or symbols more charged with the bias of the Iron Age against indigenous, "earthier" tribes? The immediate adjoining text sheds light on John's blast of unmitigated masculinism. He had just berated the church in Thyatira: "This I hold against you, that you tolerate the woman Jezebel, who calls herself a prophetess and is teaching and beguiling my servants to practice immorality and to eat food sacrificed to idols. I gave her time to repent, but she refuses to repent of her fornication" (2:20–21).

These Jezebel-identified eating practices were part of the food rituals of polytheist communities, performing participation in the cultural and economic life of the city. But some, including John, judged any such syncretism "immorality," and advocated the sort of purism that marked the Christian community as outsiders.[26] John's call to uncompromising conquest specifically targets the controversial "Jezebel." Political dominance over "the nations" is promised to the community as a reward if they will just expunge this woman's influence. His rage against her and her "children" (her disciples) waxes hysterical: "Beware, I am throwing her on a bed, and those who commit adultery with her I am throwing into great distress, unless they repent of her doings; and I will strike her children dead" (2:22–23).

"Jezebel" is John's term of derision for a Thyatiran leader. Is the fact that she is a woman incidental? We know nothing of her apart from his censure. Let me suggest the following hypothesis: to provoke such ferocity, she must have represented some widespread tendency. A parallel pattern of problems surfaces for Paul among the Corinthians, the eating of meat sacrificed to idols and other "immoral" behaviors—such as women's public speech—defended by the Corinthians in the name of their new-found freedom. He too writes them a paternalistic ultimatum: "Am I to come to you with a stick, or with love in a spirit of gentleness?" (1 Corinthians 4:21). Antoinette Wire has argued that Paul's problem in Corinth lay less with food than with women. They were exercising an unruly range of spiritual prophetic gifts. Hence Paul's great analogy (1 Corinthians 12:14–26) of the subordination of individual talents to the good of the body, whose head is Christ, is developed in parallel with his sexist vision of the man as "the head of the woman." "Headship" again lifts up its "rod." By Wire's reading, Paul considered the church endangered by these "Corinthian women prophets"—uppity women not only disregarding the legalisms of a food code but cultivating a scandalously self-authorizing spirituality *en christo*.[27]

One might read a similar situation to have arisen in Thyatira. John's anger at the power of a woman within his community invests these verses (2:26ff) with such virulence that the "earthen pots" seem to stand in for the bodies of Jezebel and her ilk. With dreamlike precision, the promise of pot-breaking power follows succinctly upon his threats against a female competitor. Even apart from such speculation about a vilified prophetess, however, the fact remains that this is the single reference in all of Revelation to a human female. All the other women are allegories, and all the persons (including 144,000 virgins) are male.

The poetics of power, of conquest, of swords and iron rods pitted against female flesh, penetrates the significatory field of the Apocalypse. A feminist ethic cannot "veil" the misogyny of its metaphors, even if, as Elisabeth Schüssler Fiorenza stresses, this *is* the one book of the New Testament dedicated to justice.[28] Yet the macho rod does not substitute remainderlessly for the subtler, double-edged s/word. Whatever else can be said of the book, its radicalism repels moderates and liberals: those "neither hot nor cold, but lukewarm, I will spit you out of my mouth" (3:15). The methodological ambivalence it demands runs not lukewarm, but hot and cold.

5

After this I looked, and lo, in heaven an open door! And the first voice . . . said, "Come up hither, and I will show you what must take place after this." Immediately, I was in the Spirit; and lo, a throne stood in heaven, and there was one seated. (Rev. 4:1–2)

A heavenly come hither initiates the unveiling of a virgin time, soon to be consummated. The prior messages to the churches established the intended audience and framed in an epistolary *inclusio* device the protracted vision to be directed by the sword-tongued spirit guide. The reader becomes voyeur of the visionary, who is himself aroused to ecstasy by the sight of the "open door." Given Hebrew strictures against the gaze–to see a parent nude, to see God face to face, were taboo–the text delivers a frisson of the forbidden. To "see" the naked future: afterwards, Christians could always indulge this titillation through the lens of Apocalypse.

As Schüssler Fiorenza argues, the "eschatological promise to the victor"–that "the one who prevails . . . may sit with me on my throne"–prepared for the vision. The throne image recurs twenty times throughout the book. True to liberation theology, this is a political leitmotif, but in the image of the *dominus* enthroned in his *domus*. "The central theological question of chapters 4–5 as well as of the whole book is: Who is the true Lord of this world?"[29] In answer we see only "lightning and voices and peals of thunder" from the throne, seven spirit-torches burning, a sea of crystal sparkling. The brilliant light re/veiling "G-d"–disclosing the divine politics of the future but no divine person–reveals and guards the Jewishness of the text.

> And around the throne were four living creatures full of eyes before them and behind them; the first living creature was like a lion, and the second living creature like an ox, and the third living creature had the face as of a man, and the fourth living creature was like an eagle flying. And the four living creatures, each of them had six wings, they were full of eyes around and within. (Rev. 4:6–8)

If we free these "creatures" from their later allegorization as the four Gospels, their wildness wings into view. Encrusted with neolithic totemism, mirroring humanoid and animal spirits, their myriad eyes stare back at us from the peripheral vision of the text. Primitive *pneumata* still blow through the Apocalypse. But they did not simply drop in as archetypes from prehistory. Every element of the scene cites a longer vision from Ezekiel 1:

> I saw a storm wind coming from the north, a vast cloud with flashes of fire a brilliant light about it; and within was a radiance like brass, glowing in the heart of the flames. In the fire was the semblance of four living creatures in human form. Each had four faces and each four wings. . . . All four had the face of a man . . . and of a lion . . . an ox and . . . an eagle. . . . The appearance of the creatures was as if fire from burning coals or torches were darting to and fro among them. (Ezek. 1:4–13)

The operative citationality bears examination. Ezekiel's creatures attach to a complex vehicular contraption (favored by UFO adepts) of wheels which "sparkled like topaz," all shaped as a wheel within a wheel: "All four had hubs and each hub had a projection which had the power of sight, and the rims of the wheels were full of eyes all round . . . they moved in whatever direction the spirit [or "wind"; Hebrew, *ruah*] would go" (Ezek. 1:16–21). But John junks Ezekiel's fantastic hovercraft, prying loose one face and a bunch of eyes. In Ezekiel the eyes succinctly edge the vision-wheels, showing the spirit where it wants to go; John affixes the multiple eyes to the creatures at random. For both, the multiocular *monstrum* (portent) suggests maximum awakeness.

But in John a totalistic randomness–eyes before and behind, around and within—refracts the gaze of an author peeping into the throne room of God. Even his syntax compares clumsily to Ezekiel's: "and . . . and . . . and . . ." suggests a frantic montage of available conventions. Images in this book pile up densely, lacking the breathing room—the space for the *ruah* of reading/hearing?—allotted to them in the poetry of Ezekiel or Isaiah, where images are allowed to reach their depth, to breathe, to dilate. In all its phantasmagoric stress, stripped, caught in rapid (and-and-and) collations, the mythopoiea of Revelation verges on myopia.

Freud defined the work of the dream as "compression" or "condensation": "The dreamwork has carried out a work of compression or *condensation* on a large scale. . . . From every element in a dream's content associative threads branch out in two or more directions."[30] Dream imagery displays a randomness and rapidity—eyes everywhere. Multiple associations contract into imagery. Dreams, supremely intertextual, endlessly recycle received images. But John is not dreaming, he is designing a dreamlike message. And John's prolific imagery serves the ends of rather simple ideas. Think of television as an analogy—its rapidity of imagery, far from freeing up the imagination, binds it to scenarios dangerously simplistic in ethics and outlook. It seems no accident that the televangelists have lodged their apocalyptic message in this medium. If reduced, against its own spirit, to conceptual content, the Apocalypse boils down to a great theological disambiguation: salvation for a martyr elite and annihilation for most of creation. This eschatology is more simplistic than that of Ezekiel's performative conditional;[31] and Jesus' parables, far leaner of image, accomplish what John Dominic Crossan calls "world subversion" and "reversal" through an open-ended ambiguity.[32] The lack of metaphoric breathing room in Revelation seems to seal in the final closure it prophesies. By the exercise of its cosmologically foregone conclusion, does the text discipline the mythopoeic productions of its own unconscious?

Of course, reading after the text's quite recent accretion of fundamentalist antipoetics, one wonders whether something in the genre made it vulnerable to its own later literalization—both by oppressors and their victims. If, as Owen Barfield has it, "literalism is the besetting sin of our age,"[33] we must ask whether John's hallucinatory compression prepares the way for a literalism contrary to its own style. Julia Kristeva lends an enigmatic, if rather generic, clue: "All literature is probably a version of the apocalypse that seems to me rooted, no matter what its socio-historical conditions might be, on the fragile border (borderline cases) where identities (subject/object, etc.) do not exist or only barely so–double, fuzzy, heterogeneous, animal, metamorphosed, altered, abject."[34] John's recycled animal spirits seem to roam the borderlands but also to guard them, to preserve a space for an absolute reality denuded of all fuzzy ambiguity, perhaps thus protecting certain psychic fragilities from further harm.

Yet we also read this text at the edge of a history of its service as the "hidden transcript" of revolutions. From this point of view, the abject marks the identity of the subaltern. According to a liberation rhetorical analysis, its author's awkward use of Greek counts as deliberate anti-elitism, as Jewish colonial subversion of a civilization which defined itself by its language: "barbarians" are those who sound like "bar-bar." According to Allen Callahan, "The Seer's language is due not to intellectual deficiency, but to an idiolectical peculiarity that is both intentional and insurgent." As "an elite victim of an imperial system," John makes use of the "'koine' of provincial elites everywhere in the East" because, like English today, it affords international communication; and "because as the language of domination it must be 'decolonized.'" Thus the closure in context creates a protected space of linguistic dissent. "In every repetition of the solecistic liturgy, in the utterance of each crude calque, the text asserts anew the authenticity of its subaltern voices, voices *subtus altare*," claims Callahan in a delightful play on Rev. 6:9; the spirits speak from "under the altar" in the Vulgate translation. "Language for that moment ceases to be an imperialist prisonhouse."[35]

At the border–*eschaton*–of the tight apocalyptic ego, identity dissolves into pluriformity, and at the same time captures those sacral animalities–purifying, enthroning, eyeing them. Literature of subaltern survival or of literalizing control? Of both together? But what single "view" of this text could survive the multiocular vision?

6

And I saw on the right of the occupant of the throne a document written on the obverse and the reverse sealed up with seven seals. And I saw a mighty angel proclaiming . . . , "Who is worthy to open the document and break its

seals?" And no one in the heaven, no one on the earth, no one under the
earth, could open the document or read it. And I mourned deeply. (Rev.
5:1–4)

Not the "occupant of the throne" but the "document" rivets John's attention. The door of heaven has opened to reveal a scroll, the ultimate "Transcendental Signified," indeed the very "signifier of signifiers"–and no one can read it.[36] No wonder the situation precipitates a paroxysm of scribal grief. The scroll's author is in no simple sense "God." The book of what is to be just *is*–less a personified providence than an impersonal karma. It is written. But not yet *read*.

A voice breaks the moment of suspense: "See, the Lion from the tribe of Judah . . ." But if *voice* announces the victorious Davidic lion, *vision* spots "a little Lamb, standing as though it had been slain." The heavenly hosts chant that "the Lamb who was slain" is the one worthy to read. And into the bargain, "is worthy to receive power and riches and wisdom and might and honor and glory and praise" (5:12).

"John of Patmos' Lamb is, we suspect, the good old lion in sheep's clothing," quips D. H. Lawrence.[37] His own last work, a commentary on John's Apocalypse, reads it as a "revelation of power, pure and simple, and of the raw lust for power." Lawrence did not object to domination– "man has his fulfillment in the gratification of his power-sense" –but to abject hypocrisy. He considered Christianity a cowering mass of ressentiment, sick with envy for the power and wealth of the Romans. In this he joined Friedrich Nietzsche, who found John's Apocalypse "the most rabid outburst of vindictiveness in all recorded history."[38]

On the other hand, Schüssler Fiorenza notes that "both [lion and lamb] images designate Christ as the fulfillment of all Jewish messianic hopes."[39] While retrospectively correct–the metaphor of the slain lamb alludes to Isaiah's suffering servant hymn, which contoured the messianism upon which Jesus, his disciples, and his after-death interpreters would presume–such Christocentric closure can appear both supercessionist and overdrawn. But, as she would stress, these messianic hopes were not of Apocalypse's triumphalist, otherworldly variety: "and they shall reign *on the earth*" (5:10). So the sacrificed lamb, a trope not just for a messiah but also for his persecuted community, deserves not just afterlife benefits but also a fair shake of political and economic

shalom. In this spirit, congregations of the two-thirds world have begun to ask not just for salvation but for democratic access to *power* and
the fair distribution of land and resources, that is, of *riches*; and many
have been awarded instead with martyrdom.

Nonetheless, one might contrast this scene with that of the Lukan
Jesus' beatitudes, which also lift up the oppressed and cast down the
arrogant and affluent. Those who are poor now will not get "wealth,"
the persecuted will not "rule with a rod of iron." The promise in Luke is
only something more realistic to achieve, if more difficult to imagine–
"the kingdom of God." Already. Resources are to be shared, enemies
"loved." Now. Rather than second-guessing Judgment Day, "judge not."
Liberation exegetes have also drawn from the potential of Jesus' parables and sermons of the *basileia* for their this-worldly strategies. Does
the "Jesus before Christianity" voice the transition from apocalypse to
counter-apocalypse, possibly quite precisely in the face of his prediction of the apocalyptic devastation of Jerusalem?[41] The Nazarene may
have discarded the apocalypticism he learned from the Baptist, as New
Testament scholar J. D. Crossan claims.[42] At any rate, he certainly dis-
rupted its facile dualism and high-pitched finality. Indeed, Crossan situates this tension in the "split between Jesus as a sapiential teacher of
wisdom versus Jesus as an apocalyptic prophet of eschatology," located
as far back "as one can ever get in the inaugural Jesus tradition." For all
its subtle antiliteralism, Jesus' path proved subversive enough to lead
him and many who followed it–in South Africa, Central America–to the
slaughter. But no appeal to "the historical Jesus" can settle these issues.
I merely mark a noteworthy first-century Christian rhetorical alternative to John's militant martyrism.

We need not collapse the vision of the Lion-who-is-announced into
the audition of the Lamb-who-appears.[43] The vision of a power from
below, what Elizabeth Janeway called "the power of the weak," does
counter the voice of dominance.[44] Perhaps the mixed medium conveys
its own message: "What is it that insures the existence of the sign, that
is of the *relation* that is a *condensation* between sound image (on the
side of word presentation) and visual image (on the side of thing presentation)?" asks Kristeva. "A language now manifests itself whose
complaint repudiates the common code, then builds itself into an *idio-
lect*, and finally resolves itself through the sudden eruption of *affect*."[45]

Neither the effects nor affects released by the unresolved inner tension of the apocalyptic ear and eye can be overestimated.

The "complaint" inspiring the apocalypse script resignified, I am suggesting, Western signs of the collective future: resentment or revolution, it whispers, whines, mourns—and bursts the "common code."

7

"Come!" And I saw, and behold, a white horse, and its rider had a bow; and a crown was given to him, and he went out conquering and to conquer. (Rev. 6:1–2)

With the breaking of the first four seals of the scroll's seven, four horses burst onto the scene. After the white comes the red, whose rider, given a sword, "was permitted to take peace from the earth, so that men should slay one another" (6:4); next the rider on the black, carrying a balance, while a voice-over announces "a quart of wheat for a denarius, and three quarts of barley for a denarius; but do not harm oil and wine!" (6:6); and then the "yellowish green" horse, "and its rider's name was Death" (6:8).[46]

The four seals implicate a cosmology. "Four" signifies all directions, all elements, all known space. The foursome bursts from the second septet, within the structure of sevens. The astrological number of the known planets (figured in the menorah) organizes creation on the lunar principle: time numerologically envelops space. In the dark of this moontime the nightmares race, riding, ridden, ridding us of world, the world of us. Pain released in fury, four primordial warrior-powers gallop in the double cross-sections between time and space, above and below, discourse and the elements. The equestrian icon of what may be dubbed the apocalyptic sublime has stormed on. On the brink of modernity, the Protestant Dürer had them trample popes; in the final horizon of Bergman's *Seventh Seal* the medieval dance of death foreshadowed modernity's end. Perhaps Lyotard's "incredulity toward metanarratives" thwarts such representations; or do we hear the hoofbeats precisely within the defining postmodern rhetoric of a "presentation of the unrepresentable"?[47] Of the "*end of* modernity"? In their condensation of the unrepresentable, the nightmare quartet can be read as Kristevan "powers of horror"—cosmological "abjects" riding *between*, at once mesmerizing and revolting—or, in Rudolf Otto's prepsychoanalytic language, "mysterium tremendum et fascinans."[48]

Lawrence rode these images hard. "These four horsemen are obviously pagan. They are not even Jewish. . . . In they ride, short and sharp, and it is over."[49] Onto John's reworking of older sources, Lawrence imports a body-loathing, *afterlife* Christianity he disdainfully associates with the Salvation Army and Methodism. But in the esoteric depth of the text, veiled from John himself and now "revealed" by Lawrence, he reads a prebiblical prescription for renewal. The white horse becomes "my sacred ego, called into a new cycle of action by the Lamb and riding forth to conquest . . . of the old self" by way of descent through the "seven psychic centers of the human body," into symbolic death. Like Blake, he discerns an interior vitality of the layered images, which he reads against the words. Unfortunately, Lawrence's more Freudian obsession tends to override his more intriguing insights: "Far back in our dark soul the horse prances. He is a dominant symbol: he gives us lordship: he links us, . . . with the ruddy-glowing Almighty of potency: he is the beginning even of our godhead in the flesh. . . . The sons of God who came down and knew the daughters of men and begot the great Titans, they had 'the members of horses,' says Enoch."[50]

As Lawrence's stallion identification swells into full view, he does us the favor of exposing what orthodox commentators cannot: an archaic masculinity, a phallicism repressed by a celibate overlay. John's text serves as vehicle of Lawrence's own final revelation. "Within the last fifty years man has lost the horse. Now man is lost."[51] John in this reading lambishly resents all that is powerful, sensual, pagan, heroic—all that is Rome-Babylon.

In this manful reading, Lawrence contrasts the ideal femininity (which he will also find in Revelation) to the "New Woman" of his day, who, "wrapped tight and tense in the folds of the Logos . . . is bodiless, abstract and driven by a self-determination terrible to behold." He discerns in equality a sorry sign of the times (as did the fundamentalists, arising as his contemporaries.[52] "Women today," he pronounces, prefiguring the antifeminist rhetoric of political correctness, prude, and puritan, "have a large streak of the police-woman in them."[53] At the thought of a vocal woman, the one cries "whore" and fantasizes his "rod of iron"; the other cries "bodiless" and conjures a stallion's penis. Equal if opposite condensations of image/sound into masculine protest?

What might the riders have signaled within their own context? The white horse's rider, wearing a triumphal wreath, suggested with his bow the Parthian cavalry, who threatened the Pax Romana.[54] Schüssler Fiorenza believes that he "reveals that the expansionistic military power of Babylon/Rome will be overcome. If so, the first rider functions as the precursor of the victorious parousia-Christ."[55] Such a political eschatology seems consonant with the text's messianism—or at least with that of Schüssler Fiorenza. Others consider him a parody of the forthcoming Armageddon messiah and therefore Antichrist.[56] Indeed the figure does seem to ride in harmony with his three vicious fellows. The fiery red horse brings the blood of war. The black horse rides for hunger, famine, and economic injustice: the balance and the voice convey the inflationary cost of the necessities (the denarius was a laborer's day wage) and the protection of luxury items for the elite (olive oil and wine), images that lampoon Roman agricultural policies, their early version of "free trade" with the colonized; also, scales signified justice. The fourth, called Hades, not a natural death but hellish nonlife, rides a corpse-colored horse.

Only with this fourth horse is the quaternity granted "power over a fourth of the earth, to kill with sword and with famine and with pestilence and by wild beasts of the earth" (6:8). In other words, ecological disturbance is understood as an *effect* of systemic injustice. Thus Boesak:

> The horses are not sent out by God, they are the inevitable consequences of the deliberate choices made by men and women. The first four seals and the horses do not denote natural disasters; the earthquake comes only later. All the disasters described thus far are the result of human action. There are wars . . . , not because wars are the will of God but because of . . . the lust for power and domination. There is hunger not merely because there is a lack of food, but because of political and economic policies that foster inequality of the distribution of resources, because of one-sided control of world markets by powerful nations who refuse to enter seriously into the search for a more just, equitable, and sustainable economic order.[57]

The violence of nature begins only here to follow upon the heels of *manmade* violence. An ambiguous victory, this. But the Lamb's performative "reading" of the scrolls *describes* rather than *prescribes* the impending violence. The Apocalypse captures a momentum of destruction already overwhelming late Jewish and early Christian history, having culminated in the destruction of the Second Temple. By prophetic convention, it projects these tribulations into a future narrative. Description slides into prediction. But such prediction does not offer literal foreknowledge of coming events. Whatever ungodly levels of future destruction remain ahead are metaphorically visible to the apocalypticist as potentialities already partly realized. The prophet's preliteralist inversion of time to authorize foreknowledge would only later be twisted into the divine determinism that mocks human efforts at social change. Really, how much better have other prescientific texts done at depicting social practices and environmental consequences that *must* stop, but that they cannot stop?

Of course the question of prediction echoes with the voice-overs of "born-again" preachers. Without homogenizing or demonizing those Christians who call themselves fundamentalists (tempting as it is to use their weapons against them), we note three striking characteristics of the movement. (1) It is, as Ernest Sandeen authoritatively argues, foundationally apocalyptic.[58] (2) At the end of the twentieth century, it is the fastest growing and arguably most influential Christianity anywhere, yet most Christianity through history has sublimated the apocalypticism that arises as fundamentalism's raison d'être. (3) In contrast to liberation theologians, who emphasize the social nature of salvation, fundamentalists stress the salvation of individuals and so gravitate logically from an apolitical to an actively conservative stance.[59]

Contrary to a common view, fundamentalism does not simply feed on uncertainty and fear. It creates a strength of commitment and community rarely found in mainstream Christianity or secular culture. Moreover, fundamentalism does not avert its gaze from the horrors of history and the bankruptcy of modernity. By finding in crisis the fulfillments of "the prophecies," it performs its tour de force: it makes the *cause of fear into the source of hope*. To this end, even the most scholarly dispensationalists such as Walvoord downplay historical context, reading "prophecy" as specifically predicting current events: John had *us* in mind, not his people.[60] They can—perhaps unlike John—greet the four horsemen as "the will of God."[61]

Here springs the "rapture" fantasy.[62] Just as things get horrible on the earth, what with the seals being broken and the beast on his way, the (born-again) Christians will be "caught up in the air with Jesus." Literally. "It will happen!" wrote Hal Lindsy in the biggest nonfiction hit since the Bible. "He is coming to meet all true believers in the air. Without benefit of science, space suits, or interplanetary rockets, there will be those who will be transported into a glorious place more beautiful, more awesome, than we can possibly comprehend." For Lindsy and the Dallas school, the coming of the red horse signifies the futility of peace. "God releases the dreaded second of the four horsemen of the Apocalypse . . . to show that the Antichrist's promises [of peace] cannot stand. The thing which man feared most, an all-out war, now rushes upon him."[63]

Peacemakers espousing biblical ideals of peace, justice, and community obstruct the premillennialist version of the Second Coming, which denounces the UN[64] and the World Council of Churches as carriers of the demonic "new world order" blended of New Age syncretism and communist economics, and dubbed "the New Age world religion."[65] Not just feminism and homosexuality, but ecumenism or even community signal the Antichrist. "In reality, Community is just another synonym for Satan," that is, part of the Babylonian conspiracy "TO DESTROY OUR FAMILIES AND OUR COUNTRY."[66] Thus, despite their own success in building community, right-wing ideologues link "community" with leftist politics (quite correctly, as a later chapter will show), but they fail to note the continuity of revolutionary communities with John's Apocalypse.

Their own congregations claim "soul-winning for Christ" as their "top priority."[67] A popular premillennialist analogy from the 1870s is often cited: "I look on this world as a wrecked vessel. God has given me a life-boat, and said to me, 'Moody, save all you can . . . the children of God don't belong to this world; they're in it, but not of it, like a ship in the water.' "[68] According to Strozier, it is mainly extremist authors and leaders who advocate Armageddon; the rest are merely willing to accept mass death and the damnation of most of humanity as the price of the Second Coming.[69]

This endist individualism reinforces the secular myopias of U.S. culture today—infantile cravings for gratification and rescue. The successful politicization of right-wing Christians, whose apocalypse had kept them largely apolitical, signals a shift in the endtime gait. It allows the right to secretly harness the revolutionary horsepower of apocalypse; it redirects the force of the text away from the liberation encoded into the text, and exploding in movements around the world, into backlash against those very movements. In terms of our other categories, retro-apocalyptic and cryptoapocalyptic effects combine against a dissident neoapocalypse.

8

Under the altar the souls of those who had been slain for the word of God ... cried out with a loud voice, "O Sovereign Lord, holy and true, how long before thou wilt judge and avenge our blood on those who dwell upon the earth?" (Rev. 6:9–10)

Now we come to a *locus classicus* of the "subaltern." This under-the-altar scene lends to the book's bad press: with its determinist numerology of martyrdom, it seems to "seal" salvation into the vengeance of victims. Mainline commentators have readily cried "subchristian!" (thereby distinguishing, via an anti-Judaic logic, Old Testament vengefulness from Gospel love). Schüssler Fiorenza retorts:

Since many exegetes do not suffer unbearable oppression and are not driven by the question of justice, they often label this outcry as un-Christian and contrary to the preaching of the gospel. However, only if this outcry for justice and for vindication, for the revenge of so many lives taken ... is understood, can the theological quest of Revelation be adjudicated.[70]

Citing the Jewish Josephus, who reports that the Zealots accepted torture and execution rather than acknowledge the Roman emperor as "sovereign," she argues that in using this title here for God, "John alludes to the fact that those whom Roman justice has failed and killed acknowledge God as true sovereign."[71]

Since, however, her call for "understanding" is somewhat circular (you can only understand what you already understand), let us for a moment crawl under the altar. However unedifying, this religiosity of woundedness depicts a rage that turns wraithlike when cut off. It resembles what Koreans call *han*—an emotion of the oppressed mixed of repressed rage, grief, and simmering resentment.[72] "An ego, wounded to the point of annulment, barricaded and untouchable, cowers somewhere, nowhere, at no other place than the one that cannot be found."[73] Kristeva, descending to the abject, writes, "Where objects are concerned he [the abject] delegates phantoms, ghosts, 'false cards': a stream of spurious egos."[74]

Opening psychoanalysis into theopolitics, the altar's ego yields no neatly customized afterlife. The global systems of persecution must be overcome before salvation can be realized. Salvation, in other words, is still constructed as social process. Yet the textual *pathos* festers "under the altar," beneath the sanctum of social surfaces or liturgical order, in the shadows of a disembodied underside that is hellish but not hell, intermediate but not purgatorial, incurable at the level of an ego, an individual.[75] It suggests the suspenseful, cumulative energy of suffering. Does the primitive Christian text share a sensibility with Leslie Marmon Silko's *Almanac of the Dead*, wherein Wiesel Tale explains the Ghost Dance? " 'We dance and we do not forget all the others before us, the little children and the old women who fought and who died, resisting the invaders and destroyers of Mother Earth!' " After a sip of water, he continues, " 'The spirits are outraged! They demand justice! The spirits are furious!' "[76] The line between justice and vengeance is subtle, since the needed changes will *feel* like hell to those who benefit most from injustice: the collapse of their privilege is its own punishment.

And the exaltation of martyrdom? The souls under the altar are to number the "144,000" before the end.[77] Elaine Pagels has argued that martyrdom represented acts of public resistance to the totalizing cult of the Roman Empire, which ought not be anachronistically read as masochism.[78] So liberation martyrology, at the end of modernity, memorializes not just giants like Archbishop Romero, but the numberless anonymous victims of neocolonialism and its client elites.

I think of another Salvadoran, whose story I heard at the women's center in San Salvador, who left her marriage, was rejected by her church, and blossomed into joyous, visible leadership among women, not just organizing teachers and working-class women for their rights but, for instance, offering a radio cooking show for women, which she peppered with comments like "You weren't meant to be a servant." After three years she was abducted for an afternoon of rape, torture, and death by the paramilitary. A global "chain of hope" in her name—María Cristina Gómez—was organized. My hair stood on end as her daughter interpreted her mother's murder: "The evil forces were not able to stop what for her had meant life." A resurrection of martyrs, indeed, of martyrology.

Under the altar of this text gathers the tension of prematurely stifled lives, a peculiarly Western mix of high expectation with deferred dream. Futurity here barricades itself into a space apart–*kadosh*, separate, holy–vulnerable to the most rabid sublimities. This intensified sense of deferral offers a clue to postmodernity. Derrida thematized deferral it-self–as *différance*, the differing which disrupts the homogenizing ego or single end and thus endlessly *defers* "presence."[79] Does deconstruction, however rightly interrogating any decisive position, end up making de-ferral into an end in itself–an endless "post-"? But let it suffice for now to touch the wound in the deferral, the haunts of hope, who never thought to wait so long.

9

Behold, there was a great earthquake; and the sun became black as sack-cloth, the full moon became like blood, and the stars of the sky fell to the earth as the fig tree sheds its winter fruit when shaken by a gale; the sky vanished like a scroll that is rolled up, and every mountain and island was removed from its place. (Rev. 6:12)

The sixth seal. The earth, ultimate ground of any stability, revolts.[80] Foundations shake down and horizons close. In effect, the openness of sky winds into a scroll: a book replaces space itself. Symbolically the scroll/book/text did, in exile with the Jews, take the place of any particu-lar place. Compared to indigenous spiritualities, the abstraction of "book peoples" from particular places is noteworthy. For Jews, this de-tachment, prepared for by the anti-idolatry cult of the Yahwists (oppos-ing indigenous earth-spiritualities), was later necessitated by exile and landlessness. For Christians, suppressing indigenous practices in Eu-rope and then in its colonies, "heaven" as site of ultimate significance kept us "pilgrims" on the earth–"This world is not my home." The mod-ern ecological ravaging of the planet followed; and the subaltern body of woman, embodying earth times and moon tides, stable or shaky, would provide the intimate foil for abstraction itself.[81]

Yet at the threshold of the vision, the assault on "chaos" is not yet an institution. "When the world is perceived to be chaotic, reversed, limi-nal, filled with anomie," writes Jonathan Z. Smith, "then man [*sic*] finds himself in a world which he does not recognize; and perhaps even more terrible, man finds himself to have a self he does not recognize. Then he will need to create a new world, to express his sense of a new place."[82]

Not just yet. Nor need we let the scholarly story of our continual self-re-creation out of the chaos brush aside the nagging materiality of the dislocation. Revelation 6 anticipates another throne-room vision, "a great white throne and him who sat upon it; from his presence earth and sky fled away, and no place was found for them" (20:11).[83] "No place" for the earth and sky, a paradox that our eco-history now performs. Nor then is there any place of refuge: "The kings of the earth and the great men and the generals and the rich and the strong, and every one, slave and free," in vain hide "in the caves and among the rocks of the mountains" (6:15–16; 19:18). Disaster creates its own democracy. In the meantime, the affluent can buy clean water, organic vegetables, and psychotherapy, continuing to consume the planetary commons. But we can't hide in our climate-controlled caves forever.

Next is sung a hymn of consolation to the white-clad crew of martyrs, they who "have bathed their robes and made them bright in the blood of the Lamb" (7:14). Note the earthiness of their desire, promising not ethereal blessings but the fulfillment of basic human needs–what Lacan calls "the Real." For denizens of the two-thirds world, such pain-washed hope, far from infantile, stirs immediate recognition: "They shall not hunger anymore or thirst anymore, neither shall the sun nor any scorching heat fall upon them, because the Lamb . . . will shepherd them and guide them to springs of living water; and God will wipe away every tear from their eyes" (Rev. 7:16–17).

10

Structurally, the six seals summarize the book and the tribulation process right up to the point of final judgment and an anticipation of the New Jerusalem, a cool, comforting utopia of nourishment and nurture. But what of the seventh seal? "And when the Lamb broke the seventh seal, there was silence in heaven for what seemed half an hour" (8:1).

An eerie silence–sinister sabbath. Now we expect some climactic devastation. Instead, the curious literary structure of the book discloses itself. The content of the seventh seal *is* the entire new septet which follows, of seven angels blowing seven trumpets. So each set of seven in fact twists like the turn of a spiral into the next set. By this compositive device the seventh item in fact *is* the entire new set: the doom of the seventh trumpet will *be* the seven signs (and again, there will be a silence upon the descent of the seventh angel, who will command that "the words of the seven thunders" be sealed up and not written down) and so on, through seven septets. This literary "technique of intercalation" lets each septet in some way recapitulate and amplify the previous one. With each twist the tribulations worsen; yet the process cannot be read either as a cyclical repetition or as a linear progression.[84] Each septet spirals back over the previous seven, not repeating, but redescribing the situation, "turning and turning in the widening gyre" (William Butler Yeats, "The Second Coming"). Yet with each cycle the narrative surges forward. As Schüssler Fiorenza puts it, "This method of composition makes Revelation end-oriented rather than cyclic or encyclopedic. . . . At the same time, [the author] conveys structurally . . . that the eschatological future gives meaning to the present situation and struggle."[85] So the promise of solace comforts *now*, and the Last Day justifies *present* commitment.

The eschatological spiral envisions the future as though it has already occurred. For the communities who listened to this letter from John of Patmos, much of the doom described in the first five seals had indeed occurred—Israel had been through cataclysmic times, including the genocidal destruction of Jerusalem and the Second Temple within the same generation (70 C.E.). In a sense its world had come to an end. And the same causal matrix of Roman oppression still obtained in John's present. The literary device of the future-past intensifies the spiral of violence to a prolepsis of total collapse, and thus, in the perennial gamble of the genre, clears the space for the new age.

Apocalypse, piercing the omega point, fathered the Western timeline. Yet it does not conform to it. The temporality of the text radiates from the spiral of its composition. In its looping dream-momentum of doom and hope, its structure remains considerably less linear than numerous Greek, Roman, and Hellenistic narratives normally relegated to the category of "timeless myth."[86] But out of this helical temporality, its omega would be afterwards abstracted as the endpoint of a line: salvation history, straightening out the apocalyptic drama, would repress the loops, the gaps, the overlaps. Such linear historicity has little to do with the Hebrew time sensibility still scripting the Apocalypse, a time which drives forward but, as Boman claimed, "rhythmically" rather than sequentially.[87] The fugue-like structure of spiraling septets is indeed cosmically, cataclysmically, "cryptogrammically" *rhythmic*. Like all secret codes it both resists and invites historic reference.

As outlined in the story of creation-Christ-*eschaton*, Western time came to mirror the structure of a book. That is, of the canonized Christian Bible precisely as a book and not a scroll. The history of the material artifact of "book" oddly reinforces the paradox, given the new device of the codex, pioneered and possibly invented by the poorly educated, lower-class Christians of the Roman Empire. According to Jack Miles's *God: A Biography*, Roman literary elites disdained the codex, adhering to the older tradition of the scroll. The Jews have retained the scroll ever since for ceremonial purposes. But the scroll, which allowed thirty pages maximum (about the length of the Book of Isaiah) and could only be stored in containers, tended to keep the parts "mentally moveable and to forestall any tendency to edit them into a single, large, closed anthology." As the flat and linear codex was not "felt to be a proper book," at first, "the separate works of the New Testament have not traditionally been called books"; we do not speak of the "Book of Matthew or Book of Paul." "True," comments Miles parenthetically, "there is the Book of Revelation, but Revelation is a late, consciously antiquarian exercise by a writer who is, among other peculiarities, fairly obsessed with the scroll as a physical object."[88] So—to clarify the paradox—the bookish fantasy of a scrolling spiral served to flatten the alpha and omega into a canonical line of closure.

In the dreamtime of apocalypse, each twist of the spiral opens and closes time: no timeless space but a *limen* or threshold tense with tenses. To let Revelation frustrate the a priori assumption of time as a causal series is to shake the construction of Western historicism from within. At the same time perhaps it scrolls Apocalypse free of the endist literalism for which it is the necessary mythic origin but not therefore sufficient cause.

11

Now is the time . . . for destroying the destroyers of the earth. (Rev. 11:18)

The notion of earth-destroyers seems prescient if read from the operative anachronism of an ecological perspective. It also clarifies theologically what most fundamentalists forget—that the destruction is not the will of this God. One tastes in the text of uncreation after all some love of the first creation. Here at the end of the second, the most environmental, series of tribulations in the text, the warning (so impossible then, so casual now) sounds explicitly: as *"the nations rage"* (11:18), the planet is dying.

Most Christian biblicists advocate some mix of dispensationalist premillennialist cum "wise use" ideology, queuing up with the destroyers. There are important exceptions, such as Billy Graham in his *Approaching Hoofbeats*, in which he makes an apocalyptic case for good stewardship in "the meantime."[89] The H. W. Armstrong Worldwide Church of God's periodical *The Plain Truth* published a frankly environmentalist issue, its cover displaying a shattered planet with the subscript "Planet EARTH: Beyond Repair?" The magazine joins current statistics and classical prophetic promises: the "deforested, abused and parched lands" will once again become productive; "with Isaiah, 'the desert shall rejoice and blossom as the rose . . . for waters shall burst forth in the wilderness.'" These exceptional evangelicals then translate eco-apocalypse into the need for "a very different economic system. . . . The inequitable system of our world–the system that leads to immense wealth and greed on the one hand and poverty and unending debt on the other–will be replaced." That "this requires global centers of cooperation" sounds like what fundamentalism identifies as the Antichrist's peace coalition.[90] The last biblical quote is Revelation 11:18, and the question is asked, "If God is going to establish a government that will take care of our environmental problems, what responsibility do today's governments have?"–a question aimed at Christian social passivity. "A loving God will . . . intervene and spare his creation from total extinction. But not without consequence. The Bible says that the time is coming when God will 'destroy those who destroy the earth.'" Such interventionism theologically reinforces the very irresponsibility it addresses. Yet given the anti-environmentalism of its audience, the warning seems well-placed. "In his love for his creation, he will right the many wrongs humanity has inflicted upon its planet and upon itself. . . . The earth will be saved." Appealing to paternal omnipotence, this argument confronts its audience within their own terms. I derive a bit of counter-apocalyptic cheer from Revelation's ability to bear correctives to its own abuse, and welcome eco-evangelicals to a conversation in which most fundamentalists by definition do not take part.

12

And a great portent appeared in heaven, a woman clothed with the sun,
with the moon under her feet, and on her head a crown of twelve stars.
(Rev. 12:1)

Suddenly we find ourselves in the atmosphere of a heavenly female
radiating all the cosmic luminaria. Even Yahweh, for all his sky symbols, never robed himself in sun, moon, and stars all at once.[91] Who is
she? What does the surplus brilliance of this text signal? Most key characters in the book bear titles; this one remains anonymous. "Woman
clothed with the sun" has apocryphally been referred to as "the Queen
of Heaven." Medieval iconography transferred the Sun Woman's celestial cyphers to the dogmatically safer (always only human) Mary.
Clothed with the sun and standing on the moon, the celestial woman
prefigured the Assumption of the Virgin.[92] Thus made cosmic, Mary
could attract goddess-accustomed folk; for instance, the Virgin of Gua-
dalupe always comes imprinted with moon beneath her feet and golden
aura around her body. But beyond the fact that she is about to give birth
to a supernatural male, the text does not support that I.D. Mainstream
Protestant tradition identifies this figure with the people Israel giving
birth to the Church; she then prefigures the New Jerusalem, who will
appear as virgin bride at the book's climax. But why rush to allegorize,
to doctrinalize, to make "her" an "it"? Since the Bible yields up so few
icons of cosmic power in the female, why foreclose our metaphoric
options?

For just a moment she hovers here, at the "centerpiece of the Apocalypse."[93] Effulgent with the lights of nature, she resists the archetypal
confinement of "the feminine" to moon, earth, and sea. If anything more
solar than lunar, her crown marking her as astrological, she embodies
the whole expanse of space.[94] The dying Lawrence's passion for the "pagan bedrock" of the *Apocalypse* unveils her misfit: "This wonder-woman
clothed in the sun and standing upon the crescent of the moon was too
splendidly suggestive of the great goddess of the east, the great Mother,
the Magna Mater as she became to the Romans.... How then does she
come to tower as the central figure in a Jewish Apocalypse?"[95]

Even steeped in such an overripe matriarchal hypothesis, Lawrence's
question, so long predating current goddess-feminism, is well taken.
While patriarchal polytheism could rape, marry, or demote, rather than

64

eliminate, most goddesses, monotheism by contrast had to strain them out of its universe. It retained here and there a "feminine" trait for the Lord, and otherwise maligned "Ashtorah" and other Ishtar/Isis variants as temptresses, their female supporters as Jezebels. So why, from a feminist rather than a Lawrencian perspective, read an anonymous goddess back *into* this grimly androcentric text?

First of all, such a reading acknowledges the contextual resonances of the imagery. Biblical scholars note the Sun Woman's resemblance to Greco-Roman revivals of the great goddess, especially to the goddess Roma, worshipped in Asia as a mother goddess.[96] But they tend to curtly dismiss the *significance* of the allusion: "It seems unlikely that a book like this apocalypse, devoted to a polemic against idolatry, should utilize pagan symbols of the faithful community."[97] Precisely. To dally with this improbability is to read the text in *spite* of its intention. Thus a second motive: to cultivate the gap between what is seen and what is said, where archaic images may break in to dance a few steps of the unacceptable. If this gap unearths some "collective unconscious," we need not thereby summon with it a static pantheon of "archetypes." Intercultural and intertextual thea/logies are already lurking within the historical margins of the text.[98] Retrospectively this cosmic "she" may display a life of her own, one not of a timeless truth but of a timely possibility, perceivable perhaps neither to sexists nor to radical feminists.

The epiphany resembles, for instance, the Egyptian sky goddess Nut and especially the Hellenistic revival of her daughter, Isis. The latter, in vogue at the time of the early Christian movement, says of herself:

> I am she that is called goddess by women . . .
> I showed the paths of the stars.
> I ordered the course of the sun and the moon . . .
> I made the right to be stronger than gold and silver.
> I ordained that the true should be thought good . . .
> I am in the rays of the sun . . .
> I set free those in bonds . . .[99]

Thus Isis joins cosmic powers to an ethic of liberation. A second aretology, or poem of praise, credits her with a less biblical accomplishment: "Thou didst make the power of women equal to that of men."[100] Since goddesses were still much in evidence, not merely unconscious archetypes, maintenance of orthodox Jewish or Christian identities required their active repression. The appearance of our Queen of Heaven's scintillating counter-patriarchal forcefield interrupts her own text's presuppositions. Why does apocalyptic discourse permit such a disruptive, if veiled, visitation? Freud found that "the return of the repressed," its "irruption," the "failure of repression," expresses itself precisely in an "end of the world."[101] *Whose* world, "she" asks back? So a third motive must be admitted, driving the first two: the need for a female image of the divine.

13

She was with child and was crying out in her birthpangs in the agony of giving birth. (Rev. 12:2)

Might we imagine that this "great sign" appears amidst cataclysm in order to bear some new possibility? Cosmogonic females routinely gave birth to universes—like Eurynome, a pre-Hellenic/Orphic figure, goddess of the primeval night, who in partnership with the cosmic serpent gave birth to the planets. The Sun Woman's labor is the book's first *glimpse* of hope; heretofore hope has been merely *voiced*.

Even among innumerable biblical deliveries this birth is noteworthy. The first condemned all daughters of Eve to painful deliveries. Yet the Greek term for Eve's suffering, *basanizomene*, "being in torment," is otherwise scripturally never applied to motherhood. (Among other, extracanonical apocalypses such as Ezra's, birth imagery recurs, but signals the moment of hope for cosmic renewal.) *Basanizomene* means "to apply the touchstone," that is, "to test the genuineness of a thing," and to use torture to do so. The *basanos* was for the ancient Greeks the "touchstone" by which, according to Page du Bois, "the process of torture takes on the metaphorical language of reproduction; truth is born from torture, it is released in painful labor that turns the informer into a woman giving birth."[102] Virginia Burrus has shown how one early Christian female martyr subverted this production of *aletheia*, proving herself "the ultimate virtuoso of torture" in her "noble refusal to speak the torturer's truth," that is, through her "speaking the Christian truth with the body itself."[103] The term for the Sun Woman's "crying out"[104] connotes "proclaiming in the face of contradiction" and articulates the cry of the martyrs to God (6:10). The simile of the mother in travail has prophetic precedents: "The daughter of Zion cries in anguish, gasping for breath like a woman in travail" (Jer. 4:31); the men of devastated Judah hold their hands on their loins "like a woman in labor" (Jer. 30:6).

Pregnant and single in the misogynist heavens, she remains an endangered protagonist on the surface of a text which robs her of name and language. If we imagine a "deep background" (in Mary Daly's phrase) against which she could recall (then, now) her cosmological productivity, then no wonder she shrieks "in the face of contradictions."

14

And another portent appeared in heaven; behold, a great red dragon, with seven heads and ten horns, and seven diadems upon his heads. His tail swept down a third of the stars of heaven, and cast them to the earth. And the dragon stood before the woman who was about to bear a child, that he might devour her child when she brought it forth; she brought forth a male child, one who is to rule all the nations with a rod of iron. (Rev. 12:3–5)

The "great sign" of the celestial woman provokes an opposite and equal omen–the red dragon of flaming evil, constellated in voracious antagonism. If earlier the book was "full of eyes," it undergoes, in the second half, a semiotic shift: once John is forced to eat the second scroll, the text is full of mouths. As the red mouth of her womb opens, the red dragon appears, perverse mimesis, mouth open to eat the issue. What *is* the issue?

Manhood? As the text translates literally, the woman gives birth to "a son, a man." "The phrase," notes Ford, "is a peculiar one and although it may sound redundant it probably stresses the 'manliness' of the son, his characteristics as a warrior."[105] This is *boy* to the second power, macho in miniature. Perhaps this "redundancy" worsens her "contradiction," itself mute, read through a tortured masculinity. Perhaps, in Kristeva's words, "abjection preserves what existed in the archaism of pre-oedipal relationship, in the immemorial violence with which a body becomes separated from another body in order to be."[106] However we may historicize any such hermeneutics of birth, the Apocalypse labors violently to separate lives from their first bodies.

"But her child was snatched away and taken to God and to his throne" (12:5). Churning with gender tensions–between the heavenly mother, the hyper-boy, and the invisible father–the text could read as a parody of the holy family. If the Synoptic Mary is only "heavenly" in her capacity to conceive without a man, the Apocalypse Kid makes baby Jesus look like a wimp. Jesus grew up to teach and heal, not to rule by the rod; his mama's anguish marks not his birth but his death. As for most promising boys, the destiny of the "son-man" of the Apocalypse lies in identification with the transcendent Male. If mom is the queen of heaven, dad is enthroned in the higher heavens. The very absence of the father invests the patriarchal throne with its power to "snatch" the boy.[107] If such supercession of mom by dad happens routinely under patriarchal childrearing circumstances, it at least reveals itself here as catastrophic.[108] And once again, when a woman appears, the "rod of iron" follows.[109]

At this instant the Apocalypse bursts into full-fledged oppositionalism: the Enemy appears in person. Or rather, in dragon. In this most dualistic book of the canon, *this* is the moment at which good and evil break into absolute polarity. Evil congeals over and against a helpless woman. In response to this danger, the forces of pure good, also masculine, constellate: "War broke out in heaven; Michael and his angels fought against the dragon" (12:7). The celestial woman's epiphany provokes—in symbolic counterbalance to her ambiguous power?—an absolute display of male forces. For the first time, the Bible introduces the two opposing teams: Michael and His Angels versus the Dragon and his. But only after the defeat of the dragon "and his angels" is evil named: "And the great dragon was thrown down, that ancient serpent, who is called the Devil and Satan, the deceiver of the whole world" (12:9). The editorial voice, labeling and literally demonizing, comes on stronger than ever. True to local mythology, John collates the dragon image with that of the ancient serpent. By identifying it as "Devil" and "Satan" the author, a victim of the West, ironically bequeaths to the West the image it would deploy for our moral superiority.

Why, however, would the dragon want to eat the baby? The text suggests that the messianic baby, destined to total power over the earth, poses a mortal threat to the dragon in heaven. At this level, the tale refracts the oedipal pattern already set forth in Sumerian and Greek cosmogonies, in which father gods try to nip their sons in the bud. Does the dragon carry Yahweh's shadow?[110] Adela Yarbro Collins has drawn the parallels to the Python-Leto-Apollo triad, as well as to the Egyptian triad of Set-Isis-Hathor.[111]

The last book of the Bible again darkly mirrors the first. At the end of time, the dragon in a cosmic tantrum knocks down the stars. But the dragon was there before the stars were up. It was resting in liquid latency, as the salty abyss, the *tehom*, out of which all things were made. In Genesis the dragon remains anonymous, masked as the "face of the deep." In Genesis 2, the noun *tehom* translates the Sumerian *tiamat*–the creator-mother-dragon of the *Enuma Elish*.[112] The cthonic spirits had begun to appear as enemy to the Bronze Age heroes, as, for instance, Marduk slaughtering Tiamat–"only a female thing"–in order to create his own cosmos from her corpse. The degradation of the goddess and the demonization of the serpent are thus corollary semiotic processes, the *locus classicus* of which, Genesis 2–3, already presupposes a widespread Middle Eastern revolt against cosmic mothers. The biblical demotion of the serpent-dragon to a "creeping, crawling thing" effectively divided and conquered the old serpent/goddess pair–a strategy key to the symbolization of sky-god monotheism and male supremacy. When Revelation 12 narratively reconfigures Genesis's mythology of creation–mother of life (*Hava*, Eve), snake, and fall (now literally from heaven to the earth)–as the defeat of the rebellious angels in heaven, the scene is set for the culminating terrestrial battle. Thus the text promotes the snake back up from garden-variety creep to cosmic Evil worthy to oppose the Good. Apocalypse does not casually *reverse* Genesis. The "fall" of the first creation narrative is *replayed*, taken into the spiral, in order to solve it–to end it.

Not that the serpent-dragon–figured slithering around so many neolithic pots, slicing through earth and water, sloughing and renewing self, uttering oracular wisdom–had represented "good." It seems to have vitalized a spatiality "beyond good and evil," beyond the binary construct which depends–for good and ill–upon heroic monotheism.

Rather than a serpentine time-cycle of perennial spatial re-creation, the Apocalypse scripts in the midst of its spiral a once-for-all-time creation, salvation, judgment, and new creation. John's mythopoeic helix *unwinds* time from its material base of particular places. The presupposition but not yet the realization of sequential time, such abstraction from space emerges only slowly, against resistance. So the serpent trope of renewal was progressively demonized. Is this why its elemental associations of water and earth contradict rather than complement "her" air and fire, threatening to extinguish her lights, eat her issue?

15

As soon as the dragon found himself thrown down to the earth, he sprang in pursuit of the woman. (Rev. 12:13)

Why? The voice-over explains. "Woe to the earth and the sea"–those serpent elements–"for the devil has come down to you in great wrath, because he knows that his time is short" (12:12). On the textual surface he vents fury at imminent defeat. But consider the logic of the dream: if a monster pursues you, you need only turn around, face it, and learn its desire, for it to reveal itself as some part of yourself, furious at having been split off.[113] It–the "id," "shadow," "other"–craves acknowledgment. The repressed returns, dragon-red in its rage, wound, and passion.

"The terror over creepy crawlies is merely an icon," suggests Morris Berman in his analysis of the Western dissociation from the body-self. "It is isomorphic to the anxiety over the body and finally attains a visible in the yearning for *Vernichtung* (extermination) *Gleichschaltung* (leveling, homogenization). . . . We shall solve it *all*, destroy any vestige of a wild, disorganized Other *entirely*, so that Self now reigns supreme in a pure, dead and totally predictable world."[114] Western orthodoxies have identified with the angelic army, hunting down the chaos dragon, whose slippery identity could readily be foisted on any socially inconvenient "others," Muslim, Jewish, heterodox, female, dark-skinned, and so on. But Berman misses the gender of this homogenizing angst. We note, however, the feminized status of whatever is "wild," "organic," "disorganized," "fluid"–bodily?[115] Not "essentially" more earthy or liquid, women remain liable to construction as such. As the god-identified masculinity "transcends" its organic ground, so the female splits into heavenly and base. Thus even in an antipuritanical period of "body conscious" commodifications, only a young, dry, tight "female thing," a minimally organic body, boundaries firm, purged of the marks of time and earth, gains approval: so we feel monstrous if our belly bulges.[116] As Foucault reads power written in the body, so power inscribes itself as apocalypse in women's flesh, publishing ever new translations of old medusas, dragons, witches, whores, and bitches. We are offered redemption within the system of homogenizing transcendence as well–on condition that we dissociate from our corporeal power base. From our red dragons.

16

But the woman was given the two wings of the great eagle, so that she could fly from the serpent into the wilderness, to her place where she is nourished for a time, and times, and half a time. (Rev. 12:14)

She "was given" the wings. In this particular case of Revelation's re-current passive voice, exegetes presume rescue by God; they disregard the divinity of the woman. Within the earth's atmosphere, the Sun Woman sprouts wings, those of an eagle, mythograph of soaring solarity. Again she flies in the face of archetypes: while Jungians label eagle, like sun, as "masculine," this anonymous goddess recalls the winged disk of Egyptian iconography, associated with soul guides like Hathor and Isis, as in the latter's flight from the dragon-crocodile Set. (I also think of Fan-chon, choreographer, Jewish feminist liturgist, at six feet and six de-cades when she first went hang-gliding; clutching the young male in-structor, she heard a huge voice rise up out of her, crying, "I am eagle queen.")

Revelation 12:14 may be read as gloss on the Exodus liberation narra-tive. "You have seen what I did to the Egyptians, and how I bore you on eagles' wings and brought you to myself" (Exod. 19:4).[117] But the winged one is God. To cite an instance of a traditional midrash, the Palestinian Targum to Deuteronomy 32:10ff:

> As an eagle stirs up and cares for his[?] nest, and hovers over his young, so
> did his Shekinah stir up the tents of Israel, and the shadow of his Shekinah
> overspread them; and as an eagle outstretches his wings over his young
> ones, bears them and carries them upon his wings, so bore he them and
> carried them, and made them dwell upon the strong places of the land.

Cagily masculinizing the eagle-mother, the Targum presents the *Sheki-nah* of God as protective presence; in exilic Judaism this feminine noun for the "presence" of God personified God dwelling with the people, guiding them in exodus and accompanying them in exile. She signifies divine immanence, painfully divided from the transcendent Yahweh. *Shekinah*, from "dwelling-place," finds—*is*—the homing Presence.[118] The desert, Hebrew site of death and renewal, loss and epiphany, raw nature and ritual culture, was dotted with "strong places." The Babylonian Tashmit was called "Lady of the Dwelling Places"; Yahweh himself was "the everlasting dwelling place" (Psalm 90:1).

More recently, Luce Irigaray would reconsider the femininity of place, recognizing our bodies as place for not just fetus or man but for ourselves (and surely also for other women?). "When separated from place, the thing feels an attraction to place as a condition of existence." Perhaps this character of place as "not the thing but that which permits

71

the thing to be" grounds the association of goddess and mother with place, as site of incarnation, of living as belonging to the earth. "I shall affirm," writes Irigaray, "that the masculine is attracted to the maternal-feminine as place. But what place does the masculine offer to attract the feminine? His soul? His relation to the divine? Can the feminine be inscribed or situated there?" In this welcome twist, according to which the masculine imaginary of Yahweh as dwelling would also find its place, she invokes a hopeful, almost counterintuitive mutualism: "If any meeting is to be possible between man and woman, each must be a place, as appropriate to and for the other, and toward which he or she may move." As below, so above.[119]

So the very sense of place, the divinity of place, has long known itself displaced, fleeing, seeking. Other ancient texts, differently divined, anticipated the flight of the divine female to her place. For instance, the intertestamental "Jewish apocalypse" of Enoch:

Wisdom went forth to make her dwelling
Among the children of men [humans]
And found no dwelling place;
Wisdom returned to her place . . . (Enoch 1:42)

Wisdom, who says of herself, "He created me from the beginning before the world and I shall never fail" (Ecclus. 24:9), was early assimilated both to Mary and to the sun-robed figure.[120] Nelle Morton, a mother of feminist theology, recognized this "pervasive wisdom" as "feminist," a female figure of the divine if such exists in the Bible.[121] If this Sophia/Hochma finds civilization inhospitable, it is no wonder. The thought of her return provoked major ecclesial convulsions even at the end of (our) second millennium.[122] In the meantime, the displaced Presence remains in retreat—at "*her* place."[123]

Then from his mouth the serpent poured water like a river after the woman, to sweep her away with the flood. But the earth came to the help of the woman; the earth opened its mouth and swallowed the river that the dragon had poured from his mouth. (Rev. 12:15)

The dragon pursues, orality accelerates: after the mouth of the womb opens to the monstrous maw, now the serpent vomits a river from his mouth—and the earth opens its lips to drink the effluvium. The veiled interplay of thwarted yearnings invests the text with an amorphous, elemental sexuality. Its female associations notwithstanding, the serpent now spews phallic aggression at a fleeing woman, a "malestream" threatening to engulf her (perhaps as reading women, yearning to remain *au courant*, get "swept away").

The earth, not "God," intervenes–mysterious in a tradition bent on disenchantment of the earth. The moment recalls a gesture, a *mudra*, from another founding moment: Gautama, meditating under the Bo tree, in the wilderness, is attacked by the Demon Lord and so touches the earth, who rescues him. Buddhism is born. The earth both times models an exemplary nonviolence towards angry demons.

Not disgusted by this gushing serpentine sensuality, the earth receives the flux. Mouth to mouth. Beneath the textual skin, a counterapocalypse mouths off, dousing dualisms of good/evil, male/female. The gender of dragon remains ticklishly ambiguous.[124] Wounded or healing, the serpentine subjectivity keeps sloughing textual identities.

17

Then the dragon took his stand on the sand of the seashore. And I saw a beast rising out of the sea ... (Rev. 13:1–2)

Wet and wily, the dragon reproduces itself from the gaping womb– the raging seas which terrified the landlubberly biblical peoples. This is the third in the set of seven signs. Beginning with the woman clothed with the sun, the portents shift style from lists (seven churches, seals, trumpets) to mini-allegories. Here is the story. The dragon, warring on "the rest of her children," witnesses a beast with ten horns and seven heads emerge. In parody of the Lamb, the latter sports a mortal/healed wound. Next, sign four, the last in a trinity of monsters, a beast rises out of the earth. Like the right-hand man of Caesar, this third beast will politically subject the world to the beast from the sea. Sign five: the Lamb stars with a cast of thousands in a musical number on Mt. Zion. The lyrics ("and they sing a new song before the throne" [14:3]) awkwardly echo Psalm 96. But rather than eschatologically opening a community into its future, the "new" seems esoterically to close it in: "No one could learn that song except the 144,000. . . . It is these who have not defiled themselves with women, for they are virgins" (14:3–4).

Nothing ambiguous about the sex of these "first fruits." How seriously must we take this sexism, given the prominence of celibate women

among the martyrs? On behalf of a liberation apocalypse, Schüssler Fiorenza attempts to forestall the "linguistic determinism" of a predictable
feminist response. "Such a feminist analysis, for instance, traces and
highlights the grammatically masculine language of Revelation that
makes women invisible or marginal in the text. . . . Such language, moreover, as when reading Revelation 14:4 . . . in a literalist sense, insists that
the true followers of the Lamb are male ascetic warriors."[125] By all means
let us not add to the strings of literalist readings of this book; but the problem lies not as much in literalism as in misogynist symbolism. The allusion to the single human woman in the text as Jezebel, the obsessional
warrior imagery, and the stereotyped purity of good femininity (let
alone the forthcoming trope of the Great Whore) combine with the quite
literal-sounding claim about "those who have not defiled themselves
with women" to sustain a higher pitch of androcentrism than most of the
Bible's. Abiding in ambivalence, we may acknowledge the misogyny
without thereby dismissing the intersecting zones of liberation.

By the seventh sign, the known world is nearly to an end. Angels "reap
the earth" in a bloody harvest, and "every living thing died that was in the
sea." Only now, the planet's doom foreseen, do we spiral back and zoom in
on the fall of Babylon. "She" appears in imperial arrogance: " 'A queen I
sit, I am no widow, mourning I shall never see' " (18:7). The graphic septet
depicting her fall, a straightforward allegory of the anticipated fall of
Rome, has offered revolutionaries special solace. Angels sing the denunciation of the empire. The "Whore of Babylon" then rides the seven-
headed beast. "This calls for a mind with wisdom:"–a conspiratorial
wink to the reader–"the seven heads are seven mountains on which the
woman is seated" (17:9), that is, of course, the seven hills of Rome. Given
Rome's repressive apparatus, it was prudent to bury the anti-imperialist
polemic in cryptograms rolled into the last third of the traveling scroll.

18

Fallen is Babylon the Great! . . . the dwelling place of demons, a haunt of
every foul spirit. . . . For all the nations have drunk of the wine of the wrath
of her fornication, and the kings of the earth have committed fornication
with her, and the merchants of the earth have grown rich from the power
of her luxury. (Rev. 18:2–3)

For the first time, John discloses the historical identity of the "destroyers of the earth." The vision pans to Rome-Babylon's clients. As Bab-

ylon falls, the "kings of the earth, who committed fornication and were wanton with her," who will "wail over her when they see the smoke of her burning," sing a lament; then the "merchants of the earth" mourn "since no one buys their cargo any more, cargo of gold, silver, jewels, and pearls," for "in one hour all this wealth has been laid waste," and then the shipmasters, whose business in trade is now devastated. Their songs, in counterpoint to the secret virgin-song, concretize what is lost in the collapse of global colonialism. The Apocalypse, in other words, "reveals" the global sin as less traditionally religious than economic. The spiritual foulness of the empire emanates from the gross capital accumulation of its elites.

The angel announces catastrophe in almost tragic terms–perhaps the only expression of empathy for the doomed. "The sound of harper and minstrels, of flute players and trumpeters, shall be heard in thee no more; and a craftsman of any craft, shall be found in thee no more; the voice of bridegroom and bride shall be heard in thee no more . . ." (18:22–23). Lamenting the loss of humble joys, the angel's song acknowledges that the common people suffer from socioeconomic collapse as much as their oppressors.

John depicts the cause of the system's collapse in terms of its internal contradictions. Babylon will be burnt and devoured by "her" own beasts, an apt allegory of the voracious power drives at the top of the pyramid as well as of the nonsustainable practices which eat up its base. Evil will collapse under the weight of its own corruption. Then the city will burn. "Hallelujah!" they sing in heaven. "The smoke goes up from her forever and ever" (19:3). The Babylons of today are also flammable. A *Village Voice* headline, in huge red letters, played subliminally on Revelation 19: "APOCALYPSE '92–It Takes a Nation of Millions to Make L.A. Burn."[126] After the hallelujah, the rest is always history.

19

They will make her desolate and naked, and devour her flesh and burn her up with fire. (Rev. 17:16)

But we have not yet faced the signifier *herself*. The motif of eating clamps together the sixth with the final septet. It is proclaimed that "the Great Whore, the Queen" is to be burnt and eaten by her own henchmen, the beasts: the systemic contradictions take flesh. Almost at once, an in-

vitation is issued to "the marriage supper of the Lamb" (19:9), the ultimate promise of eschatological consummation. Then the angel announces a third feast, "the supper of God, to eat the flesh of kings, the
flesh of captains, the flesh of mighty men, the flesh of horses and their
riders, and the flesh of all men, both free and slave, both small and great"
(19:17–19). This invitation is literally for the birds: after the victory at Armageddon over the empire and its allies, the vultures will be "gorged
with their flesh" (19:21).

In terms of literary structure, these three feasts merge together. As
fire consumes the city–that is, as the beasts cook and consume the
whore–the angel issues the twin invitations. The composition thus collates the cooking and eating of the queen, the battleground supper of
God's consuming wrath, and the supper of consummate fulfillment. In a
Christian context, "the supper of God" can only connote the Last Supper.
The Lord's Supper of the man-eating birds: John's little satire seems
to spoof the charge of anthropophagy which Romans sometimes leveled
against the early Christian practice of eating "Christ's body." It is as
though the text sniggers, "You call us cannibals–the time is coming
when you really *will* be eaten." Prophetic eschatology depends upon inversions–the high are cast down, the valleys raised up–but normally not
upon hallucinatory omnicide. In the dreamlike rapidity of the images,
the wedding invitation merges with the vultures' feast. Juxtaposing the
meal of doom with the banquet of celebration, John pushes prophetic oppositionalism towards its biblical climax.[127] The inversions mount at in-
digestibly high speed, blending in a bitter imagistic aftertaste. This is
one kind of echatology. But Jesus, rehearsing the eschatological banquet
by eating with the outcasts, notoriously ate *with* the whores. Here–mor-
dant irony indeed–the whore is dined not with but *upon*. There is no veil-
ing the way this vision of justice boils down to the burning and devouring of a woman's body.

The angel had announced that the two beasts, initially the Babylonian queen's cohorts, will "hate the harlot; they will make her desolate
and naked, and devour her flesh and burn her up with fire, for God has
put it into their hearts to carry out his purpose" (17:16). Why this trope to
depict the defeat of the oppressor? In God's name, a powerful, sexual, bejeweled woman is stripped, humiliated, and devoured by hairy and
horny beasts. Vision becomes voyeurism: a pious snuff picture unfolds.

In Kristeva's words, "Voyeurism accompanies the writing of abjection."[128] Like earlier prophetic writers, John portrays economic injustice as a debauched and spoiled woman. "Whore!"–the most satisfying derision–hurls itself into the vocabulary of future apocalypses. Of course "Whore of Babylon," whether later identified as a pope, a political system, an emperor, never literally designated "women." The term serves rather to vilify especially the enemy male, to feminize and abject, mock and reduce him (to ashes). But to claim that because the text does not intend misogyny it is innocent of its metaphoric subtext is to sweep *women's* ashes under the carpet.

Right on cue, Mary Daly reallegorizes the allegory. For her it illustrates the "Sado-Ritual Syndrome" she has spotted at the heart of gynocidal, "de*a*cidal" civilization: "The harlot 'deserves' to be hated and destroyed, of course, for she symbolizes the uncontrollable Babylon, the wicked city. No one asks who are the agents of wickedness. It is enough to have a scapegoat, a victim for dismemberment. Everyone knows that the woman is at fault."[129]

Given the Whore's resemblance to the class of sensuous goddesses popular in the ancient world–Astarte, Ishtar, Inanna, Aphrodite–her demise surely counts as a cryptic case of cosmogonic goddess-murder. "Continual complicity in the crime of Goddess-killing is mandatory in the Man's world," says Daly.[130] But since the text has named kings, merchants, and false prophets, it is not quite right to say that "no one asks who are the agents of wickedness."

To stabilize the methodological ambivalence of the present project: John's prophetic rage lashes out laudably at unjust patterns of "consumption," but, like most prophets, he fails to question his own participation in the all-*consuming* paradigm of gender. Standing neither with the lascivious beasts of wealth and power, nor with the ascetic males who project all that is sensual and tempting onto the woman's body, we may behold the Whore of Babylon as a great "queen" indeed: imperial patriarchy in drag.

20

Then I saw heaven opened, and there was a white horse! Its rider is called Faithful and True, and in righteousness he judges and makes war. (Rev. 19:11)

The prototype of Christian heroes, shining and pure, arrives–in a re-capitulation of the fall of Babylon–to fight the war to end all wars, the war to end the world. At Armageddon, "mother of all battles,"[131] he will vanquish the beasts and the "kings of the earth with their armies" (19:19). The Alpha/Omega, director of the vision, returns as its star.

> His eyes are like a flame of fire. . . ; and he has a name inscribed that no one knows but himself. He is clothed in a robe dipped in blood, and his name is called The Word of God. And the armies of heaven, . . . were following him on white horses. From his mouth comes a sharp sword . . . and he will rule [the nations] with a rod of iron. On his robe and on his thigh he has a name inscribed, King of kings and Lord of lords. (Rev. 19:12–16)

This polynomial superhero is none other than the son of the Sun Woman, grown to supermanhood and come into his "rod of iron," holy machismo. The Exodus scripted redemption as liberation by a divine military hero: "The Lord is a warrior; the Lord is his name. . . . In the greatness of your majesty you overthrew your adversaries; you sent out your fury, it consumed them like stubble" (Exod. 15:3, 7). The prophets had picked up the theme (for example, Isaiah 42:13) and passed it on to the apocalypticists, such as the Qumran community of the Dead Sea Scrolls and possibly of John the Baptist, who center on God as warrior. The Qumran texts admonish God to crush his enemies and "devour" them with his sword, "and all the peoples shall his sword judge."[132] The divine warrior motif upholds the just war tradition invoked by rulers and revolutionaries alike. The reincarnation of the Word of God as end-time hero thus canonizes holy war for Christendom. Almost an antitype (thus Antichrist?) to the cheek-turning Jesus of the Synoptics, the war-rior is posited as Christ. "On his robe and on his thigh he has a name in-scribed, King of kings and Lord of lords." His "thigh," a common ancient euphemism for genitals,[133] thus manfully sows the seeds for Handel's Hallelujah Chorus.

Armored over with "names"–no anonymity for him–"the Word of God" is literally, letter by letter, written in blood. Unlike the fourth Gos-pel's oral Word become flesh, this messiah "comes again" as the *written word* incarnate. But his secret name is known only to himself; it is a proper name "inscribed" but illegible to all but its proprietor. In his Sec-ond Coming, the Word of God is the consummate self-reader.

21

Then I saw an angel coming down from heaven, holding in his hand the
key to the bottomless pit. . . . He seized the dragon . . . and bound him for a
thousand years, and threw him into the pit, and locked and sealed it over
him, so that he would deceive the nations no more, until the thousand
years were ended. (Rev. 20:1–3)

Here, sealing up "evil" like toxic waste with a thousand-year half-life,
the angel inaugurates "the millennium" (*chilia*). The 144,000 are now
physically raised to reign with Christ in a kind of theocratic protectorate.
The Western history of utopian struggle roots in this blip of hope for a
worldly justice short of final judgment. Amillenialists make the millennium the church; premillennialists wedge in the "rapture." Thus conservative Christianity has sought to "seal over" that turbulent hope.

When the thousand years are ended, Satan will be released from his
prison and will come out to deceive the nations. . . . They marched up over
the breadth of the earth and surrounded the camp of the saints. . . . And
fire came down from heaven and consumed them. And the devil . . . was
thrown into the lake of fire and sulphur, where the beast and the false
prophet were, and they will be tormented day and night for ever and ever.
(Rev. 20:7–10)

"Just as the first creation appears to have involved a struggle between
Yahweh and the water monster of chaos, so the new creation is preceded
by similar victories," notes Ford.[134] No surrender, no conversion, no rec-
onciliation: "Let the evildoer still do evil . . . and the righteous still do
right" (Rev. 22:11). The dream of total victory cannot abide the "nightmare scenario" of negotiation.[135] In the effective history of holy war, utopian millennium has always miscarried, while technology has mastered
"fire from heaven"–napalm or nuclear, "daisy cutters" or smart bombs.
The state can rain down fire with omnipotent impersonality in our time.
But genocide, once a dirty business of face-to-face slaughter, was best
left to angels in the second century.

And I saw the dead, great and small, standing before the throne, and books
were opened. . . . And the dead were judged according to their works, as
recorded in the books. . . . And anyone whose name was not found written
in the book of life was thrown into the lake of fire. (Rev. 20:11–15)

The opening of final scrolls: you will be unmasked, unveiled, opened and read like a book. These books are closed canon, no room for midrash. No talking back. Hell is being out of print; those whose names are "not found written" come not just under erasure but eternal torture. After lambasting chiliasts as literalists, Augustine displays an obsessive literalism when it comes to holy torture. He mounts a massive argument that the body, materially resurrected, not only should but can endure eternal pain, "that it is possible for human bodies, possessed of soul and life, not only to escape disintegration by death but even to persist in the torments of everlasting fires."[136]

22

I saw a new heaven and a new earth; for the first heaven and the first earth had passed away, and the sea was no more. And I saw the holy city, the new Jerusalem, coming down out of heaven from God, prepared as a bride adorned for her husband. (Rev. 21:1–3)

"Earth and heaven fled from his presence" (Rev. 20:11). Like an old, used-up wife, the consumed matrix of life is cast aside. Into the space, the *outopos* which is "no place," descends the virginal new order. An urban architecture supersedes the organic topologies of earth and sea. The text thereby pulls the plug on sea dragons, draining from the universe once and for all the salty fluids of our bioplasmic genesis. Postmodern cosmopolitanism, founded on antipathy toward origin, nature, and depth, may find here a premodern prototype. By this point in the narrative (especially as read in our spacetime of displaced, replaceable urban masses) the "destroyers of the earth" have left little in "place." And so, in the ultimate act of urban renewal, the New Jerusalem descends, adorned—*kekosmenen*, from *kosmos*, meaning "world," "beautiful order," and "decoration." Yet more than a glistening cityscape is promised:

"See, the home of God is among mortals.
He will dwell with them as their God; they will be his peoples. . . ; he will
    wipe every tear from their eyes.
Death will be no more;
mourning and crying and pain will be no more,
for the first things have passed away." (Rev. 21:3–4)

The salt-water of tears and of sea have evaporated together. The poem's poignant paternal message (derivative from Isaiah) might comfort anyone who "feels like a motherless child." Nowhere, however, is the difference between the prophetic and the apocalyptic eschatologies more evident. Contrast Isaiah on the "new creation": "No more shall there be . . . an infant that lives but a few days, or an old person who does not live out a lifetime" (Isa. 65:20). Unlike John, Isaiah has not banished finitude, only premature death. "They shall build houses and inhabit them; they shall plant vineyards and eat their fruit. They shall not build and another inhabit; they shall not plant and another eat. . . . They shall not labor in vain" (Isa. 65:21–24). While the classical prophet portrays an earthy *shalom*, material life lived in justice and delight, the Apocalypse envisions a bodily immortality. Apocalypticism does remain Jewish: bodiless souls are ghosts. But if there is a fine line between death-defying and death-denying attitudes, this Apocalypse ecstatically crosses it. For Isaiah the new age must be constructed within history through a divinely infused *human* effort; here–after too much despair?–it has floated out of reach of human agency. It must "come down out of heaven from God." So just what comes down?

"The twelve gates are twelve pearls . . . and the street of the city is pure gold, transparent as glass" (21:21). Most striking in the architectural detail of the New Jerusalem is its gemology. "It has the glory of God and a radiance like a very rare jewel" (21:11). The twelve foundations of the wall of the city (named for the apostles) are "adorned with every jewel" (21:19). Thomas Hardy thus whimsically characterizes an explorer, "He was always beholding a gorgeous city–the fancied place he had likened to the New Jerusalem, though there was perhaps more of the painter's imagination and less of the diamond merchant's in his dreams thereof than in those of the Apocalyptic writer."[137] At the moment of unveiling, the bride's baubles crystallize the vision. (Isaiah preferred the organic imagery of the lion lying with the lamb, a little child leading them.) Yet this "mystic crystal revelation" conveys after all not the mercantile but the iconic value of light, refracted multicolored from luminous textual surfaces.[138] Have the multiple eyes of the vision turned to gems?[139]

The four-walled, twelve-gated design lays out a utopian space. Architecture has its own utopian millennialist tradition, from Campanella in the sixteenth century, to Paolo Soleri in the twentieth.[140] Doris Lessing named her apocalyptic "space fiction," culminating in a post-cataclysmic utopia, *The Four-Gated City*.[141] John's prophecy becomes blueprint. "Its length and width and height are equal"–fifteen hundred miles each (21:16): the New Jersualem is an impossible, colossal cube! (Strange that modern architecture has shaped urban life cubically, with shiny surfaces adorning its formal geometry.) "The city has no need of sun or moon to shine on it, for the glory of God is its light, and its lamp is the Lamb" (22:23). The text now imagines divine immanence, God as the invisible medium of all vision will be all in all. The Christological lamb-lamp furnishes a visible mediator of the invisible light source. But this high-wattage Presence, like an aesthetic of fluorescently bright windowless rooms, obviates natural lights. In chilling indifference to the first creation, the author terminates sun, moon, and stars. Were these attributes of the Sun Woman lost with her in her descent? Certainly her naturalist style is passé: Miss New Jerusalem in her bijoux wears the "Last Word" in fashion.

23

Then the angel showed me the river of the water of life, bright as crystal, flowing from the throne of God and of the Lamb through the middle of the street of the city. On either side of the river, is the tree of life with its . . . fruit . . . and the leaves of the tree are for the healing of the nations. (Rev. 22:1–2)

So this city is not dry. Traces of natural life (geometrically landscaped) support the promise of a global civil society. Nor is it apolitical. However denatured and posthistorical, this city remains a *polis*. As antitype to Rome, "the nations will walk by its light, and the kings of the earth will bring their glory into it. Its gates will never be shut" (21:24–25). Contrary to the views of our own religious right, John envisions a pluralist polity of "the nations" rather than a monolithic theocracy; even in utopia, the nations require "healing." The medicinal leaves suggest realistically that any future order will need constant care lest the old abuses return. The theme of "the nations" would later spawn myriad political enactments of the New Jerusalem. Blake's poem "Jerusalem" synthesizes radical pro-democracy ideology with mystical apocalypticism:

I will not cease from Mental Fight
Nor shall my Sword sleep in my hand

Till we have built Jerusalem
In England's green & pleasant Land.

Still, even if the persona of the bride exhausts itself in the allegory of the city, I wonder who "she" is. Traditionally, she is identified as "the Church," which in its purity supersedes the Jews in exile (the woman in the wilderness). But she can only "be" the solar Queen of Heaven through incest, since the bride marries the Lamb, the son of the Queen of Heaven. Is the bride then something like the Queen's daughter–or daughter-in-law–descending (like Athena born of Zeus' head) with no memory of a mother?

At any rate, I would not want to identify the anonymous Sun Woman of Apocalypse 12 with the over-named New Jerusalem. I do not want to surrender her agonizing autonomies to the ultimate in passive brides, to sacrifice her sun and moon and stars to this city lit by the Lord's twenty-four-hour neon. But a hint of their female solidarity–veiled from the text–suggests itself. The voice proclaims that "the home of God is among mortals; that God will dwell with them" (21:3); the Greek for "dwelling," "tabernacle," *skene*, resembles the root of *shekinah*, "God's Presence."[142] Behind the conventional personification of city as female shimmers a memory of the Lady of Dwellings, where history and place, transcendence and immanence, may coinhere. In her margins we have begun to read for a counter-apocalypse.

But the apocalyptic hope feels as brittle as an old scroll. The scribal voice of the epistolary *inclusio* now takes over:

I warn everyone who hears the words of the prophecy of this book: if anyone adds to them, God will add to that person the plagues described in this book; if anyone takes away from the words of the book of this prophecy, God will take away that person's share in the tree of life and in the holy city. (Rev. 22:18–19)

John could not tolerate some jubilant generosity of open ending. An editor himself, he understood what it means to mess with a text. He won't have it done to *him*: let the final dis/closure close down history, nature, revelation, and book. Forever. Nonetheless, here at the end of The End, where the curse comes, let it be noted: we have neither added nor subtracted. This midrash leaves the text intact, hard grains captured in its own intertextuality. In the irritation, pearls form like gates.

3. Time

Temporizing Tales

no sudden revelation but the slow
turn of consciousness, while every day
climbs on the back of the days before:

no new day, only a list of days,
no task you expect to see finished, but
you can't hold back from the task.

Adrienne Rich, from "Turning"

But why do you not know how to interpret
the present time?

Luke 12:56

1

Present time exists, or ends, as a daily cadence. We slouch not toward the Last Day, but the next one. In the Western economics of time, the day-to-day nonetheless routinely bristles with apocalypse. Everyone who works runs out of time, while around us the displaced, the unemployed, the migrant, improvise lives outside of history. Nervously we glance over our shoulder. The planet itself seems to be running out of time; the rhythmic hoofbeats at the horizon, ringing hollow, closer, strike their quadruple time.

An ontology of time, hugging close to the nuance of the moment, seems to offer some saving space. Moment-to-moment we might just evade the grand narratives of dread, hope, and closure. There, we might–

in the face of all anxiety or desire—just be, if only for that moment. In Heidegger's analysis, for instance, "being toward death" frames and judges every moment anyway; for Whitehead, every "actual entity" is a momentary event which arises and perishes.

From the vantage point of such "perpetual perishing," one might ask, Is the apocalypse pattern just one particularly histrionic response to human finitude, a sensationalist twist on some perennial "sense of an ending"? We all face death. But although the pressure of finitude is, if anything is, a universal condition, the constructions of that finitude, even *as* finitude, are not. So what needs to be explained is the uniqueness of the high-pitched eschatology that our civilization canonized. In apocalypse, we must all face finitude together, at once. Indeed the text *kills time* before it kills us. At its liveliest, the fantasy of the end of time itself renders every moment a battleground of meaning, with not a moment to waste. But amidst our current death-denying cryptoapocalypse, the phrase "killing time" means, by contrast, wasting it.

Most cultures experience death as some kind of dilemma, and weave ritual stories to ease the suffering. Death can be undergone with ecological dignity, with spiritual integrity and communal regenerativity. But that would be more likely where a time-full death could be expected, the death of those the ancient Hebrews called "full of days," where the power drives of history have not yet filled life with unjust and untimely demise. Apocalypse, we have seen, rages out of the bitter heart of systemic suffering: if history itself must end to staunch the tears, to stop the time of suffering, so be it. If even amidst the numbed death-denials of consumer culture, apocalypse in some sense scripts our time-stress, it does so precisely from the eerie margins of canon, culture, and consciousness. This is what I would guess: no temporal ontology which ignores the apocalypse at its Western edges can ease the causes of suffering. Which is to say, we cannot ignore the politics of time.

2

When Frances Fukuyama declared "the end of history," he meant to applaud "the triumph of the West," not to ally himself with either John of Patmos or his fundamentalist interpreters. "What we may be witnessing is not just the end of the Cold War, or the passing of a particular period of postwar history, but the end of history as such: that is, the end point of mankind's ideological evolution and the universalization of Western liberal democracy as the final form of human government." Even less would he identify with the aspirations of the motley revolutionaries in between who declared the end of their age and the eruption of the New: it is precisely *over* their heritage, indeed over their hope, still lingering when he wrote in 1989, of a "convergence between capitalism and socialism," that he discloses the "unabashed victory of economic and political liberalism."[1]

Of course, late capitalist millennialism rarely has cause to break into such conspicuous apocalypse. But it behooves us, as ambivalent beneficiaries of posthistory, to back off a bit and consider the kinship between such ultramodern claims of "the end," usually cryptic, and those of an archaic text. From the pre-modern through to our uncertainly postmodern period, the vision of the end of history—"not just of a particular period"—has recurrently encroached upon the historical imagination. Our millennial moment, distinctly structured of thermonuclear and environmental edges, economic mirage and systemic stress, may still bear the time signature of the old manuscript. In this chapter we listen to the entangled tempos of narrative, historical, and apocalyptic time, syncopated by counter-apocalypse.

Time running out: we stand within a history of "the end of history," optimistic or pessimistic, hopeful or nostalgic, within continuity of discontinuity, an interminability of termination. From this perspective, the Apocalypse of John provides a narrative origin for this drive toward historical closure. But one can hardly construe the Apocalypse as a historical narrative. It is supremely uninterested in the past: its Omega in effect devours the Alpha. In its privileging of the future, John's text stands in stark contrast to both the Hebrew chroniclers and pagan historians. In its occlusion of human agency and its choice of a purely mythopoeic vocabulary, it also differs from the eschatological prophets. Certainly John resists anything remotely resembling a modern historical "fact." Later literalists might try to decode the Apocalypse as the history of the future, always pointing to a few already realized predictions to prove the claim of its reference to "our time," then readjust facts and dates as needed, carrying on a multinational endtime industry. The social force of apocalyptic literalism (by repeated polls, a fourth of U.S. citizens expect the end of the world and the rapture soon) underlines the paradox of a stubbornly nonlinear text founding caricatures of Western linear time.

My thesis runs something like this: the Apocalypse, itself marginal within the canon, canonized for Western civilization the outer edges of our time frame. Its own narrative historicity is neither that of a history nor that of modern historicism. Nonetheless, the text is not simply ahistorical. It takes aim at historical events. Its narrative does not mirror facts past or future, but offers an interpretive framework for them. Paul Ricoeur rightly affirms that biblical interpretation requires a narrative theology, if not that of the Yale School's self-encapsulated variety. *Qua* narrative, the Apocalypse does not unfold *in* time—and certainly not outside of time—but rather constitutes a specific form *of* time.

3

Any influential narratives, their rhythms meshed with other stories and entrained with the life of a people, serve this temporalizing function.[2] But the biblical temporalizing style differs from the stories of other peoples in its moments of overweening singleness of purpose. This monotheism, especially in its Christian and thus internally contested form, reaches its fevered fruition in the temporality of the Apocalypse, that is, in the fantasy of a single, all-consuming outcome of history. By concluding "God's biography" with the climactic closures of Revelation, the Christian canon, unlike the Jewish, gives form to an unprecedented finalism.[3]

Of course the Christian version of the Bible tells no seamless story, though it presents itself as a determinate totality. It seeks at once to retain and to contain not only its own complex little library but the vast Hebrew multiplicity of tales, once literally only stored in jars, but now, as Christian canon, strung out in a codex. If Hebrew scripture labors to produce a unifying salvation history, even the expectation of the Day of Yahweh did not lay upon time any foregone conclusion. The security of a single history numbered from The Beginning to The End is an effect of the text of Revelation—but only as placed by pro-imperial theologians long after its composition and placement in its canonical location.

Yet already in John's hands a relentless temporal oneness penetrates its confusing multiplicity of images: the Alpha which is one with the Omega, one global history directed by one God, culminating in one final judgment issuing in one redemption—for those "at one" with its End. While the narrative structure of Apocalypse does still express, like a basso continuo, the rhythmic Hebrew sense of time—neither line nor circle, but "purely and simply a rhythmic alternation"[4]–its cadences propel it frantically forward, towards its unnerving *ultimo*. Thus we saw a mythogrammatic spiral, bearing no resemblance to the narratives of the modern timeline, plant the "post-" to which all posthistory would attach itself–"The End."

As a pre-modern narrative that refuses either to relinquish its claim on history or to separate history from myth, Revelation may, perversely, bring us round to a postmodern and in another sense posthistorical "narrative." Postmodern theories unveil modern historicism as foundationally teleological and therefore implicitly eschatological, indeed apocalyptic. Thus Foucault: "The historian's history finds its support outside of time and pretends to base its judgments on an apocalyptic objectivity."[5] This conflation of apocalypse with objectivism is of course grossly inaccurate in its allusion to the biblical genre. Yet it does bespeak the current end of history–as a discipline purporting to purge fiction from fact.

Narrative, according to Roland Barthes, describes that linguistic experience which "ceaselessly substitutes meaning for the straightforward copy of the events recounted."[6] The concept of narrative is pivotal here, for the narrative structure–the story-form of a clear beginning, middle, and end–did not casually or necessarily become inflated into the monolithic structure of universal history. This is the peculiar transmogrification of Western history. Narrative, as Barthes remarked, "is simply there like life itself . . . international, transhistorical, transcultural."[7] Unlike the modern historian, a storyteller does not pretend to be rendering something single, objective, true beyond the telling itself. But this much may then be retrieved from Foucault's claim: the narrative of the Apocalypse may after all channel the transition from the intersubjective, imaginative truth-claims of myth and parable to the objectified universals of theocratic Christianity. Through the force of its apocalyptic imaginary, did Christian theology become the conduit for the narrative structuring of history into a modern objectivism that finally shuns the object of theology but retains its essential universalism, its teleology, its oneness of truth?

Barthes asks rhetorically, "Does the narration of past events, which in our culture from the time of the Greeks onwards, has generally been subject to the sanction of historical 'science,' bound to the underlying standard of the 'real,' . . . –does this form of narration really differ, . . . from imaginary narration, as we find it in the epic, the novel and the drama?" Moving to a less Hellenocentric perspective, one might paraphrase the question: Does the narration of past events really differ from the mythic narration of an apocalypse? Well, the latter narrates the future, one might respond. Yet John *re*-narrates the future as the story of his already *past* revelation. The tense is that of the future-past, which only makes its character as "imaginary narration" all the more transparent.

Once one challenges "the distinction, basic to historicism in all its forms, between 'historical' and 'fictional' discourse,"[8] the distinction between the mythological rhetoric of a religious apocalypse and the "real" exposition of history becomes less impressive than the question of narrative structure itself. The specific narrativity by which a single-minded movement toward closure comes to structure our sense of our common life–our common sense–comes into focus. The point is that this particular inscription of the future as though it has already transpired, this strange privilege of The End, has framed the Western story. It at once wedges open and slams shut that future.

Still, if the Apocalypse is not a history, if it betrays only coded, dream-dense traces of history, then by what route of effects might it have come to serve as a major source of Western historical consciousness? The answer, I believe, depends upon a theory about theories of history. The two first and major theologians of history are Augustine and Joachim da Fiore. A millennium apart, these two may be read as primary sources of Western time sensibility. They provide certain missing links between primitive Christianity and Western modernity. And both, in sharply juxtaposed ways, with quite contrary political consequences, reread John's Apocalypse as primary text of human history. If we (like Gadamer) are curious as to the *Wirkungsgeschichte* of the Apocalypse, that is, as to the history of its effects as a text on other texts, we may begin to spot the pattern in the tension of Augustinian and Fiorite readings of John. The history of a text makes history when its own vision of history gives rise to "history" as a theoretical production arising from and issuing into sociopolitical lifeworlds. This history of history requires more than academic urgency if we suspect that Revelation's effects do not remain confined to historical texts, that it has been working all along as a self-fulfilling prophecy.

4

If the Apocalypse configures a persistent historical fiction, it cannot, however, be read as a timeless archetype underlying history. It may drive toward an end of time, time as finitude, but it knows no abstract eternity. Yet there is nothing elsewhere, apart from its influence, to compete with the *temporalizing* force its endism—its final judgment accompanied by the total consummation of the world and its once-for-all regeneration. So it will not do to homologize the apocalypse pattern with pre–Bronze Age agrarian mythologies of rhythmic death and rebirth. Rather, it radically rescripts, denatures, and singularizes that cyclical sense of beginnings out of endings.

With its roots in prophetic, wisdom, and Zoroastrian literatures, the Book of Revelation became a source, marginalized yet canonized, sublimated yet effectual, for all subsequent Western history. Its script of binary time, a before and an after, of the age of captivity to evil and the age of redemption, takes on divergent and contradictory meanings within different historical circumstances. And within its story it eludes the time frames to which it was reduced: How does one count the millennium in relation to the New Jerusalem? Are there a total of three ages after all? This would become, in the dissident subtext of the West, a world-historic question.

In the meantime, however the devotees of apocalypse count time, time poses a question to us only inasmuch as we bump up against its edges. I imagine the present, collective momentum of the developed world, bloated with the effulgences of technological progress, has brought this edginess to a pitch of terror. Many of us most of the time have the luxury of numbing our fears into free-floating stress. But even when we attend to its realities, we cannot get our minds around the total present threat to livable life on our planet. And because that threat presses with unrelenting and mostly subliminal relevance upon our temporal sense, the Apocalypse, as the privileged text of any global annihilation, indelibly winds its narrative around our present perspectives.

Thus its temporal edges serve as a kind of epistemic *eschaton*, not unlike "time" as a constitutive idea within the Kantian transcendental limit of reason, which limits and so shapes our capacity to conceptualize our situation; but then it is not a matter of time as such, but of specific temporalities, among which apocalypticism represents one branching cluster. If this is true, apocalypse may disclose *an* (i.e., not *the*) inner logic of Western, patriarchal time. The tension between the desire for and the deferral of apocalypse, a tension which emerged within the first four centuries of the text's influence, may be an organizing force behind the tenses of what we know as time.

5

How might we retell the tale of apocalyptic effects, then? The narrative could start much earlier, it could reach much further into nonbiblical mythological contrasts, it could mean much else. To reconstruct its history, precisely not as the only possible account but as the most persuasive I can now collect, is to resist its own compulsion toward the one right, true, and moral account.

It might commence thus, in Palestine. A charismatic Jewish teacher and healer from the countryside became too influential, performed provocative public acts in the big city, and was summarily executed by the imperial authorities. A number of his friends experienced some kind of psychic-somatic contact with the dead young rabbi soon thereafter and interpreted these disparate spirit encounters under the category (then still largely reserved for a future and collective event) of "resurrection."

These apparitions were short-lived, while the Roman occupation was not. This made for a rather anticlimactic denouement of a movement charged with great expectations. Some decoded certain of Jesus' comments on the Book of Daniel (or rather, comments reported as his by the Markan community) as a solution to the problem of his early demise: that when Jesus was referring to "the son of man," he must have meant himself; indeed that Daniel, writing around 156 B.C.E., must have been predicting Jesus when he referred to a glorious return of the "son of man" as apocalyptic judge. Hence the Christian preoccupation with the Parousia. The ephemeral communal visions of resurrection were not enough. For some, he would have to come *again.* But scholars argue that "son of man" was not a title and therefore, on Jesus' lips, not a circumlocution for himself. His audience would have taken the expression, John Dominic Crossan contends, "in either a generic (everyone) or an indefinite (anyone) sense. . . . An unchauvinistic English translation would be 'the human one.'" Only Mark 13 uses the phrase as a title, and that not in an evidently self-referential sense. But the post-resurrection tradition soon turned the generic into the titular "Son of Man," and "generated thereby a magnificent stream of theological confusion."[9]

There is no evidence that the Nazarene was preoccupied with his own future status. He was obsessed with the present work of the "kingdom of God"—the subtle transformations of life possible right now, when the people would break bread and boundaries together, when the bakerwoman kneads the yeast through the dough of the everyday.

6

Though there is no evidence that he predicted his own "second coming," and considerable evidence that he kept such expectation low and deliteralized—"But about that day or that hour no one knows, not even the angels in heaven, not even the Son" (Mark 13:32)—some of Jesus' followers could not resist the hope of an imminent, final, transparent, indeed *visual* vindication of their dependency ("every eye will see him, every one who pierced him" [Rev. 1:7]).[10] This visualization of end things, as we have noted, endows them with "the real." To reopen history—"the new" of the prophetic hope—was not enough for some with more futurist yearnings. They would instead close the loopholes of time and deposit their faith in a guaranteed return, a "Second Coming in Glory." The vulnerability of the first appears shoddy in the glaring light of the second: Jesus turned his cheek one too many times—never again! Needless to say, in the transition to his rod-wielding Parousia, Jesus is stripped of the personality which endears him to antiauthoritarians of every stripe, including feminists.

At the same time, we may assume that during the first two centuries of Christianity, the unassuaged suffering within some communities demanded more than trust in a holiness which reveals itself "in time." It craved closure. No more finitude. Time becomes the placeless site of final judgment and thus of its own end. After all, the celestial bodies which mark earthly time were banned from the new heaven and earth. Yet the New Jerusalem did not suggest a purely ahistorical heaven, however hard we will see Augustine try to make it into such. Rather, it promised a historical temporality denuded of natural cycles and thus, most importantly, of suffering. A denatured universalism, in which time is closed— if not in any literal sense terminated—sealed Christian moral dualism into the dualism of two ages. *This* time is running out, and soon will be over; the coming time, or *aeon*, discontinuous with this one, will succeed it. Thus the way was cleared for the moral dualism upon which the dualism of aeons was predicated. Only this place-free binary of time secured the mirage of Jesus' immediate return, to dry all the tears . . .

But too much time went by. Quotidian, struggling time. And still no power-messiah. The Christian apocalypticism of the first century could not sustain its first fervor. Some historians have interpreted this crisis as the formative problem of Christianity. As Martin Werner, their champion, put it, "The delay of the Parousia of Jesus, which after his Death became increasingly obvious, must, in view of the non-fulfillment of the eschatological expectation, have grown into a problem which was conducive to the transformation of the original eschatological doctrine."[11] The churches increasingly focused on sacramental presence, orthodox teaching, and institutional order, displacing apocalyptic hope onto the individual destiny of the soul after death. Even the formal apocalypses of the patristic period (C.E. 100–400) neglect the classical apocalyptic concern with history and its imminent crisis, securing instead the fate of the individual soul.

The "delay of the Parousia" wedges into the foundations of Western temporality a primal deferral. Christian history pivots around this embarrassing non-event. Did the delay inscribe upon Western temporality a certain subterranean tension of disappointed anticipation? Ernst Käsemann declared that the "apocalyptic is the mother of Christian theology." But it would seem that "she" revealed a "bad breast," in Melanie Klein's metaphor for that maternal withdrawal from the infant's mouth, inevitable and enraging, filling the child with a "persecutory anxiety."[12] But "mother-of" tropes exist to bear filial projections. It was the so-called consistent eschatology of modern biblical historians, rather than any consistent picture presented by the texts themselves, which led to the scholarly assumption that early Christians, instructed by their Lord, subscribed to a literalist expectation that the present world was soon ending, and Jesus physically returning.[13] The situation was more complex. It would seem, rather, that those communities who entertained, in the spirit of Paul or John of Patmos, and later of the Montanists, a foundational apocalypticism would have been those vulnerable to the delay/disappointment complex. Yet historical literalism in our factual sense was not yet possible, even among those whose faith provided the sine qua non of such literalism. Certainly mystical groups such as the Corinthians (whose women proved too uppity for Paul) and most forms of "gnostic" Christians leave no trace of interest in a physical return and end. The polyvalent parables of a harvest reaped, dough kneaded, or treasure found were not lost on all.

Apocalyptic expectations about history nonetheless continued to develop during the patristic period, albeit outside of the originating form.[14] The tension of desire and deferral now became institutionalized. "The apocalyptic tradition continued to renew itself, not only through the study of texts of the classical period, but also by the creation of new scenes in the drama of the end."[15] The church fathers especially contemplated the theme of the Antichrist (as dragon/beast) and the number and duration of the ages of the world. Conceptualization of time was intimately linked with that of evil: the polarity of good versus evil was from its incipience inseparable from a linearizing temporality in which the past and present were subsumed under the power of evil, while the imminent future remained pristine.[16] Yet already in Revelation the time dualism of the two ages contained wrinkles such as the brief allusion to a thousand-year millennium. Patristic theologians worked out the details of the scheme. "The determination of ages does not play a large part in the New Testament texts, but by the second century a number of patristic writings not only show a revived interest but also indicate a preference for a scheme based on seven periods of one thousand years each, or the 'cosmic week' theme."[17] This neat pattern adds the thousand-year kingdom of Revelation to the traditional six thousand years of creation as its preordained Sabbath.

Here lay the basis of a "chiliasm" (from the Greek *chilia*, one thousand) which accommodated a quite literal reading of the millennial kingdom.[18] The successive times of time finally lead to a totality of divine presence, but still, for chiliasts, a totality more or less *within* history. This utopian hope—noticeably worked out not in the narrative form of Apocalypse but in the discursive and polemical prose of theological treatises—inaugurates the specifically Christian preoccupation with chronology. Each passing year brought humanity closer to the Second Coming. The first coming, as the incarnation of the Word once and for all in Jesus, separated all that came before from all that came after, into B.C. and A.D., in what Robert Markus calls a "strained time-scheme"; the historical sense of Christianity now stretches between "two 'ends,' one already achieved, the other still in the waiting."[19] Though the Incarnation would increasingly mark the middle point of sacred history, it already represented a climax. Therefore the time between the two climaxes—whatever counts as the present time—droops, gaps, waits, reads in itself as anti- and ante-climax:

> These were the "last times." Whatever world-shaking events, disasters or revolutions intervened, nothing could now have a decisive significance in the history of salvation. In this long perspective—and nobody could say how long it might be—events could henceforth only be neutral, devoid of sacred significance. . . . The "sacred history" of the last times was a blank, an open space between the Lord's two comings.[20]

Even the growing hierarchy, building ecclesial continuity, found apocalyptic thought indispensable inasmuch as it could be retooled from drama of radical disruption to single, universal sacred history.

To the new Christian elite, the deferral of The End (which would after all terminate the world over which they were presiding) offers relief, not disappointment. Irenaeus, the major Christian writer of the patristic period, bishop of Lyons from 178 to 200, incorporated a popular materialistic reading of the thousand-year kingdom into speculation on the cosmic week. In so doing he carefully shifted emphasis to the authority of the church as enshrined in the episcopal office. Tertullian prays for the further delay of the Parousia, not for its speedy advent. Hippolytus (160–234) places Jesus in the middle of the sixth millennium, rather than at its end, proving from his exegesis of Daniel that the end is *not* imminent. Lactantius's doctrine of the ages of the world, likewise placing Jesus' birth in the middle of the sixth, contains the richest surviving account of the refigured apocalypse.

> Perhaps someone will now ask when these things we have spoken of will take place. I showed before that the transformation has to happen after six thousand years and that the final day of the last end is already drawing near. We can know this much concerning the signs predicted by the prophets; they foretold signs by means of which we could day-by-day await and fear the end of time. Those who have written about the ages deduce the number of years from the beginning of the world out of holy

scripture and different histories and teach when the *whole sum will be completed*. . . . No expectation seems to be more than two hundred years. The current situation indicates that the collapse and ruin of everything will soon take place, unless nothing is to be feared because the city of Rome is still unharmed. But when the capital of the world will have fallen and begun to be a street, as the Sibyls say will happen, who can come? This is the city that still upholds all things. *Let us entreat and implore heaven's God to put off his decisions and decrees, if possible.*[21]

The entreaties worked! Time now appears as a "sum" to be completed: the helical numerology of the Apocalypse straightens into a serial arithmetic. A shift in social location may be pertinent. Lactantius, a teacher of rhetoric, served Diocletian, left when this emperor began to persecute Christians in 303, and as an old man was called back into imperial service by Constantine in 317. However inconsistent, the privilege of his imperial associations seems to inhibit enthusiasm for Rome's collapse—in striking contrast to the jubilation of John's angels. Yet still the Parousia is anticipated and the destruction of the empire assumed.

We note the reference to the popular Sibyls. The oracles of the female Sibyllines were treated with great respect by the Christian fathers from the second century, a respect that was not to decline until the Enlightenment. Augustine admitted "the Sibyl" to the City of God. Ostensibly Jewish and Christian, the fourteen Sibylline Books contained much pagan material attributable to the tradition of the female seer known as the Sibyl in the eighth century B.C.E. According to Plutarch, in the earliest attestation, "the Sibyl with frenzied lips, uttering words mirthless, unembellished, unperfumed, penetrates through the centuries by the powers of the gods." Uttering doom for the manmade citadels of power, this enshrined Cassandra-type hints at the solidarity of women of wisdom with the prophetic radicals, a kinship of "frenzied lips." A female-identified and pagan authority startles one in the midst of the time-paternity. But the output of ecstatic spirit-disclosures, so readily female-embodied (as Corinthian and Montanist women demonstrate) and already controlled in the Apocalypse, now only distantly suffuses the intertextual field of a new, discursive prose, polemical, apologetic, and preoccupied with its own orthodoxy.

Hammering the sequence of time into a finite line, the church now preferred to defer the end. More time goes by. The religions and political situation shifted dramatically with the conversion of Constantine. And, correspondingly, the religious politics of time itself would undergo a sharp alteration. Eusebius of Caesarea (263–339), theologian at the court of Constantine, spearheads what we may recognize as the first major anti-apocalypse. From Origen, Eusebius absorbed an allegorical reading of Revelation.[22] His tremendously influential *Chronicles* adopted the scheme of world ages. But in an important shift, he focused attention on the *past* of the Christian truth rather than its future. As to the promised millennial kingdom, Eusebius hardly differentiates it from Constantine's empire. If the Apocalypse had pitted the churches *against* the power of Rome, Eusebius now identifies Rome with the Church Triumphant: their time is one. Millennialism, at its official origin, identifies the church as the millennium itself.

Describing the banquet thrown by Constantine to honor the Council of Nicaea–which had just constructed, under the patronage of the emperor, a unifying credal orthodoxy which would undergird the empire–Eusebius draws an ominous comparison:

> Detachments of the body-guard and troops surrounded the entrance of the palace with drawn swords, and through the midst of them the men of God proceeded without fear into the innermost of the Imperial apartments, in which some were the Emperor's companions at table. . . . One might have thought that a picture of Christ's kingdom was thus shadowed forth, and a dream rather than reality.[23]

Thus the eschatological banquet translates into the feast of imperial Christianity. If the angels of Revelation invited the birds to feast on the carcass of Rome, Rome now appears as the consummate host.

7

The anti-apocalypse, necessarily wrought of interpretations of the Apocalypse, now gels as the form of orthodox Christianity. Without question it was Augustine of Hippo (354–430) who was "the most incisive opponent of the apocalyptic interpretation of history in the patristic period."[24] He rejected the euphoric linkage of the destinies of Rome and the church which had led some chiliasts to construe the conversion of emperors and the end of persecution as the onset of the messianic age. Troubles such as the sack of Rome in 410 undermined any smug triumphalism—as surely as the failure of Christ to return in glory had undermined a naive apocalypticism. Indeed, Augustine's magnum opus, *The City of God*, systematically uncouples divine providence from the history of nations. The spiritual history of the City of God is invisibly intertwined with the secular history of the City of Man. The first represents the collectivity of the saved, the second the "lump of perdition." In the latter "the lust for domination lords it over its princes as over the nations it subjugates; in the other, both those put in authority and those subject to them serve one another in love, the rulers by their counsel, the subjects by obedience."[25] While feminists might be unimpressed by the distinction between "dominance" and willful "obedience," it forms the basis of his ideal social order.

Only in the end, a time he refused to predict, at the Last Judgment, will these cities separate from each other finally and visibly. Then the City of God will appear as the New Jerusalem, but a New Jerusalem with nothing to do with politics (contrast the "healing of the nations" of Revelation 21), a resurrection beyond all history, beyond time—a blissful state of eternal stasis. His allegorical dualism of the cities rescues eschatology from any future embarrassment. Keying in great flexibility as to historical vicissitudes, it simultaneously reinforces a foundational (if not uncritical) loyalty to the imperial and civil order. Christian faith "looks forward to the blessings which are promised as eternal in the future, making use of earthly and temporal things like a pilgrim in a foreign land, who does not let himself be taken in by them or distracted from his course toward God . . . and yet does not hesitate to obey the laws of the earthly city."[26] The trope of the *civitas pellegrina*, the pilgrim city passing through the degraded *civitas terrena*, obeying its rules but not becoming attached enough to challenge the unjust ones, requires, like that of Paul in Romans 13, quite a theological balancing act: to value worldly law and order as divinely ordained while devaluing the fallen world which requires them. This sublime aloofness seems to position itself as the most realistic of stances toward the present and the most idealistic toward the future. The Augustinian reduction of all things creaturely to means to the timeless End secures the Western disconnection of spirit from the time rhythms of the earth.

It is this dissociative temporality that a counter-apocalypse seeks to heal. The pilgrim metaphor still exercises profound resonances among mainline Christians and secular progressives, who read there a healthy discontentment with the status quo, a utopian refusal of any static "place." But in Augustine it is positioned precisely *against* the utopianism of hope. He thoroughly lambastes those who turn the Apocalypse into "ridiculous fables" and is at pains to retrieve the book from the materialism of the chiliasts, "who assert that those who have risen again will spend their rest in the most unrestrained material feasts."[27] This caricature must have been a response to a real threat. A historicizing interpretation of the Book of Revelation—perhaps akin to that of Lactantius, but evidently more utopian and materialist—must have held sway over significant numbers of Christians. Augustine's reading of Revelation reroutes the thousand years as a metaphor for "all time," that is, all the time remaining until Christ returns. Thus he separates the millennial theocratic rule of the saints on earth from the eternal New Jerusalem, which he identifies as "heaven," site of the final resurrection. The binding of Satan so as not to "seduce the nations" means in his reading that Satan will not be able to deconvert the Christianized nations of the empire, not that evil has been conquered. And as to "the thrones" perceived during the vision of the millennial kingdom, the bishop ingeniously interprets them "as the seats of the authorities by whom the Church is now governed, and those sitting on them as the authorities themselves."[28] In this way he scrubs the Apocalypse clean of its earthy, material, and especially its antiauthoritarian, anti-imperial insinuations. Revelation is skillfully de-revolutionized.

In his critique of millennialists, Augustine deploys a hermeneutical polemic: "The indolence of the flesh and the slowness of an uninstructed and untrained mind is content with the superficial, literal meaning and thinks that no inner meaning is to be sought."[29] In the face of the current spread of fundamentalism, it is tempting to identify with Augustine's elitist critique of literalism. But there is an irony of historic proportions at work here. To be sure, Augustine, like Eusebius (and most fundamentalists now), eschews any attempt to pinpoint the "hour and the day." But he protests too much. As do those content, in their defense of the apocalyptic tradition, to categorize his philosophy as *merely* anti-apocalyptic. If one subtracted the apocalyptic elements from *The City of God*, the text would be mercifully shorter but unrecognizable. The very structure of Augustine's vision, like that of the other above patristic writers, derives from his *literal* reading of key apocalyptic themes. For instance, he lists, among others, the following features of the future, which faith must accept as predetermined to occur *in fact*, not in figure:

> And so . . . we have learnt that those events are to come about: Elijah . . . will come; Jews will accept the faith; Antichrist will persecute; Christ will judge; the dead will rise again; the good and the evil will be separated; the earth will be destroyed in the flames and then will be renewed. All those events we must believe, will come about.[30]

This particular slate of eventualities does not derive from the Apocalypse, but rather presupposes already that peculiar amalgam of apocalypticisms through which John's version was read (mixed of Daniel, Ezekiel, Paul, et al.) and which would characterize the apocalyptic subtext in all times.[31] It is this intertextual brew that fundamentalism claims—by an amazing leap of faith in itself—as its literal reading of scripture. The "belief" demanded by this calendar of coming events constructs historical literalism, shutting down the future in advance, and thus closing out the polyvalences and possibilities of present times. To be sure, Augustine's tone suggests mere assent to accepted tenets; these external markers of salvation history hardly inspire him. But this is precisely the point: a certain shape of history is becoming Christian common sense. In fact he has reconstructed time (a topic which had earlier exercised such great fascination upon him) as a movement through the key moments canonized in the Apocalypse—the coming resurrection of the dead, the final judgment, and its eternal results.

These eschatological doctrines *do* now excite him. I cannot read his construal of these final events as anything but a rather gross literalism couched in his indefatigably brilliant prose. Augustine devotes the two final and climactic books of *The City of God* to the details of hell and heaven respectively, to either of which every resurrected body will at the end of the world be teleported. We noted earlier how he argues obsessively that yes, contrary to skeptics and as John promised in the vision of the lake of fire, resurrected bodies, unlike mortal ones, *will* be able to suffer eternally without dying.[32] Invoking the "omnipotence of the Creator" as guarantor of a miraculous technology for the eternal torture of real bodies, he proceeds to refute all arguments for mercy as impious, irrational, or wimpy—from Origen's belief in the eventual salvation of all, to a Platonic understanding of hell as purification, to those who argue that eternal damnation for finite sins is unfair.[33] Again the belief in absolute and incurable evil, deserving endless punishment, seems to go hand in hand with the closure of time—moral and time dualisms require each other.

Augustine's apocalyptic literalism receives equal elaboration in his descriptions of the physical bodies of the saved, who will be resurrected at age thirty-three, recognizably themselves but perfected. They come in male and female, contrary, I hasten to admit, to worse chauvinists who imputed redemptive perfection only to a male form. Finally, in heaven we will be free again of lust, that punishing lack of control he bemoaned as a result of the Fall. Bodies will exist in an undisturbed equilibrium of aesthetic harmony. Moreover, the Bishop of Hippo has not only reserved but legitimated for subsequent Western thought the apocalyptic theory of the ages of the world, now rendered in voluminous philosophical intricacy. History is a closed unity, and we are approaching the end of it, for it is sealed at the beginning by its *creatio ex nihilo* (no chaos, no Tehom!) and at the end by the New Creation, the paradise of posthistory, in which time, movement, change, and death do not obtain.

The younger Augustine is generally recognized to have propounded the first systematic Western thoughts on the nature of time. His *Confessions* defined time as a matter of the succession of intervals of different lengths; the present is the razor's edge dividing past from future, lacking width of its own, therefore belying time itself. The perspective of eternity thus shrinks time, rendering it strangely insignificant. This thought is given an eschatological context in *The City of God*: "But any space of time which starts from a beginning and is brought to an end, however vast its extent, must be reckoned when compared with that which has no beginning, as minimal, or rather as nothing at all."[34] He argues that "without motion and change there is no time, while in eternity there is no change." In other words, changelessness is the very essence of the immovable God, whose omnipotence is steering us unwaveringly through time towards the final confrontation. Then life will be frozen eternally into one of the two possible conditions. Although he does not say when, he assumes that time is running out: "The world is passing away, the world is losing its grip, the world is short of breath. Do not fear, thy youth shall be renewed as an eagle."[35] Renewal, as for conservative Christians

101

today, would be that merely of the individual soul in Christ; time itself, comments Marjorie Reeves, was "positively decaying, a world grown old whose only significance lay in the miracle of new growth in Christ happening in its moribund carcass."[36] Time feels weak, earth itself exhausted.

History becomes Plato's "moving image of eternity." But the mirror is soiled. Free of time, the self will again reflect the image of God, in which it was created. Or rather, in which men were created. For Augustine, women, while redeemable as such, only possess the image of God inasmuch as they are coupled with men, as body with head. Women within classical discourses were more kin to the corruptible, time-wracked flesh. Now that Christianity had become the imperial religion, things were as good as could be hoped for within time. So hope properly directs itself to the private futures of timeless and immaterial bodies. As "the fountainhead of all anti-apocalyptic eschatology in the Middle Ages,"[37] Augustine provides a framework for an obsession with the fate of the individual soul and its eternal body. Out of it medieval theologians could construct the (hardly Augustinian) myth that the Church Triumphant was identical with the millennial Kingdom of God.

I want to stress, however, that it is not apocalypse per se which has been undermined by the Augustinian triumph, but rather the apocalypse of collective, utopian aspirations for greater justice in history. The anti-apocalyptic impulse produces an anti-apocalypse *precisely as a form of apocalypse*. It is as though the patristic period has achieved the *sublimation* of apocalypse. Freudian sublimation entails something more gross being pushed downward while a more "sublime" analogue for it ascends. While the more concrete, material hopes carried in the apocalypse pattern were repressed, its temporal and moral dualisms were driven "upward," as the loftier spirituality of the theocratic hierarchy. In this "sublimed" condition, it riveted attention to "higher" things, that is, to an individualized and supernaturalized intensification of apocalyptic dualism.

Exploiting Augustine's complex insinuations, an ecclesial triumphalism gradually took over, willing to identify "the church" with the predicted thousand-year theocracy. Thus history, closed into a meaning-deprived deferral, coordinated with the closure exercised by an increasingly monolithic orthodoxy. This latter had effectively, often brutally, purged any paganism that it identified as religious and not merely cultural.[38] It was then prepared to project the shadow of its "evil" onto any obtrusive "other"–eventually to liquidate not just pagan but Jew, certainly Muslim, and eventually countless women (the latter as witches). And, remarkably, it served within the conservative framework of the sublimated apocalypse to keep history at once status quo and terminal, a foreclosed unity. It closed not so much by the force of historical prediction as by enervation. An abstract eternity sucked the energy out of the experience of time. By thus accommodating apocalypse to the empire it was born to oppose, the historical and revolutionary implications of millennialism were not in fact lost but rather driven deep into the political unconscious of the West. All the Western explosions to come will take the form of apocalypse freeing itself from history as anti-apocalypse.

Having spent a bit of my youth in proximity to medieval cathedrals, I remember the *feeling* of that enshrined theology of history. How readily one is absorbed into the kaleidoscoping colors of the rose windows of European cathedrals, all built around the blossoming Mother of God. There no linearity figures. But I had to struggle to find interest in either the form or content of the endless representations of the Last Judgment dominating the portals: the static symmetry of barred lines rising up hierarchically, with Jesus top center and a jury of male apostles and angels arrayed around him, a serene Mary perhaps to the side, and often more men just below, to represent the "first fruit" male virgins. From Jesus' lower right ascend the saved, while the damned are dragged screaming and writhing in their nakedness down to his left. As ever in Christian iconography, scenes of the devils tormenting the damned provide the emotional intensity, the bodily gesticulations, the dynamic movements which hold the interest (Milton's later Satan syndrome). They break up the passive crowds crammed into either/or, the linear up/down movement, the boring (as Mary Daly would have it, *boring*, that is, penetrating) gaze from the judgment seat. At this moment I gaze back at two photographs of such portals: an eleventh-century fresco in Formis, Italy, and the Gothic relief of Bourges. In both cases, a sprinkling of crowns and other headgear mark the patrons of the church and other elite on Jesus' right side. On his wrong side there are none. In this period the church, as we shall see, was striving aggressively to overwhelm its flock into obedience to itself and to the dominant class–tempting alternatives were offering themselves.

8

In the winter of 1190–1191, Richard the Lionhearted, en route to the Third Crusade, stopped at Messina and asked to see the renowned Abbot Joachim. Fetched down from the Calabrian mountains "to stand in the eager and curious circle of English courtiers," Joachim, whose face was said to look (but for moments of illumination) like "a dried-up leaf," was asked to prophesy concerning the fate of Jerusalem. Instead he expounded "the whole pattern of history, as it impinged upon the present," interpreting the seven heads of the dragon as leading up to the present one, the sixth, Saladin, with one yet to come. Therefore he could read only an ambiguous and postponed victory.[39]

The crusader and the prophet–a portentous pair. The crusader incarnated the apocalyptic holy warrior, now fully literalized after centuries of state Christendom. In spite of the theological repression of apocalypse, the resurgence of its themes is flagrant: the royalty of Islam was readily identified by the established church as Antichrist. Not so paradoxically, given the leaky character of Augustine's own sublimation of apocalypse, this irruption is in fact fueled by an Augustinian orthodoxy whose "militant we/they attitude and uncompromising hostility toward all sorts of unbelievers . . . formed the basis of expectations of a literal victory over the enemies of Christ."[40] The desublimated apocalypse ignites the moribund violence of Europe, which was well reinforcing the Augustinian expectation of gradual degeneration. Now the construct of the Muslim as "infidel" arises. Pope Urban had preached the First Crusade in 1095, deploying the theme of the common, indeed the transcendent Enemy as a device for European unity, challenging the nobles of Europe to "turn the weapons which you have stained unlawfully in the slaughter of one another against the enemies of the faith."

But now (roll over, Augustine) the glittering vision of the City of God gets literalized with a vengeance: the hope for the "spiritual" triumph of Europe fastened itself upon the acquisition of the fabulous wealth of the *old* Jerusalem. From the beginning, the Pope's plan got out of hand. What he envisioned as a succinct campaign of the feudal nobility mushroomed into a desperate mass movement, simultaneously genocidal and suicidal. On the way to the Holy Land, the crusaders subjected the Jews of European cities to a first taste of holocaust.

And they would go on to sack and plunder with a self-righteous brutality identified with the messianic hosts of Armageddon. After all, the Book of Revelation, with its bejeweled Jerusalem, had promised them her riches. A contemporary, Archbishop of Tyre, commented on the mind-numbing carnage with which the crusaders descended upon city after city of "enemies," as it climaxes in Jerusalem:

> It was not alone the spectacle of headless bodies and mutilated limbs strewn in all directions that roused the horror of all who looked on them. Still more dreadful was it to gaze upon the victors themselves, dripping with blood from head to foot, an ominous sight.... It is reported that within the Temple enclosure alone about ten thousand infidels perished.[42]

All survivors, the bishop continued, indeed whole families, "were dragged out into public view and slain like sheep.... For before the capture of the city the pilgrims had agreed that, after it had been taken by force, whatever each man might win for himself should be his forever by right of possession.... Consequently the pilgrims searched the city most carefully and boldly killed the citizens."[43]

This "pilgrimage" in time has not ended. Have the subsequent wars of Europe and America ever forfeited this self-righteous religious zeal, unprecedented in world history, of armed apocalypse? Other patriarchal civilizations have proven just as brutal, yet never so moralistic, so "good" in their genocidal acts. Raining down "fire from above," the Gulf War of 1991, quickly dubbed by numerous Arab critics of U.S. intervention as "the Last Crusade," presaged further crusades for the sake of whatever other precious resource the West claims "by right of possession." Certainly either Christian or Islamic fundamentalists are willing to work out the "final" implications. The crusaders' extermination of Jews and Saracens bequeathed to history the model of the purge, to be applied to all manner of heresy or irritant, close or distant. There seemed never enough infidels, witches, and heretics to purge, never enough blood in which to bathe, renew, and unite the West.

Frederick Turner suggests that the precipitating crisis, however, did not lie in "the fate of the empire, nor the survival of Western Civilization. The crisis was in the religion itself, bereft of its vitality but presiding with its symbols, sacred texts, liturgical calendar, and ecclesiastical hierarchy over the states of the West."[44] I might not so cleanly lift "the religion itself" from its political topology, but Turner's point is well taken. A spiritual apparatus bent on postponing—especially for the common people and rigorously for women—bodily renewal and social justice until some point beyond death would surely have drained social life of its vitality. Plague, urbanization, and early capitalist oppression, however powerful, do not add up to an explanation for the throbbing, bloody desperation of much medieval life. It is as though the sanctified dualism of deferral and desire, of now and then, came at points to fester feverishly in the daily life of these Europeans; as though life in a time thus tensed erupted chronically into the intolerable.

Perhaps Apocalypse, promising material gratification—"the real," not just empty afterlife hopes—set off a violent chain reaction of renewal. No matter how short-lived each New Jerusalem. But the picture is more complex. Hidden in the smoke of the upheavals lies a little-told story of millennialist attempts to thaw out that vitality frozen in the church. Some of them blend too well with the spirit of annihilation, like the anonymous "Revolutionary of the Upper Rhein," frothing in the new medium of print with fantasies of the extirpation of all his enemies, the clerics and aristocrats especially, who add up to the Antichrist: "Go on hitting them from the Pope right down to the little students! Kill every one of them!"[45] But others, from the Franciscan radicals onward, disclose more appealing spiritual and political countercultures. These were doomed by the unity of church and state powers in their time to fail. But recent social movements—among them feminism—may prove indebted to these antecedents for their opening in time, for reopening history.

9

Let us peer now under the hood of that monk at Messina. Given his abstruse apocalyptic speculations on how to translate seven seals into three ages, complete with eidetic diagrams, it is understandable that Joachim of Fiore is not normally noticed by feminists, theologians, or feminist theologians. Moreover, the authors of church history, lacking enough evidence to hereticize him outright, have pursued obfuscation rather than refutation. But if in the pursuit of counter-apocalyptic possibilities we seek precedents for a post-Augustinian dis/closure of history, we cannot bypass the Joachite contribution. And it has not been ignored by all modern commentators.

Joachim of Fiore appears as a patron saint of socialism in Ernst

Bloch's *The Principle of Hope*: "Joachim was cogently the spirit of revolutionary Christian social utopianism."[46] Morton Bloomfield, pursuing no apparent political agenda, positions Joachim as "the first systematic thinker about the nature and meaning of history.... The significance of history ... and an eschatology of hope, were deeply embedded in the Judaeo-Christian tradition long before Joachim, but he was the first to make a discipline, a subject, out of these notions and produce a coherent and articulated philosophy of history."[47] Actually, more or less the same "first" is normally predicated for Augustine. But it is Joachim who presents the great anti-Augustinian alternative for the doctrine of history, and he does so through a visionary revival of the genre of apocalypse. He is credited with the first creative apocalypticism in a thousand years.

Joachim broke through to a construct of history as a time not just for waiting but for growth.[48] Indeed, one of his favorite images (he drew an arboreal ideogram) was of "the Tree of History." Drawing on an eleventh-century hermeneutical trend, he reinterprets John's Apocalypse. Like earlier prophets, he announces an imminent time of worsening crisis (despite the crusaders' hopes) before the new "state" could be realized. By elaborating the textual possibility swatted away by the antimillennialists, he constructs the first theology of history according to which there is something to hope for *within* history. What he does with time is crucial: against Augustine, he again positions the millennium as a symbolic period *in* history, just ahead, and binds it to the Spirit, that untoward agency of ferment. Indeed a trinity becomes his template for the unfolding of time: each of the three Persons presides over a *"status,"* or condition (something very like an aeon, or age), but he avoids literalizing the periods, instead reinforcing their overlaps.

I will spare us his painstaking collations of Old and New Testament figures, his intercalations of the number three with the seven seals, his numerological diagrams. The visual dimension of his intellect is often noted, and obviously attuned his intertextual radar to John's visual proclivities. "Joachim's imagination had a kaleidoscopic quality: the pieces in his mind were always forming new patterns."[49] Schüssler Fiorenza had also noted the kaleidoscopic structure of Revelation. Joachim's seven *etates* and three *statuses* send time through loops and spirals less gloomy, but structurally homologous, to John's septet of septets. But however arcane the vocabulary, the drama of the reopening of history did not go unnoticed. Here is a sample of his revolutionary trinitarianism of *etates*:

> The first was lived in the servitude of slaves, the second in the servitude of sons, but the third will be in *liberty*; the first was a time of chastisings, the second of action, but the third will be the time of *contemplation*; the first was lived in fear, the second in faith, the third in *love*; the first was the status of slaves, the second of sons, but the third will be that of *friends*; the first of old men, the second of young men, the third of *children* . . .[50]

According to the standard trinitarian economy of time, the Age of the Son passes as quickly as Jesus himself and ushers in the final age, that of the church as the vehicle of the Holy Spirit converting the rest of the earth. Instead, Joachim subsumes the entire period of Christendom until his own time under the Second Person, the Son. He thus frees the Third Person, the Spirit, to preside over the coming age. In this Joachim anticipates the realization of eschatological values more reminiscent of the classical prophets and the Gospels than one is wont to encounter in the history of theology. A gender-sensitive reader will note the unmistakable if inadvertent leap beyond the Father & Son. The Spirit-driven movement beyond every state of subjugation implies a move beyond masculine imagery into the gender-inclusive metaphors of "friend" and "child." If the gender politics of time twist open here, the revolutionary reading has not been effected simply by revolving back to the text. On the contrary, Joachim has read John's text beyond, if not against, itself.[51] Deconstructing through the medium of time itself the imagery of divine dominance, he generates a humanly appealing utopia, different in tone from *Revelation*'s bitter quest for a vindicative justice: freedom, meditation, love, friendship.

As Marjorie Reeves dryly comments, "The third *status* could quickly become a third age, with a new 'testament,' a new authority and new institutions. There was concealed dynamite here."[52] If he did not intend to declare a coming age of liberation from ecclesial fetters and all private property, his images nonetheless gave form to a long suppressed depth of egalitarian yearnings in Europe. Joachim himself never during his life forfeited the blessing of Rome, and in his last decade, although he had retreated into the Calabrian mountains, he was frequently contacted by heads of state and church for prophetic counsel. Yet the long-term impact of his doctrine of a radical immanence of the Spirit entering history was not thus contained. His entire doctrine of the historical trinity was posthumously condemned. Centuries of those for whom he ranked as *magnus propheta* derived from often free-floating allusions to Joachim their heterodoxies of spiritual community and historical concreteness. This influence would transmit itself under the heretical cyphers "the eternal Gospel," "the third age," and "the age of the Free Spirit."

The effective history of Joachim—a major chapter in the *Wirkungsgeschichte* of the Apocalypse—channels out by way of the "Spiritual Franciscans," who first synthesized Joachimist prophecy with economics. In opposition to the "Conventual Franciscans," the Spirituals were insisting on the mendicant path, in imitation of Christ's poverty and Francis' renewed example. The ecclesial authorities came down hard in defense of the sacred rights of property. The "barefoot order" did not keep its "improprieties" to itself, and their "bitter opposition to the growth of the Order in terms of buildings, legacies and libraries" along with their "passionate devotion to their patched and skimpy habits" resonated too well with popular resentment.[53] They seem to have proclaimed the advent of a third age of universally shared, contemplative poverty, in which the two testaments would be superseded by a third—the eternal Evangel.

The Fraticelli, a persecuted party of Franciscans, brought the threat out of latency. By the late fourteenth century the latter were assailing the Pope as Antichrist—a trope of which thus long antedates the Protestant Reformation.[54] In a certain sense the Apocalypse comes full circle: if the church persecuted by Rome became the Roman persecutor, how fitting that the epithets of Beast, Antichrist, and Whore of Babylon now turn upon it.

Of course the terms suffered from characteristic apocalyptic excess—at least as cited by their enemies, who destroyed most of their writings. The Fraticelli saw themselves as the "saving remnant gathered into the frail ark of the true Church, the Noah's Ark of the last age."[55] Olivi, a scholastic philosopher whose tone was anything but fanatic, emerged as the major intellect to fuse Joachite prophecy with Franciscan opposition to property. A charismatic personality as well, he developed a strong following for the idea of a flowering of history after the defeat of Antichrist and before the final consummation, in that temporal wedge of the chiliast metaphor. Several Olivists who refused to rescind these notions were burnt at the stake in 1316. Soon the Brethren of the Free Spirit began to move through Europe, teaching their own blend of church-free and unpropertied mysticism. Students of one of their great thinkers, Amaurus, at the University of Paris, who developed a full cosmology of the Free Spirit, were exposed by an infiltrator; the fourteen who would not recant were burnt. These little holocausts announced the new Roman cure for heresy. If Rome earlier deemed censure and exile strong enough medicine, it now applied to internal dissent the techniques rehearsed in the Crusades: the purge, once a bloody biblical fantasy of divine wrath, becomes a mechanism of social control. Apocalypse versus apocalypse.

10

The politics of time had found its economic battleground. Forged in the medieval turmoil from which modernity would issue, the notion that a new age in real time was dawning came into play inseparably from the hope for a communal sharing of all resources, made possible by the spontaneous democracy of the Spirit. But, not surprisingly, such anticipation exercised considerably more charm for the poor, and exposed its adherents to persecution by those for whom neither the end of the known world nor the redistribution of their property held any redemptive allure. The story of the extent and challenge of these countercultural movements from the eleventh through the sixteenth century has been virtually expunged from the standard accounts of church and state history, which figure them as mad, enthusiastic, or heretical if they could not be erased. Cohn's *Pursuit of the Millennium*, if imbued with the familiar distaste for these motley groups and the revolutionary trajectory they opened, first comprehensively tracked the wildfire of apocalyptic dissent and the wrath of theocracies stamping it out. The heresy of the Free Spirit stirred the discontents of Europe into forms both fanatic and attractive, drawing from the laboring and peasant classes as well as from the dissident fringe of the elite. As the church in the thirteenth and fourteenth centuries closed that period of relative openness in which time itself had been reopened, the politics of chronology constructed a spiral of spiritual resistance (pacifist or armed) and ecclesial counterinsurgency.[56]

11

These short-lived countercultures shifted the spiritual economies of gender as well. Women's desires came into public time, announcing a new age incarnate in a woman's body. The new dis/closure of time unveiled another horror: where his/story became her/esy. Then the burning anticipated in the demise of the Whore of Babylon, the burning of disobedient female flesh, would be literally enacted in the public squares of Europe. Eventually tens and perhaps hundreds of thousands of women would die for the heresy of witchcraft.

Guglielma made her mysterious appearance in Milan circa 1271. The only record of her teachings is that of the Inquisition's proceeding thirty years later against her followers, the Guglielmiti, who had persisted under the leadership of her main disciple, Saramita, and his female companion, Manfreda, who leave their testimony for the record: "As the Word had been incarnate in a Man, so the Holy Spirit had now become incarnate in a woman"; Guglielma herself would rise from the dead and send her followers the Holy Spirit as tongues of flame.

Again, the Age of the Spirit is dawning. The extant hierarchy had forfeited its authority. New spiritual offices were to be appointed, primarily to women. Manfreda would be pope and her cardinals would be women. Saramita would be the scribe of the "Eternal Evangel." "The sect was too mad to be really dangerous and soon disappeared," comments Marjorie Reeves archly. "It reveals the most . . . absurd lengths to which the logic of a Trinitarian interpretation of history could be pushed." Odd to hear a woman scholar identify so comfortably with the Inquisitors. Adding class to gender bias, she notes, "though, curiously enough, [the movement of Guglielmiti] was drawn mainly from the well-to-do and Manfreda was probably the cousin of Matteo Visconti."[57] That she fails to interrogate the inquisitors' own recordings of their victims' confessions suggests the anxiety which gender stirs in history and historians. Beneath the inquisitorial text one may read, rather than insanity, a radical cultural critique, symbolically performed as well as theorized in the religio-cultural terms of the time. Reeves wants to defend her favorite, Joachim, against the taint of such protofeminist usage, but some might value him all the more for this unforeseen effect of his time-opening.

Then there was Prous Boneta. A disciple of Olivi, she, like the Guglielmiti, emphasized the new age of the Holy Spirit just breaking in. "As Eve had been the downfall of human nature, so Prous would be the instrument of all men's salvation." According again to the transcript of the inquisitorial confessors, she described herself as an incarnation of the Holy Spirit, being crucified by the condemnation of Olivi's works and by her own persecution.

Certainly a gender crisis has manifested itself in these martyrdoms for a new aeon. Such women as these were not content to seek institutional equality in a culture which had strictly cloistered their leadership capacities. They moved right to the level of the symbolic, announcing a new female dispensation of the Spirit. Their choice of the Holy Spirit–the only gender-neutral and traditionally even sometimes feminine symbol within the trinitarian economy–to represent their struggle prophetically anticipates, as we shall see, nineteenth- and twentieth-century women's movements.[58] In the Spirit, though not necessarily in gender-analytic consciousness, they announced the coming of *their* spirit. Even Reeves acknowledges the salience of gender in these medieval apocalypses: "The human desire to find an enhanced role within the historical process lies at the root in both cases, but the women bring to the surface in a dramatic way the problem of sex in the Christian religion."[59]

Let us note the stunning power of Spirit–as movement and as representation of a movement, as medium and as message–to question the presuppositions by which history is framed. As with the biblical prophets, the new aeon is always declared "in the Spirit." Women and Spirit, as we shall witness again in the final chapters of this work, make dangerous new allies in and counter- apocalypse. The opening of time into the expectation of a new and better history will again and again release an experience of the divine spirit from within, one so immanent as to be embodied in the flesh of a woman. Or vice versa: a particular spirit-consciousness can so empower certain persons (even female) as to begin to reopen history then and there, already, within their incarnate existences. Six hundred years later, when a recent and spirited heresiarch declared again "the Second Coming of Woman," the same church reacted with the same intensity of condemnation; so Mary Daly, instead of retorting with the now tired trope of the papal Antichrist, would in exasperation celebrate feminism as Antichrist.[60] Fortunately, in the meantime Rome had had its matches confiscated.

But in the late thirteenth century the burning had only begun. The first mass women's movement of Europe was gathering momentum at the time. Especially in the North, women were choosing to gather together under a new social form known as Beguinages. These communities of women often lived together, but included married women living with their families; they pursued a spiritual vocation, but chose to remain outside of the jurisdiction of religious orders; and they combined contemplative mysticism with social activism. They preferred the wandering Brethren of the Free Spirit, the Beghards, to priests. When the Beghards were proscribed, the Beguines continued to shelter and converse with them. As to the links between these two groups, Cohn comments that "the Millennium of the Free Spirit had become an invisible empire, held together by the emotional bonds—which of course were often erotic bonds—between men and women."[61] But the bonds between *women* defined Beguine life. The Beguines soon came under persecution, but by agreeing to supervision by male clerics, some groups did survive for centuries. A Franciscan of Tournai reported that

> though untrained in theology, the Beguines rejoiced in new and oversubtle ideas. They had translated Scripture into French and interpreted its mysteries, on which they discoursed irreverently in their meetings and on the streets. Vernacular Bibles, full of errors and heresies, were available to the public at Paris. An east German Bishop complained that these women were idle, gossiping vagabonds who refused obedience to men under the pretext that God was best served in freedom.[62]

Their vernacular translations in an era in which the Bible was retained in clerically controlled Latin versions performed a radical job usually credited to the Reformation. Indeed, Bernard McGinn credits these women with the development of a "vernacular theology," a theology in which "women, for the first time in the history of Christianity, took on an important, even a preponderant, role," and which belies the normal categorization of theology into "monastic" or "scholastic."[63] The notion of women "rejoicing" in textual hermeneutics and intellectual conversation (subtle speculations and idle gossip) while refusing subjugation to men, was just too much free spirit.

The Beguine Marguerite de Porete in particular had developed a wide reputation for her learning and mysticism. She pursued the peripatetic path of male adepts of the Spirit, walking and teaching her way through

Europe. While her book, *A Mirror for Simple Souls*, affirms the Trinity and other dogmas, one may read here a revolution in spirituality. As with so many of the women mystics of the medieval period, the path of mystic renunciation let her be "free from all slaveries and possess complete freedom of being."[64] It is composed in a free-form, lightly allegorical style, as a conversation of Love with Reason, Soul, and a few other denizens of her consciousness. Love emerges, among the Beguines, as the supreme authority.[65] The *Mirror* text playfully jilts scholastic Reason—the epistemological edifice of orthodoxy—and dramatizes its own rhetoric of ecstatic spirit possession in the form of a multivocal conversation between Love, Reason, Soul, and so on. The other published Beguines like Hadewijch and Mechthild similarly scripted a pneumatology in which a spirit discourse of divine immanence and intuitive response supersedes the unmistakably androcentric order of Reason, to whose centers women had no access. Marguerite's renunciatory Love teaching,[66] like Buddhist doctrines of nonattachment, leads to release from all wanting—even the desire for God and salvation—and issues into "the life of true freedom." Thus "Love" argues, "Let's take one soul as an example: she seeks neither disgrace nor poverty, worries nor cares; she needs no masses or sermons, or fasting or prayers; she gives nature all she asks willingly and ungrudgingly."[67]

This freedom, performed by a wandering and writing woman, struck the authorities as anarchy. It had evident associations to the heresy of the Free Spirit. The one man to have stood by her once she was imprisoned, the Beghard Guiard of Cressonessart, "held millenarian views related to those of Joachim of Fiore."[68] (He avoided the stake by confessing to errors.) This is not to say that women then or ever depend for liberation upon a Joachite or other apocalypse. The Bible was the available text, and the Book of Revelation its most radical critique of the status quo, mythologically relevant to any situation of historic rupture. Prophetic women, often with the support of male soulmates, made use of the millennialist opening, as today we make use of postmodern or liberation or psychoanalytic paradigms, to theorize their freedom.

The *Mirror* mentions no literal Second Coming or dawning Age of the Spirit at all; however, its discourse does not resemble the Apocalypse. Rather, the Spirit, intimately immanent to the experience of its practitioners, makes freedom available already. Hints of counter-apocalypse? After a bishop had her book burned in 1306, Marguerite sought and re-

ceived written endorsements from three male theologians. She repub-
lished the book, and the authorities ignored her sponsors. She was burnt
with her book in Paris in 1310. She had not compromised what she called
her "perfect freedom."

The feudal church was evidently intent on aborting any new age, let
alone divine incarnation of the female. To do this they would resort to the
most rabid apocalyptic dualism of good and evil, divorced from the dual-
ity of ages. In a bit of truculent intertextuality, the Dominican witch-
hunters Kramer and Sprenger would justify the systematic war against
women with a parenthetical quote from the great female apocalypticist
of the medieval church. The irony is double, as this seems to be both their
only citation either of millennialism or of female authority. Describing
the way the devil, working through witches, stirs up adulterous lusts in
men, they cite Abbess Hildegard of Bingen, known in her time as the
Sibyl of the Rhine:

> When a man is so bound in the meshes of carnal lust and desire that he can
> be made to desist from it by no shame, words, laws or action . . . when it
> is found that those of noblest birth . . . are the most miserably involved in
> this sin (for this age is dominated by women, and was foretold by S. Hilde-
> gard . . .) of what use is it to speak of remedies to those who desire no
> remedy?[69]

The alternative treatment they spread would perform on earth Augustine's vision of hell, where masses of bodies are tortured and burned
for the glory of God. Understanding themselves as strict purveyors of Augustinian orthodoxy, they did not subscribe to Hildegard's creative apocalypticism. It is as though they sniffed out her moment of what we might
call internalized sexism—her rhetorical strategy of a debased age dominated by women—by which she had claimed the space that men, having
proved irresponsible leaders, had left to the likes of her.

In form the abbess fit her visions to the Augustinian scheme of the
seven days; but the Sabbath day, symbolizing the New Creation, implied
a more hopeful End of the World. As though to counter the apocalyptic
tone of bitter rage, she claims it "will be brought forth openly with gentle
words—just as the words of this book are—on the seventh day of quietness." *Ecriture feminine?* She anticipates an eschatological yet open-
ended Sabbath. Not that it will be without devastation and judgment. But
her sense of creation leads to a very different sense of the New Creation.

The old will not simply flee away, to be replaced with a supernatural replica. "On the last day, even the very land itself will be disturbed when I–God–wash the four elements clean." Indeed the cosmic elements will come to their full lustration: they will *be* the sparkling gems of the New Jerusalem. "The sun, moon, and stars–just like embellished things–shone with a reddish gleam full of brightness and beauty." They then became fixed and no longer went around in a circle, "so that day and night were no longer distinguished ... And so it ended."[70] A different sense of earth, of place, of cosmos emanates from Hildegard's apocalypse; though like all orthodoxy, she stops time, she does not thereby vaporize the great spatial symbols of time, the luminarias of the Queen of Heaven, but on the contrary, grants them pride of place.[71]

The "gentle words" did not soften the discourse of Kramer and Sprenger, whose expropriation of her prophecy lends a pseudo-apocalyptic legitimation for extending the church's prosecution of heretical (usually apocalyptic) prophets to the persecution of women. Not that they required a quote from a woman. Still, the sinister citation warns that there is nothing necessarily liberating about the female voice of prophecy–she may precisely at that juncture avail herself of some rhetoric of misogyny to be deployed later by others against her entire gender. This tangle anticipates the larger question of this book, How are we to assess the dependence of modern feminism upon the essentially sexist script of apocalypse?

12

Subsequent chapters will pick up the chronological threads. But I want to meditate for a moment on the leap through a half millennium of modern times. What happened to time? How did we get from the tightening medieval *kairos* of deferrals and eruptions to the banal *chronos* of late capitalism? What does the theocratic performance of final purpose have to do with a time standardized for production, universalized for global liquidation, transmitted in electronic impulses, and marketed as the technofix *now*? When *are* we?

The evacuation of sacredness from time was already well advanced by the church's deferrals unto eternity of any meaningful future. The sacrality of the present was mainly captured in the denatured sacrament of a past saving event. Counting down towards the end, official Christian time was self-secularizing: the sense of purpose preserved by apocalyptic hope would soon translate itself into the modern myth of Progress. This shift seems to tighten rather than to resolve the Western tension of postponement. Pertaining to this futurist continuum, Turner points to a fundamental alienation which would be later routinized in early modern European history:

> Robbed of ... old comforts, and unable to feel reattached to the great events sealed off by subsequent history, the Christian West had to live onward, set its face resolutely forward in the hope of recovering in an apocalyptic future what it had once had in the past. The historical interpretation of Christian mythology thus became the very engine of history.[72]

By these "comforts" Turner has in mind a certain earth-based integrity of time, place, and meaning already sacrificed to the church.[73] Turner draws the consequences widely, tracing the path of this "engine" which will thunder along the tracks of "progress," crushing the earth and its indigenous peoples under its wheels.

There are good reasons for the historical convention of reading the modern sense of historical progress as a secularization of the Christian myth of apocalypse.[74] It is, after all, the apocalypse which produces the very notion that the future holds out something *better* for us, and modernity receives the faith filtered through the Joachite rereading of the millennium into history. Indeed, even such a rude positivist as August Comte in the nineteenth century, schematizing history in a triune progression from the Age of Faith to the Age of Reason, to the Age of Science, reinscribes the tradition of the Three Ages transmitted through the Free Spirit heresies. Freed from the Spirit—or rather, having successfully translated "spirit" into "mind" (*Geist*)—the Enlightenment could render salvation history as temporal progress of the *humanum* toward the universal and eternal truths of Reason. The Enlightenment could thus effect both an appropriation and an overthrow of apocalypticism, that is, it will eschew the supernaturalism and authoritarian particularism with which Christendom had institutionalized the Final Judgment. The ultimate deadline would be lifted, graciously, if perhaps self-deceptively, from history.

As critics of the Enlightenment have demonstrated, however, the generic Reason and Science which were to replace religious bigotry carried the same unacknowledged bias; they universalized the privilege of the white male Eurocentrism which produced them.[75] With its manly faith in its own civilizing capacities, the modern trajectory of Reason would fortify the crusading animus of Christendom into a previously unimaginable scope of colonization. As Australian political philosopher Joseph Camilleri claims, "Underlying the history of the expanding, conquering, 'sovereign' state is the notion of continuity yet 'progress' across time, of history unfolding . . . as the ordering of time and space, as mastery of people and nature."[76]

Politics inscribes its control within the sensorium of daily life, within its most intimate spatiotemporality. But the critique of the modern does not often note that this rationalizing of time and space–by which national, international, and, in time, a global market emerged–could only develop on the basis of the medieval regularization of earthly time, syncopated into preparation for the next world and so de-emphasizing the natural rhythms of this one. Lewis Mumford analyzed how the routines of monasteries regularized European time; Pope Sabiniasnus required that the bells be rung seven times every twenty-four hours, a mechanical regularization that sonically came to dominate the daily life of the continent. Thus time, mechanically measured, grew "dissociated from organic sequences." Centuries later, the Pueblo Indians' sacred clowns would use alarm clocks in their dances as a way of "ridiculing the whites' enslavement to the marching minute hand."[77] Church bells have become computerized carillons, and the circling of the hands of the clock–which did at least recap the motion of cosmic bodies–has been replaced by the electronic blips of digital time. No allusion to the *space* of time remains. Yet hand or digit, they still mark the progression of the modern state's capacity to regularize the spirits and the labor of its citizens, *to keep them in place by controlling their time.*

Camilleri continues:

As the main carrier for the ideology of modernity . . . the system of sovereign states was predicated on the erection of boundaries not only between geographical territories but between segments of time. In addition to fostering a pervasive disjunction between the traditional and the modern, the sovereign state sought to control the flow of time by measuring, standardizing and segmenting it, by distinguishing private and public time, work time and leisure time. The application of the market principle to the workplace made possible the buying and selling of labor time, that is, the commodification of time.[78]

118

As Laguna-Pueblo-Sioux critic Paula Gunn Allen writes, "Chronological time . . . the idea that everything has a starting point and an ending point reflects accurately the process by which industry produces goods. . . . There is a connection between factories and clocks, and there is a connection between colonial imperialism and factories."[79] The point here is that the chronologizing modern sense of time, which she contrasts to mythic-achronological time, found its mythic justification in John's distinctly premodern text, whose alpha-omega at once founds The End as the goal of time and motivates the Western drive to the future.

Modern time did not just casually synchronize the colonization of planetary space. Conscription now required all young males to place their time at the disposal of the state, thus both universalizing the foundational warrior ethos and providing forceful support for the new markets. Time in the nineteenth century served as a political instrument forged "to adjust human life more rationally to the constraints of an absolute time and space."[80]

To accomplish this massive social abstraction of time from the recalcitrant local rhythms of daily life, indeed, to do the dirty work of empire and commerce, public time/space was separated from private. In the newly constructed private time, men refresh themselves at the bosom of ideal women. At least this is the dream of the Victorian white middle class, in which the household angel presides over a feminized domestic space temporalized by economically trivial rituals. Here the male was to find his respite from the routines of history. Women of the rising middle classes, expected to humanize this mechanized temporality of their men, were increasingly locked into a complementary private space where an ahistorical time of quotidian cycles ruled. Mary Daly, with characteristic apocalyptic flair, captures the transition in "the contrast between captured time, the clocking/clacking of clonedom, and the Tidal Timing of the Race of Raging Women."[81]

We will ask, Is it the *spatiality* of time from which projects of universal dominance, apocalyptic or modern, must textually abstract history? For a universal missionary faith must by definition disdain the roots of peoples in their *places*. Secularization theory assumes that a humanistic historicism replaced the mission of salvation history. But if, rather, certain biblical narratives were already well on the way to voiding the spatiotemporality of God, then modernity stood prepared to absorb the divine potencies fully into itself, concealing them within the universal

119

parameters of the new mechanics of "absolute space and time." But then the God of the biblical text gradually loses the capacity to exercise even the medieval level of moral constraint over *men's* secular powers. Cut loose in modernity from theistic moorings and textual accountability, the universal chronology of the apocalyptic vision came to subserve the manmade ends of the state, technology, and the market.

As Christian eschatology turns into secular teleology it massively, materially literalizes apocalyptic time. We will later consider its utopian optimism. But a cinematic image reveals its new hell: the workers chained to the hands of giant clocks in the industrial hell of Chaplin's *Modern Times.*

13

How we read time—our time—may pertain *liter*/ally to how we *read*. The medieval period was an elaboration on one text, read by few, mimed by most. It gave way to the mass literacy and publication of the modern press. If the book-centered history of Christendom mirrors the temporality of the Book of Revelation—its hypertextual alpha and omega scrolling out a sequential salvation history of the Word—it seems no coincidence that finally the civilization of the Book developed the linear sense of history into its own end. That is, it would eventually escape the limits of Beginning and End, translating divine Author/ity into human control.

Is there is an apocalypse-prone relationship between the act of reading and the narrativity of time? From the vantage point of the current "end of reading" we may note with Sven Birkerts the coordination of text and temporality:

> The depth of field that is our sense of the past is not only a linguistic function, it is in some essential way represented by the book and the physical accumulation of books in the library space. In the contemplation of the single volume, or mass of volumes, we form a picture of time past as an accumulation of sediment; we capture a sense of its depth and dimensionality.[82]

Insightfully exposing the spatial field of time, Birkerts predicts that as "the electronic order" supersedes the order of the written word, we will experience a "flattening of historical perspectives." Both visual and nonvisual technology works against historical perspective, "which must depend upon the notions of logic and sequential succession." Instead, it heightens the user's focus on the present—the *now*—where the entertainment industry will seize the advantage: "The past will be rendered ever more glorious, ever more a fantasy play with heroes, villains, and quaint settings and props."[83]

Not that Birkerts's nostalgia for the book will not gain much support in even a bookish feminist counter-apocalypse. Besides, by the tone of his announcement of the imminent "death of the book" and advent of "the electronic millennium" he postures as a kind of endtime prophet of writing, like the book-fixated John of Patmos, with the electronic media as Antichrist. Yet his McLuhanite warning is well taken. The leveling of history into a controllable, commodifiable present is proceeding at eerie speed through the hyper mechanics of the socio-communicative field. The hegemony of writing, which still among academic elites struggles to maintain its edge over oral culture, faces the revenge of the sound bite!

What is this high-tech "now" which Birkerts dreads? It equates growing "rooted in the consciousness of the *now*" with an ahistorical cult of instant gratification. But is it not, on the contrary, the loss of the now, of a certain *kind* of present, that we must face—a "now" translucent upon its past, like the Woolfian trope of memory as surface upon the ocean, pulsing tide-like toward its future? Such a presence itself resists the dissociative digital now-point.

This flat "now" can be analyzed as another unintended effect of the old eschatological tension of deferred hope and anticipatory fulfillment. Suspended between gratification and catastrophe, postmodern capitalism sates the hunger for immediacy with electronic junk food. Such a present finds momentary relief from the tension, indeed, from hope itself. The mediations of texts have given way to the illusory immediacy of the media, whose sale of sex and horror packages the time of Babylon as our own. The *Clockwork Orange* of late "modern times," of late modern temporality.

14

"Hope is women's most powerful revolutionary tool," commented Peggy Korneger in a feminist dictionary entry early in the second wave of feminism. "It is what we give each other every time we share our lives, our work and our love. It pulls us forward out of self-hatred, self-blame, and the fatalism which keeps us prisoners in separate cells."[84] A couple of decades earlier, socialist philosopher Ernst Bloch had argued in the three-volume *Philosophy of Hope* that "because true hope moves in the world, via the world and works in mediation with its objective process, it stands together with this process in a hazardous business, *that of the Front.*"[85] Hope as revolutionary tool, as motive force of "the Front." Western social progressivism, including feminism, is from the outset founded on the eschatology of *hope*.

An orthodox atheist, Bloch traced all Western revolutionary hope to its biblical sources in the prophetic tradition. He keyed in on Apocalypse as funneled into modernity through the influence of Joachim of Fiore. His understanding of hope's "objectivity" will help to illuminate a path from apocalyptic time, within which he is willingly ensconced, to a present tense of the social movements. Their radicalism lies precisely in the habit of hope. But then does hope itself hold us to the time frame of apocalypse? For Bloch, hope cannot be reduced to a subjective emotion, hence it has a kind of ontological status, that is, it drives the desire for the new, for transformation, for justice and community throughout world history. Hope for a utopian fruition of human life leaves its tracks throughout the pre-Marxist history of human signifying activity. "The Authentic or essence is that which is not yet," Bloch wrote, "which in the core of things drives towards itself, *which awaits its genesis in the tendency-latency of process*; it is itself only now founded, objective–real–hope."[86]

The Blochian "not yet" works like a magnet of the future lodged in the "essential" present. Inverted Hegelian metaphysics aside, to honor this genesis of the possible, we would have to sacrifice any notion of the symmetry of the tenses for the sake of that theopolitical dynamism of which the eschatological prophets created "hope." In his philosophical expedition through world history, Bloch certainly lends temporal depth—no "flattened historical perspectives" amidst this dramatic metanarrative—to the conventional left-progressive privilege of the future. We might further nudge his high modern objectivism toward an intersubjective field theory of relations. Yet in the ripening history of progressive social movements lies also the germ of a sense of time beyond even the softened, enriched Marxism of Bloch, of a temporalism that had outgrown the time of state socialism before the latter ended, that found its institutionalized hope impossibly flat as well.

"The new social movements" writes Camilleri, "are helping to redefine the conception of history and time on which the modern state has constructed the edifice of sovereignty."[87] That means the edifice of the revolutionary state as well as that of the capitalist one. Thus, from the crucible of the social movements—feminist, liberative, ecological, anti-racist—emerge slowly the contours of a new temporality:

> To begin with, their praxis implies a rebellion against the decoupling of private and public time, against the segmentation, flattening and abstraction of time. They privilege personal relationships and forms of communal life which endow the experience of time with an organic quality and allow for a more creative coalescence of past, present and future. . . . [The new attitude toward time] enables the subject to develop a deeper sense of collective purpose . . . and facilitates the emergence of new communicative structures and forms of collective identity.[88]

That "creative coalescence" of tenses does not imply their symmetry. Indeed Bloch's phrase "tendency-latency" may provide a clue for movement beyond the time-binaries of apocalypticism. The question, however, is whether the root–*radical*–hope of progressivism is contaminated at the core by the endist complex of righteous dualism and aggressive conquest.

Progressive temporalizations of hope resonate, as German feminist Christina Thürmer-Rohr makes vivid, with the young white man's idealist adventure to the new frontier or the old white man's yearning for immortality. Thus she finds feminist presumption of the categories of futurity and hope demoralizing. Instead she eschews the colonizing manhood underlying revolutionary as well as reactionary ideology. Thürmer-Rohr proposes instead "living hope-lessly in the present."[89]

Given the apocalyptic womb of the very ideal of hope, a counter-apocalyptic feminism will need to take seriously the challenge of such decolonizing "anti-hope." Indeed, her critique parallels the anti-utopianism of French feminist poststructuralism. But what if those who count as the colonized consider hope, even hope founded on apocalyptic time, as a necessity of survival? Would we mark unwhite hopes merely as "other," irrelevant to gender- and class-based yearning among European cultures?

For example, Karen Fields, author of *Revival and Rebellion in Colonial Central Africa*, argues that she has discovered a "deep connection" between the "theologically principled" law-breaking of colonized villagers (in such actions as refusal to pay taxes or accept wage work) and "millenarian and messianic visions of the world's End."[90] Any white feminism which seeks solidarity with antiracist movements will find the subversive uses of apocalyptic hope before them—perhaps even "essential." As the slaves sang, for whom eschatology was neither a luxury nor a crusade but a matter of the courage to rise and survive, "In that great getting up morning/Fare you well, fare you well."

Must counter-apocalypse, if it *hopes* to remain in service of the crosscutting voices of multiple social movements, problematize, contextualize, and nuance rather than jettison hope? Consider in its context the hope of Matilda Elena Lopez, the Salvadoran poet of resistance, in these lines uttered in the midst of the twelve-year Armageddon of the civil war:

> I cry in the cocoon
> for the wings of tomorrow
> the future is a tortured today
> that doesn't yet have wings.[91]

The trope of the future as "a tortured today," all too resonant for one living amidst victims of physical torture and in daily danger herself, reopens the wound at the heart of hope. As the midrash of the souls under the altar encrypted it, *hope* addresses a kind of damage that exposes the tinny superficiality of optimism. The apocalypse script proves indispensable to Lopez's expression of the drama of oppression:

> heaven
> opens part way
> demons guard the entrance
> with swords of fire.

As in John's Apocalypse, the omega has absorbed the Eden of the alpha, leaving little difference between endtime angels and the fiery demons. Here, as there, the future is glimpsed, in Bloch's words, as the "not yet, which in the core of things drives towards itself." As Mary de Shazer comments, in her moving work on women's "poetics of resistance," "The future's frail wings are not yet strong enough to permit flight, and the present is tortured by demonic gate guardians bearing fiery swords— apocalyptic imagery, to be sure. All we can do, the poet asserts, is to live intensely in this moment."[92] Indeed, in Lopez's recourse to genesis-apocalypse, the cocoon of the present "awaits its genesis in the tendency-latency of process."

The counter-hegemonic temporality of these movements will no doubt continue to radicalize the discursive edge between doom and utopia: "All of the critical social movements are to a greater or lesser extent animated by a radical assumption about the future."[93] As the chapter on communities in revolt will show, the "radical assumption" can never purge itself of apocalyptic residues. But that assumption, which in Camelleri's analysis "perceives and enlivens the progressive, at times tortuous, often painful unfolding of the possibilities latent in individual and collective life," contains the germs of its own counter-apocalypse–inasmuch, I will argue, as the future, precisely *as* the possible, is firmly rerooted in the "organic quality" of the present. The "tortured tomorrow" growing its wings? For, unlike the messianic future of John of Patmos, Marx or Bloch, Lopez's hope comes with no guarantee: those wings might be already crippled.

15

If we recognize a persistent spirit of the possible in the cocoon of the moment–not in the hard core of some scientific utopia–we might trace from it the course of a vast intersubjective process. We might, indeed, grant that spirit a more honestly theological status. For the language of hope not only roots in biblical eschatology, it brings with it the assumption of the social character of human existence and the spiritual work of possibility in time.

Given the biblical freight of Bloch's atheistic hope, its foundational influence upon the German theologian Jürgen Moltmann poses little inconsistency. "The God spoken of here is no intra-worldly or extra-worldly Gods, but the 'God of hope' (Romans 15:13), a God with 'future as his [*sic*] essential nature' (as Ernst Bloch puts it)."[94] Moltmann's theology of hope, jointly fathered by Bloch and Karl Barth, is premised on the assertion that biblical eschatology is not about the end of time, but about hope. This is a valuable clarification. Moltmann recognized the limits of any ideological application of eschatology. He points to the continual receding of the "horizon of hope"–the future–and therefore to the idolatry of any attempt to stabilize it as a church, a program, or a party.

Oddly enough, I find the patriarch Barth himself illuminating on the matter of hope. For Barth, a theologian suspended somewhere between anti- and neoapocalyptic theology, the genuine hope which is derived within Christianity from an eschatological hope "for the Last Day, for the eternal year" enables hope "for the next day and the next year." The promise for a post-Barthian theology of the Barthian hope manifests itself in three characteristics. Hope is not bound to optimism or pessimism, since even in desperate situations one "may still dare to hope for indications of the ultimate." "Hope takes place in the act of taking the next step. Hope is action and as such it is genuine hope." And "the Christian does not think or act as a private individual" but rather "hopes in and with the community, and in and for the world, that there will not be lacking to the world, even in all its needs and perplexities, provisional lights, concrete aids and deliverances and preservations and advancements, but also salutary crises."[95] Dislodged from the parochial context of Barth's relentless Christocentrism, not to mention his unrepentant male supremacism, I would want to submit these three criteria of hope to counter-apocalyptic consideration.

That a useable hope would not be *optimism*—no distinction is more critical to the present project. For the cycle of pessimism and optimism which virtually convulses Western, and especially U.S. culture—including preeminently its social activists—may be a prime production of the repressed cycle of apocalyptic doom and millennial expectancy. Yet that such hope is not a passive expectancy but an actualization of real possibility indicates its temporalizing power. The communality of hope, inasmuch as it critically enhances the sociality of being in time, would require a relationalist account of temporality.

The "next step": a non-endist, detotalizing move, potentially leading beyond both religious and Blochian certainties about the future, hovering closer to the earth and the present. Outgrowing Barth's chauvinism, Moltmann later ceased to pit a Christian "future" against a pagan "present" and emphasized rather the embodiment of the Spirit in the media of presence. Though his eschatology still falls prey to the andromorphic iconography of orthodoxy, Moltmann does offer "hope" to church feminists, opening Christology into cosmological and even "Sophialogical" zones—loci of potential solidarity with the Sun Woman. Such emergent affinities might be read as portents of her time, the time of her coming.

16

Now I become myself. It's taken
Time, many years and places;
I have been dissolved and shaken,
Worn other people's faces. . . .[96]

The text of a counter-apocalypse already comes inscribed by the subject of "women's time." Or the question. Women have been scapegoats for time, or more exactly, for a masculine escape from time. We have carried for the benefit of dominant males the onus of finitude, mortality, and corruption itself. As material girls or abandoned hags, women—seen as the more bodily, the more changeable, the more fickle and lustful—have borne a special cross of human mortality, indeed have provided the "subaltern" that supports a construct of a masculine immortality, a male approximation of the timelessness of male divinity. This judgment of our temporality from the vantage point of a masculinized eternity takes the form of the internalized male gaze. Thus Sandra Lee Bartky beautifully "disciplines" Foucault's concept of the "synopticon," metaphor of the model prison in which prisoners stand under twenty-four-hour surveillance, for feminist analysis: "In contemporary patriarchal culture, a panoptical male connoisseur resides within the consciousness of most women: They stand perpetually before his gaze and under his judgment."[97] As Edith Wharton describes Lily's self-scrutiny: "and she was frightened by two little lines near her mouth, faint flaws in the smooth curve of the cheek."[98] Timelines inscribing slow death in the flesh of the androcentric female.

But these interpretive stereotypes are also faintly flawed. For it seems just as self-evident, after this generation's excavations, that woman is to place as man is to time, "As for woman, she is place," writes Irigaray laconically.[99] Thus motherland and mother earth, the Whore of Babylon and the Virgin Jerusalem, would locate femininity with that which lays itself open to the interpretation of male time-travelers. As Yahweh took charge of salvation history, so the sons of men would take charge of global history.

In other words, when (as is more characteristic of biblical eschatology) the juxtaposition is of time over space, masculinity is temporal, femininity ahistorical. When (as is more typical of classical influence and thus of a Christian anti-apocalypse) it is a matter of eternity over time, women are temporalized. The binary axes of dominance and subjugation are context-specific, and will be tangled into endless temporalizations and detemporalizations through the added binaries of race, of class, of age, of sexual affinity, each announcing its own time, its own apocalypse.

So, inevitably, in response to our irruption into history and its writing, there emerges a sense at once of the end of the world of the old timelords and of the start of a new one for ourselves. Yet we waver over these decades between our own perilous optimism–"the end of patriarchy"– and acquiescence to their refrain, "the end of feminism." We suspect that our "new day" has neither dawned nor not dawned.

To evade the apocalypse habit, before complacently or triumphantly locating ourselves in "the time of women" we had best remember all the women's movements which have arisen and perished. And yet a sustaining hope is operative in the persistent spread of global women's networks well beyond the private, the voluntary, and the marginal spheres of the past–and beyond the public spaces controlled by white middleclass straight women. Perhaps this is a hope whose time has come. But then let us think the trope of "women's time" through Julia Kristeva's classic essay by that title.[100] She considers women's time both as the epoch of the women's movement and also as a possible female sense of temporality.

Noting the associations of femininity with space rather than time, with reference to the Platonic *chora*, she parses the topic into varying time modes linked to the feminine or feminism, such as "repetition and eternity" and therefore the "cyclical and monumental." By contrast, "history," or "linear temporality," which is the time "of language considered as the enunciation of sentences (noun + verb . . . beginning-ending)" has been labeled masculine. Kristeva characterizes the latter as "both civilizational and obsessional."[101] We have noted, however, the apocalypse habit in the effects of an endist obsession, which first took radically *anti*-civilizational form. While it fathered the progress linearity of the civilization, apocalyptic futurism will not be surfaced by Kristeva's gendering of time.

Tracing, then, three phases of feminism, Kristeva shows the first struggling to be included in history, that is, in civilizational time defined by men (the suffragists through de Beauvoir). The second phase (meaning, I presume, U.S. "radical feminism" and French "*ecriture feminine*") "almost totally refused" the projects of linear time in favor of "intrasubjective and corporeal experiences left mute by culture in the past." She comments that "such a feminism rejoins, on the one hand the archaic (mythical) memory and, on the other, the cyclical or monumental temporality of marginal movements.[102] But even allowing for her animus against this phase one wonders at these leaps. What makes the temporality of marginal movements either "cyclical" or "monumental," given their own apocalyptic futurism and their inherent hostility to any self-monumentalizing, self-eternalizing status quo? Again one notes the tendency of philosophers to neglect the complexity and the force of the biblical influence on history.

I would think, rather, that feminism, precisely as a marginal movement, had all along been breaking into history, refusing not language itself but the temporal grammar of a linear logic. (The equally articulate rivals Kristeva seems to target, Irigaray and Cixous, are no more vulnerable to charges of biological essentialism than she.) Kristeva proposes the third way, that of a "new generation of women," who seek at once "*insertion* into history and the radical *refusal* of the subjective limitations imposed by this history's time."[103] We duly note the unconscious Joachite element of her chronology: while she would categorize her thinking as anti-apocalypse, it reveals the irresistible pattern of the three intersecting ages converging on the "new" third—as ever, the best—about to break in.

We might say, rather, that by entering into the masculinist discourse of history we come close enough to entrain ourselves in its time, indeed to mimic its discourse, in the Irigarayan sense of a subversive mimesis. Yet if this is some kind of "age of women"—overlapping as in the Joachite iconography with prior periods, lacking a distinct beginning or end, or his confidence—then perhaps the women's movement is bringing enough critical mass to history to alter its beat. Perhaps, without surrendering to Kristeva's Freudian apparatus (our "insertion" into history seems to reduce to the feminine right to corporal pleasure cum phallic speech), we might "refuse" to let our time any longer veil over its specific temporal base of bodily cycles.

We might resist liberal, phase-one feminism's trivialization of embodiment, as though it invariably will capture us in static, "immanent" circles. We might yet find historical language for the pulsing periodicities of personal and collective history without surrendering to the immature romanticisms of "cultural" feminism. But also we might question tendencies in Kristeva's preferred, stage-three feminism—which became in the U.S. that of a genealogical poststructuralism, again dictating feminist "theory," again proscribing any discourse of "nature" or "organicism," of a cosmology by which "the body" might insert itself not just into history but into *time*.[104]

Perhaps we need a stage four—eco-social feminism. It would not need to sink into a discourse of women's "more natural" bodies, while attending to the dramatic temporal-material fluctuations which accompany our every thought. Avoiding with Kristeva the dualisms of crusading misogyny or of feminist reaction formations, while claiming nonetheless the "radical assumption" of a social temporality perhaps means at the moment not trying to isolate a single normative feminine temporality. We may then think time from a perspective insistently temporal and female without serving up a feminist or feminine time as something that could be subtracted from or added to history, like a dinner course. As something that could free itself from the intermingling, confusing time-flavors of class, race, religion, culture. The ecological diversity of our bodily times, rather, may require of us a certain philosophical refraction.

17

So what sense of time would germinate in the spaces where the divergent movements of women intersect other social movements? Wherever else we also are, however else we script our mortality, we may find ourselves still habituated to apocalypse. At least this is the plot of the present narrative. We who are part of Western history cannot step clean and clear of it, to a place beyond its time. After all, to end one time and move into another is by definition to do an apocalypse. So, to put the same question differently, What then is the time sense of counter-apocalypse?

First of all it is just that—a sense of time. Not the eye shifting mechanically to the watch, the gut clutching at the deadline, the mad dash. Sensing time means having rhythm, paying attention to the sensory alterations—the breath, the pulse—which punctuate each moment's fleeting density. Such mindfulness, I suggest, begins to massage "history" into "time." In other words, counter-apocalyptic time would relax the omni-cidal tensions of "history," a history apocalyptically fused from the start.

If we grant "time" a certain heuristic priority over "history"—that is, over the specifically Western narrative of human time in abstraction from all other times—we might remember the other temporalities. For instance, we might again mind the effects of galactic bodies upon our own: stars, sun, moon, tides and seasons. Yet such cosmological synchro-nizers are inscribed by the apocalypse as superfluous or monstrous, by modernism as ahistorical or merely useful, and so far by postmodernism as mere cultural constructs too dumb for language. All three Western "ages" are prepared to replace nonhuman nature by some kind of tran-scendent supernature—some realm treasured precisely as beyond "na-ture," constituted by theological or atheist projections of cultural nor-mativity.

In the light of the cosmic bodies, how might we rematerialize history —resensitize, indeed perhaps even renaturalize it—without flattening its dynamics of human struggle and self-signification? As physicist Karl Friedrick von Weiszacker argued, the new cosmology must understand history to be part of nature and nature to be part of history, in a universe which is itself historical, that is, involved in dynamic processes of change.[105]

We would then not dehistoricize time but rather retemporalize his-tory, setting it in the context of galactic, geological, arboreal, animal rhythms, practicing what for us would be new habits in order to loosen the grip of self-destructive ones. Such as, for instance, the drive to domi-nate in time, by staying "on" time.

Being-on-time (to mimic Heidegger for a moment) metabolizes the ontology of the West: managing, using, making time, being on top, on top of time. To master time one does not merely control one's own time and that of others, but one finally transcends it. Thus time-control guaran-tees personal immunity to apocalypse; come what may—even the End of History—being-on-time ensures that the successful time manager will not be left behind. Premillennialist fundamentalists offer the strangest symptom of this Western rush to be "on time": the rapture is coming very soon but without warning (like a thief in the night), and if one is not ready (on time) one will be literally left behind as mere refuse of the time before. These alternate Western modernisms share an acute sense of imminent deadline. From the vantage point of non-Western peoples our treasured creative tension appears as *koyaaniqatsi*–the Hopi word for "life out of balance."[106]

Being-on-time carries in itself the explosive dialectic of the sublimation and desublimation of apocalypse: the manic movement between order and rupture, timelessness and futurism. The old religious forms yield to flattened secular idolatries. Stress, for instance, which counts as a sacrificial symptom of professional prestige, reveals its own hypermodern sublime, degenerate heir of Augustine's ennoblement of restlessness. Faith cannot calm itself in time–"my heart is restless until it rests in thee"–but its milieu offers no "thou" who would assuage it. Its optimistic corollary, the modern faith in "the new" (whether in consumer products or social movements) partakes of a tinsel version of the apocalypse habit, ever exposing "the old" as a used-up drudge or a sold-out whore, and the future as the youthful beloved. Of course the creativity of the Western time trajectory is as indubitable as its destructiveness; I can hardly finish a paragraph without recourse to our sacred hope for "the new." For the present Western time sits tensed on the classic razor's edge between past and future.

Might we consider something like being-*in*-time as a less cutting way to become who we are? Neither negligible nor enduring, such being just *is*–for the moment. It connotes something akin to Heidegger's "within-time-ness," without conceding his radical subordination of space to time. Time (he would agree) is not an endurance but a relation. But are we not then "in" time as inside of something, like air, or inside of nothing, like a vacuum? The reversal of "time is of the essence," a cliché deployed to enforce being-on-time, is disclosive: whatever is "essential," that is, whatever is constitutive of what I at this moment am, is *in* and *of* time. My subjectivity, such as it momentarily configures itself out of the complexities of our overlapping histories, is no timeless essence but rather can only be imagined from this viewpoint as a temporalizing process–an act of timing.

If being is timing, and subjectivity is thus what we may call a performative temporalization, then of course there is no escape from finitude. Or rather, finitude is not a sphere, a place "in" which one abides or "from" which one moves. "Temporality, as an ecstatical unity, has something like a horizon."[107] We "stand out" (*ekstasis*) of being as the very act of *ex-istence*. But for Heidegger, death, my death, has the primary temporalizing power. It provides the horizon, moment by moment, and thus provokes existence/ecstasy. The apocalyptic hope for "no more death" is then a hope for no more existence, *and* for an ecstasy only imaginable in a deferred future existence.

Certainly Heidegger's words to a heaven-bent tradition of death-transcendence return the focus to the present, where any counter-apocalyptic existence must plant itself. But might we consider whether it is the horizon of our *relations*, not of death itself, that exercises the primary time-power? The relationships making up the discursive context of my finitude interpret death to me long before death begins to interpret my relations. Likewise, the quality of relations at the end of life may be more definitive of the death process than the mere fact of dying. The existences, human and not, which nurture my subjectivity within the field of intersignifications, at the same time dramatically limit my options. Yet such a field will have fuzzier boundaries and a less unifying ecstasy. Its borders run through "the valley of the shadow of death." But the shadow itself varies in its shades, like the cinematographic chiaroscuro of Kurosawa's *Ikiru*.

To sense time is, then, to attend to the ambiguity at the edge, the permeable border between now and then, which is simultaneously the *eschaton* between self and other. Difference–posed by the being of another–does not stand here presenting either damnation or salvation, absence or presence: it both "defers" and "presents" itself. It is precisely the fixed boundary which counter-apocalyptic time dissolves. Thus the play of finitude cannot be reduced to the moment of biological death. To exist is to inscribe upon reality a momentary act of becoming and passing away–Plato's *genesis kai phtora*, or Whitehead's "perpetual perishing."

Whitehead, Heidegger's contemporary, in his own attempt to retemporalize Western self-awareness, worked on a relativity theory to counteract the relativism of the Einsteinian version (as it twisted time back on itself, into a circle). Time and space are understood not as axes or horizons initially but as *relations*. "Temporalisation is realisation," he asserted. Subjects–human and otherwise–are related through a "process" of reciprocal influence and self-concretization. As they selectively realize the potentiality that their relationships offer–for good or ill–they become actual. "In realization the potentiality becomes actuality. But the potential pattern requires a duration. . . . Thus time is the succession of elements in themselves divisible and contiguous."[108] This divisibility unhinges the substance metaphysics of the underlying "individual"–the Western monad undergoing its pilgrimage in time.

Time as succession may be then imagined as a series of relations configured as differences. Thus the individual, as the subject who is different from any other, exists only for a moment, a duration, of indivisibility, the embodiment of a present which is neither a mere now-point nor an unwinding line, but a complex eco-social location.

To temporalize is to relativize selfhood and difference to each other. Inasmuch as time is of the essence, so are the others whom I willy-nilly internalize. For good and evil, the others become part of who I am and cannot be purged–not, at any rate, without more apocalypse. They can be judged, distanced, reconstructed. The subject can be firmed and the edges softened. But the edges of (my) being at any given moment are the edges of (my) time: eschatology, posing its questions of collective ultimacy, meets us if at all in the minute acts of timing constitutive of our life's rhythm, the rhythm of our relations. Edge, *eschatos*, limit or opening, boundary or freedom: we cannot sense time, a time, without edges. Time comes tensed, edgy, rimmed by tragedy, edged by all of our deaths: the frame of finite relations which constitutes the moving boundary of any moment, from the complex of relations which I have become to a new (but barely new) complex I have yet to embody.

If we do not seek to flee from finitude and thus from tragedy into an arrhythmic utopia–if instead, as feminist theologian Kathleen Sands advocates in another challenge to feminist utopianism, we "escape from paradise"–perhaps a certain fleeting ecstasy makes itself available even in the midst of suffering:

> Were our hopes to rely on perfect beginnings and ends, this would surely be cause for despair. But if hope, instead, is our messy, multiform continuance, then what we need is rather to mourn and laugh and dance until our flesh remembers how the world goes on.[109]

Performative temporalization may then require rituals, new and old, by which the work of grieving and remembering, the "work of the people" (*leiturgos*, liturgy), can go on.

18

To be sensually in time means to step out of the theatre of the absolute beginning and end, of a first "Big Bang" and a final one. What remains are the moments and the transitions between them, and the transitions between transitions, constituting whole societies of moments. Moments are events, and are as such the closest thing to what is meant by an "individual." And they have moment—these events and whole societies of events, they matter. They have body. Unlike the razor-edge present of Augustine's *Confessions*, let alone the flattened history of time-bites, they have what William James called "thickness." Humans script the succession of moments into "history"—into sequences like stories, shaping the relations between moments, forgetting most, highlighting "the momentous."

Because, like a sautéed mushroom, the moment itself renders up what is possible, a feminist counter-apocalypse will not reduce itself to a few "great moments," as in the Creation, the Fall, or the Second Coming, or as in Matriarchy, the onslaught of Patriarchy, and the Birth of Feminism. Perhaps such master narratives can only take over in an undernourished history of deferral, of postponed moments, where one story conquers, where it subdues the parabolic openings and prophetic possibilities tucked even into the biblical narratives. Amidst the habitual deferral, the subtler lure of timeful possibility fades into insignificance. Its little parables of the moment cannot hold up to the exaggerated predictions, the dooms and the utopias.

The fullness of present time—"the palm at the end of the mind" (W. Stevens)—does not grow of timelessness. Only of clocklessness. Timefulness brooks no radical break between human and nonhuman time. We tend to think of nonhuman time as cycling emptily, statically, devoid of awareness. Yet earth time, englobed in a galaxy of intricate cycles, does not only move in circles. It spirals; it shifts; it evolves. According to Hawking, "The cosmological arrow of time . . . is the direction of time in which the universe is expanding rather than contracting."[110]

Counter-apocalypse, unlike an anti-apocalypse, which merely opposes the Western preference for future, avoids the rhetoric of "arrows" and "expansion," yet it does recapitulate a trajectory of nonrepeatability. While the relations marking time recycle the past, the moment never merely repeats it: if it tries to, it becomes rigid or stale but still does not stay the same. The cumulative, helical movement of time enfolds the inevitability of a relational process but not of a predictable progress. It is how every moment absorbs into itself the energies of its prior history—that of its own private history and of public relationships. Only when the West abstracted this cumulative tendency from the recycling narratives of creaturely relations could the time of process metabolize as "progress."

Dis/closing time, therefore, directs attention at once to the sustaining and the transforming sequences of our lives. Certain relationships, expressed perhaps in Hildegard's "gentle words," "open" time for us—and in their moment we do not feel stressed or bored, rushed or frozen. Or, in the feminist theology of Rebecca Chopp, time appears in contrasting qualities of the Sabbath celebration. It is at once as "cosmic time," the "temporality of relatedness, the ceaseless rhythms of natural time, not progress toward an end, not cause from an origin, but an endless flow of connectedness"; and as "kairotic time." *Kairos*, Paul Tillich's biblical evocation of the time of revolution and revelation, when "eternity breaks into time," is here beautifully translated into a dissident time, "admitting the possibility of radical change, radical chaos, radical openness." In the spirit of dis/closure, Chopp's discourse of "proclamation" thus identifies this apocalyptic side of history—disarmed by its confluence with cosmic-connective time, as "the incredible openness of time."[111] Time thus con/figures counter-apocalypse. In kairotic time, relationship itself, one presumes, at once judges and is judged: if it is not timely—embodying the possible within the limits of the real—it is assigned "time out."

19

This timely relationality, however, as read cosmologically, cannot rest content with anthropocentric rhetoric. Process thought rightly inscribes all subjects of experience—animal, vegetable, mineral—as agents composing themselves out of social relations. With loss of the dualism of beginning and end, of two ages, is also dissolved the dualism of public and private, outer and inner. At the heart of this cosmologically disseminated process operates also a Spirit, a Wisdom, identified by Whitehead as the "divine element in the universe"—the "lure to actualization,"[112] a preconscious purposefulness, evolutionary as well as cultural. Thus the

God of process theology emerges at precisely that point which marked off the "tendency-latency of process" or the possibility inherent in the organic coalescence of tenses.

Because sensory time, as the rhythm of the flesh, nests in a vast, impersonal, bio-geological time, relativizing human history as small time, it may quite literally ground the stress of clashing human projects. In our terrestrial places, even our wildernesses, the earth would—as it did for the fleeing woman clothed in the sun—come to our aid. But given the modern quest for utopia through the exploitation of the earth, a historic deadline, a death-line, is after all unwinding. Still, only if we can shake the tale of "too late," can we hear something of the stories our crusading culture crushed:

> The right timing for a tribal Indian is the time when he or she is in balance with the four rivers of life. That is, Indian time rests on a perception of individuals as part of an entire gestalt in which fittingness is not a matter of how gear teeth mesh with each other but rather how the person meshes with the revolving of the seasons, the land, and the mythic reality that shapes all life into significance.[113]

Thus Paula Gunn Allen analyzes the achronicity of American Indian rituals and novels—and refusal to "be on time"! She studies how mythic narratives and rituals of signification perform "right timing." Telling time is telling stories. "Where pain is the prime number/and soft stepping feet/praise water from the skies"—Allen invokes a "ceremonial time."[114] Perhaps reflecting preapocalyptic time, such ritual time marries human and cosmic stories; it echoes sometimes still in sacramental time-sensibilities within Christian ritual recollection. Feminist rituals within Christianity have provoked waves of backlash precisely because they attempt, however awkwardly, to retrieve some elemental rhythms, some repressed presences, some timely localities. They reveal the reflexive character of "worship" as *weorthscipe*–"deeming worthy": the timely work of "worshiping women," as Heather Elkins writes of women's liturgies.[115]

A renewed sense of ceremonial time stems from the attempt to locate ourselves not just socially but historically, in the space-time of social movements sensing their time as sacred and their sacredness as social. There, in "the incredible openness of time," ritual actions may take on the original character of *leitourgos*, "liturgy" as the "work of the people." Unlike the sacraments of timeless truth, which lift us off the earth, time-ful ceremony reinvests attention in the communal tensions and material realities of the people. It can do this perhaps only inasmuch as it learns to rest *in* time. In this it practices, whether or not it grafts itself onto the living Jewish tradition, some Sabbath-like, de-mechanized, rhythm of attentive relation to the living and the dead.[116] Thus ceremonial time may rehearse within the horizon of its community a *sustainably* political time, a temporality which performs a widening gyre of influence. From which, even as it spirals, there is "no turning back."

20

But even to ruminate on time as the first "dimension" of counter-apocalypse risks reestablishing the privilege of time which only the culture of apocalypse could accomplish. We have yet barely addressed the uprooting of times from their places. Thus in the next chapter, in which it is hoped that space will put time in its place, we will move through some history of the displacement of place, which at the same time dislocates time. As cosmic and bodily, periodic, ceremonial, political, and hopeful, time does not exist outside of place. As Leslie Marmon Silko puts it: "He did not think time was absolute or universal; rather each location, each place, was a living organism with time running inside it like blood, time that was unique to that place alone."[117]

Lounging in her desert hide-a-way, she takes a cool sip of mint water. She gazes at the dusty horizon, solemnly cradling the clay bowl on her bronze belly. Curled up beside her, the red dragon growls up from his nap. She passes the water to him and scratches his head. This desert is spreading everywhere, she shudders. So fast. She blinks away the time-lapse optics of her older perspective. She has struggled to love this bound-less wilderness, its gritty resistance, its dry wit, its blusters of manic ruach. For herself, the strategy has worked—to wrap her body around its slow and sudden times, to tend its understated habitats, to build her invisible pyramid among the rocks. She has made herself at home. Per-haps she no longer misses the voluptuous densities of green, the spray of whitewater, the scent of lilies she has relished on other sojourns. Thirsty emissaries have come from the city, leaving in desert veils of her own mak-ing. Reaching over to add a few stitches to a new one, she chuckles at her artwork—it will camouflage its wearer in sun, moon, or starlight. In its iri-descence she has secretly embroidered another chapter.

De/Colon/izing Spaces

> "I tell time through space. I remember
> time by place."
>
> *Karen Brown*

1

Having grown up in perpetual geographic motion, I read my youth as a paradigmatic case of late modern Euroamerican displacement. I try with limited success to remember my past, to find places for memory. In nocturnal dreamscapes, a crumbled inner city, a crowded house not yet unpacked, and an eroded coastline junky with tourist overdevelopment recur as spatial atmospheres capturing no literal location. Most of the places, private or public, seem dim, chaotic, and temporary, depressing in their jumbled exteriority. Icons of deteriorating modernity, they lack ecological or communal density. Perennially packing and unpacking, migrants moved by something between choice and necessity, my family hardly had *time* in which to develop a relationship to a *place*. But we moved on without nostalgia, cultivating no thicket of relationships, no kin or community, no local history or ecological practice that could tie us to the places. Indeed, within the philosophy of our existence, the topic of "place" came off as superficial, clingy, materialistic.

Unconsciously, to be sure, our seminomadism interpreted itself along eschatological lines. Our survival-driven, explosion-filled, hope-edged transitions were felt to lend us mysterious spiritual and cultural advantages over the smug, the secure, and the sedentary. In order to construct continuity amidst spatial dislocation we devalued–"transcended"–place itself. As in any apocalyptic spaciality, the cathexis withdrawn from particular pasts got wholly displaced onto the *new* place. For my family, the aureole of hope surrounding the *next* place–at least until we settled there–shone with a brightness inversely proportional to the doom that had befallen us in the place before. Indeed, as we fled toward the new, the past world collapsing about us, we understood ourselves as a tiny band of the persecuted, socially and economically on the edge, requiring impossibly unified internal cohesion, barely escaping mounting tribulations. So though no actual place–and thus no idea of place as such–could accrue the moss of ordinary time, the ever mythical *future* place held all promise. Indeed that place felt more like a time. It lacked the concreteness of a place, the peculiarities of landscape and social history. Utopia: the "good place" is always "no place."

2

If I grew up apocalyptic, I have since had the luck or instinct to stay put and begin to heal from this dislocating spatiality, to revitalize bit by bit my numbed sense of habitat. Likewise, in the interest of counter-apocalyptic spatial therapeutics, this chapter will consider certain trans-historical, indeed transcontinental, dislocations of Western sensibility. To this end, I trace the emergence of apocalyptic mythology against the background of a prehistory of cultural relations to natural habitat. At the foreground, initiating the monumental time of modernity, the Apocalypse will be seen inscribing itself into the colonizing topography of "the New World." We will consider the objectification of the apocalyptic millennial future which has been accomplished in the demi-millennium of modernity. During the past five hundred years, the Joachite hope for a radical realization of the *new age* seems to have fueled the progress into a future in which real–European–bodies did (violently) find *new space* for themselves.

Rendered static, conquerable, and consumable, space cannot keep pace with history. Finally, *place itself could not keep its place.* Those who invade what they believe they have discovered enter from the raw outside of the given space; they do not know themselves as beings grown in delicate reciprocity with the relations constituting a place. The new place is called "paradise" and then "wilderness" and "wasteland"–it throbs with mystery, resources, sex, and threat. In short–again–with femininity. Or, then again, space bifurcates into that wild place of "natural" femininity to be colonized and that already domesticated femininity awaiting the hero upon his return. According to geographer Doreen Massey:

> The construction of "home" as a woman's place has, moreover, carried through into those views of place itself as a source of stability, reliability and authenticity. Such views of place, which reverberate with nostalgia for something lost, are coded female. Home is where the heart is (if you happen to have the spatial mobility to have left) and where the woman (mother, lover-to-whom-you-will-one-day-return) is also.[1]

I hope such spatial spadework will expose the textual imprint of the consummate Christian *utopos* upon the present consumer society, the economics of which consumes *topos* itself. Which, I argue, only a "topical" spatiality can heal.

3

My home over there, my home over there,
My home over there, now I remember it!
And when I see that mountain far away,
Why, then I weep. Alas! what can I do?
What can I do? Alas! What can I do?
My home over there, now I remember it.[2]

How sorrowful a prospect had read itself into the space of history. After the desolation of the ecosphere and the holocaust of the city, after the millennial respite, when, at last, comes the intervention of interventions, *then* John of Patmos has "earth and sea flee"–"no place is found for them." Used up, expendable, they duck out of the picture. No place for place itself–at least for the terrestrial spaces in which, *as* which, "earth-bodies" come to be.[3]

The biblical apocalypse, unlike the "ecological apocalyptic," did anticipate the re-placement of heaven and earth: a future world will be supernaturally manufactured to take the place of the devastated old one.[4] Like the Jewish prophetic tradition, the Christian Apocalypse projected the true home into a redeemed future. But by bringing "Jerusalem" down from a supernatural Above, it cut hope free of geography. Time, the dimension of transcendence in which biblical salvation history writes itself, lifts free in the Apocalypse of all former places. It is not, therefore, that the apocalyptic vision leaps to a state of immaterial placelessness; rather, it fantasizes a new space for new bodies. Yet the text conveys no tragic regret that something irreplaceable–the space embracing earth's lives, memories, and potentialities–would disappear. It does not grieve the passing of all known places.

The communities responsive to Revelation seem to have undergone such fundamental dislocations that the replacement of all worldly places seemed not only possible but desirable. Out of place even in the Jewish diaspora, these early Christians knew no strength of place equal to the force of history. Instead they could hope for new spaces, supernaturally produced, erasing the past of suffering, displacing death itself. Not that this represents the only way for colonized people to construct a sense of place. The Jews never forfeited their claim on the land from which they were forced into diaspora: its past contained their future. On this conti-nent, the Tewa lament (quoted above) performs the grief of coerced dis-placement, where "home" situates itself unforgettably in the lost geogra-phy of the first nations, and conquest holds place captive to the past.

If the end of the modern millennium did not threaten to nudge out the living spaces of earth and sea as though they were expendable, to deposit us in a series of mass-produced pseudo-places, if it did not uproot with casual brutality mass populations, if it did not create a universe of dis-placed persons and other animals living isolated, replaceable lives–well, then, one might now (two millennia beyond the apocalyptic text) read its syndrome of displacement/replacement with detached compas-sion. But given the Constantinian conversion of Christianity and its modern uses, we can read the Apocalypse only through the warp of its own subsequent history.

4

To sense better the contours of the ongoing apocalypse of place, we had better first get this analysis situated within the contemporary discourses of place. Unlike "space," with its tendency toward galactic dissipation, the term "place" insists on the particularity of the relations which con-stitute a particular situation–a site of entangled spatiotemporal experiences.[5] Place–precisely in its homey particularity–can less easily be vaporized into mathematical abstractions. I will depend upon Doreen Massey's definition:

> If *space* is conceptualized in terms of a four-dimensional "space-time" and . . . as taking the form not of some abstract dimension but of the simultaneous coexistence of social interrelations at all geographical scales, from the intimacy of the household to the wide space of transglobal connections, then *place* can be reconceptualized too. . . . It is the vast complexity of the interlocking and articulating nets of social relations which is social space. Given that conception of space, a "place" is formed out of the particular set of social relations which interact at a particular location.[6]

Of course "space" may begin to take on the characteristics of "place." But let us define "place" as *the relationality of space*, therefore as intersubjectively occupied space. Geography in this way becomes a branch of social analysis. Manuel Castells sheds light on the relations between space, class, and society:

> Spatial forms . . . will express and perform the interests of the dominant class according to a given mode of production and to a specific mode of development. They will express and implement the power relationships of the state in a historically defined society. They will be realised and shaped by gender domination and by state-enforced family life. At the same time, spatial forms will also be marked by resistance from exploited classes, oppressed subjects, and abused women.[7]

Place articulates the complex and fluid relationships which interlace and thereby constitute the earth but interact significantly always at particular sites. Relationships *take place*. Building on A. N. Whitehead's account of space and time as mutually dependent modes of relationship, an account which displaced Newtonian treatments of space and time as static axes *within* which relations take place, we may thus contextualize any geographic enterprise within the discursive relations of the geographer. Only so can we bring into view the social mythology underpinning the geography that Columbus bequeathed to us as common sense for the modern world. Once excavated, that geo-mythology tells the tale of the genocide and ecocide which, far from static, violently overturned the space and time of much of the earth.

Beyond the cosmological and phenomenological philosophies just alluded to, four streams, or voices, of contemporary theory refocus a definition of space in terms of the particularity of place. Each entails a project of decolonization. Poststructuralism, abdicating the Western privilege of universal metanarratives and their salvation-history underpinnings, privileges instead "local knowledges" (Foucault) or "local determinisms" (Lyotard). Next, "locality studies" constitutes an intriguing counter-colonialist discourse, mainly within the British study of geography; redefining "space" in terms of a socialist analysis, radical geographers like David Harvey, H. Lefebvre, and Doreen Massey investigate the local implications of global economic trends in terms of social relations of class, and sometimes of gender.

Less easy to categorize, the third "place voice" speaks in the plural and precedes theory. This is the spatial sensibility currently audible as postcolonialism, largely defined by indigenous movements of resistance to the colonial history of displacement. People such as Vandana Shiva of India, Vítor Westhelle of Peru, Inez Talamantes, George Tinker, Paula Gunn Allen, and almost every other Native American writer articulate at once a political spirituality of place. The fourth voice, that of ecofeminism, overlaps with indigenous sensibility in the effort to liberate our socially, sexually, and ecologically oppressed realities from the historical forces of male, white, and human supremacy.

Without detailing their arguments, a counter-apocalypse of place will divulge certain salient convergences and divergences of these locality advocates. For instance, while the radical geographers, with their structural analysis of global economic forces impinging on localities, come into tension with poststructuralist resistance to any "totalizing discourse," both share a massive omission. Adherents of both schools fail almost absolutely to consider nonhuman place. Both discuss locality exhaustively in terms of human relations, whether conceived primarily in linguistic, gender, or economic categories. The anthropocentric paradigm apotheosized in the hope of the New Jerusalem holds.

Even in theories meant to deconstruct the imperialist and indeed teleological "thrust" of Western history, however, the reconstruction of place lacks all but a dismissive or pejorative language of nature. Indeed, both discourses are nicely eager to avoid the "essentialism" which upholds as "natural" the status quo of class, gender, or identity. But unfortunately they merely repeat the displacement of the entire biosphere of relations which precede, surround, and comprise the human. Material-

ity becomes a matter of human cultural production or economic trans-
action. May we partake of their de-essentializing accounts of locality
without also neglecting the subhuman density of layered bodies, including our own, which together constitute a habitat?

For indigenous and ecofeminist sensibilities, place is first of all habitat, the reality in which—or more precisely, as *part of which*—one dwells.
While habitat tends to call up the image of an inert container or passive
preserve, these alternate sensibilities suggest instead the socioecologi-
cal connectedness of which such habitation is configured. Nor does their
operative notion of habitat reduce place to a solipsistic locality. For instance, Vandana Shiva, an Indian scientist-activist in whose work ecofeminist and indigenous sensibilities join, finds in the symbiosis of the
local and the global the key to ecological justice:

> Ecology movements are political movements for a non-violent world order
> in which nature is conserved for conserving the options for survival.
> These movements are small, but they are growing. *They are local, but their*
> *success lies in non-local impact.* . . . With the success of these grassroots
> movements is linked the issue of global survival. Unless the world is re-
> structured ecologically at the level of world-views and life-styles, peace
> and justice will continue to be violated and ultimately the very survival of
> humanity will be threatened.[8]

Her work models a counter-apocalyptic sense of place: "global survival" is at risk, and the annihilative apocalypse represents the inevitable outcome of present trends *if* they persist. But conversion remains not
only possible but already under way—the "not-yet" we recall from prophetic eschatology is taking place "already." The politics of place—unlike
the Western politics of time—will neither defer utopia nor possess it. Its
local practices will not be restricted by some postmodern abdication of
the global to the merely regional—"the fetichisms of locality."[9] The local
situation is both shaped by and aimed toward global processes.

Those peoples most sensitive to the micro-stories and local spirits
dwelling in particular mountains, springs, woods are just as vividly attuned to the macrosphere of stars, sun, and moon. But cosmology is then
narratively distilled into the particular places of the people who tell the
tale.

In a Hopi creation story, Spider Grandmother spirals down (as is her
wont) from outer space to the still sterile earth ball, and creates two

handsome young men by taking two handfuls of dirt and spitting into them. The three meditate together. Then one man goes to each pole: from the crystalline north, Poquanghoya works the magic of form, creating the patterns of life; from the south, Palonghoya, in a trance, picks up the heartbeat of Tiowa, the Great Spirit, and begins to drum out the same rhythm. Thus a vibratory field is generated between the poles and finally rushes up from a crystal at the center of the earth. As energy breaks through the earth's surface, the planet bursts into life. But at some points, due to Poquanghoya's patterns, the power became more concentrated. These are the "spots on the fawn," luminous places of healing energy. They are, according to Hopi elders, the sacred places—places sometimes fabulously beautiful, sometimes undistinguished but by marks of prior pilgrimages. Without these places and ceremonial access to them, the world would fall apart.[10]

Space, with time as its heartbeat, condenses itself into narrative places. Such a sensibility feeds itself from the special places, where energy is concentrated in nature. Certainly Christianity built on the sacred spaces of more earth-tuned peoples, but it built Romanesque enclosures, then cathedrals with stained-glass windows, gorgeously blocking the view into the merely natural world. As the medieval church increasingly standardized its ceremonies, it sometimes absorbed but often demonized the preexisting traditions that kept local peoples synchronized with the rhythms of place. As Catholicism and Protestantism entered into conflict, both competed to establish universal, place-independent liturgical rules.

In other words, all residues of the sacred time-spaces attended to by the indigenous cultures of Europe were finally bleached out of the fabric of Christian worship. And what could not be thus homogenized—in Europe, for instance, the practice of "local knowledges" in the form of the herbal therapies and other vestiges of regional nature religions kept in practice by the rural women known as witches—was burned. The colonial missions at best manipulated, and routinely annihilated, the particularities of native spatiotemporalities.

This universalizing spatiality of the "Church Triumphant"—the realized eschatology that after Augustine identified its theocracy as the millennium—at once culminated and broke precisely as the modern age arose. It seems to have bequeathed its spirit of uniformity to the secular polities which would take the *place* of institutional religion. As David

Harvey elucidates it, the modern project unfolds as a progressive unification of space—in precise sync with what we have in the last chapter characterized as "modern time," or, in his own cryptoapocalyptic phrase, "the annihilation of space by time." Modern cartography would compose a unified text of space, homogenized for the sake of conquest and trade—Babylon redux. Erased would be the sacred nodes, the unchartable differences of a particular place. How unlikely it remains for most of us urban folk today, whose visual fields mirror the spatial flatness laid out as the condition of progress (indeed, of our high-tech New Jerusalem), to perceive the "spots on the fawn."

5

The Apocalypse, pitting its good city against the bad, displayed a typical urban uprootedness from its nonhuman habitat. The New Jerusalem will be landscaped like a neoclassical park. (As in formal gardens, the point is always that nature did *not* do this.)[11] But to understand the sense of place to which apocalypse gives rise, which perhaps still holds us, let us ask the converse question: What sense of place gave rise to apocalypse—to the story, told long before manmade omnicide was conceivable, that the natural world will come to a cataclysmic end?

Let us momentarily re-narrate the times of our species' relationships to its spaces. In her typology of the history of human interaction with the habitat, anthropologist Felicitas Goodman sheds light on the causes of apocalyptic expectation. She invokes five principal types, or "lifeways," of adaptation to the natural environment: those of hunter-gatherers, horticulturalists, agriculturalists, nomadic pastoralists, and city dwellers.

According to Goodman, the hunter-gatherer culture, with its laidback and egalitarian practices came "as close to paradise as humans have ever been able to achieve" and "was such . . . a successful adaptation, that it did not materially alter for many thousands of years."[12] Peggy Reeves Sanday finds also a rare balance of gender powers.[13] These humans know the habitat through which they wander and so "live a life of total balance, because *they do not aspire to controlling their habitat*, they are a part of it."[14] Unique among the lifeways is the mutuality of their relationship with place: "When a hunter dies, such as a Pygmy of the Ituri rainforest . . . the Forest, representing the habitat, needs to be consoled with a feast."[15] Though pursuing its own romance, Goodman's narrative counters both the modern myth of progress and the feminist privilege of agricultural matricentrism.

In the horticultural phase which arose in response to pressure exerted on the environment by the growth of population, women's knowledge of plants lent them special authority. But Goodman surmises that the need to force from a personified Earth what "she" does not freely give wounded the relationship of mutuality: "Humans distanced themselves from the habitat. Burial customs reveal no trace that the habitat needed to be consoled when someone died." Here she offers a clue: "While no doubt the cultivation of plants was a solution in a period of great need, what was experienced as a rape of the Mother still produced a massive feeling of guilt. It is with the horticulturalists that we encounter for the first time a prediction about the end of the world as ultimate retribution for this sacrilege."[16]

The anticipation of cosmic cataclysm stems, in other words, from the angst of detachment *from* the cosmos. Certainly horticulturalists tell apocalyptic tales. For instance, the Hopi predict the end of the present fourth world and the emergence of humanity into the fifth world: "That time is not far off. It will come when the Saquaschuh Kachina dances in the plaza. He represents a blue star, far off and yet invisible, which will make its appearance soon."[17] Apocalyptic expectation of this sort, however clothed in indigenous imagery, may well emerge, as it did in Judaea, in response to genocidal encounters with a city-centered empire; Hopis, for example, had already been "contaminated" by exposure to the Christian apocalypse. Nonetheless, the Hopi apocalypse differs significantly in form: it is not a once-for-all end of the world, but part of a cycle of periodic world changes. Indeed, one might wonder if Goodman's metanarrative of guilt and retribution itself draws energy from a much later apocalypse habit. And yet something crucial comes into view, perhaps only through the overstatement: a predisposition for apocalypse forms itself in the eviction from the hunter-gatherer habitat. If not at the genesis moment itself, then in the stories told from the vantage point of the lost Eden. Interpretations of apocalypse rarely consider ecological motives in addition to sociological ones.

The habitability of a place, however, depends from the outset upon the justice with which humans share with each other as well as upon their ecological integrity. Goodman locates a social distortion of the agricultural lifeway as it developed to feed the high Neolithic and early

Bronze Age cities. Women may have retained some prestige as geniuses of agriculture (the Demeter configuration), but the rise of animal "husbandry" accompanied, as Gerda Lerner has argued, the systematic militarization, enslavements, and class and gender stratification that define these "cradles" of civilization.[18] "What all agriculturalists have in common," writes Goodman, "is the illusion of power, of being able to exert control over the habitat."[19] Maintaining the illusion comes at a cost: when "domesticated animals and plants provided the major or only sustenance, humans unwittingly bent their necks to the yoke. Certainly some more than others became enslaved: yet all forfeited the freedom to roam." Habitat becomes private property. House and field must be guarded and tended.

In the new epic literature, only the heroes roam, but no longer in collaboration with the landscape; they wander recklessly, in quest of "name and fame" (Gilgamesh). No longer do guilt feelings attend the despoiling of the earth, a passive woman-identified partner in the newly crystallizing arrangement. Paranoia toward "bad" plants, animals, and humans characterizes "agriculturalist apocalyptic prophecies." These envision "a catastrophe, a kind of ultimate exorcism" which will "rid the world of all evil people, and the good will survive and carry on undisturbed in their pure and sacred confines."[20]

As the theopolitics of this new anthropocentric dualism spreads, it achieves its once-for-all universalism among Zoroastrians and Jews. The earlier Hebrews, with their formative legends of nomadic patriarchs competing with agricultural pagans (Cain and Abel), had an uneasy relationship to their own agriculturalism. According to Goodman, nomadic pastoralists ("although they do not actively modify their natural environment, they are not part of it, either"), possess "no tradition of end-of-the-world, apocalyptic prophecies. Conflicts between humans and their habitat can be mediated by the sacrifice."[21] Perhaps it is for this reason that Hebrew myth irrupts into Christian apocalypse through a sacrificial trope—the pastoral picture of a slaughtered lamb. The text of Revelation, its *Sitz-im-Leben* urban, does not mourn the loss of habitat. It seems not to remember. So it forgets forward, into a supernaturally artificial environment.

Then and now, urbanites as a class "are divorced from the habitat. The earth, the sky, the rain, the plants and the animals are not their partners in the struggle for subsistence." This urban alienation has steadily intensified, moving along a continuum marked by qualitative leaps such as industrialization and now a final destruction of the traditional peasantry through agribusiness. When Goodman notes that city-dwellers "evince a morbid curiosity about cataclysmic prophecies" in which one day "the habitat, distant, incomprehensible, . . . the ultimate outside force, will one day ineluctably strike," she has in mind New Age apocalyptic syncretisms of UFOs and Native Americanisms.[22]

But surely it is not that city-dwellers, however beset by apocalypse, have no vital sense of place. On the contrary, not just the elites enthroned in penthouses and skyscrapers, but all people in the perennial diversity of classes and survival strategies generate their own artful sense of place. However, city space tends to eclipse its own embeddedness within the natural habitat. With their ghettoes and suburbs expanding proportionately, the cities are sucking into themselves an unsustainable proportion of populations and natural resources—indeed "the city" appears in eco-apocalypse as the carnivorous cosmopolis which rends nature into "resources." If throughout the centuries cities have been beacons of possibility to those forced or lured from their rural habitat, they have just as often become the festering ground for apocalyptic revivals.[23]

Perhaps the apocalyptic habit heightened implosively by prolonged urbanizations helps account for the lack of adequate urban resistance to ecocide: the expectation of doom realizes its prophecy. But to romanticize away the city becomes a kind of Earth First! apocalypse. As John of Patmos, deeply alienated by the City of his time, already sensed, there is no way back. Nonetheless, there are different ways ahead.[24] The choice depends upon how we face the legacy of the five hundred years during which an urban civilization inflicted the manmade apocalypse upon countless habitats.

6

I know only the bright hunger
in my belly,
centered and true
as a child's question; it leads
me on in this motherless geography.[25]

I can't remember the first mountain. But I do know that "bright hunger in the belly" that Elaine Orr invokes in her poem. So we creep back into "this motherless geography." Having traced a particular set of place relations let us zoom in on the particular urban civilization of which most of us reading now are profiting members. It behooves Euroamericans, who unlike Europeans lack deep roots into our own habitat, to pick up where the commemoration of the Columbus quincentennial left off. It is a matter of "placing" ourselves in the history of apocalypse. Without this, we lose track of ourselves.

The Spanish name *Colón* seems eerily to prophesy his inauguration of the new era of colonialism. For purposes of this book, Colón provides the missing link—if the question is, What, through chains of historical determination, does the text of Apocalypse have to do with the late twentieth-century level of apocalyptic threat? In our previous chapter's exploration of time, the dialectic of Augustinian and Fiorite eschatology suggested opposing modes of reception of apocalypse into and as history. The Augustinian mainstream *sublimated* the Apocalypse, making its final vision apply to a strictly supernatural hell and heaven, while it transferred millennialism to a *realized* eschatology of the church. The radical traditions, making use of Joachim's eleventh-century apocalyptic revival, took up again the Hebrew resonances of prophecy, thus anticipating a "third age" of the Spirit *within* history and so within real terrestrial places—not a realized but a *performative* eschatology. But how does that ongoing tension of endless deferral and imminent enactment push through to today's specifically spatial dooms? Beyond Goodman's clue as to the passive urban acquiescence in twentieth-century techno-threat, is there any historical reason to believe that the text of Apocalypse has served as an *actively* self-fulfilling prophecy?

I will argue that the case of Colón, read as a genealogy of modern apocalypse, displays the configuration of colonialism, sexism, racism, capitalism, and religion undergirding the power relations of the present age. "Modernity," I believe, is best grasped as those five centuries whose terms now vie for a hypermodern control of the postmodern possibility. In the period of "the end of" modernity, it is apropos to track the apocalyptic impulse into early modern geography, for we may read there the hidden cartography of modern colonialism. Far more than any prior history, the early modern breakout of Europe into the world altered the particular places of the planet and displaced their human, animal, and plant inhabitants.[26]

In his aptly titled *Year 501: The Conquest Continues*, Noam Chomsky argues that the "fundamental themes of the conquest [of the New World] retain their vitality and resilience, and will continue to do so until the reality and causes of the 'savage injustice' [Adam Smith] are honestly addressed." The politically sponsored market forces by which the "third world" in the (global) South and the "third world at home" continue to suffer are among the results of this heritage, which Chomsky (rereading Smith) traces from "two vast demographic catastrophes, unparalleled in history: the virtual destruction of the indigenous population of the Western hemisphere, and the devastation of Africa as the slave trade rapidly expanded. Much of Asia too suffered 'dreadful misfortunes' [Smith's phrase]."[27]

But let us add to the litany of racial and economic devastation the ecological. Demography is embedded in geography, the "writing of the earth." The earth, our blue-green oasis of galactic habitability, suffers its own dual catastrophe: the number of human inhabitants increases exponentially, while the earth's habitability more or less proportionately decreases.[28] However, it is not Southern fertility, but the neocolonial market that creates the conditions for both demographic imbalance and the shutdown of the planetary life-systems, as this market funnels three quarters of all resources to its Northern beneficiaries. The corollary expansion and displacement of human populations has made space itself a luxury commodity.

7

Each of us has some version of the discredited narrative. I remember the image from some grammar-school text of a blue-eyed boy Columbus staring at ships crossing the horizon of the matching blue sea. He prepares to make his famous induction—the horizon is not the end of the world. But the tale of this gaze is itself a retroactive myth of modern science. No sailor of Colón's time feared they would fall off the edge. (His journals never report any of his own crew to have been concerned about that, and the Hellenic hypothesis of a round globe was common among the educated.) Now we look back at the look itself: the youthful male gaze of the modern age. Unlike the vision of its premodern fathers, which radiated upward along the vertical axis, this masculinity looks *forward*, penetrating its future, piercing horizons. Its eschatology will render the planet endlessly available to cartography, to conquest, to commodification.

Colón referred to the newly encountered land as *otro mundo*, the "other world" (the language of "*new* world" came a bit later). That world across the seas turned out to be populated with "others." We find in Colón's journals a clear progression—from a honeymoon phase, to scorn, to plans for conversion and exploitation, and on swiftly to enslavement, wanton mayhem, and genocide. Let me suggest that without attending to the gender code structuring the entire colonial enterprise, its five-hundred-year persistence, indeed its spatiohistorical passion, cannot be understood. The subjects of all four Columbian expeditions, including that of the seventeen-ship colonizing fleet of the second voyage, are all male. That its masculinity is uninterrupted is precisely why it has been and should not be taken for granted.

The gender code is revealed in the iconography of the first contact, in which Colón is depicted in his first moments upon this new place with upraised standards, sword and cross. He is there to enact the written mandate of his sovereigns "to discover and acquire."[29] The *otro mundo*—as both land and people—presents itself in the spatiality of a feminized "other." "Planting" the standards of Spain and the cross of Christ, he inseminates the "virgin" space. Not only would the dark woman provide, like the dark soil, the "other" for these adventurers, the entire "other world," mysterious and fertile, lies before them like its dark and wild women, to be taken in that act of possession which will result in "the birth of a nation."

A juxtaposition of historians' comments suggests the ambiguity of the moment. Samuel Eliot Morison, a leading authority on Columbus, writes of the early scenes rhapsodically: "Never again may mortal men hope to recapture the amazement, the wonder, the delight of those October days in 1492 when the New World gracefully yielded her virginity to the conquering Castilians."[30] Kirkpatrick Sale, the revisionist historian, pinpoints the lineage of Morison's reading strategy: "This the watching Indians would have known, as they did come to know it, as rape."[31] In what follows, I rely upon his rereading of Columbus. He senses in the admiral's wooden prose little sense of any "amazement" or "wonder" in the face of the "other world," rather a kind of admiring assessment. From the longboat of the Santa Maria, Colón reports the first sight of the island, with "very green trees, many streams, and fruits of different kinds . . . the whole of it so green it is a pleasure to gaze upon." ("Green" and "very green" exhaust his place vocabulary.) At that distance he recognized "naked people . . . of very handsome bodies and very fine faces."[32] Here begins the projection onto the natives and their land of the old European fantasy of the lost paradise.[33]

The honeymoon phase carries within it the seeds of abuse.[34] The Tainos, as Colón named the Arawaks after their own word for "good," still astound the invaders with their gracious and happy demeanor, the "sweetness" of their talk, their "fulfillment of the love commandment." And yet these same traits quickly inspire disdain: "Like beasts [*como bestii*] [they] gave what they had."[35] Childlike or bestial, "they ought to be good servants and of good skill ... I believe that they would easily be made Christians, because it seemed to me that they belonged to no religion. I, please Our Lord, will carry off six of them at my departure to Your Highnesses, that they may learn to speak."[36] Just as he declares for the first time his intention to displace and to enslave, he describes their "sweet talk" as no language at all; this inconsistency speaks worlds. In this phase, these aliens seem to talk and love, yet with no discernible language or religion. For their invaders, they seem to slide down into the "semiotic"–Julia Kristeva's sublinguistic realm of the sensual, rhythm, the maternal, and indeed of the spatial–as the conquerors gather themselves back into the "symbolic," the realm of language, history and the law of the Father.[37]

The honeymoon was consummated in literal rape. Early on the admiral sent his crew ashore to capture "seven head of women, young ones and adults, and three small children" for his sex-deprived sailors. Later, the garrison of forty Spaniards which Colón had left on Hispaniola (the island of Haiti and the Dominican Republic) was found destroyed, its men killed.[38] In the gluttony for the paradise of endlessly available women's bodies, along with labor and land, the first orgy backfired–native men seem to have taken vengeance. Colón had already learned to distinguish from the "good Tainos" the "fierce Caribs" as cannibalistic, darker, and warlike. Now the myth of the "man-eating Caribs" served to justify the change of agenda from supposed generosity to unmitigated genocide. It also finessed the policy toward women, as appears in the first narrative of a "new world" sexual encounter. Thus a nobleman on the second voyage:

> I captured a very beautiful Carib woman, whom the said Lord Admiral gave to me, and with whom having taken her into my cabin, she being naked according to their custom, I conceived desire to take pleasure. I

155

wanted to put my desire into execution but she did not want it. . . . I took a rope and thrashed her well, for which she raised such unheard of screams that you would not have believed your ears. Finally we came to an agreement in such manner that I can tell you that she seemed to have been brought up in a school of harlots.[39]

Sale responds cogently: "It is every rape fantasy ever penned, dripping with ugly macho triumph. One longs to know the young woman's version."[40] Discovery, acquisition, and mastery are depicted as male adult conquest at once of women and of feminized space. Place, which may have signified prepatriarchal female spirits (Lady of Dwellings) itself had long been subject to patriarchal feminization, whether as Mother Nature or Heavenly Jerusalem. But here we sense the transmutation of paradise into an erotic place of commodification.

The heady dream of paradise meant mass enslavement of natives and nature. Soon the distinction between the good Tainos and the fierce Caribs dissolved—all natives were savages for the taking. The islands contained enough gold to whet an appetite that would only be satisfied by the next wave of conquistadores. Las Casas describes Colón's brutal system of gold quotas as "impossible and intolerable."[41] On Hispaniola, half of the 250,000 Tainos died in two years through "murder, mutilation, or suicide," after their sorrowful attempt at resistance; through slave labor, the population shrank to 50,000 by 1515, 500 in 1550, and by 1650—none.[42] Ironically, 1650 is the date which Colón had set for Armageddon. (The end of the world proved, as ever, more local, less equal than predicted.)

Though the uncontained destructiveness of the colony engulfed the Spaniards themselves—mutinies, executions of Spaniards, etc.—Colón still managed funding for a third expedition.[43] On this journey a new discourse enters his text. Heading southward, he encounters evidence of a continent (*tierra firma*) at the mouth of the Orinoco River and its four tributaries. He promptly sails into a "state of disarray."[44] He pivots in the waters, leaving suddenly and swiftly, and sailing (despite a proscription) back to Hispaniola, citing various practical reasons. But in the journal entry of August 17 he writes that the land he had found was in fact the lost Eden: "I am completely persuaded in my own mind that the Terrestrial Paradise is the place I have said."[45] He now states that his reason for leaving was fear of entering paradise without a directive from God. Thus the fantasy of the terrestrial paradise bursts into hallucinogenic early modern clarity. Colón finds that these rivers match the four biblical rivers flowing from Eden. Moreover, as legend predicted, he has found at the fringes of this Eden people "whiter than any others I have seen in the Indies," and "more intelligent." The racist note harmonizes with the tones of early capitalism, for even at this moment of overwhelming awe, he writes that these people would have "plenty of gold."

On the basis of the medieval legend of Eden, reinforced by his astrological calculations, the new geography for the modern world begins to unfold. The cosmological vision continues: the distinctively shaped mountain panorama, in conjunction with sightings of the North Star, convinced Colón that the earth after all was not round but rather "has the shape of a pear, which is all very round, except at the stem, where it is very prominent, or that it is as if one had a very round ball, and one part of it was placed something like a woman's nipple (*una teta de mujer*)."[46]

The world shaped like a woman's breast culminating at its nipple in paradise—so Colón, poised at its aureole, focuses the colonial adventure. He repeats the images of pear and breast: this is no casual analogy but the basis for serious cartography—indeed, carto-pornography! The continent looms as forbidden fruit, the virgin body ripe for the plucking, the mother breast ready to a suckle death-ridden, depressed Europe into its rebirth.[47] This moment of renaissance merges infantile intensity with material desire. Gaia's nipple arises in the sterility of the all-male world of the conqueror, promising not relationship but suckle. Having infantilized the natives, Colón, this emblem of modernity's manhood, reveals the depth of its infantile yearning. Yet, not surprisingly, renewal through the nourishing breast is impossible—he flees. The sacrality of the oral paradise of the Mother presents itself at the same time as a powerful taboo, forbidden by the oedipal Father. Colón—now the "deject" in relation to his "abject"—invites a Kristeven exegesis. "There looms within abjection ... one of those violent, dark revolts of being, directed against a threat that seems to emanate from an exorbitant outside or inside, ejected beyond the scope of the possible. ... That leap is drawn toward an *elsewhere* as tempting as it is condemned."[48]

The *abject* roots in the preoedipal situation, prior to the formation of the (m)other as *object*. The source of violent ambivalence, its apocalypse binds the "deject" to the space he flees. "Instead of sounding himself as to his 'being,' 'the abjector' does so concerning his place. '*Where* am I?' instead of 'Who am I?'"[49] Like Columbus, he is also characterized as a perpetual exile–"the more he strays, the more he is saved." The subject constituting himself in relation to the abject is twisting and turning in relation, always, to the Mother, seeking "the desirable and terrifying, nourishing and murderous, fascinating and abject inside of the maternal body"–yet always "the hoped rebirth is short-circuited."[50] Colón cannot but flee, scheming immediately to return, to conquer, to keep his boundaries clear and yet at the same time transgress them. The tempting *elsewhere* of this daunting, unconquered world-space taunts the Europe he embodies.

The breast of a maternal continent, swelling to the Edenic nipple, becomes the subject not only of lengthy epistolary outpourings back on Hispaniola, on "the terrestrial paradise," but also on his plans for its conquest. The mother to be fled can be turned into the virgin to be taken. But the virgin is colored by the dark aura of the sacred and the bestial, the taboo and the threat. The cycle of abuse can begin again. The sublime breast, which Colón lays unhesitating plans to colonize, is already the "savage breast." This ambivalence, alternating between repulsion and fascination, mirrors his bifurcation of the indigenous peoples into good Indians and cannibals, which in Europe would constitute the complementary traditions of the Noble Savage and the cannibal. Good breast and bad.[51]

At the dawn of the epoch of rationalization, the unconscious of its wandering hero, having now erupted into the vision of the breast, becomes manifest in the mode not of a dream, a story, an artwork, or a ritual, but of a *map*. For all his confabulations, the product is a quite precise chart of the coastline of Paria in relation to Cuba and the other islands, the map which would make possible the work of Cortés. The trope of the map rewrites the earth for early modernity, which required new–literal–maps, maps literalizing the space of conquest. "The [modern] map is, in effect, a homogenization and reification of the rich diversity of spatial itineraries and spatial stories."[52] Ferdinand of Spain kept the new maps locked as a state secret in his trunk. Thus we may today read the map as a "totalizing device" which "eliminates little by little" all traces of "the practices that produce it."[53] If earlier maps had been illumined with exotic bits of history and myth, displaying little interest in geometric proportions, the abstract mathematicizing of maps now makes its appearance, erasing from its surface the "spatial stories" of strange peoples and lands.

8

Of the New Heaven and Earth which our Lord made, as St. John writes in the Apocalypse, after He had spoken it by the mouth of Isaiah, He made me the messenger thereof and showed me where to go.[54]

Colón wrote these words in 1500, while he was busy mapping out the nipple of paradise. We are not accustomed to hearing of his apocalypse: it jars the heroic icon of the brilliant navigator and cartographer of the horizontal. His exegesis betrays a startling sleight-of-hand. He reads the object of apocalyptic hope, of the New Creation, by God the Creator *already* created—and therefore available to "discovery." As would be confirmed by later outpourings, the admiral's words cannot be dismissed as a casual Christian convention. If anything, his messianic self-designation risks blasphemy in a culture just mastering the art of burning heretics. Indeed, the "unveiling" of *apokalypsis* can be translated as "dis-covery." He is no biblical illiterate, as his correct alignment of Isaiah and John demonstrates. A fateful bit of retroapocalyptic conflation has taken place. Colón has collapsed the expectation of a future creation into the medieval tradition of a Garden east of Eden, denied to humanity since the Fall.

A new approach to space became possible: the symbolism of the new heaven and earth now reduces to geographic literalism. In this temporal inversion, the symbolic future has been remade as a literal past. To grasp hold of the mammarian *axis mundi*, he bends time backwards, translating it into his new, commodifiable *space*. This move expedited the "discover and acquire" project. When the new heaven and earth lies "before" in space rather than in a numinous spacetime, human control of space and what lies "in" it gains force. Regarding the theological implications of modern maps, David Harvey argues that "since space is a 'fact' of nature, this meant the conquest and rational ordering of space became an integral part of the modernizing project. The difference this time was that space and time had to be organized not to reflect the glory of God, but to celebrate and facilitate the liberation of 'Man' as a free and active individual."[55] But Harvey underestimates how this celebration of a new, autonomous ego must first mobilize the spiritual energies of its culture. "The liberation of Man" from the constraints of feudal theocracy needed a potent eschatological charge.

Imagery of the first and the coming paradise had readily mingled at the edges of the medieval imagination. But the identification of an actual geographic discovery, both with "the Terrestrial Paradise" and with the "New Creation," turns the apocalypse pattern to unprecedented use. In Colón's small library was Pierre d'Ailly's fanciful *Imago Mundi*. This text intertwines legends of Eden and of the adjacent land of blessed peoples with the eleventh-century chiliast prophecies of Joachim. Colón had pored over this book. And he had consistently underlined and annotated the Joachite prophecies of a new age, inferring that "the world will come to an end" around 1650. If the new heaven and earth have already been created (contrary to any Joachite view), it follows that this end of history will not herald a new beginning. In this he shared what Johan Huizinga called "the confessed pessimism"[56] of late medieval Europe. This diffuse sense of impending calamity seems to have meant for Colón that little time remained for the Christianization of the earth, of which he would rightly understand himself to be the key agent. The Franciscans of Spain, with whom he often boarded and to whom he had entrusted his son's care, seem to have instructed him carefully in the theology of his mission.

When Colón returns to Spain again, now in dishonor due to the mismanagement of the colony, frantic for his glory and his money, he writes two books, whose titles already signal the complementary motives of heroic journeying. The first, *Las Privilegias*, cites arguments and accounts of all that he has achieved for Spain and all that is owed to him and his descendants.

But the twin book, *Las Profecías*, is virtually unknown. It was published in English only in 1991,[57] and indeed only a few years earlier in the original Spanish. Its plot line: the Lord chose Colón as the divine instrument for the fulfillment of the ancient prophecies. He would be the one to rescue Christianity before the apocalypse (only 155 years away) by spreading Christianity to the unsaved pagan populations around the world, and providing the gold for financing the crusade to recapture the Holy Sepulcher from the infidels. This is why God led Colón to the *otro mundo,* where so many heathens and so much gold were to be found. To this end, he bestowed upon his herald not only the requisite marine talents, but also special illumination–a "light, which comforted me with its rays of marvelous clarity . . . and urged me onward with great haste continuously without a moment's pause." "You may rejoice," he writes to Ferdinand and Isabella, "when I tell you by the same authorities [his prophetic precedents] that you are assured of certain victory in the enterprise of Jerusalem if you have faith."[58] (They were not thus assured.) In his rhetoric of a new crusade, twin apocalyptic spatial objectifications transpire, that of the New Jerusalem literalized as the conquest of the old Jerusalem, and that of the new heaven and earth literalized as the conquest of an old garden, South America.

Colón thus consolidated both his worldly and his theological claims. Taking a fresh stance among historians, Sale stresses that "bizarre though [the claim of *Las Profecías*] was, to disparage it as simple madness or dismiss out of hand the apocalyptic vision and religious zeal that gave rise to it would be a mistake." The direct influence of Colón's personal beliefs may have been trivial. But they focused those "rays of marvelous clarity" directing his endlessly influential voyages. Left there, the apocalyptic construction of the "other world" might be accounted for as mere biography, as the private motivations of a monumental personage. But even if Colón's own apocalyptic delusions were ignored, they shed light on Europe's movement into its next phase. "It was an authentic expression of that deeply embedded millenarianism we have seen in medieval European culture," writes Sale, "and Colón would not be the only colonist motivated by this passion in the subsequent conquest of the New World. The apocalyptic vision . . . provided many with the essential justification for–the overarching *rightness* of–the Christian mission of expansion, as it was appealed to as often by the Puritan English and the evangelical French as by the Catholic Spanish in the decades to come."[59]

In 1493, Colón adopted a new identity device. Using the abbreviation in Greek letters for Christ, he signed his name xro-ferens–"Christ-carrier." He has cunningly rewritten "Christopher," patron of sailors (!), whose name he bore and who had borne Christ across the river as now Colón bore Christendom across an ocean. Choosing a single name in the style of saints and royalty, he fashions himself as messianic sign. The signifying system of modernity would erase this self-inscription, which might have signed away Columbus as the rational hero. But his own "technology of the self" (Foucault) marks the space of the Great Discovery with the sign—indeed sign/nature—of an ancient messianism.

There is a certain textual irony about the economics of Colón's apocalypse. Joachim did not focus upon the end of the world but rather upon the coming millennium, or rather the "third age" of the Free Spirit—free also of private property. In this sense, the medieval rebirth of apocalypticism had expressed fidelity to the economic communism and the anti-imperialism of the biblical vision. After all, the biblical apocalypse constitutes one long protest on the part of a colonized people against the world-colonizer, Rome as Whore of Babylon. Despite its own ambiguous totalism, the Book of Revelation itself, we have argued, houses an anti-imperialist animus, opposed to precisely the Rome-like concentration of colonizing power and wealth which Spain was emulating. But the Crusades, as an apocalyptically inspired movement against dark unchristian peoples, had in fact already accomplished a conversion of apocalypse into imperial aggression—always justifiable by constructing the Moor or the Turk as the demonic superpower.

In Colón's version, there will be no residue of the actual content Joachim ascribed to the coming period, no recourse to the hope for a communism of spiritually mature love. On the contrary. The identification of the "third age" with legends of a paradisiacal land allows a rather less subtle set of hopes to supervene, hopes well summarized in the constant refrain of Colón's journals: "There may be many things that I don't know, for I do not wish to delay but to discover and go to many islands to find gold."[60] He never did turn up the fabulous quantities he tirelessly sought, but those who followed immediately in his wake would so flood Europe with the gold and silver of America that a new economic system would arise. Thus the global capitalist economy is directly indebted to the native peoples and the silver, gold, and resources their slave labor produced.[61] The "New Heaven and Earth" of which Colón was the messenger would liberate Europeans not *from* private property but *for* its limitless pursuit.

The perversion of the apocalyptic tradition takes place, nonetheless, along a continuum. The Book of Revelation remains militantly androcentric and culminates in an unveiling of virgin territory, but the New Jerusalem, bride of the Lamb, comes down from heaven miraculously—it cannot be "discovered" horizontally. The patriarchy of premodern transcendence differs from, yet prepares the way for the patriarchy of commodification. For both, women appear only as whores and virgins, not as subjects of relationship but as abject emblems of male dread and desire. And if in John the messiah presents himself as hypermasculine hero, the Lamb returned to lead the slaughter, then its shift in "rhetorical situation" (Schüssler Fiorenza) to undercover the book of empire has (not surprisingly) dire consequences. As we see in Colón's self-understanding, the apocalyptic contortion sanctifies a genocidal mission. Thus the new creation becomes the icon of a stabilized paradise fixed in space, *there*, dis/covered like its naked woman by heroes. Were the anti-imperialist impulses of apocalypticism transformed into the modern energy for empire only by way of the spirituality of its relentless warrior-fixation?[62]

9

Feminist theory has long recognized the structural parallelism of early modern white man's ambivalence toward women and toward "savages." As Carolyn Merchant writes, "Animal passions believed to govern the Indian and to be present in all human beings were also symbolized by the lust of women and the disorder wrought by the witch."[63] An already ancient interplay of desire and disgust entered a new phase of collective abjection. Its explosive charge, well stoked by the ambitions of the imperial nation state, expresses the force of apocalypse with a diminishing return on its faith.

While the global organs of "free trade" work to keep the colonized dependent on the colonizer, the colonized have become conscious of their dependency and claim postcolonial self-definitions. The dependency of the colonizer, mixed of endless oral gratifications (of coffee, sugar, fruit, meat), is repressed and therefore lethal. Hidden like the mother beneath Colón's map, it perpetuates the cycle of desire and loathing. Still the breast of paradise threatens to elude the grasp of the conqueror–it churns up revolution, its exotic exuda run dry, its spaces turn inhospitable.

But the paradise paradigm keeps the conquerors coming. "The paradises of western men–and of their wives, mostly sent for later–are their colonies," writes Christina Thürmer-Rohr, in her critique of Ernst Bloch, who in rhapsodizing on the spirit of Columbus "describes them not as the sites of robbery, of oppression, of presumption, of rape and murder, but rather as 'geographic utopias,' earthly paradises, since heavenly paradise had proved unattainable." The bodies of colonized women—at home and abroad—absorb the full force of the sexualized and racialized apocalypse. One need only think of the quest for the dark breast of paradise pursued by millions of average white men in the sexual tourism and traffic in "third world" women.[64] Perhaps, even without purging hope, "we should let paradises alone."[65] Thürmer-Rohr strikes a sardonic note of European remorse. She recognizes the acquisitive aggression which has organized itself around the Western passion for apocalypse and utopia.

Colón's objectification of apocalypse fueled an entire epoch with this paradise hope, the motive force of the modern religion of progress. In the secularization of the apocalyptic hope into the open future of perpetual conquest lies the foundation of modern science. Where the colonial warrior laid bloody claims to space and resources for Western affluence, the Western scientist would offer a serene and humanistic vision of the continual perfection of "the human race." The manful collaboration of power and knowledge, of military and scientific messianisms, have crafted Euroamerican civilization.

The magisterial "universalism" of the modern scientific paradigm, extrapolated from its elite white masculine subjectivity, has well served the economics and politics of Western nation states. Suffice it here to note the apocalyptic sincerity of its terms—even as freed from dependency upon the church for truth and upon God for the New Jerusalem. Its utopias contain genuinely egalitarian aspirations. Francis Bacon's *New Atlantis*, like such other fanciful plans as More's and Campanella's, will depend on solely human resources to overcome human misery. Storming heaven, these utopians take the Joachite vision of the millennium within history to its logical conclusion, as does Bacon in *The Masculine Birth of Time*:

> My dear, dear boy, what I plan for you is to unite you with things themselves in chaste, holy and legal wedlock. And from this association you will secure an increase beyond all the hopes and prayers of ordinary marriages, to wit, a blessed race of Heroes and Supermen who will overcome the immeasurable helplessness and poverty of the human race, which cause it more destruction than all giants, monsters, or tyrants, and will make you peaceful, happy, prosperous, and secure.[66]

This hope for a manmade heaven on earth picks up precisely where Columbus leaves off, as at a geopolitical level Bacon's mentor King James did with the founding of Jamestown. The heroic masculinity of the scientist shrouds itself in the eschatological aura of the coming "Supermen," an entire race of revelatory "discoverers." But if for the conquistadores "she"–the "other" as place, the Place of the Other–was the exotic world of the natives and their lands, for the scientist she is Nature herself. "The things themselves" refers in the above honeymoon mode to the material world. The scientist is now the messianic bridegroom taking to himself matter as his virgin bride. With the "I" of biblical revelation, Bacon proclaims of himself: "I am come to you in very truth leading to you Nature with all her children to bind her to your service and make her your slave." The new virile rationalism thus reinscribes apocalypse in the material bodies and the intertextual tropes of slaves, women, children, and nature.[67] Time in its "masculine birth" exults in its emancipation from all places, from maternal constraint; as purified rationality, purged both of nature and of supernature, it is free to use uninhibitedly that materiality which no longer mars its own origin. For Western epistemology, "Nature" now marks the place of every "other."

Almost two centuries later, in the ambiance of the French Revolution, Condorcet would anoint himself the prophet of the new religion. Progress in his text explicitly replaces God ("Progress–the new god of the age"), arrogating to itself the sacrality of faith and hope. "Long since persuaded that the human species is infinitely perfectible . . . I considered the task of hastening progress to be one of my sweetest occupations, one of the first duties of a man who has strengthened his reason by study and meditation."[68] Unlike Bacon's, his social vision of *égalité* mirrors the utopias of More and Muntzer in their passion for the extirpation of slavery everywhere, even sounding promising notes for the equality of women. I honor such enlightening propensities. Yet the construction of Nature as the new and ultimate "other," the recipient of the messianic aggressions of Progress, continued in Condorcet and the scientific idealists to gain force: "Interrogated everywhere, observed in all its aspects, attacked simultaneously by a variety of methods and instruments capable of tearing away its secrets, nature will at last be forced to let them escape." Again the tropes of the inquisition, the technology of modernity deployed against its own resistant cornucopia, its withheld breast. Finally the master metaphor of "dis-covery" as the new *apokalypsis* prevails: "Every discovery is a conquest over nature."[69] This scientific confidence indelibly pervades the Western progressive spirit. Progressive politics remains even now barely separable from this piety of "discovery." Only pessimists like Malthus and royalist-theist conservatives like De Bonald revealed its underlying motive force. The latter anathematized the new science of the eighteenth century by declaring Condorcet's *Esquisse* "the Apocalypse of the new Gospel."

How might we, now, displace at once the immanent force of this objectified progress-apocalypse while evading the stasis of a postmodern anti-apocalypse, as potentially conservative in its implications for politics as the early reaction against the modern? Pitting space against time merely runs us aground, like lost colonial ships. It is rather that, as Frederick Jameson suggests, "the distinction is between two forms of interrelationship between time and space rather than between these two inseparable categories themselves."[70] Postmodernism, he suggests, evokes spatialization as "the will to use and to subject time to the service of space, if that is now the right word for it." Perhaps the flattening of time into the spatiality of electronic digits, flashing images, and dissociated local knowledges exemplifies his critique.

Modernity, we have argued, had (inversely) subjected space to the service of its new time lords. But Harvey's "annihilation of space by time" leaves us with a detemporalized, denarratized space. A space without place. So it is not a matter now of our sense of space in itself becoming omnivorous, but rather of cryptoapocalyptic displacements of space itself, as dissociated from its own multilayered temporal complexity, and thus from its ability to *place* us.

Already our analysis of the configurative dimension of time required thinking toward a consistent spatiotemporality—without letting the dimensions simply merge. So now perhaps this story of place comes round to making its own demand for a mutual implication, indeed a counter-apocalyptic mutualism of location and history.

10

When Columbus for a moment terrified himself with his own spatial trespassing, he did not resort to a philosophy of time but to a theology of apocalypse. Properly so. He was initiating the end of one world for the redemption of his own. His gaze was fixed relentlessly ahead, abstracting space from its inhabitants, subordinating their place to his time. "Over abstract space," reflects H. Lefebvre, "reigns phallic solitude and the self-destruction of desire." Musing on Picasso as herald of the space of modernity, Lefebvre nonetheless points to the gaze of an earlier heraldry, a "cruelty toward the body, particularly the female body, which he tortures in a thousand ways and caricatures without mercy, is dictated by the dominant form of space, by the eye and by the phallus–in short, by violence."[71]

In its movement toward a universal, if not quite abstract, space, the original Apocalypse had prefigured a phallic synergy of vision and violence, celibate rather than solitary, acquainted with the torture of bodies. At the end of the modern epoch, "the self-destruction of desire" unveils new collective formats. Modern space was desacralized, then desocialized. We meet it as background, as stage, as hollow container, as mother's body, as storeroom of commodities, as poisoned environment. Social significance, history itself, has been violently extracted from place, reinscribed for the computerized classes in the Cartesian purity of globally and instantaneously available "information." For the rest, the violation of public and private place, of habitat and body, goes on with unremitting literalism. At the edges of all habitats, however, the ecological apocalypse merges the destruction of the *otro mundo*, the world of "the other," with modern *self*-destruction.

Within the electronic network of late modern abstraction from living, communal habitat, a social analysis of place, may prove essential to resistance and persistence. Kin to the radical geographers in their analysis of the sociality of space, Camilleri, the political philosopher who had such cogent insight into the time of social movements, further concretizes such an analysis:

> The experience of disruption and alienation evokes varied responses: total withdrawal into private spaces on the part of some; grudging adaptation to technocratic requirements on the part of others; but also various forms of rebellion designed to defend against encroachment and discover new, more congenial spaces. Such categories as gender, class, ethnicity and neighbourhood assume greater importance as a focus of organized resistance.[72]

He cites as examples women gathering in support groups, workers refusing relocation, urban ethnic communities demanding better services; there is more than a figure of speech at work in "alternative spaces." The new movements of resistance gain focus as they challenge the map of social space imposed by state and market forces. For dominative power (not only in the organized hierarchies of state and economic manipulation but in local "microprocesses") demands the desocialization of space. Space, reduced to binaries of inside/outside, up/down, suburb/slum, north/south, civilization/wilderness, public/private, each inscribed as masculine penetration/feminine absorption, cannot resist the increasingly region-transcendent forces of late capitalism.[73]

Camilleri discerns an increasing capacity on the part of social movements, despite their often competing differences of purpose, to "place a given struggle, however specific or immediate, in a wider context informed by many of the connections to which we have already alluded." Beyond the guilt-drenched cynicism of many former caucus activists, beyond the "infighting and shrinking," hope appears under the banner of coalitions of diversity: "It is precisely this fluid interaction at the level of ideas and analysis which explains the growing tendency towards overlapping membership, networking between movements, and coalition-building across geographical issue boundaries."[74] A coalescence of social movements grounded locally and regionally and registering globally presents an unprecedented possibility in history. As events such as the 1995 gathering of UN and NGO women's organizations in Beijing illustrated, it configures a dynamic spatiality that has some chance of providing effective resistance to "free market" forces, that is, transnational forces "freed" to desecrate habitat unrestrained by local accountabilities.

This hope requires a counter-apocalyptic sense of place–that is, a sense of differentiating reciprocity between persons, groups, and species, a sensibility that has matured beyond the apocalyptic dualisms, and single-issue absolutisms of the social movements themselves. This task evinces a spirituality of its own. Indeed, I would suggest that because the present geopolitical situation derives and legitimates itself from the colonial cryptotheology, only a certain *honestly theological counter-gesture–a discourse of spirit–*can sustain the needed correlation of politics and spatiality.

Such a correlation is modeled in liberation theologian Vítor Westhelle's essay on the Latin American search for a "vital space." As it works within the immediate field of Columbus's effects, a close reading of this remarkable piece will launch the counter-apocalypse of place through his text:

> Common to the multiple contexts in our continent is the problem of place. From the struggle of the native inhabitants' right to their nation's land to the reality of the *favelas* (urban slums), from agrarian reform to the conflicts in Central America, from the demands of Black people for a social space to the women's movement, signs of change and consciousness of displacement are commonly found. *Time, history, is a function of geopolitics.*[75]

I take Westhelle not to mean any sense of time, but the time of colonialism, the time of conquest—U.S. Fruit, the Uruguay round, the ever more precise clockwork ticking away inside the "fruits" of U.S. consumerism. In other words, the geopolitical moves of modernity found "time," that is, the timeline of Western progress. The heir of Columbus now appears as the corporate exec, flying first class and heard to say, "Nationality is irrelevant; the hotels I stay in in Singapore, Rio, Paris, or New York are all pretty much the same," and whose frequent glances to the watch orient him upon his place-transcending flight. The Western priority of time over space—of hearing over vision, of the invisible over the visible, of the abstract over the concrete—now funds the movement of transnational corporate capital. This is why Harvey defines the economics of the postmodern as the "annihilation of space by time."

Westhelle suggests that Hegel "was wrong *precisely* in saying that 'the truth of space is time.' In our experience, if time does not convert itself into space, there is no time at all. The relativity of time *and space* is a common sociological experience."[76] Time, in other words, remains discarnate and unaccountable unless it *takes place.* Time abstracted from the material circumstances of places charted the abstract space of modernity, preparing the way for the terrors of mass displacement. The alternative, however, is not mere reversal—space up, time down—but a mutual correlation of space and time. Difference, as Derrida charmingly hints, is the "spacing of time and the timing of space." I take this to imply that the very rub of the "other" against what tries to sustain its own identity creates a displacement, and thus a new space, the timing of which *defers* any new fixity.

Space and time, as the cosmological matrices of all relation, suffer objectification by virtue of their dissociation from each other. For they do not exist in and of themselves, but only in relation to each other, as the joint and fluid form of relation itself: configural dimensions of all subjects of relationship. I do not relate to you *in* time, or greet you *in* some preestablished space; rather, our relationship will constitute its own spacetime. Such attention to space brings into the foreground once again and at once the local, the carnal, the cosmic. And therefore at once the temporal, that finitude which allows its members no pretense of their own infinity.

To embed time in a particular place already interrupts the priority of time over space, letting time again beat at the heart of concrete relationships *taking place*. Place, then, locates me within the relationships through which I come to exist–to stand forth (in Heideggerian ecstasy, displaced from time to spacetime)–at this particular moment. The particularity of a place is not to be discerned, anymore than is that of its time, by separating it off from other place-times, but rather by tracing its dense aura of relations to them. These relationships–nicely problematized by liberation theology, feminism, and Foucault–require analysis as loci of power–of domination, subjugation, and resistance.[77] Yet power, like place, is not some *thing*, but an irrepressibly fluid relationship, not a substance or a possession or an intrinsic evil. Thus those who resist do so "in place." They need not wait for others to spring them loose, or conversely to bring them power. I think of Salvadoran activist Marta Benevides, noting that "it is not a matter of 'empowering' the poor but of recognizing that all life has power."

Now let us take an apocalyptic clue from Westhelle. "This is our task: to discern the signs of places in which we do not yet belong but in which we will belong–'*no places*' that will become concrete *utopias*."[78] Signs of places rather than signs of the times: such utopias are "no place" because those who are displaced cannot yet inhabit them, yet they may glimpse there the signs of future belonging, for instance, in the farmland that a group of indigenous peasants in El Salvador is trying desperately to find money to buy in order to preserve their community and their livelihood, or in a shelter for battered women in my suburb. In such local sites of struggle–each subject to systemic, global effects of colonialism or of sexism–the temporal "not yet" of a liberation eschatology already begins to *take place*.

For purposes of the present counter-apocalypse we may assert that the utopia of the displaced will be, paradoxically, *topical*. The Greek *topos*, also the root of "topography," means "place" (in contrast to the more generic *chora*, "space.") A concrete, or topical, utopia embodies issues like race and gender and ecology, otherwise "transcended" in the construct of the universal utopia. Liberation discourses commit this transcendence when they become fixated on a singular metanarrative which subdues all issues but their own. The notion of the topical, on the other hand, recognizes issues as after all relative to the place and time. The word "topical" means not just regional but contemporary, hence impermanent and current; a properly topical issue enters (or "issues") into these currents powerfully but fluidly. The topical utopia remains a contradiction as long as the conditions of injustice obtain. Acknowledging its own internal contradictions, such a hope incorporates the political with the geographic, evoking the social density of place. It protects habitat as the vital space not merely to be preserved but to be co-constituted by just relations among its multi-specied members.

Unlike "theologians of the developed world" who stress the "order of creation" in the tradition both of Karl Barth and of the scientific liberalism he opposed (and who tend therefore to sacralize the social status quo), Westhelle prefers Ernst Bloch's materialist reception of biblical apocalypse, in which creation is viewed through the eschatological lens of the "new creation." "Thus," Westhelle writes approvingly, "rather than justification of the old order, creation would be the theological expression of the belief in the *novum*: 'Behold, I make all things new!' (Rev. 21:5; Is. 43:19)." But for reasons not unrelated to Thürmer-Rohr's argument, he also takes issue with Bloch (and by implication with Moltmann's *Theology of Hope*): "It is not clear, though, what this novelty is. It is only clear that it is 'not yet,' i.e., eschatological. . . . The fundamental question that emerges in the dialectic of displacement and belonging is not addressed by horizontal transcendence and its appeal to history. The question of transcendence, for the displaced people on earth, is much more related to fences and walls than to a shiny new day to come."[79] In other words, for displaced people transcendence involves very real places and the concrete means by which capital and the state keep improper people, unpropertied peoples, out of them. Even within the propertied classes, the old order managed to deny half of itself "a room of her own."

In the Apocalypse, utopia broke the limits of the topical, replacing any particular relation to a particular place with a yearning for the perfect new creation—a creation out of something very close to nothing. Not surprisingly for a liberation theologian, Westhelle seems all too trustful of the apocalypse-move, indeed even translating it into the later doctrine of *creatio ex nihilo*: "In the experience of total negation, *creatio ex nihilo* is the affirmation of hope in a God who will not succumb to negation."[80] Like Moltmann, he interprets the "new creation" as a new act of "creation from nothing." He cites Gunkel's "*Endzeit gleicht Urzeit*" (the end of time is the same as the beginning) with approval, noting that only as "protology and eschatology" converge, is faith "assured that the maker of heaven and earth can make all things new and is not bound, even by what already exists." This may be a paradigm case of wishful thinking in the service of a worthy cause.

Not to bind "God" to what already exists sounds fine if Westhelle simply identifies "the already"—the world—with an oppressive social status quo; but "already" here includes the intimate, social, and cosmological matrix of all sentient life. Westhelle gets caught in the tension between his Christian progressive eschatology and an indigenous attention to issues of place. Creation out of nothing, presupposing the omnipotent Lord, provides a troubling enough model of power and an awkward, post-biblical account of the universe—but what *on earth* does the metaphor of *creatio ex nihilo* do when transposed to "the end"? Doesn't it collude all too readily with the requisite an*nihil*ation?

If place is the unique space of our relations in community and ecology, then a God unbound by the matrix of relations becomes exposed as the idol of Displacement. Such a deity, suggested by the most cherished texts of the prophetic tradition, must be held accountable—along with "his" theologians—to the *old* creation. Otherwise will not the "vital space," the living space from which so many are being excluded, become utopianized in just the sense Westhelle wishes to oppose?[81]

So a cosmology of counter-apocalypse will translate the notion of creation out of that of absolute *origin* and into that of *perpetual origination*. "Relevant possibilities," in Whitehead's language, locate themselves in the process of a *creatio continua* going on in particular places. That is, if the possibilities—of which any future is a realization—deserve to be lifted up (*relevé* into relevance for the present), then they are not free-floating (or frequent flying) Platonic abstractions. They have *topos*. Therefore why not reaffirm Whitehead's wry empiricism "everything must be somewhere." This axiom preempts Descartes's substantialism ("an existent thing which requires nothing but itself to exist"); in other words, the actual entity, in virtue of being *what* it is, is also *where* it is. It is somewhere because it is some actual thing with its correlated actual world. So even pure possibilities–the "not-yet"–must be located *somewhere*. Ergo, according to Whitehead, God must exist, in order to provide a place for them.[82]

But then this "God" does not exist apart from a body any more than any other being. If the universe is God's body, as Sallie McFague suggests,[83] then these possibilities housed in the mind of God are not nowhere. I take the metaphysics tongue in cheek, but I take the story seriously. Like the production of the two figures created by Spider Grandmother, patterns of possibility interact with the throbbing energy of Spirit at particular places. The flesh of the world dis/closes its holiness precisely as it opens into its own site-specific futures. Embodied but still unactualized, they rim the topology of "vital space." A topical eschatology is once spatial and temporal: it narrates that potentiality at the edge of (our) time where place comes to life.

11

"The Earth is the breast that feeds us. The land is an extension of our body. Anything that causes damage to the Earth causes the same to [us]."[84]

The earth-breast, seen from another side. This topical rhetoric feminizes the place of the Lumad, a mountain people of the Philippines, not to justify conquest but to decry it.[85] Here the mammillary trope expresses that nonpropertarianism which Colón ridiculed as childish and uncivilized. Yet derision is not limited to forthright capitalists. Feminist theorists also get edgy at any association of "woman" with "earth"–identifications of femaleness with nature threaten to congeal women as static, maternalized places of nurture.[86] Indeed, it is arguable that earth mother metaphors are best left in the care of indigenous peoples. For Euroamericans, they may connote an infantile return to the *teta de mujer* our people have nearly sucked dry, they may reinvest greed for the nipple of paradise. By contrast, the animating, if not animist, sensibility of the

Aeta people (also indigenous Filipinos) exemplifies an identification with the land ("land is life") which invites personification and eschews private ownership. Place is inseparable from self, at least from a self which knows itself as bodily and communal.

A postmodern pluralism rightly warns of a discursive chasm between colonizing white, even female, experiences of "mother earth" and indigenous symbolizations. Yet as long as our material and political relations configure a near total–and infantile–dependency on the commodified spaces of the *otro mundo*, respect for "them" will require attention to what our culture had to violate *in ourselves* in order to violate "them." A place of counter-apocalyptic communication with the Aeta and other "others" begins to open. Space in the indigenous vision cannot be divided and conquered–except at the cost of natural apocalypse. Thus the Aeta, still living in the horticultural life-way, interpreted the 1991 eruption of the sacred Mount Pinatubo, as "the end of the world." Like *Revelation*'s cosmic quake, the earth-mountain "had finally said no to its desecration by man [*sic*],"[87] that is, by the civilization of the invading destroyers. A geothermal apocalypse responding to urban intrusion: Mother Earth blows her top.

In our urbanized habitats, we have less poetic ways of articulating the anxiety. It is as though our turn-of-the-millennium fear of nature's vengeance blends somehow with a more intimate anxiety–that of the abject mother, rage smoldering, in whom subjectivity may dissolve. Do we fear the holism of indigenous mother-earth spatiality, as though it could obliterate difference? As though it is incapable of high levels of differentiation? Yet there is no sign that "her" body parts blur into undifferentiated totality. On the contrary, it was the conquest which spearheaded the mass reduction of difference both biological and ethnic.

Alternatively? "To become dwellers in the land," writes Sale in another venue, "to relearn the laws of Gaea, to come to know the earth fully and honestly, the crucial and perhaps only and all-encompassing task is to understand *place*, the immediate specific place where we live." Bioregionalism, a movement by which we might shelter the spectrum of diversities, has ancient, spirit-drenched roots. The earlier settlers of the North American continent "distributed themselves to a remarkable degree along the lines of what we now recognize as bioregions."[88] For us–in both urban and rural settings–it means awkwardly relearning the place specificity which our culture has systematically leveled. But here, let us link this gaiacentric attention to place with a fuller reading of place as site of social relations. Otherwise we remain captive to the dichotomy of ecology and sociology, a pernicious outcropping of mind-body dualism that invariably locates spirit on the side of the speaking *socius*. As noted, even when a feminist geographer "attempts to think the spatial in terms of social relations," she did so with no reference whatsoever to the earth.[89] Western anthropocentrism, however progressive, opposes the social to the natural.

The conceptual link between a sociological and an ecological re-trieval of place must be situated within the terms of social relations. Any imaginable site of human social relations is at the same time a complex of multilayered inorganic and organic relations. Some, like bodies, rep-resent highly organized communities of biogenetic interaction. Other relations, as of nerve endings to light waves or lungs to air molecules, represent looser social interchanges. No human dwelling "in the earth," however urban, can with any honesty abstract itself from the skins and fluids and vapors of the earth-body of which it is part. Our bodies are not containers contained within larger spatial containers, cultural linguis-tic mentalities. As Merleau Ponty put it, our intersubjective sociality weaves itself as the "flesh of the world." Politically, this suggests that eco-logical commitment to place will take the form of a social activism on be-half of place itself, in and as the right of peoples "to dwell in the land."

To inscribe within counter-apocalypse the sociality of place, we might then reinforce the noncompetitive possibilities of the interface of social movements as they mature beyond caucus identity politics.[90] "Even when they are reactive, negative or one-dimensional, the forms of expression, organization and mobilisation developed by the social movements foreshadow a new conception of politics. Their collective struggles are catalysts for the reconstruction of time as well as physical and social space."[91] This is an apt statement of the *space* of counter-apocalyptic hope.

Perhaps it is in rendering space *place* again that spiritual attention plays a crucial role. For instance, Vandana Shiva shows that within In-dian eco-social space–as, for instance, that constituted by the Chipco, or tree-hugging, women's movement–ancient animism and goddesses as well as Gandhian religiosity emit guiding resonances. And the present project stays close to the space of biblical mythos precisely in order to translate its more salutary emissions into presence. Moltmann similarly lifted up–albeit with minimal exegetical warrant–biblical pneumatology as invocative of a spirit which is our living space. A spiritualization of place consciousness, an attention to the spirit of place, may prove a critical power for sustaining struggle beyond its apocalyptic moments of mere revolution. For *grounding* eschatology in incarnation.

12

The body is a self's ownmost place, "the geography closest in."[92] Not that the self lives in the body as in a house, but that *as body the self takes place.* The refiguring, the configuring, and the occasional transfiguring of the flesh incessently manifest our plastic spatiality. Inter-subjectivity is inter-spatiality. None of the political coalitions of coalitions of communities of relationships make a difference–or respect difference–unless their members keep faith with the body, with the incarnate spatiality of each as enmeshed in the material processes of all. Movements for social and ecological justice, whatever their messianic pitch, exist first of all to resist the bodily degradation of particular sets of sentient beings. For instance, the women's movement has from the start engaged a daunting multiplicity of fleshly violations: rape, battering and sexual harassment, incest, violence against women of color and lesbians, anti-abortion politics and the global interrelationship of sexual politics with population, female infanticide, resource consumption, and the malnutrition and starvation of women and their children in situations of mass dislocation. More than any theoretical nondualism, the spacetime of the social movements has begun to provide a massive if vulnerable force for the deconstruction of two millennia of mind-body dissociation: the topicality of its utopias grounds them in the suffering of present bodies, bodies whose pain cannot be deferred, pain which in a dissociative society exceeds the vicissitudes of mortality.

Thus a counter-apocalypse of social space will situate its theology in the body, site of any doctrine of incarnation. But ironically, traditional doctrines of "the Incarnation" siphoned energy away from all bodies but one, that tortured, executed body, whose resurrection was not enough. He needed to "come again," to guarantee for the rest of us a literal resurrection of the flesh. In this ancient hope the suffering of a colonized people sought healing. Yet as persecuted Christianity accrued the power to persecute, the single and unique incarnation of God as "His Son" came to function as the exception which proved the rule–the rule of a fleshless Father through his Word. The apocalyptic hope of a collective reanimation of the flesh in history was quelled along with the subtler wisdoms of transformation. For if apocalypse effected a certain dissociation through the deferral of spirit-flesh integrity, the classical dissociation disciplined the spirit for permanent separation.

The concept of the final resurrection became, with the development of classical orthodoxy, quite anti-apocalyptically correlated with the doctrine of the incarnation of the Son. Thus it could drain all but prurient interest from the flesh, to reinscribe the classical mind-body dualism on the very body that might have enabled its healing. Much twentieth-century theology labors to correct the classical discourse of spiritual dissociation from materiality. In ecofeminist modalities, it brings a width of context-mirroring apocalyptic hope for a new creation without replicating the supernaturalist assumptions of final resurrection or the misogynist assumptions of the celibate martyr ideal. Thus McFague's ecological theology, which is based "on the model of embodiment," is conceived of as "a theology of space and place." "It is a theology that begins with the body, each and every body, which is the most basic, primary notion of space: each life-form is a body that occupies and needs space." She means this language to be materially concrete: "for the first thing bodies need is space to obtain the necessities to exist–food, water, air."[95] Yet even the metaphor of "occupation"–contrary to her intention, which is to signify a rich indwelling–can reinforce the notion that space is something *in which* a body exists, that is, the container I use. Indeed, the very discourse of "the body" within a culture of classical dissociation and a hidden habit of apocalyptic dualism proves extraordinarily resistant to revitalization without mere psychoanalytic fetichism. It is not the project of this book to resignify embodiment. I merely affirm here such attempts as McFague's to lift human bodiliness into a time and place wide enough to keep it from imploding–and that width may translate into nothing less than the zone of creation itself, renewable as "realm of God" in theological parlance.

But the space in which to counter apocalypse tends to shut down even within feminist rhetoric around "the body." The tendency to abstract

177

ourselves from the incarnate relations by which human subjectivity takes place not surprisingly continues to pervade our best attempts to re-incarnation. For instance, Judith Butler deconstructs the feminist convention of distinguishing "sex" from "gender." If "sex is to gender as nature is to culture," she writes in *Gender Trouble*, feminists might hope to distinguish an underlying "natural" body from that cultural text written upon it by patriarchy. But such hope belongs to the cultural text itself. Demonstrating the impossibility of any residual nature, culture-free "sex" evading the impact of the heterosexist formations of social power, Butler implicitly confirms the radical sociality of embodiment. There is no "natural" body, in the sense of some untouched essence that transcends the effects of the sociocultural system. We cannot simply step beyond the sex/gender system, whether into some subjective transcendence or into some bodily innocence. Thus strategies of "performance" and "parody" replace the revolutionary, that is, apocalyptic, utopianism of earlier feminisms.[94]

Yet Butler's proposed metaphor for the body colludes with classic Western disembodiment. She proposes to frame the body as a "denatured" social construction, indeed a "moving boundary," hence effectively emptying it of any prelinguistic pulp. In her subsequent work, *Bodies That Matter*, she puts forth the notion of "materialization" to rectify the appearance of idealism in her constructivism.[95] Yet her performance of the poststructuralist body seems still to find itself raptured out of the fallen realm of materiality. Her fleshless imagery of the boundary–the *eschaton*, after all–sounds the apocalyptic underside: the new body is the one signified ex nihilo by the Word, at the boundary of history, where "nature" has been dismissed once again into insignificance. And that Word proves for her, no less than for St. Paul, to be the incarnation of the Father's Law (through Lacan's), which cannot be abrogated, but rather which itself produces the attempts to subvert it.

How will parody open new social spaces for the sexual body, however, unless it embraces the materializing sociality of place itself, offering topologies vastly preceding and perchance therefore resisting paternal order?

Rather than container or boundary, we might consider the body as a spatiotemporal complex. "Complex" in the original Latin signifies "surrounding, encompassing, ... embrace, connexion in discourse."

In the course of English usage it came to include "its analytical sense of 'plaited together, interwoven . . . formed by combination of different elements, composite, compound."[96] The human body suggests in the present discourse the most complex of complexes, interwoven into the encompassing space of environing complexes which constitute its topical world. Of course we endlessly contest its meanings, speaking as it, for it, from it, over and against it–but if the body constitutes the most intimate and persistent place *as* which we understand ourselves to dwell, it partakes at the same time of vastly prehuman, prelinguistic forces colliding and colluding with the sociolinguistic ones, which are equally as impersonal. The complex can be experienced as colonized and invaded, as delusional, as pathological, as extrinsic; and it can be felt as vulnerable, labile, and actively participating in its own discursive self-formation. Only by locating the renewed body within the larger ecologies in which it dwells–of which it is a shifting configural space–do we allow renewed powers of desire and of healing to release themselves into feedback loops large enough to "embrace" us, to feed us back to ourselves more animate.

Some men, we have noted, have begun to address the colonial space-complex of the commodifying patriarchal spatiality *as* patriarchal. Glen Mazis, a phenomenologically oriented philosopher, rediscovers body as "the waystation of the currents of our relations with the world–our emotions." To be a finite human bodily being interconnected with others, he argues, will necessarily involve pain. Masculinity has evolved into one great defense against that pain, which therefore makes others–especially women, people of color, animals, and the earth–feel men's pain for them.[97] Men in the context of male supremacy are the bodies who are able to defer the suffering of finitude, displacing it onto the bodies of the others who cannot. Gender has functioned as a binary procedure, in which one pole separates itself and displaces its carnal vulnerability onto the flesh of another, while remaining unconsciously dependent upon that other. We may conclude that this operation has created and continues to create our intimate and our geopolitical spaces.

In the creation of a new geography of relations, perhaps, the women, the people of color, the beasts of the field and the birds of the air, indeed even the pale males, will refuse to stay in their assigned places. The "phallogocentric" law (as French feminists name it) will not thereupon dissolve; the old creation will remain, marred and scarred, to be mourned, healed, teased, its lonely phallic signifiers danced around like ancient maypoles.

13

A sacred space if ever there was one. Now soft and mound-like, covered with grassy soil, ringed by equidistant mountains and charged with centuries of ritual presence. Marta had brought our group, half gringo students and half indigenous peasants, to the pyramid. The Nauhats descend from the Mayas of western El Salvador, 60,000 of whom were slaughtered during the *matanza*, the "killing," of 1932 by the troops of the descendents of the Spanish; perhaps 6,000, still frightened to reveal their identity, survive. This was their first encounter with the ancient ritual center of their own people (they could afford with our dollars to rent a bus to get to the site).

Provoked by Marta to feel the energy emanating from the site—she was dancing it—an old Maya woman quietly came forward, kneeled, and raised her hands; she began to pray aloud to the Madre Tierra, announcing that the spirits of the ancestors were present, thanking the Great Spirit, calling above all for strength in the face of so much injustice (here she burst into sobs), for strength to persist, and turning to all directions to thank their spirits, returning always to the invocation of the Mother. Her prayer for her did not contradict her Catholicism. Marta noted that at a certain point Maria, or Hermana Salvadora as she liked to be called, switched into an eloquence of Spanish of which her unschooled speech is normally incapable. Afterward, we picked up the ubiquitous trash that preceded us, picnicked, and played childhood circle games in the sun at the foot of the pyramid. To be honest, most of us gringos soon dropped out, clutching our souls under cover of shade. In ways too diverse, too intimate, too elusive to narrate, spirit "took place" among us that day.

5. Community

Congregating
Conflagrations

1

Community is in apocalypse. Those fragile, hope-fraught groupings by which we configure our relations in time and place, in which we sometimes huddle for warmth and focus, may seem hardly up to the name of "community." *In apocalypse*: not just that social forms of cohesion are under threat by, for instance, the economics of "the end of history" and its individualism, but that the ideal of community may have become suspect among precisely such progressives as in the past might have been its primary advocates. But there is a more positive sense in which community stands within apocalypse. The concept of community can arguably be situated within the larger set of apocalyptic movements, as their product. What bonds individuals "called out"–*ek-klesia*–of the larger society to the common goal of the New Jerusalem proves to be revolt. This chapter will examine the configural zone of community as the mutual articulation of *apocalypse* and *revolution*.

The link between the apocalypse script and Western patterns of rebellion has already been elicited. Foucault confirms its vocabulary:

> We can understand why revolts have easily been able to find their expression and their mode of performance in religious themes: the promise of the beyond, the return of time, the waiting for the saviour or the empire of

the last days, the indisputable reign of good. When the particular religion
has permitted, these themes have furnished throughout the centuries not
an ideological cloak but the very way to live revolts.[1]

In order to anchor the question of counter-apocalyptic sociality
within its history, we will consider several apocalyptic tales of early modernity. These narratives will serve to complicate both the modern romanticism of community and the postmodern sacrifice of the ideal of
community. Since "community" colors itself of heavily normative memories and hopes, the term is identical neither with "group" nor with
"society."

For present purposes, we may distinguish between three overlapping
phases of community: (1) *indigenous*, that is, tribal or local community,
from the hunter-gatherer period on through various village peasantries
and their urban residues, rooted in a place, and therefore in a bottom-
lessly shared past woven of stories and ancestors, on principal end-lessly
recyclable; (2) *state* community, including most of the historical social
forms of the West, which rearranges once indigenous peoples into class
hierarchies subservient to the needs of the urban elites: in this long process, imperial, anti-apocalyptic theocracy has served to homogenize
populations mixed together in the rearrangement; (3) *dissident* community, which raises into consciousness its alienation under the empire
and tries to restore the holistic accountabilities of an originative phase,
often remembered as a lost Eden, in some new spiritual solidarity.

It is only as the latter, our narratives will suggest, that "community"
articulates itself. That is, only in the mode of rebellion and epiphany
does it become intentional and self-conscious. As such, sociality reverses
its orientation in time: originally grounded in an organic and place-
bound past, it comes in the anti-state, the state of resistance, to orient itself to the future, to a common goal, an *eschatos*, that coming time which
has yet no *topos*.

If the very ideal of community in the West is redolent of revolt, it is
nonetheless the case that its futurism often mingles with a myth of origin. Thus a nostalgia for the lost harmony may, as in contemporary communitarianism, overpower the eschatological element and import a reactionary coloration. But, as the following excavations of the layered
apocalypse in revolt may display, one would be hard-pressed to judge
"community" an essentially conservative desire.

2

What is at work here is the longing for that *rightness* which, in religious or philosophical vision, is experienced as revelation or idea, and which of its very nature cannot be realized in the individual, but only in human community.[2]

As Martin Buber, in his advocacy of utopian socialism demonstrates historically, the eschatological longing for rightness that he refers to above takes the form of community; when eschatology moves into apocalypse, the way is opened for revolution—and with it the violent dualism of a homogenizing anti-state. Ernst Bloch, a fan of the apocalyptic force of "Christian social utopias," recaptures the leap from earliest Christianity to Joachim of Fiore, of "an anger born of hope . . . which had hardly been heard since the days of John the Baptist." Here we pick up the trail of apocalyptic time. "They deck the altars, and the poor man suffers bitter hunger," said Joachim. We discussed earlier the medieval consequences of this "most momentous social utopia." Bloch's socialist approbation of the monastic and apolitical Joachim rings with a double anachronism perhaps (from him to Joachim, from our postcommunist present to Bloch), but brings to salience the apocalyptic production of revolution. Joachim's greatness for Bloch consists in having transformed the traditional "trinity of mere *viewpoints* into a threefold gradation *within history itself.* Connected with this was the complete transfer of the kingdom of light *from the other world* and the empty promises of the other world into history." Bloch then points forward to the Joachite influence in Bohemia, Germany, and Russia, then England: "Only the heretical sects, with Joachim among them, allowed revelation to spring up anew even in the west, and the Holy Spirit accordingly recommended astonishing Pentecosts to them. It recommended social principles of Christianity which . . . were not cringing and did not treat the proletariat as a rabble."[3]

Moved by the myth of the Third Person coming into its aeon, Bloch inadvertently honors the biblical warning: to blaspheme against the Spirit is to forfeit hope itself. Moving to the holy writ of his own community, Bloch's apocalyptic metanarrative forges via Engels the crucial link to its own Marxist modernity:

A remark by the young Engels in 1842 (MEGA I, 2, p. 225f) contains an echo from Joachim, only a few years before the Communist Manifesto:

"The self-confidence of humanity, the new Grail around whose throne the nations jubilantly gather . . . This is our vocation: to become the Templars of this Grail, to gird our swords about our loins for its sake and cheerfully risk our lives in the last holy war, which will be followed by the millennium of freedom."[4]

Bloch amplifies this "echo" into an illumining thesis: "Utopian unconditionality comes from the Bible and the idea of the kingdom, and the latter remained the apse of every New Moral World." Just as unconditionally, Bloch reinvests hope with his own eschatological fervor, confirmed by the discernment of this pneumatic current rushing along, *all* along, to the "not-yet."

A feminist can only deconstruct the symbolism trumpeted by Engels in Bloch's proud apocalyptic intertextuality. Performing a near archetypal condensation, the passage rhapsodically invokes the medieval imagery of the crusade, the apocalyptic final battle, and the pure brotherhood of the warrior-heroes, in a guarantee of the millennial triumph. That "last holy war"—which took place as the Russian Revolution—proved to be one more in a series of wars to end all wars. But then those of us still enmeshed in communalist egalitarian hopes must ask, Just how definitive of the communal-egalitarian impetus in the West is this macho millennium and its failed communist project?

Today the communist apocalypse may look like some once grand dream lying homeless on the pavement of "posthistory." But perhaps by the same token progressives may now grapple more honestly with the way the metanarratives of an egalitarian, just, and *peaceful* community, from the biblical warrior myth onward, have marched earnestly, sword in hand, into historical horror. So now let us back up to consider another trajectory of early modernity, whose crusades run simultaneously with Colón's conquest of the New World or Bacon's of the natural. These heirs of the Joachite vision rarely conquered. They communed. Violently.

1419, Bohemia

The radical wing of the Hussite movement, born after the execution of John Huss (who had challenged Rome's hierarchical clericalism, corruption, and the sale of indulgences—grievances the Protestant Reformation would reheat) fled from persecution to the hilltops of South Bohemia. They called themselves Taborites after Mount Tabor (the name of the mountain where, according to an old tradition, Jesus had foretold his Second Coming and to which he would return at the millennium), and formed settlements where life was lived in imitation of the original Christians.

"Together these communities formed an embryonic society," according to Norman Cohn, "which was wholly outside the feudal order and which attempted to regulate its affairs on the basis of brotherly love instead of force."[5] Influenced by millenarians carrying the doctrine of the Free Spirit, they read the Church of Rome as Whore of Babylon. They denounced the prelates who ignored Christ's injunction to poverty and instead exploited the poor. Living at the threshold of the new age, which would be the Third (and last) Aeon, the community prefigured the time when no sacraments would be needed for salvation, the church would disappear, nobody would suffer physical hardship or deprivation, women would bear children without pain, and death would disappear. They declared that "All shall live together as brothers, none shall be subject to another.... The Lord shall reign, and the Kingdom shall be handed over to the people of the earth. The Saints would live together in a community of love and peace."[6]

In these Bohemian traces we discern one of the first intentionally egalitarian but nonmonastic communities of the West. Based upon the futurist narrative of resistance to a theocratic empire, it inherits a myth of origins as well. As Cohn notes, the first historian of Bohemia, Cosmas of Prague, had three centuries earlier recalled the first Bohemians as living in a state of total community: "Like the radiance of the sun, or the wetness of the water, so the ploughed fields and the pastures, yea even the very marriages, were all in common.... Nor did anyone know how to say 'Mine,' but, as in the monastic life, they called whatever they had 'Ours ... ' But alas! they exchange prosperity for its opposite, and communal for private property." The legend of a lost "anarcho-communist order"—perhaps mythically recollecting hunter-gatherer existence and its village remnants—indigenizes the apocalyptic inheritance. The mix replaces nostalgia with a historical project.

Before "the Kingdom shall be handed over to the people," however, the old world—the orders of Roman Church, Empire, and Wealth—must topple. But the faithful will no longer wait for God to devastate the godless. They take history into their own hands. Soon, not surprisingly, the extremists among the persecuted begin to take over. One widely circulated tract declared, "Accursed be the man who withholds his sword from shedding the blood of the enemies of Christ. Every believer must wash his hands in that blood." And take sword in hand they do. So what was a first experiment in intentional community also marks the point at which apocalyptically detonated violence becomes intentional revolt. The medieval outbreaks had been sporadic and disorganized; Colón's use of the myth of apocalypse at the end of the same century would remain private and would form no community but rather serve the state. Now we begin to witness the formation of a third trajectory, anti-statist and organized.

There remains the poignant text of another Taborite, Peter Chelčický, who decried the change in his movement. He wrote that Satan had seduced his colleagues into regarding themselves as angels called to purify Christ's world of all sins and destined to judge the world; thus they "committed many killings and impoverished many people." Closer to the pacifism of the biblical context, Chelčický prophecies *against* this new self-literalizing apocalypse. True to form, it was especially the urban rich who were to be eradicated; towns were to be burnt, and Prague was identified as Babylon. Armageddon would be a final "class war against 'the great' "–" 'All lords, nobles and knights shall be cut down and exterminated in the forests like outlaws.' "[7] Taborite armies took over towns, expropriated their wealth, and declared the peasants free of all feudal bonds. But neglecting all production in their endtime rush to share others' property, they soon began collecting dues from the peasants just as onerous as the feudal ones. The Taborite army, led by Zizka, soon had to face more radical offshoots of themselves, such as the Adamites, who practiced nudism, free love, and nocturnal raids on surrounding villages, reportedly killing every man, woman, and child they found. Zizka exterminated the Adamites. Yet the entire movement understood itself to be living in the tribulations and therefore obliged to kill not just evil leaders, but sinners who would not join their community. "The just . . . will now rejoice, seeing vengeance and washing their hands in the blood of the sinners."[8] But it was soon the Taborites whose elimination would be cruelly celebrated.

Those interested in trivializing the egalitarian utopia of community will find it easy to discount the Bohemians and their heirs as fanatics. The Taborites represent a first major outbreak of apocalyptic revolution, that is, of rebellion carried by a faith exceeding local protest. Those of us who are moved by the originative force of the popular hope cannot so lightly cure our ambivalence. We may wonder how many of the nonviolent voices like that of Chelčický were silenced as persecution mounted and the warriors, biblically inspired to purification by violence, came to the fore; and we may wonder how the women, all the women who lived and died for this revolt, thought and felt about it.

1525, Germany

"Go to it, go to it, while the fire is hot! Don't let your sword grow cold, don't let it hang down limply! . . . One cannot say anything to you about God as long as they rule over you. Go to it . . . while it is day!"[9] Thus Thomas Münzer, manfully arousing his community of peasants for the climactic battle of the German Peasant Wars.

A proficient biblical scholar, Münzer himself tracks the apocalyptic subtext of the new class war: "The whole business can be read up in Matthew 24, Ezekiel 34, Daniel 7, Ezra 16, Revelation 6 and all these texts are explained by Romans 13." The "business" here is that of the messianic kingdom, the Second Coming, the Day of Wrath and the Four Horsemen. But why Romans 13, ultimate proof-text of Christian tyrants and magistrates (as indeed it was of Luther in his antirevolutionary and anti-Anabaptist doctrine of the two kingdoms): "Let every person be subject to the governing authorities; . . . those [authorities] that exist have been instituted by God" (13:1)? In a confrontive letter to a count, Münzer performs a midrashic tour de force: "But the key to the knowledge of God is this: to rule the people so that they learn to fear God alone" (Romans 13). The authorities *have* no authority unless that authority is godly, for, as Paul continues, "rulers are not a terror to good conduct, but to bad" (13:3). Thus Münzer reads these Pauline postulates as prescriptive norms for rule rather than ontological descriptions. Indeed, Münzer first calls upon the princes to wield the sword "necessary to eliminate the godless" (Romans 14), and later chooses to wield it against them when they will not.[10]

In the tradition of apocalyptic signature, Münzer once signed himself "the Sword of God," yet it is only in his last two years that his occasional writings turn militantly—though never literally—millennialist. He begins with the radical rhetoric of the other reformers, appealing to Luther as "model and beacon to the friends of God!" and choosing chiefly religious targets.[11] Yet already he declares that "the Lord is with me as a strong warrior." It took a long series of humiliations and migrations, coupled with a rash of peasant tax revolts, to suck him into the undiluted vortex of revelation as revolution: "The sweat of the working people tastes sweet, sweet to [the authorities] but it will turn into bitter gall. . . . The truth will out. No counterfeit enthusiasm for the gospel [á la Luther's reformers] will avail them. The people are hungry; they must eat; they intend to eat, as Amos says, and Matthew 5, too."[12]

Indeed, his writings record some of the first Western moments of radical social analysis. Against Luther, who uses Romans 13 to justify the princes' rule, who inveighs against the "murdering and plundering gangs of the peasants" and demands their blood, Münzer argues,

> He suppresses here, however, the basic *reason* for all theft. . . . What is the evil brew from which all usury, theft and robbery springs but the assumption of our lords and princes that all creatures are their property? The fish in the water, the birds in the air, the plants on the face of the earth—it all has to belong to them! [Isaiah] 5. To add insult to injury, they have God's commandment proclaimed to the poor: God has commanded that you should not steal. But it avails them nothing. For while they do violence to everyone, flay and fleece the poor farm worker, tradesman and everything that breathes, [Michah] 3, yet should any of the latter commit the pettiest crime, he must hang. And Doctor Liar [Luther] responds, Amen. It is the lords themselves who make the poor man their enemy. *If they refuse to do away with the causes of insurrection how can trouble be avoided in the long run?*[13]

In other words, the system is set up to blame its own victims. What a grand grope toward what now calls itself "systemic analysis." Five hundred years later the same analysis of the criminalization of the poor obtains. Within the church, only the social gospel and liberation theologies have reclaimed this root prophetic insight.

At the same time there is no mistaking the mounting and obsessive violence of Münzer's rhetoric as it presses toward its own enactment; the fantasy of purification bleeds through his correspondence. He rails against the "counterfeit clemency" of any who disagree that "one should kill the godless rulers, and especially the monks and priests who denounce the holy gospel as heresy and yet count themselves the best Christians."[14] In the end, the army of the princes would effortlessly slaughter five thousand peasants–and within a few weeks, a hundred thousand. As with the Taborites, whose influence had secretly worked itself into the German towns for a century, the vision of a community where "all things are to be held in common and distribution should be to each according to his need, as occasion arises," has irrupted–and gone berserk.

Cohn comments acerbically, "To judge by his writings he certainly showed far less interest in the nature of the future society than in the mass extermination which was supposed to precede it." Cohn scorns the "naive" Marxist inflation of Münzer into "a prodigious hero in the history of the 'class war.'" But Cohn's political animus drives him to reductionism: "Münzer was a *propheta* obsessed by eschatological phantasies which he attempted to translate into reality by exploiting social discontent."[15] Cohn's accusation that one of the first Europeans to expose exploitation was himself the true exploiter, insane and hypocritical, incites one to contrast Cohn's version with that of his ideological opposite. Bloch (whom Cohn would count as a "naïf") maintained that "humanity actively comprehending itself" culminates in Marx, "this impassioned man" who "feels that he is himself a human being and . . . others are human beings too and yet for the most part are treated like dogs."

> Those who maltreat them thus are therefore not included in any mercy, on the contrary: to tolerate them would be to act inhumanly towards the humiliated and the insulted. The 'feigned goodness,' as Münzer called this in Luther, who condemned so tenderly for the masters all violence not perpetrated by them, is a far remove from Marx.[16]

Bloch's inverse irony at once resonates with all liberation movements and veils the messianic horror of their triumphs. But however heinous or self-defeating the revolting violence may become, to fail to note its first causes, the systemic violence of the state against which the poor first seek defense, is indeed to "feign goodness."

With pastoral fidelity, Münzer writes to "the community." The trope of the *Gemeynde*, the "congregation," has nothing to do with formal parish structures, but encodes "the common person," *der Gemeyne*, as the historic site of apocalypse and agent of God's cause. "For the common man (God be praised) is acknowledging the truth almost everywhere."[17] Münzer's understanding of commonality even hints at a religious universalism (almost unheard of in his day) needed "if we Christians are now to agree peaceably [Psalm] 72, with all the chosen ones among all scatterings or races of every kind of faith." "If a man in his whole life had neither heard nor seen the Bible, he could still, through the right teaching of the spirit, have an unerring Christian faith, just as all those who wrote the Holy Scriptures without any books."[18]

Such pneumatological width, pitted against Luther's biblicism, is rooted in a mysticism familiar for centuries to adepts of the Free Spirit. "Just as happens to all of us when we come to faith: we must believe that we fleshly, earthly men are to become gods through Christ's becoming man, and thus become God's pupils with him—to be taught by Christ himself, and become divine, yes and far more—to be totally transfigured into him, so that this earthly life swings up into heaven."[19] This mysticism of theosis (divinization), heresy in the West, orthodoxy in the East, transforms earthly life from within. In Münzer's apocalyptic communalism it seeks concrete, social manifestation. Refusing the Augustinian-Lutheran dualism of two kingdoms, heavenly versus earthly domains, the Joachite utopia, reference to which appears in Münzer's documents, inspires him to imagine heaven on earth for all.

His vision crashes, however, against the realism of the state power in its collusion with even reforming religion—and he sees red, blood red, "as high as a horse's bridle." Stumbling into suicidal literalism, his potent hysteria setting back the cause of the peasants for centuries, he "opens the gates to that tragic coupling of utopia with creative violence whose force as a revolutionary idea is not yet spent."[20]

And women in this new epoch of swords raised in revolt? We hear only from the nun Münzer married, Ottilie von Gersen. She bore him a son on Easter 1524, and, according to Agricola, the father demonstrated his spirituality by showing no pleasure at the news. The only note of personal warmth one finds in Münzer's writings is his request, just before his execution, that she be cared for. Bereaved and destitute, the remnants of *Gemeynde* abandoning her, Duke George never responding to her sad petition for Münzer's property (his books and few household items), she asks to return to the convent. Nothing more is known: no place for her among the triumphant and tragic heroes of Armageddon.

And there remains Melanchton's letter upon the occasion of Münzer's execution: "Dear God, of what prophecies did he lead the stupid mass of the people to take up arms? How many promises that in the near future the order of the state would change on command of the heavenly oracles?"[21]

1534, *Münster*

Within a decade, in a city swollen with Anabaptist immigrants and bands of the homeless, the ferment resurfaced. It is said that women (many recently rebaptized ex-nuns) began to see apocalyptic visions in the streets, writhing on the ground, screaming, foaming at the mouth. Winning control of the town council, the Münster Anabaptists determined to create "a New Jerusalem purified of all uncleanness."[22] Guided by the "Dutch prophets" Jan Matthys and Jan Bockelson, armed bands expelled all Roman Catholics and Lutherans who would not submit to rebaptism. Preparing for siege, the city sent out requests for supplies and mercenaries along with pamphlets. Community was the theme:

> Amongst us God ... has restored community, as it was in the beginning. ... We hope too that amongst us community is as vigorous and glorious, and is by God's grace observed with as pure a heart. ... For not only have we put all our belongings into a common pool under the care of deacons, and live from it according to our needs: we praise God through Christ with one heart and mind and are eager to help one another. ... Everything which has served the purposes of self-seeking and private property, ... eating and drinking the sweat of the poor ... and indeed everything which offends against love—all such things are abolished amongst us by the power of love and community. ... And indeed no Christian or Saint can satisfy God if he does not live in such community.[23]

In the light of what follows such rhetoric may read as propaganda. The "power of love and community" soon revealed its face. With two thirds of the population female, polygamy was declared and defended biblically, shocking the strictly monogamous Anabaptists. About fifty dissenters, men and women, were executed. Bockelson gathered a harem of fifty wives and a court by which he had himself declared the messianic king. In preparation for the Second Coming, the court lived in ostentatious luxury while the rest began to starve. The terror was intensified: all who sinned against the revealed truth would henceforth be brought before the king, executed, and their memory expunged from the Chosen. "The first victims were women: one was beheaded for denying her husband his marital rights, another for bigamy—for the practice of polygamy was of course entirely a male prerogative—and a third for insulting a preacher and mocking his doctrine."[24]

Maintenance of this New Jerusalem of sex and violence required strict control of the female saints. Always undergirding apocalyptic politics, male supremacy flares into a savagery bearing no resemblance to the hopes which had gathered the new *Gemeynde*.

Consistent with prior movements, the aim was "to kill all monks and priests and all rulers that there are in the world." Again, the bloody wrath they invoke backs up upon the community. The starving, besieged population is mercilessly massacred. Throughout the region, Anabaptism— "re-baptism"—was made a capital offense, and "countless men and women in the towns were beheaded, drowned, burnt or broken on the wheel."[25] Münster's particularly revolting violence can only be read against a background of prior state violence, whose reactive slaughter as usual grossly exceeded that of the radicals in quantity and brutality.

If revolutionary violence mirrors that of the rising patriarchal nation state, it adds a fanaticism driven by desperation and apocalypse. Apocalyptic community obsessively presses toward purification, toward homogenization—"to praise God through Christ with one heart and mind." It gathers its strength to dissent against heretofore barely questionable authorities by eliminating internal dissent. It forges its oneness through the purge, its actualization through the sword. But recall the time frame. Noticeably lacking in these early modern enactments of endtime is any planning for the future. Since Christ would take charge in the wake of the imminent bloodbath, there was no time and no need for patient community-building, for suffering and sorting through disappointments in each other and ambiguities of vision, let alone for developing long-term strategies of resistance. (Analysis of the means of production awaits later apocalypses.) Revolution, son of Revelation, offers all or nothing, now or never—anything lukewarm is to be spit out of the messianic mouth.

And repeatedly the women comrades, bringing their hopes for liberation to the struggle, would be betrayed. One must suspect that then and
now their full participation, essential to these struggles, would demand
a counter-apocalyptic practice of daily deference to difference.

1652, England

Forced underground with increasing rigor on the Continent, the center
of the revolutionary apocalypse seems to have shifted to England. When
it sublimates its warrior-violence, when it notices the needs of the earth,
it may be less likely to make an impact in history. But these other
branches of utopia, eschewing the dream of rebirth through violence,
belong also to the apocalyptic heritage.

As does, for instance, the communalism of Gerard Winstanley, a key
player in what revisionist historian Christopher Hill dubbed "the revolution within the revolution" of seventeenth-century England. The Puritans had fought perhaps the first successful apocalyptic revolution, de-
capitated a king, established the Protectorate of Oliver Cromwell and
with it the Parliament. Abolishing feudal tenures and arbitrary taxation,
they enfranchised a new class—the men of property. Thus the Puritans
replaced the divine right of kings not with apocalyptic communism but
with the sacred rights of property. But before they instituted the "imperialist foreign policy" of the 1608 settlement, creating a new world "safe for
business men to make profits in," there was a period of "glorious flux"
and intellectual excitement. As Winstanley put it, "The old world . . . is
running up like parchment in the fire." According to Hill, the revolution
which "never happened, though from time to time it threatened . . .
might have established communal property, a far wider democracy in
political and legal institutions, might have disestablished the state
church and rejected the protestant ethic."[26] This revolutionary counterculture woven of Quakers, Fifth Monarchy Men, Ranters, Levellers,
Diggers, and others shared the millennialist excitement of the moment
and a disappointment in the Commonwealth articulated here by Winstanley:

> While this kingly power reigned in one man called Charles, all sorts of
> people complained of oppression. . . . Thereupon you that were the gentry,
> when you were assembled in Parliament, you called upon the poor com-

mon people to come and help you. . . . That top bough is lopped off the tree of tyranny, and the kingly power in that one particular is cast out. But alas, oppression is a great tree still, and keeps off the sun of freedom from the poor commons still.[27]

The revisionist Hill warns against the conventional "lunatic fringe" label for these remarkably diverse groups flourishing during the two decades before the Restoration brutally suppressed them. Indeed, he suggests that "a partial lapse from 'sanity' may have been the price to be paid for certain insights." Thus Winstanley, knowing himself referred to as madman, counters that "the declaration of righteous law shall spring up from the poor, the base and despised ones and fools of the world."[28]

Winstanley, the intellectual leader of the colony of Diggers, left much more text than did most of the early modern prophets. The project was to dig up the massive commons of England for the use of the poor, the "commoners," who had traditional rights in the common–rights long abrogated by the aristocracy and even more by the bourgeois Puritans. Winstanley's argument–that the communal cultivation of the commons must provide the starting point from which common people could build up an equal community–stands as the only democratic and realistic solution proposed by the radicals. "The bondage the poor complain of," he wrote, is "that they are kept poor by their brethren in a land where there is so much plenty for everyone." He proposed a sophisticated agricultural program based on intensive manuring: "True religion and undefiled is to let every one quietly have earth to manure"[29] (a splendid metaphor for theology itself).

The Diggers sowed their land with carrots, parsnips, and beans, crops which were to transform English agriculture by keeping cattle alive through the winter in order to fertilize the land. Winstanley founded his vision on a kind of midrash on the *Genesis* text of creation and original sin:

> The great creator, Reason, made the earth to be a common treasury, to preserve beasts, birds, fishes and man. . . . Not one word was spoken in the beginning that one branch of mankind should rule over another. . . . But . . . selfish imaginations . . . did set up one man to teach and rule over another. And thereby . . . man . . . became a greater slave to such of his own kind than the beasts of the field were to him. And hereupon the earth . . .

was hedged into enclosures by the teachers and rulers, and the others were made ... slaves ... whereby the great Creator is mightily dishonoured, as if he were delighting in the comfortable livelihood of some and rejoicing in the miserable poverty ... of others.[30]

Domination counts as the original sin, and the enclosure of habitat as its first symptom. The shift of God to "Reason"–recalling the classical Logos–references Bacon and the rudimentary development of natural science. But Winstanley's is an immanent rather than a deist deity: "To know the secrets of nature is to know the works of God."[31] His theology soon outgrew notions of an apocalyptic intervention, indeed of any controlling providence. His critique of otherworldly eschatology scathingly anticipates Feuerbach. Thus the priests of state religion

lay claim to heaven after they are dead, and yet they require their heaven in this world too, and grumble mightily against the people that will not give them a large temporal maintenance. And yet they tell the poor people that they must be content with their poverty, and they shall have their heaven hereafter. ... While men are gazing up to heaven, imagining after a happiness or fearing a hell after they are dead, their eyes are put out, that they see not what is their birthright, and what is to be done by them here on earth while they are living.[32]

This is modern emancipatory discourse: vision means opening our eyes. It no longer simply pits the supernatural against the establishment, but exposes the collusion of supernaturalism *with* the establishment–without losing any of the righteous fervor and futurist faith of apocalypse. Denouncing the "bloody and thieving power," he does not resort to threats of blood; he is preoccupied not with vindication and purification but with economic justice. Nor does his millennialism depend any longer upon any last minute divine intervention (as, poignantly, it did for Münzer). He represents a prophetic conditional: "But when once the earth becomes a common treasury again, as it must ... then this enmity of all lands will cease, and none shall dare to seek dominion over others, neither shall any dare to kill another."[33]

The colony of Diggers endured for two years. After its collapse, Winstanley wrote of a communal utopia. But, unlike those of More and Bacon, courtiers of middle-class origin who never founded communities, his utopia is rarely mentioned. In it education is pivotal–the world would be persisting. Rare for seventeenth-century imagination, this vision of education in "all arts and languages" was to include both sexes and all classes. Winstanley's philosophical views of gender complementarity do not imply an equality in practice, and leave much to be desired. Yet his passing warning to women against joining the Ranters, a radical sect which actually practiced the libertinism of which most radical communities are accused, indicates a protectionist but respectful awareness of the concrete circumstances of women: "The mother and child begotten in this manner is like to have the worst of it, for the man will be gone and leave them, and regard them no more than other women . . . after he hath had his pleasure. Therefore you women beware, for this ranting practice is not the restoring but the destroying power of the creation. By seeking their own freedom they embondage others."[34] Even more in the pre-contraceptive age, women's liberation–as we rediscovered in the sixties of this century–hardly equaled sexual liberation.

With Winstanley we come close to the counter-apocalyptic impulse, a place-conscious practice of community grounded in an economic theory of the commons in a world renewed not by divine fiat, but by human action. It lives life for the long run. Evil is redefined as dominative power, and so God also forfeits the transcendent trappings of sovereignty. If the possibility of an eco-democratic approach brooded fleetingly here, let us retain the clue of the commons: that "community" of common people requires the justice of common access to the earth. At the end of the twentieth century, the ecological movement had reclaimed the critique of enclosure and the idea of a global commons in resistance to eco-apocalypse. Indeed, environmentally oriented communities (often led by third-world women) such as the Chipco movement enact the clearest analogy to the Diggers.

1812, Southeastern United States

By definition we cannot construct a counter-apocalyptic conception of community on the basis of white European sources only, without interrupting the seeming continuity of the foregoing narrative. Joel W. Martin's case study of the Muskogees' "struggle for a new world," *Sacred Revolt*, performs a kind of Foucaultian archeology of a particular, millennialist revolution among the largest nation of Southeastern (U.S.) Native Americans.[35] I choose it to consider because it is far less known than the case of the apocalyptic Ghost Dance movement, crushed at Wounded Knee, and also because of a certain multiracial intricacy.

In 1813, "the Muskogees were confronting a difficult complex of political changes and cultural challenges, internal conflicts and economic crises."[36] Conquest, trade, and alcohol were devastating traditional spirituality; Muskogee communities were subject to an increasingly uneasy peace with the Georgia settlers, who lusted after their land and had ruled that any offense by any Muskogee was grounds for indiscriminate retribution against any Muskogee person or village. Given constant incursion into their hunting grounds and a recent plan to build a road right through their territory, the chiefs could not always restrain warriors from acts of defiance. An earthquake set the apocalyptic mood. But the precipitant occurred in 1812, when several chiefs, pressured by the New York Treaty and by governor Hawkins, put to death several Muskogee men for crimes against Anglo-American settlers.

A group of "critical shamans" sprang into existence, fingering the shaman of the "friendly chiefs" as led by a "diabolical spirit." Between 1812 and 1814 the Maker of Breath—the Creator—granted the critical shamans the revelation that the time was ripe for revolt. The shamans, as prophets, announced that the Spirit of the Universe opposed the colonial invasion and the despiritualization of Muskogee.[37] The spirits of the land and the ancestors demanded the expulsion of the invaders and their native collaborators as the only means to restore order and balance. The campaign was launched with the killing of the colluding shaman, then the chiefs of numerous other towns, first those friendly with U.S. agents, and then—by a familiar pattern—any who opposed the revolt. Increasing numbers of Muskogees defected to the prophets.

The rebels' purificatory process involved a radical surrender of their colonized identity, hence they killed cattle and shed ornaments of silver and brass, farm implements, and other trade goods. The rebel women burned their muslin dresses. Martin likens the process to initiation rituals: "Acts of destruction were necessary as a kind of prelude . . . within a larger transformation drama." In the spring of 1813 the rebels moved their camps away from the towns into the woods, the site of the traditional rites—and, we note, a recursion to the hunter-gatherer lifeway. "Movement in space was correlated with a passage toward sacred transformation.... By resettling in the wild woods where so many of their rites of passage occurred, Muskogees embraced communal rebirth, their collective initiation into the New World identity of 'red people.'"[38] In the overhunted wilderness they came to depend on women's gathering skills. And, above all, the rebels danced—a complex, traditional but transformed set of ritual steps prepared them both for war and the new world. "On the verge of receiving a new identity, the Muskogee rebels felt more than ever the need to dance a radically new dance, to move their bodies in a new way in and into a new space/time."[39] (Whereas Hebrews had needed to "sing a new song.")

Though the Redsticks—the name given the rebels, after a red baton they carried—directed their fury mainly against collaborators, the whites inevitably got involved. The violence escalated horribly. In 1814, nine thousand Muskogees, with few firearms, were annihilated by a force of fifteen hundred Anglo-Americans, five hundred Cherokees, and one hundred "friendly" Muskogees. The revolt was extinguished, the aftermath horrific for the "friendly" Muskogees as well, resulting in the greatest land cession of the Southeast. But there is more to excavate.

The analogies of the Redstick revolt to the European precedents expose a pattern of community desperately attempting to redeem an original identity—whether of the first church or of tribal tradition—by a purifying violence that willy-nilly results in group martyrdom. But let us contextualize the similarity within the multicultural ambiguity of an *anti*-Christian apocalypse. Millennial revolutions seeking to restore lost community along egalitarian spiritual lines have a long history in Africa, Asia, Oceania, and Latin America, as Bryan Wilson, Kenelm Burridge, and others point out.[40] Their prophets teach a new revelation, in which resurgent indigenous symbols authorize the new imagery of a final, cleansing conflict in which the indigenous people, reborn, overcome the colonial powers with the help of the spirit(s) and so open a new age of communal integrity and abundance. Almost always, these movements take the form of communities resisting the annihilation of their identities by modernity—and they almost always fail. Not surprisingly, this apocalyptic pattern does not seem to occur apart from Christian influence. Thus among Christians or pagans, apocalypse catalyzes revolution against the received Christianity; the text of the apocalypse finds its way to mostly preliterate peoples suffering from dislocation—like the early Christians, but that the imperialists now come bearing bibles.

In the case of the Muskogees, the plot thickens: white missionaries do not seem to have been the key transmitters of the millennial myth. Martin makes an intriguing case that the revolutionary potentiality of apocalyptic teaching was relayed by black slaves and runaways. Among African Americans, he notes, "conversion was both a colonial and a counter-colonial process."[41] With no access to the long tradition of European resistance, African American slaves had on their own decoded the Exodus and Apocalypse symbols: in prayer and song, they invoked a God who would bring judgment on the oppressors, liberate the slaves, heal the suffering, and usher them into a Promised Land "where the streets are pearl and the gates are gold." Though the role of eschatology is subject to debate among African American scholars, some have argued that blacks used the idea of heaven to justify their belief that in spite of all, "God was liberating them from earthly bondage."[42]

In Goose Creek, South Carolina, a center for trade with the Muskogees, in 1710 an Anglican missionary was disturbed upon finding a local African American community entranced by apocalyptic teachings:

> The best scholar of all the negroes in my parish and a very sober and honest liver, through his learning was like to create some confusion among all the negroes in this country. He had a book wherein he read some description of the several judgments that chastise men because of their sins in these latter days . . . and he told his master abruptly there would be a dismal time and the moon would be turned into blood and there would be a dearth of darkness and went away.[43]

In the following century, hundreds of African American slaves ran away yearly to join Muskogee villages, sometimes as free persons, sometimes as slaves (accepting a more humane form of bondage—they could marry into the family, and their children were born free). Two German Moravian missionaries in 1812(!) report being refused permission to preach to the African American slaves of a Muskogee chief, who complained that the slaves "had been made sullen and crazy" by the message of a black preacher named Phil. This preacher had urged African American and Native American residents of Muskogee "to anticipate a fiery final judgment against the powerful." Some Muskogees did not share the chief's irritation with apocalypse.[44]

Yet something nags at this racial picture. The story of an African American delivery of the germs of millennialism to the Muskogees may be valid. At least it illustrates the strange history of Apocalypse spiralling back to make its intercultural impact upon colonized peoples. But there have been no major millennialist movements among African Americans. "Curiously," notes Charles Lippy in a reflection on the Ghost Dance, "chiliastic expectations have not flourished among the other group of Americans, the Blacks, who have suffered as much, if not more, repression and oppression than the Indians." Why not? Because slavery "frequently snuffed out obvious remnants of African tribal traditions. . . . Black Americans were deprived of an historical past and even of a mythological past," Lippy suggests. "History and myth have generally provided the springboard for millennial dreams." Given the eradication of community through the systematic separation of members of language groups upon arrival and routine selling of family members, it is a matter not just of the loss of tradition, but of some communal continuity in which tradition could be remembered—and restored for revolutionary solidarity. Lippy finds the apocalyptic element in slave religion minimal, that black Christianity stresses instead "conversion, sanctification, perfection, and rigid morality."[45]

These emphases, however, went hand in hand with apocalypse. Black scholars tend to agree with James Cone that "Black slaves also expressed their anticipation of God's new future with apocalyptic imagination. 'Where shall I be when the first trumpet soun'; soun' so loud till it woke up de dead?'" God's kingdom, or Heaven, "was God's eschatological promise; it was a place of 'golden streets,' 'pearly gates,' and 'the long white robes.' There would be no more sadness, no more sorrow and more hunger—for everybody is 'goin' feast off'n milk an' honey.'"[46] With Exodus, the New Jerusalem supplies a constant refrain in the religion of African Americans.[47] How then account for the lack of a millennial movement?

James Cone throws light on the much-debated issue of the supernatural eschatology: "What could freedom mean for black slaves who could never expect to participate in the determination of the laws governing their lives? Must they continue to define freedom in terms of the possibility of escape and insurrection, as if their humanity depended on their willingness to commit suicide?"[48] Slaves had far less opportunity than other colonized groups to arm and organize. But since their own millennialist revolts almost invariably led to self-destruction, might we venture to guess that African American Christianity worked its eschatological future free of the suicidal literalizations of the New Jerusalem—and yet managed to do so in a way that maintained a tradition of self-affirming apocalyptic dissent, fostering the survival of body, soul, and community?

"Even where there is no overt or hidden reference to specific historical events," argues Cone, "the spirituals employ eschatological language to express transcendence in the slaves' recent existence. 'I've *started* to make heaven my home,' 'Marching up the heavenly road, I'm bound to fight til I die'—such lines make clear that black slaves were not passively waiting for the future; they were actively living as if the future was already present in their community."[49] African Americans have kept alive—however marginally and uncertainly—a tradition of spirituality at work to sustain community under ungodly stress. Womanist theologian Delores Williams would lift into prominence the value of survival in distinction from liberation—which is often dualistic, macho, and unavailable.[50] One suspects the powerful hands of women in this network of nonviolent subversion (consider the work of Harriet Tubman).

In this the black community would be simmering its own apocalyptic elements into counter-apocalypse—a practice of resistance to white supremacist genocide. As in their own way did Native Americans. Most tribers never engaged in suicidal revolutions, and within them all are groups (such as the Native American Church) who have learned to bide their time, with complex ritual syncretisms fostering spiritual integrity and communal memory rather than purity and once-for-all apocalypse. I have not wished to dishonor the revolutionary impulse—only somehow to loosen the grip of its self-victimizing, violent absolutes on the possibility of community.

3

"Into these 'utopian' social systems there enters all the force of dispossessed Messianism," writes Martin Buber.[51] But because of the economic momentum of the end of the millennium—a global force for which apocalyptic beast imagery is tempting—"community" and "individuality" cannot be addressed apart from economics. The transnational marketplace is busy destroying any social and ecological basis for community.[52] And the loss of the socialist alternative makes it all the more important to dredge up the links from religious apocalyptic revolt to the socialist forms of communitarianism which have shaped all Western progressive movements. Else we lose track of the story before it reaches us.

In his under-read *Paths in Utopia*, Martin Buber hunts down the concomitants of a decisive polarization: Engels and Marx's rejection of their utopian socialist predecessors. It would seem that communism—like Christianity—could have evolved differently. This is not a merely abstract claim. There was a powerful option, highly developed in theory and in practice, which could have carried the day. (The could-have-been becomes meaningful when what-has-been collapses, sucking all related options toward its black hole.) As Soviet communism was coming into its own, just before the revelation of the horrors of Stalin, Buber raised "a still small voice" on behalf of socialist communalism, dismissed by the left as utopian. Yet his experience of the kibbutz movement, "an experiment that did not fail," motivated him to thus marginalize himself.

Buber, like Ernst Bloch, derived the entire history of socialism, utopian and postutopian, from its biblical roots. Thus "the social system of modern socialism or communism has, like eschatology, the character of an annunciation." He distinguishes between the nineteenth-century effects of "apocalyptic eschatology" on the one hand, and those of "prophetic eschatology" on the other, as they issue through the bottleneck of the French Revolution.

> The whole force of dispossessed eschatology was converted into Utopia at the time of the French Revolution.... In the socialist secularization of eschatology they work out separately: the prophetic form in some of the systems of the so-called Utopians, the apocalyptic one above all in Marxism (which is not to say that no prophetic element is operative here—it has only been overpowered by the apocalyptic).[53]

Let me emphasize: We cannot evaluate our own sociality without some sense of how the earlier, ruder religious apocalypses pattern this secularization. Although we cannot here detail the extraordinary wave of utopianism which suffused Europe and America in the nineteenth century, to understand Buber's claim that the French Revolution translates religious apocalypse into secular modernity we must take note of where its precedents and antecedents pick up the torch of apocalypse.

After its radical convulsions were stifled, the spirit of utopia passed mainly from seventeenth-century England to eighteenth-century France. There, retaining perhaps a refined philosophical theism of Love, it freed itself not just from clericalism but from the narratives of Christian faith. Repelled by the millenarian Anabaptists, the Enlightened *philosophes* for the most part mocked or ignored the hundreds of utopias based on the model of More or disseminated in pamphlets and novels.

On this Jean-Jacques Rousseau broke rank. *Le Contrat Social* sounds a theme nearly lost with Winstanley: "Man was born free, and everywhere he is in chains." Rousseau's naturalist utopia, the dream of the "new man," in whom love would erase the boundary between the individual and the collective will, infused a new age of millennialism with a mesmerizing psychological complexity; its multilayered tinder would catch fire in the French Revolution. At once confessing his own psychology of masochistic "femininity" and espousing a militantly masculine upbringing for boys, Rousseau inseminated revolutionary sensibility with an erotic atmosphere of dissident honesty and recalcitrant misogyny.

Rousseau captured another, more distant "other" within his text–the fantasy of the Noble Savage so prevalent throughout Europe since the conquest. Voltaire, by contrast, consistent with his anti-utopian stance, considered the genocide of Native Americans all to the good. Thus the myth of the Savage Beast shadowed that of the Noble Savage. It is no small irony that the renewal of the Christian millennium for the modern age borrowed some of its concreteness, its sense of historic possibility, from the stories of quite egalitarian, peaceful democracies of pagans in a "state of nature." (Although most genealogies of the American Revolution and the U.S. Constitution emphasize their roots in the European and especially the French Enlightenment, and they often neglect to consider the contribution of *natively* Americans to the Enlightenment.) Yet one reads here no triumphal of return of Native elements but a dialectic of colonization, loving and hating, desiring and thieving, disguising and romanticizing goods which would always eventually be used against the giver. Rousseau signalled no more than an influential moment in the transformation of apocalyptic millennialism in the conquest of the Americas. Yet certain nativist-Rousseauesque influences perhaps kept alive an old indigenous egalitarian hope of Europe, offering it to a New World which to this day withholds equality from those inspiring "savages."

The apocalyptic utopia continued to issue in and resist the revolutions which erected Western democracy and communism. Condorcet, touched by Rousseau, proclaimed endless progress via *Raison* toward a pure and communist egalitarianism reminiscent of the previous century's religious revolutionaries. But it was a chillier order that prevailed. The Jacobins saw themselves as fighting communists on the one hand and aristocrats on the other; they forged the revolutionary triumph of the bourgeoisie. Rejecting Enlightenment gradualism, the Jacobins resorted to a speedier transformation through violence. "In this respect," comment Frank Manuel and Fritzie Manuel, "they resemble in spirit the ancient Judeo-Christian writers who foretold the apocalypse–widespread destruction followed by an eternal Sabbath." An unchanging state of "virtue" not unlike the timeless fixity of the New Jerusalem will be plucked from the fires of the revolution: "Saint-Just and Robespierre were among the last of the great static utopians of calm felicity."[54] "What do they want," wrote Saint-Just, Rousseau's disciple and Robespierre's utopian partner, "those who want neither virtue nor terror? Force does not make a thing either reasonable or right. But it is perhaps impossible to do without it, in order to make right and reason respected."[55] The head of this "archangel of the Terror" (universally praised as erect and handsome) rolled along with Robespierre's.

Another fan of Rousseau, François Babeuf, would revive the communist egalitarianism. An early enthusiast of the revolution, he was disillusioned by the ensuing economic misery. Soon his journal, *Le Tribun du Peuple*, called for a new apocalypse: "All evils have reached their peak. Things cannot get worse. A cure can come about only through a total upheaval!!!! Let confusion reign! Let all the elements be confounded and entangled, let them clash with one another! . . . Out of the chaos may a new, regenerated world be born."[56]

When his "conspiracy of the equals" to overthrow the revolutionary Directorate was uncovered, Babeuf and his manifesto were liquidated. The latter was revived by Buonarroti in the French communist tradition of the next century, and would serve the later Marxist movement as precursor. Buonarotti called for "*égalité réelle*,"[57] not the laissez-faire economics of the French Revolution: full commonality of food and property. "Community" would encompass the nation. His blueprints for the period after the revolution became a manual for the next century's revolutionaries, especially the idea which came to be known as "the dictator-ship of the proletariat."

In the following century, a new revolutionary doctrine of love would permeate the vision of the just community. Saint-Simon, Charles Fou-rier, and Robert Owen inspired simultaneous movements charged with millennialist rhetoric of a new moral age. Youthful idealists throughout Europe and the United States—among whom were a number of women of all classes—flocked to these figures and formed societies discussing and enacting their ideas. Despite the inevitable rivalries between the three schools, they all preferred persuasion to violence and conceived of the new social order as built up of small communities in association. They taught a mutual alignment of work and love, in which work would be done equitably but from desire—and desire would express itself as well in a new sexual freedom. One possibility of apocalypse barely hinted at heretofore now broke into the open: in the new order, women's equality with men in all things is declared.

Perilously and prophetically blended with what Saint-Simon called the rehabilitation of the body—especially sexual practice freed from bourgeois hypocrisies—"the emancipation of women became the symbol of the liberation of bodily desires."[58] The Saint-Simonian Enfantin en-gaged in a quixotic quest for the "Female Messiah" and preached a God of both sexes; he analyzed the psychic debasement as well as material enslavement of women, to be replaced by a new sexual order of human affections in equality. In this regard the trope of the Great Whore under-goes a stunning rhetorical transformation. Writing on the dependence of bourgeois morality upon prostitutes, Enfantin condemns the men who safeguard the chastity of their own daughters by "levying a tribute upon the daughters of the poor who walked the streets."[59]

> They squeeze and they tread upon the flesh of these women as if they were grapes of the vine—women glowing with freshness or already stained with mud, women plucked before their time or savory and mature—they bring them all to their lips only in order to cast them away with contempt. . . . All in this great Babylon drink the wine of a frenzied prostitution.[60]

Fourier also engaged the needs and wants of women in his critique of the institution of marriage. He would finally make a proposal that would hold some interest to poststructuralist feminists or queer theorists interested in breaking out of any gender twoness. "To confound the tyranny of men there should exist for a century a third sex, male and female, one stronger than man." He considered himself an *omnigyne*, a male "Sapphianist or a protector of lesbians."[61] When Marxism picked up elements of the utopian polemic against bourgeois marital hypocrisy, it omitted the socialists' sexuality and spirituality.

The leaders of these erotico-eschatological movements adopted the role of religious messiah. Saint-Simon apparently thought himself the reincarnation of Socrates and Charlemagne, and his disciples likened him to Jesus; Fourier found his own appearance foretold from scripture. "Dry your tears and rejoice, for I have come in the name of God, of Saint-Simon, and of my Fathers to make you see the brilliant colors that will soon burst forth before your eyes," announced Enfantin in 1832. Owen, author of *The New Moral World*, identified not just with Jesus but with Columbus, and announced the imminent age in 1834: "This . . . is the Great Advent of the World, the second coming of Christ. . . . The first coming of Christ was a partial development of Truth to the few. . . . The second coming of Christ will make Truth known to the many. . . . The time is therefore arrived when the foretold millennium is about to commence."[62] The letters *C. M.* were carved above the entrance to Owenite buildings, inscribing the Commencement of the Millennium. While these nineteenth-century utopians do not engage in a deterministic apocalypse so much as in prophetic confidence, their optimistic millennialism (despite Buber's distinction) does not avoid John and hail only to Isaiah. It transmogrifies, quite continuously with Joachim's Age of the Free Spirit, the mythology of the Christian apocalypse.

Saint-Simon, Fourier, and Owen, acknowledged in this by Engels as the founders of socialism, anticipated the analysis of "the alienation of work." They advocated the formation of communities of free solidarity (the "secret of association") in opposition to the French Revolution, which had dissolved guilds and association in favor of free competition. Fourier's "association communale sur le terrain de la production et de la consummation" would be developed by Owen into a transformation of society as a whole as well as in its communal cells. This, comments Buber, "is the foundation of socialism."

In the next generation, Pierre Proudhon would dissociate himself from these "systems" while continuing their line of development. Warning above all against absolutism, he insistently entered into the complex contradictions of the social order, proclaiming "defatalization" as the delivering principle. His full-scale economic analysis of oppression proposed a principle of "mutualism," the building up of an economy on reciprocity of service.

Why did Marx then move from an acknowledgment of these forerunners to a polemic against their "hodgepodge of Anglo-French socialism or communism and Hegelian philosophy," especially against Proudhon, representative of the French workers' movement, for his "sham opposition to the Utopians"? It turns out that six months before he denounced Proudhon in 1846, Marx had invited him to collaborate in a "correspondence," for "as regards France we all believe we could find no better correspondent than yourself." Proudhon refused. His reasons ring prophetic:

> Let us, if you wish, look together for the laws of society, the manner in which they are realized, but after we have cleared away all these *a priori* dogmatisms, let us not, for God's sake, think of tangling people up in doctrines in our turn! Let us not fall into the contradiction of your countryman Martin Luther who, after having overthrown the catholic theology, immediately set about founding a protestant theology of his own amid a great clamor of excommunications and anathemas.... Because we stand in the van of a new movement let us not make ourselves the protagonists of a new religion, even if it be a religion ... of reason.[63]

The differences become stark: Proudhon opposed all centralization beyond that which the immediate context required, and opposed any order imposed from above. Of the ascendent German socialism he wrote, "This dictatorial, authoritarian, doctrinaire system starts from the axiom that the individual is subordinate in the very nature of things to the collectivity; ... the citizen belongs to the State as the child to his family, he is in its power and possession, and he owes it submission and obedience in all things."[64] It was the socialism of Marx and Engels, intent on the production of doctrines and the state apparatus for their absolute and universal establishment, which carried history. Proudhon, decried by Marx as "the tapeworm of socialism," wanted to multiply the local associations and organic communities which the Marxist revolution would crush even more surely than the French.

"This is not to say," comments Buber regarding the totalitarian authority of this centralism, "that Lenin was a centralist pure and simple":

But the revolutionary-political motif dominated as with Marx and Engels and suppressed the vital social motif which requires decentralized community-living. . . . The upshot of all this was that there was no trace in the new State-order of any agency aiming at the liquidation of State centralism and accumulation of power. As Lenin remarked in 1918: 'When has any State begun to wither away.'[65]

How ironic that the great example history has since bequeathed to us of a state's self-liquidation is that of the Soviet Union. And that its voluntary dissolution has decentralized power in such a way as to betray—despite Gorbachev's efforts—not only any socialist hope but the vestiges of community as well. Yet, even if Buber's concluding prophecy lurches toward the apocalyptic, it may be that he divined the depth of the danger: "For the last three decades we have felt that we were living in the initial phases of the greatest crisis humanity has ever known." At the end of the Second World War, he did not perceive even its Holocaust as the ultimate order of doom, but as a "symptom" of this crisis: "It is not merely the crisis of one economic and social system being superseded by another, more or less ready to take its place; rather all systems, old and new, are equally involved. . . . What is in question . . . is nothing less than man's [sic] whole existence in the world."[66]

Yet Buber's neoapocalypse, like all eschatology which resists the temptation to invest some determinist agency with the power to purvey the utopia, avoids retrograde literalism by means of his prophetic conditional. Unlike Marx and Engels, he makes no promise of annihilation or salvation, nor does he relinquish what he deems "the primary aspiration of all history," that of "genuine community of human beings—genuine because it is *community all through*." He offers the sturdy kibbutzim as an icon of the persistent possibility of a commonwealth of communities. Today the very notion of a community as locus of multiple I-Thou relationships arrayed round a "common center" wears a Buberian halo, perhaps despite his effort to guard it "against all contamination by sentimentality or emotionalism." Let us nonetheless distill from his meditation a criterion of community:

Community should not be made into a principle; it, too, should always satisfy a situation rather than an abstraction. The realization of community, like the realization of any idea, cannot occur once and for all time: always it must be the moment's answer to the moment's question, and nothing more.[67]

We may presume that the apocalypticism he decries in its hardening into a centralized "end" finds its cure in such a wariness of universalizing and eternalizing abstraction, even of his own "common center."

4

We recall that the Book of Revelation conceives of both salvation and damnation only collectively. Yet we caught hardly a whiff of intentional community in the sense Proudhon suggests, of relatively autonomous groupings working not for another but for *one another*, collaborating in production and consumption. Such communities live on the strength of their internal relations and enter into federation–what today we call co-alition–with other free associations.

By contrast, the communities constitutive of apocalyptic Christianity, like apocalyptic communism, derive from something outside, from a transcendent unifying center. In the New Jerusalem, the tearless citizens are not shown communing with *each other*. The practice of mutuality finds biblical representation in the Gospels' ethic of the commonwealth of God, in Paul's image for the Corinthians of the body of mutual participation, in the *agape* communism of Acts–but not in Revelation. "The throne of God and the Lamb will be in it; and His slaves will serve Him. And they will see His face; and His name will be on their foreheads" (Rev. 22:3f). The elect, the slaves of God, seem riveted to a fixed center, to an eternal vision of the divine throne. If the pharaohs and the caesars had already provided a prototype of centralized power, the anti-imperialist John, like his Marxist heirs, opposes unjust power with the absolute righteousness of a higher center. The former pursues the certainty of faith, the latter that of reason. First the sword of the brotherhood is lifted in holy writ, then in revolutionary history.

Is the subtext of community after all indelibly apocalyptic–a righteous dream of unity, enclosed in sparkling multicolored love that dries all tears? One where, cleansed of shadows and swamps, freed from the sordid reminders of pain and mortality, not only oppression but its very possibility has been rooted out? What dissident "we," no doubt liberated from any belief in atonement, is not still stained–or bleached–by the blood of the Lamb? "One in heart and mind": how else fight the "diabolical spirit"? What feminist or ecological or racial or social justice solidarity does not define and simplify itself by its common enemy? In the name of our difference, do we also wound the impure, the unsure, the abject closest by (insiders who disappoint, who want too much or give too little) as often as we make a dent in the kingdom of the same? Always of course because we know "the system" seduces our movements. Thus even insider critiques seek to shame into confession rather than to engage in dialogue. Not to be seen as "lukewarm," white feminists, for instance, have spit at each other indignant charges–"male-identified," for instance, or "essentialist."

Is it this: That inasmuch as we succumb to the ancient nostalgia for a perfect future, we are likely to recapitulate its apocalyptic teleologies of unification? Or that when in reaction against this totalism we renege on the communality itself, we dissociate from the Western history of radical hope? For the dissociated, there awaits the cryptoapocalypse–the economic continuum of uninterrupted, *liberally* veiled sexism-colonialism-racism-speciesism, absorbing disillusioned bourgeois dissidents back into the business-as-usual bosom of Babylon. One by one.

5

So there he hung, and there I stood
The LAST MAN left alive,
To have my own will of all the earth:
Quoth I, now I shall thrive![68]

Individualism, which North American intellectuals at the end of this millennium both enact and deny, has also at certain moments unveiled its own apocalypse. Literary critic Steven Goldsmith describes a "brooding representation of eschatological themes that appeared around the French Revolution and peaked with the several 'last Man' works written between 1823 and 1826" as symptomatic of an "apocalyptic idealism." Thomas Hood's nineteenth-century quatrain, quoted above, parodies the genre. A species of romanticism, individualism's "struggle to liberate the self into an apocalyptic space free of all material contingency and social relations" reverses the communalism of the revolutionary apocalypses.[69] It has thus taken the motif of purification to its logical conclusion: not just the "bad" other but the other as such thwarts the integrity of the individual. Goldsmith reads Harold Bloom's "anxiety of influence" through this romantic solipsism. Bloom himself cites Thomas Mann with approval: "To be reminded that one is not alone in the world–always unpleasant." And then he adds, "It is another version of Goethe's question: 'Do we then live if others live?' "[70]

If on one extreme romanticism transposed apocalypse into a Rousseauesque psychology of relational merger, on the other its individual knows "himself" (always "him-") diminished by relationships with others. Others limit, impinge, demand, deplete; they mirror and so subdivide the self. Only the "last man" stands undivided, *individus*.[71] Thus a dysrelational, anerotic romanticism oddly mirrors the male virginity, the warrior celibacy, of the original Apocalypse.

Now, however, in the anticlimactic endtime of modernity, the dregs of both apocalypses, the revolutionary communalist and the anti-revolutionary individualist, slosh around in our subjectivities: a nostalgia for a solitary "we" and an allergy to "them." Moreover, whether in theological or atheist form, both edges of the romantic apocalypse construct the "I" as masculine sublime.[72] Feminist schools of psychoanalysis at least give an account of this double-edged ego-apocalypse. Nancy Chodorow and Dorothy Dinnerstein first theorized that bourgeois family units produce a separative male ego by way of an oedipal wound–the mark of the Lamb, inflicted in the painful "rapture" up out of the arms of the mother into paternal transcendence? Such an over-simplified male identity will alternately crave and dread intimacy with the m/other so early pushed off from, abjected. Not surprisingly, then, a foundational anxiety quivers along the edges of "subjects" (persons) sensing in themselves and toward themselves the flow of relations, subjects which to remain firmly self-enclosed as individuals must ever again spit out the mucous, the flux, of all that in-fluency. Or else erupt in spasms of communing dis/closure, which may open radically new space for the healing of the wound. But then such a community may no better tolerate otherness than the separative individual it opposes.

In a philosophical rather than a psychoanalytic key, Iris Marion Young has likewise argued that community and individualism confront each other as opposite poles of the same. Her feminist postulate comes attached to poststructuralist premises, the examination of which will allow us to pose the possibility of a feminist counter-apocalypse of community self-critically. Addressing the "ideal of community" as it emerges both in contemporary communitarianism and in the feminist movement, Young notes how "too often contemporary discussion of these issues sets up an exhaustive dichotomy between individualism and community. Community appears in the oppositions of individualism/community, separated self/shared self, private/public." In other words, current discourse tends to leave us no third option between the either/or of a "return" to a unifying community or the ongoing advance into a fragmenting individualism. But Young points to the "common logic underlying their polarity":

> Each entails a denial of difference and a desire to bring multiplicity and heterogeneity into unity, though in opposing ways. Liberal individualism denies difference by positing the self as a solid, self-sufficient unity, not defined by anything or anyone other than itself. . . . Proponents of community, on the other hand, deny difference by positing fusion rather than separation as the social ideal.[73]

Young sharply questions the ideal of community for its tendency to subordinate difference to unity. (Postmodernists, as Gore Vidal once quipped, always seek "more *pluribus* and less *unum*.") Since progressives have already delegitimated individualism, she launches a critique of communalism. Of course Young does not consider the apocalyptic subscript of community, yet her deconstruction of community as a "hopelessly utopian" denial of difference in some respects dovetails with the results of the foregoing history of revolutionary communities. "The most serious political consequence of the desire for community," she argues, "is that it often operates to exclude or oppress those experienced as different. Commitment to an ideal of community tends to value and enforce homogeneity."[74] Hence the revolutionary communalism presupposed by most progressivism (including my own) can revolve full circle, into reactionary format.

Indeed, in common parlance, "community" tends to refer to "the neighborhood," and appeals for its preservation come saturated with racist and classist regionalisms, along with nostalgia for the patriarchal family as the basic social unit. Right-wing hope may or may not lather into millennialist militias and mythologies, foaming with the apocalyptic discourse of revolt. Young targets the implicit conservatism of the politically moderate "communitarians," represented by theorists such as Michael Sandel, who had posed their community ideal as the only alternative to liberal individualism.[75] But her critique primarily addresses the new left. A "mystical ideal of community," she notes, "fails to solve the problem of how local communities, however successfully they integrate their differences within, are to relate to each other."[76] Therefore she seeks another framework within which to resolve the tension between democratic, regional decentralization and the wider exchange of resources, goods, and culture in which communities must partake. Proposing "empowerment" rather than "autonomy" for local communities in relation to the larger democratic process, she seems to echo the pre-Marxist socialist vision of loose federations of free, communal associations—minus of course its utopian grammar of love.

At the level of the social macrostructure, Young's proposal of a "politics of difference" replaces the model of the beloved community with that of the "good city." Politics must be conceived as a relationship of strangers who do not understand one another in a subjective and immediate sense, relating across time and distance."[77] While her critique of the political metanarrative of an overarching community of communities seems to me indispensable, its philosophical pre-text inspires less confidence. Out of her critique of postliberalism she pounces upon feminist relationalism per se—whether or not it in any sense implies such a macro-communitarianism. She positions as her foil Seyla Benhabib's notion of a "community of needs and solidarity," which involves a recuperation of earlier theories such as those of Carol Gilligan and Nancy Chodorow.

Advancing an ethic that conjoins justice with the female-identified values of care and responsibility, Benhabib had sought to defend feminist articulations of the social nature of the self. But Young philosophically suspects *any* appeal to mutuality and community of homogenism, pointing—as many white feminists now do routinely—to white feminist racism to make her case. While her "unveiling" of the deceptively inclusive utopia of sisters surely advances feminist self-critique, her argument shifts toward caricature just as she reveals her philosophical patrimony:

> In this ideal each understands the others and recognizes the others in the same way they understand themselves, and all recognize that the others understand them as they understand themselves. This ideal thus submits to what Derrida calls the metaphysics of presence.... This ideal of community denies the ontological difference within and between subjects. In community persons cease to be other, opaque, not understood and instead become mutually sympathetic ... fused.[78]

In other words, she cannot distinguish between fusion and mutuality, between the "Rousseauesque dream" and the mutuality of intersubjective selves. In her uncritical dependency upon Derrida, she indicts all mutualism for imagining the "copresence of subjects." Such ontological fusion as she diagnoses, predicated upon the ultimate transparency of final judgment, is surely implicated in apocalyptic community. But because Young fuses all relationality with fusion itself, she fails to do justice to the emerging feminist relationalism.

Certainly the ideal of mutuality allows for slippage into interpersonal merger–with all the attendant "exclusionary impulses." Yet the texts of Benhabib and the early work of Gilligan and Chodorow that Young retrieves, as well as the work of Sara Ruddick and "thealogians" such as Rita Nakashima Brock and Carter Heyward, all labor against just such a "feminized" misconstrual of community. I have also found it fruitful to distinguish a "connective" self from both the "separative" ego of modern white manhood and the "soluble" psyche toward which its female counterpart is socialized. Young's eye for Derridian *différance* blinds her to a pivotal feminist difference: between fusion and relation; between total consensus or transparency (understanding the others as they understand themselves) on the one hand, and "critical empathy" in the service of understanding on the other.[79]

On behalf of a "dialogical model of ethics," Benhabib has challenged Young's misreading of "mutual care and responsibility":

> Young is not heeding the distinction between 'consensus' and 'reaching understanding' introduced above. Admittedly, rationalistic theories of the Enlightenment and, in particular, Rousseau's theory of democracy were based on the illusion that a perfect consensus was possible; but ... this book envisages a continuous process of conversation in which understanding and misunderstanding, agreement as well as disagreement are intertwined and always at work.[80]

If apocalypse is the all-time conversation-stopper, we do well to build such a "dialogic model" of continuous conversation into a feminist counter-apocalypse. I think we can at the same time heed Young's exposé of the homogenizing tendency of community. But by rendering "community" the fall gal and giving no comparable energy to the critique of individualism, Young seems to play into the same dualism she decried—that of individualism versus communalism. Her own equivalent binary of opacity versus transparency replicates the logic of the "excluded middle."

Such a move illustrates a pitfall of poststructuralism for progressives—that it heralds "difference" while undercutting any theory of an interdependent subject and the ethics of its connections, and so quietly reconstitutes the privilege and practice of the old Enlightenment subject. As anti-essentialists often do, she herself performs the crucial essentialism: she fixes all relationalist voices within an identity most would not recognize as their own.[81] Given the messianic undertones of her own socialist-postmodern-feminist position, binary logic combines with political passion to homogenize its own other. Thus the apocalypse habit serves the trendy anti-apocalypse of "difference." "Difference"—as long as it is not gender difference—seems in this discourse to provide a wedge against some backslide into a feminine destiny, into a retrograde merger with mom and a lot of other white women. But perhaps a critically sharpened mutuality would protect us better than a reversion to manly opacity.

6

We have chosen each other
and the edge of each others battles
the war is the same
if we lose
someday women's blood will congeal
upon a dead planet
if we win
there is no telling
we seek beyond history
for a new and more possible meeting[82]

The moral objection to "community" applies to its unifying dynamic of exclusion. Therefore the self-articulation of the ethnic group most systematically and apocalyptically oppressed within United States cities (rather than Euroamerican arguments on its behalf) will serve as a test case. For instance, early on Audre Lorde–who also wrote the verses above–declared that "it is not those differences which are between us that are separating us. It is rather our refusal to recognize those differences, and to examine the distortions which have resulted from our misnaming them and their effects upon human behavior and expectation."[83]

In other words, the second-wave feminist tendency to obliterate differences of race–not to mention of economics, class, and in some circumstances sexual orientation–for the sake of the messianic unity of sisterhood inhibited our capacity to *connect*, "to use each other's difference to enrich our visions and our joint struggles."[84] By insisting that women must start with our differences, African American women were not recommending "opacity." The point was never to affirm difference as such–some differences, such as those of privilege, were obstacles to the "joint struggle" of the women's movement. Difference, like relation, is not to be uncritically celebrated but negotiated, discerned, transformed. In other words, though Lorde's community of revolt may echo the militant optimism of an earlier decade's apocalypse, it presupposes the vital interdependence of women's struggles and thus of women's communities. To evade the ricocheting bipolarities of the apocalypse habit, any relationalism worth defending works to hold the feet of our differences to the fire of mutuality.

Relative to the U.S. apocalypticism, in which all "black-and-white" dualisms carry the racial subtext, Lorde swings into counter-apocalypse: "The future of our earth may depend upon the ability of all women to identify and develop new definitions of power and new patterns of relating across difference."[85] The point of acknowledging difference is not to swat away our fleeting "copresences," but to right our relations. The "new and more possible meeting" inscribes in the cross-racial movements of women a shamelessly utopic hope. Yet what else would motivate the requisite depth of engagement with the white supremacy metabolizing not just in repressed collective attitudes but in the daily options of, for instance, any white feminist?

In the form of a dialogue–which reflects at the level of genre its relational content–performed for the sake of a text by bell hooks and Cornel West, we glean more evidence of African American (by contrast to white feminist antiracist) attitudes toward community: "It is important to note the degree to which Black people in particular and progressive people in general, are alienated and estranged from communities that would sustain and support us," comments West, whose "we" carefully avoids either pseudo-universalism or inverse exclusivism. "We are often homeless. Our struggles against a sense of nothingness and attempts to reduce us to nothing are ongoing. . . . That sense of home can only be found in our construction of those communities of resistance bell talks about and the solidarity we can experience within them. Renewal comes through participating in community."[86]

All progressives stand in danger of the alienation that comes from taking a prophetic stance, of then losing the capacity, as John of Patmos would call it, "to overcome" (Rev. 3:20). "In community one can feel that we are moving forward and that struggle can be sustained." West and hooks make the point for counter-apocalypse: "As we go forward as Black progressives"–and the following holds for other groups as well– "we must remember that community is not about homogeneity."[87]

In a move rewarding to a theologian, hooks, who (like West) freely, without parochialism, taps black church roots, gently challenges younger African American readers to a forthrightly spiritual discipline, "to be alone in that sense of Christ going into the garden of Gethsemane or going into the desert, or Buddha sitting under the Bodi tree." When West asks how such solitariness pertains to community, she replies: "It actually enables you to reenter community more fully. . . . The great gift of enlightenment . . . is the sense that only after we are able to experience ourselves in a context of autonomy, aloneness . . . are we able to come into community with knowledge of our place, and feeling that what we have to give is for the good of the whole."[88] It takes a special postmodern courage–of "knowledge of our place"–to invoke again the language of religious practice as essential to the common good. Perhaps at this moment it can only be conjured so disarmingly by a black feminist.

Similarly, Martin Buber had relativized his ideal of community, in its spacetime of associative "mutuality" to a particular context and moment. Yet if the moment of the kibbutz evokes the hope of another place, another era, his discourse seems to share the "spirit" of the foregoing minority writers. Buber, carefully circumambulating apocalypticism in its Marxist form, articulates three criteria: "It is community of tribulation and only because of that community of spirit; community of toil and only because of that community of salvation."[89] Again, pneumatological discourse enters to divert suffering from the loneliness of mere tragedy. Or rather, it tugs tragedy into good company.

In the blinding neon light of the New Jerusalems, in which the "other" stands with the self transparently disclosed, we readily retreat behind the blinders of an urbane opacity. But perhaps our very relations with those who have refused to acquiesce in just being "different" lead us to glimpse a subtler luminosity. In its shadowed glow, mutuality itself marks differences. We may there attend without pessimism or optimism to the conditions under which mutual understanding takes time and takes place. For those negotiating what might be shareable in the face of what appears incommensurable, both fusion and solipsism cease to be possibilities. Such a counter-apocalyptic sociality demands a critical sympathy working not just to understand the situation of the other person but to reconfigure my own situation accordingly.

Without this "feeling with," tinged as it may be by the pathos of love, social ethics reduces to virtuous abstractions. Young rightly warns against privileging face-to-face relations, in which intimacy barely reaches beyond the private realm. The point is precisely to conduct energy across the boundaries of individual and group self-enclosure into "the commons." But the motivation to go beyond resistance, to persist in insisting upon a just and sustainable social ecology, will require more than moralist extrapolations of difference. Beyond inevitable pronouncements of who is oppressed and who is oppressor, this endeavor demands some sense of overlapping project, of shareable timespace, indeed, of common good. Such sociality cannot draw opaque boundaries around either its individuals or its communities. Its place, constituted by shifting relationships rooted but not fixed in space and time, does not yield to a cartographically stable point or plane, to what Whitehead called "the fallacy of simple location." Rather, it clusters locally and vines globally.

Counter-apocalyptic sociality rehearses what mujerista ethicist Ada María Isasi-Díaz has defined as "solidarity"–"the practice of mutuality." It does not aim at any overarching community, but neither will it eschew crisscrossing communal solidarities. While affinity groups will likely comprise our nearest "community," nonetheless, if the homogenism of group identities is not to prevail, then a more radical mutuality, that of marked difference, must assert itself. In such moments a perilously high hope may be kindled, an eros (as Audre Lorde would say)[90] for some global solidarity of difference. We momentarily prefigure it, support it by institutional restructuring, but we only stabilize or substantialize its communal utopia by yielding to its apocalyptic subtext. And probably soon to the corollary disappointment of anti-apocalypse.

Benhabib claims that postmodernism has produced a "retreat from utopia" within feminism. We have highlighted such in the work of Thürmer-Rohr as well as that of Young. Not surprisingly, Benhabib dips into Bloch for her concluding consideration: "As the longing for the 'wholly other' (*das ganz Andere*), for that which is not yet, such utopian thinking is a practical-moral imperative. Without such a regulative principle of hope, not only morality but also radical transformation is unthinkable."[91]

Beset as my discipline remains by the theological neo-orthodoxy of the phrase "wholly other" (for Karl Barth it signified the sovereign difference of the exclusive One), I still want to agree with the spirit of her suggestion. But the longing for that other could dwell here and now. It could divest the endless deferral of a "wholly other," the eros of apocalypse, and instead practice its own present "be-longing."[92] It neither centers in nor plucks out that utopian eye, with which it inscribes upon the unknown its architectures of many-mansioned complexity, of multi-hued translucencies.

But where? Young's model of the "good city" may not strike readers of either John's Apocalypse or Augustine's *City of God* as any fresher than the ideal of community. "City"–Babylon or New Jerusalem–needs every bit as much cleanup work as "community" if it is not to reflect the injustices, numbness, and homelessness that it currently connotes. While it surely stimulates multicultural creativity, "city" suffers more than "community" from ecological oblivion of modern anthropocentrism. "The predilection of urbanites for apocalypse" concerns us because the city will remain for the foreseeable future the site for both the centering and decentering of civi/lization.[93] As normative ideal, "city" does not address the intrinsic sociality of self in the way that "community," as dissident counterculture, usually does. But city as place of civic interaction sustains the counter-apocalyptic possibility of a "global civil society."

Prefigured in the intersections of social movements and ethnic group-ings, indeed already advancing through the cooperation of nongovern-mental organizations standing close by but over and against the United Nations, such a civil society might struggle through to enough solidarity to counter the inertias of the free market cryptoapocalypse. It cannot be called a "community of communities," but rather at most a coalescence of communities.

What I am arguing is this: that there is no way to define where "com-munity" ends and mere coalition begins without thereby entrapping communities within the boundaries of their difference. This entrap-ment sabotages the fragile possibility of the larger solidarity. Regarding community, counter-apocalypse again invokes a healing ambivalence rather than a position "for" or "against." For if I try to name "my commu-nity" I come up against a mental wall: not identical with profession, church or social movement, nor with feminism, nor with a network of friends many of whom do not relate with each other. What *is* it then? Un-til engaging Young's challenge, I had seen this wall as my own, or as my sociological deficiency—my failure to quite find or recognize or produce "my community." So it is liberating not to need to wrap myself in some single, bounded community that could confer upon me that missing, unitary identity and purpose. I do not have this substantive community any more than I know a substantive self.

If not the substantive, the noun, how about the verb? "To commune" may risk a relational mysticism. But perhaps the risk is worth taking. Communing recalls a depth of social and spiritual practice that stays in process, that need not purge homogeneity and requires no idealized and stable community. For it does not posit a single end. It dis/closes the in-ternal sociality of a self composing itself out of its spatiotemporal rela-tions. It does not put a stop to the conversations which articulate its prac-tice. To commune intimates therefore a sociality of "congregating," that is, "gathering together": The *Gemeynde* as the commons, referring both to the common people and to that which is held in common economically and which holds us in common ecologically. And I mean to evoke a cer-tain nonexclusively ecclesial spirit: "to congregate" is to publicly cherish the communing moments and therefore to foster structures which sus-tain, remember, widen, and challenge its participating subjectivities. Communing here takes visible form. In its apocalyptic moments, Christianity sought to purge itself of impurities; yet in its concept of the "invisible church" it recognizes that it cannot rid itself of the ambiguities of visibility until that ever-deferred "end." But through the "communion of the holy spirit" congregants might empower themselves to resist, in German theologian Michael Welker's words, "the powers and principalities." "Their isolation as weak, consumeristically corrupted individualities, intoxicated by the mass media and without public resonance, is dissolved both for them and through them."[94] Not as isolated minds and lonely bodies do we find the solidity to practice alternate civilities. Rather, in the spirited embodiment tragically known as the Body of Christ—tragic because what was crucified was symbolically resurrected as that community, the *corpus christi*, only to be continually recrucified at the exclusionary boundaries of the triumphal Body.

To commune with one another, as bodies and as a body, "members one of another . . . grieving with each other's griefs, delighting in each other's joys" (1 Cor. 12:26). Too close for difference? Perhaps often. But if in the name of a politics of difference we draw the line around the communing body—these empathies stop here, community goes no further—then we perform a theoretical version of the orthodoxy which early possessed "the Body of Christ." The Word becomes flesh only when need, facing the absence of the m/other, articulates desire (Lacan). We grow into wordy bodies, socialities humming with conversation, each of us biotic communities in microcosm and in motion within the biotic community of the earth: the word materializes. Our ever momentary at-onement is not won by blood and violence but by the redemption of the flesh: "What is not assumed is not saved." The ancient mythology invests the flesh of the representative body, the Christ, with power to "save"—not to waste—by virtue of the sociality of enfleshment. This is the hope that the enlightened embodiment of one who had been in full mutuality with the others could permeate, through its re-membering, the common body. But contrary to the master narrative, it is we—in solitude and solidarity—who must reassume the bodies which Babylon violates and numbs. Only in the community which is a merged, simple unity rather than a complex "one" can a single heroic individual serve as a surrogate for the suffering of the rest, fusing to himself the destinies of his codependents. In the conspiracies of feminist counter-apocalypse, we release Jesus from endless recrucifixion "for our sins." This chapter, perhaps a secret

221

ecclesiology all along, grieves what-might-have-become of his body. It frees the man from the obligation to come again. It is only the living body which can.

7

In El Salvador, the term *convivencia* is used to express the postwar, post-revolutionary peace process, requiring grueling patience in the face of intolerable disappointments. But this "living-together" (often far from a city), more than communing or congregating, includes not only the comrades in solidarity but the enemies at the negotiation table: no choice, short of apocalypse. Apocalypse does not loom before us all equally, either as annihilation or as revolution. The subaltern *convivencia* of counter-apocalypse has much to teach those who, because of their economic, racial, or sexual placement, know neither crucifixion at the hands of the oppressor nor the spirit of a hope which will not stay in the grave. Such almost impossible endurance nurtures itself from the joy of its communing moments. Yet its conviviality might be contagious beyond its social locations.

In sum, temporary acts of mutuality, however they transfigure the real and prefigure the possible, do not for most of us congeal into "the community." Nor will these acts march forth, swords uplifted, to one more short-lived revolution. Their time does not revolve but spirals, their place is not utopia but topical. As in Buber's practice of shared work and suffering, moments of mutuality do motivate persistence and even a certain solidity in the face of "the tribulations." Communing moments, in the heat of history, can cook themselves into sustaining solidarities. "A new and more possible meeting": the mana appears. Not beasts feeding on a woman's body while angels gloat at the fall of the City, but the nurturant conviviality which notices moment by moment our relations to not-so-wholly others, the human, animal, vegetable, mineral, and possibly angelic others who do not cease to come, again.

She had been waiting impatiently for her friends from the city to arrive. This time she had come the distance and they were both late. Surprising, she smirked irritably. One is never on time, busy primping or flirting or otherwise sensualizing her transitions. But the other is usually so prissily prompt that she herself had rushed, despite the danger, to be on time, and now found herself alone and unwelcomed in this dank suburban cave. The eucalyptus leaves they had spread at their last meeting barely disguised its scent of moldering papyri and bat guano. Had they gotten cold feet? Had the impatience of the younger friends annoyed them? Sisterhood, she sneered at a spider repairing a web at the entrance, is unlikely. Taking a draught of night air, she relaxed a bit, remembering how little her anxiety had to do with their differences. A wave of affection rippled through her body. Regal Babs delighted her with sudden parodies of heterosexualism—and then with her laid-back, fleshy realism, indispensable to the plan. Whereas virginal Jeri, with her ebony elegance, always offered some new gem, some illumination that offset her condescensions. Was that their shadow in the distance, astride Babs's favorite beast? She laid her cloak down, and upon it some ripe figs and a manuscript. They had a long night's work ahead.

Silly Women
of the Last Days

> We are poised on the edge of the
> millennium—ruin behind us, no map
> before us, the taste of fear sharp on our
> tongues. Yet we will leap.
>
> *Women's Environment and Development*
> *Organization, "A Woman's Creed"*

> We cannot be excused from our own role
> in history because we could not know so
> as to be reassured that we were 'right' in
> advance.
>
> *Drucilla Cornell*

1

The Apocalypse had en/gendered hope in the burning of the Great
Whore. What follows will meditate on the paradox of a women's movement still inspired by a master myth that can hardly tolerate the sex of
women. Would it be surprising if at certain key moments we can hardly
tolerate that "sex" ourselves? But the operative paradox—just as in the
first meaning of that word, "that which runs contrary to doxa, to dogma,
to received opinion"—pushes here beyond mere contradiction, toward a
principled ambivalence of the sort which struck me at first so divided, so
uncertain, so gray. Now, however, it feels considerably more ethically

engaging, more multichromatic, than the options—either a dogmatic monopolitics or a self-dispersing postmodern undecidability.

The former option replays the script of purificatory unity in order to bind together a movement seething with difference. That "difference" differs from any single articulation—whether of "la différence" of sex as gender, or of the deconstruction of any sex or gender, or of the differences of sex/gender construction among cultures, races, classes, traditions. But if white feminist dogmas have lost their revolutionary innocence, the diverse movement of women still pulses and flows in and around them. Whether or not in opposing the cryptoapocalypse of our own heritage we must surrender our agency as decision-making subjects of a worldwide, heterogeneous and living movement—that is the present question.

At the double edge of that question, forged in the tension between modern emancipatory assumptions and the pluralizing propensities of postmodernity, feminism may benefit from attention to the apocalyptic unconscious of our own movement. The "eyes all over" stare back at us from its throne room, strangely multiplying and refracting the Male Gaze enthroned in transcendent invisibility. Would we modestly avert our own gaze? New Testament scholar Tina Pippin suggests, "Gazing at the biblical apocalypse enables women to gaze at the contemporary apocalypse."[1] The "courage to see"[2] may not, however, lead us only into the recesses of an endist patriarchy. The eyes mirror us back to ourselves precisely as feminists.

At least it is my contention that contemporary women's consciousness cannot be cut clean of the tradition of apocalyptic utopianism that at the same time contradicts our existence as female and/or sexual beings. How would we disconnect present surges and insurgencies of the movements of women from the dream of a once-for-all triumph of our solidarity? By the late nineteenth century, the "New Woman" represented a powerful movement, already the survivor of major backlash. Yet in its jaunty apocalypse, this movement reinscribes the millennialist dream of its own innocence, as toasted, for instance, at the Illinois Women's Press Club in 1891:

'Pealing! The clock of Time has struck the woman's hour,
We hear it on our knees.'
All crimes shall cease, and ancient wrongs shall fail;

> Justice returning lifts aloft her scales,
>
> Peace o'er the world her olive wands extends,
>
> And white-robed Innocence from Heaven descends.[3]

Similarly, in 1915 Charlotte Perkins Gilman tucked decades of aspiration into her feminist utopia: "You see, they had no wars. They had no kings, and no priests, and no aristocracies. They were sisters, and as they grew, they grew together—not by competition, but by united action."[4]

Contemporary pluralism shrinks from the prospect of such "united action." In our disappointment with the whole history of white sisterhood, we may instead leap into the anti-utopic, anti-apocalyptic trajectory, which identifies all such hopes for community with the essentialism of identity politics.[5] Academic feminists and postfeminists alike are learning to debunk the assumption of any group identity as a foundation for justice, or even for understanding "difference." The modus vivendi of such identity politics is with good reason viewed as a utopianism, which, to the extent that it succeeds, closes into some form of totalizing unity. That poststructuralist diagnosis has been to some extent reinforced, I presume, by the foregoing glimpses of the apocalyptic theology undergirding the politics of hope.

Feminist theorists, unimpressed by the foundations, essences, and aims of Western modernity, attempt to protect "difference" from the grand narratives—patriarchal or feminist—which would grind it into the dust of their revolutionary marches through history. Presumably the subalternity of race as well as sex/gender—those differences waiting "beneath the altar"—receive theoretical haven here. We needed the break. But what are the terms? Diane Elam has proposed a postmodern feminism of "undecidability." "It is this dispersal of the modern horizon of social justice that feminism and deconstruction work for," she straightforwardly submits. She aptly characterizes the Western emancipatory heritage as a "political project that ignores tradition and looks toward the New Jerusalem."[6] Postmodernists thus rightly recognize the endtime glow at modernity's horizon, but do we spy here another apocalyptic anti-apocalypse? Fortunately Elam, like most deconstructionist feminists, still insists on the ethical/political task, but would distinguish it from modern utopianisms as "political *movement*, which attempts to think its own uncertain relation to tradition."[7]

Within a widening gyre of undecidabilities, it is precisely our uncertain relation to tradition which counter-apocalyptic ambivalence re-thinks. Here, for instance, the tradition of the New Jerusalem, descend-ing as an enlightening "white-robed Innocence" from the white wom-en's movement, requires consideration. Nonetheless, we will note how the anti-essentialist convention of late twentieth-century academics, derisive of such top-down universalisms, also surrenders to some eerie overviews.

In this chapter we first examine the gender-zone via a few women's apocalypses, observing their mysticism move into utopian experiments and social policy. We then time-vault to the revolutionary styles of Mary Daly and Monique Wittig. Having at last moved into apocalypses of now, we will then consider the rhetorical "unveiling" of the racism of femi-nism. Then we will consider the postmodern assimilation of that chal-lenge into the politics of difference. But in the emergent discussion of "the essential difference" a different difference, a counter-apocalyptic configuration of sex/gender difference, suggests itself.

2

We have witnessed in earlier chapters certain irruptions of protofemi-nist consciousness. In such moments of heightened possibility, the myth of the millennium worked itself free of apocalyptic pessimism—and so of its most bitter misogyny. Gender parity gets performed in heaven and on earth. I have, for instance, alluded to the Guglielmites, about whom so little is known except for their stunning trinitarianism: the God whose incarnation was Christ must now in the Third Aeon become incarnate as the Holy Spirit in a woman. The Second Coming in female form had not merely been anticipated. She had come. That revolution incarnate was not crucified, but as befits the fleshly facsimile of the sacrificial whore, burnt alive. The visions, however, could not be extinguished: eyes open-ing onto the heavens of forbidden sight dot the history of women.

Within the Roman church, Hildegard arose as a prophet and a leader, entertaining apocalyptic visions of a divine Sophia. She even announced an age of women, if only due to men's abdication of responsibility. Still, against all odds, she found her voice within it. As did other mystics, nota-bly Julian, who from her anchorite's cell refigured Christ as milky-breasted Mother. Merely a male androgyne touting a feminine essence? No doubt. And yet what exceeds such iconoclastic gynomorphism? In seventeenth-century Britain, Jane Leade, freed from a cumbersome marriage by her husband's death, received visions on the themes of the Book of Revelation, and in writing of them radically deliteralized the endtime scenario, drawing on the Protestant mysticism of Jakob Böhme. She entertained visitations of divine Sophia, who offered esoterically apocalyptic discourses on freedom, the Holy Spirit, and the New Jerusalem, the "mother city." Leade identified this "Lady Wisdom" with the "woman clothed with the sun" of Revelation 12 and referred to her repeatedly as "goddess," "Omnipotent Virgin," "the Wonder of all Wonders," attended by an "illustrious Troop of Heroine Divine/Celestial Amazons; untaught to yield." The soul *becomes* her. "In thy light, Sweet Sophia, we are come to a discovery, where long have lain our lost forgotten dowry."[8]

This Wisdom haunting the visions of women hasn't gone away. Where does the mystical apocalypse begin explicitly to enact egalitarian community–to move from esoteric code into public life? In other words, what is the relation of the effective history of apocalypse to feminism?

A number of male utopians–such as Winstanley, the Saint-Simonians, the Oneida community–imagined gender equality. But practice lagged behind. Enfantin, for instance, could only fantasize the presence of an absent Mother. He even kept a chair empty for her at banquets, to symbolize "the lack." But when the proletarian women of the movement formed their own journal, the *Tribune*, when they found voice and visibility, he recoiled. Like other visionaries dreaming of union with the heavenly Virgin, he designated himself rather than any female the judge and channel of the coming Woman. He thus dismissed the work of the journal ("All that is a preparation for the public work of woman, but it is not a work of woman") and arrogated that work to himself: "It is we who give birth in pain to woman."[9] (Shades of the painful birth of Revelation 12–but now to a male mother goddess.) The extraordinary young women, themselves doomed but dauntless, linked class and gender oppression through the medium of a thealogical postulate: "The word of the WOMAN REDEEMER WILL BE A SUPREMELY REVOLTING WORD," wrote Claire Demar.[10]

Leslie Rabine constructs an intriguing analogy between the work of these utopianist working-class women and that of feminist theorists today, arguing that while the former use a clearly essentialist model of maternity as the universal bond uniting all women, they use it for purposes of dissent and dissemination. Demar evoked "the Mother with her thousand voices" embodied in all women as an immanent principle of revolt against unitary masculine repression. Anticipating by over a century not just Mary Daly's "revolting hag" but the *écriture feminine* which would also draw accusations of essence, Demar referred to her own writing as "*parole de femme*." The "woman redeemer" would release multiplicity and sexual pleasure—*jouissance*. This "word," wrote Demar, "will be the broadest, and consequently the most satisfying to every [sexual] nature, to every humor."[11] Rabine thus argues that "instead of perpetuating conservative essentialist ideals of womanhood, their discourse opens the jarring contradiction between the meanings of its vocabulary and the social meanings attached to its speakers, while, in addition, calling attention to the yawning gap between the social world and its ideal representation."[12]

This community of single, working-class women, constantly subjected to accusations of prostitution, partakes of no static identity. In other words, their rhetoric taps apocalypse rhythmically, cryptogrammically, to disrupt any established identity. Oppressed by gender and class outside of and even within the Saint-Simonian community, these feminists were "not recognized as occupying either pole of the gender system." Thus "on the level of social practice [they] turn their own stigmatized lack into a play that articulates this energy which challenges the symbolic order."[13] They mimic the bourgeois ideals of femininity in order to craft a universal bond of women. By mustering motherhood as a massive solidarity for resistance under the name of the yet absent Mother, they could partake of a writing and an organizing power reserved for men while disputing both bourgeois and Enfantinian patriarchy. For their revolution within a revolution, many of the women paid the price of isolation, suicide, or imprisonment for labor organizing.

It is tempting to dally with the Saint-Simoniennes and other feminist millennialist utopians (like Flora Tristan, a women's advocate and labor organizer who slogged through France trying to inspire a worker's movement which would include equal rights for women and confronted priests and bishops with her own brand of immanentist, justice-driven Christianity); however much the rhetoric of these precursors laid claim to the power of a universal feminine imaginary, however much they would hold us accountable to terms uncomfortably immense and messianic, they cannot be said to have pursued anything like the identity politics of a single-issue feminism. Inasmuch as their work altered the template of gender possibilities and subtly shifted the apocalyptic unconscious, do these utopian women not encrypt a might-have-been which holds alive a might-yet-be?

But, for the sake of cultural self-understanding, let us migrate to United States history. Here we examine narratives which bring us far from *raison*, into a more flagrant religiosity of women's apocalypse. In colonial America, still churning with the excitement and the ambiguity of the New World, female messiahs actually began to come (again).

3

As long as we have all male Gods in the heavens we shall have all male rulers on the earth. But when the heavenly Mother is revealed, and is sought unto as freely and confidingly as the Heavenly Father, then will woman find her proper sphere of action.[14]

The Shakers were a small English millennialist sect of Quakers, formed a hundred years after "the world turned upside down," named for their singing and dancing worship—a bodily, convulsive, rhythmic ritual of dissent against establishment religion. Ann Lee, a member for twelve years, experienced persecution early. Her brother tried to break her resolve by savagely beating her about the face and head with a stick, but Ann Lee cried for help to God. "While he [her brother] continued striking, I felt my breath, like a healing balsam streaming from my mouth and nose . . . so that I felt no harm from his stroke."[15] We note how the *pneuma*, "breath," con/spires with a woman for her bodily and mental survival.

In 1770 a vision informed Lee that "she was received and acknowledged as the first Mother, or spiritual Parent in the line of the female."[16] Those who became her followers henceforth understood themselves as the embryonic realm of God through which the millennium would be disseminated to all the world. She arrived with a group of followers in America in 1774. After several years of poverty and harassment the community began to flourish.

Unlike the proponents of the free-love egalitarianism of the French secular millenarians, Lee had already come to insist on the priority of celibacy. (She had given birth and burial to numerous children, and her husband went his own way.) In the dawning new dispensation of communing celibates, gender hierarchy no longer applied. Yet Lee herself never disputed the assumption of the "headship" of the male within marriage; instead she relegated marriage itself to the "old dispensation." She never identified herself with Christ—she called herself the "bride of Christ," and he remained for her the "head." Thus her own self-iconography synthesized imagery of New Jersualem, nunhood, and Pauline patriarchy. But the community which grew into a two-hundred-year utopia would identify her as the Second Christ, the incarnation of the Spirit Christ. Shades of Guglielma.

After Lee's death in 1784, the community expanded both in size and gender egalitarianism. The English radical Frederick Evans explained in 1830 why he joined the American Shakers: "Woman's Rights are fully recognized, by first giving her a Mother in Deity, to explain and protect them; where equal suffrage for men and women, and equal participation in the government of an Order founded by a woman, was an inevitable necessity."[17] As Linda Mercadante argues in her monograph on the Shakers, it is not that the inclusive image of the divine precedes inclusive praxis; rather, it was the interpretation of this experience of a woman's leadership which led to one of the most gender-inclusive theological visions yet articulated on biblical terrain.

Not surprisingly, such a disruption of millennia of symbolic habit had found its hermeneutical way to chapter 12 of John's Apocalypse. Reports from insiders and complaints from outsiders report Ann Lee's identification as "the woman spoken of in . . . Revelation . . . who was clothed with the sun."[18] In the most systematic Shaker theology, *Testimony of Christ's Second Appearing* (1816), Benjamin Young rejected the trinity itself, not only as artificial, lacking analogies in heaven or earth, but for its exclusive masculinity. As Ann Lee incarnated the Spirit Christ, or the Mother, Holy Wisdom, so Jesus Christ had embodied the Father. So Young questions theological patriarchy: "From whence this subversion of the pure law and order of God, to the exclusion of the female from her equitable right and participation with the male in the order and government of God's household, the same, as if in God, the female had no existence?" In the poem concluding the work, Young (in the tradition of radical reformers) identifies the age of the Antichrist—extending from approximately the onset of orthodox Constantinian Christendom to the time of the Shakers—with that of the trinity itself:

> The monstrous beast, and bloody whore
> Reign'd thirteen hundred years and more;
> And under foot the truth was trod,
> By their mysterious threefold God:
> But while they placed in the *He*
> Their sacred co-eternal *Three*,
> A righteous persecuted few
> Ador'd the everlasting *Two*.[19]

The Shakers held that no theological gender inclusiveness could be worked out on a trinitarian model: three, after all, is as indivisible as one. As apocalypse turns feminist, it is perhaps not surprising that its old preference for twoness reasserts itself! It would be easy from the vantage point of feminist triumphalism to dismiss this androgynous theology as another misguided essentialism: the eternal essence of maternity enthroned along with the Father hardly guarantees a long-term emancipation of (celibate!) women. But what strategy does? Viewed pragmatically, the relative success of the Shakers *counts*. In its little community of unmarried, uncoupled gender twoness, it subverts the social and symbolic order.

In 1837, the Shakers underwent a decade of revival in which gender-inclusive imagery for God reached "unprecedented proportions."[20] The Shakers received a series of visitations from Shaker ancestresses and, once again, from Sophia herself. This female aspect of the divine, called repeatedly "Holy and Eternal Wisdom," was thereby fully hypostatized (earlier the Shakers had addressed her as attribute of the Father), and now these visitations assumed ritual form. Each member came, clothed in Sunday best, to greet her before the elders, saying "Holy, Holy Mother Wisdom! I thank thee for thy great condescension and blessing, and for thy love and mercy to me." Wisdom "marked" each member (likely an allusion to the sealing of the 144,400 with marks on their foreheads), saying,

> On the right side of thy forehead I will write with my finger the name of the
> Lord thy God and also my name, Holy Mother Wisdom: And on the left side

of thy forehead I will write the name of your blessed Savior and also blessed Mother Ann's name. These names ... will abide with you thro time and thro Eternity if you are faithful. But if you are not faithful, these names are to be rubbed out.[21]

Mark her words: in this extraordinary coalescence of Revelation with the wisdom tradition, the correspondence of the "woman clothed with the sun" at the end of creation with the precreation figure of "Woman Wisdom" pursues its intertextual subplot. One of the Harvard Shaker women expressed her epiphany of Wisdom thus: "I sensibly felt her presence.... I have passed thro scenes of sorrow to do her holy will. But I have felt fully rewarded ... for her love is like healing balsam to the wounded soul."[22] The inscription of Wisdom on the subjectivities of women both emboldens them for risky action and heals the wounds which ensue.

It is well to neither romanticize nor trivialize the "subordinated knowledge" of a group like the Shakers. As a radical pacifist transformation of apocalyptic millennialism into an economic and gender egalitarian community, it did persist—even with its celibacy—solidly beyond most other utopian experiments.

4

Jemima Wilkinson, a young New England Quaker farm girl, left motherless at twelve, was converted during the New Light Revival of 1774, was soon expelled by the Quakers, and became critically ill. Few firsthand or sympathetic accounts remain of her life, but one describes this initial experience.

The heavens were open'd and she saw two Archangels descending from the east, with golden crowns on their heads, clothed in long white Robes ...[b]ringing a sealed Pardon from the living God; and putting their trumpets to their mouth, [they] proclaimed saying, Room, Room, Room, in the many Mansions of eternal glory for Thee and for everyone ... and the day of grace is not yet over with them. For every one that will come, may come, and partake of the waters of life freely, which is offered to Sinners without money and without price.[23]

She seems to have read her own epiphany through the biblical apocalypse, omitting the violence and the exclusive masculine agency of the original vision. Room for all. Whatever crowding this girl had known in her large family, whatever roomlessness women in general had suffered, whatever exclusivism other forms of Christianity may preach–now everyone could share both in the free waters of John of Patmos and in this generous sense of place. Its time was of course imminent.

> And the angels said, The time is at hand, when God will lift up his hand, a second time, to recover the remnant of his People, whose day is not yet over; and the Angels said, The Spirit of Life from God had descended to earth, to warn a . . . perishing, dying World, to flee from the wrath which is to come; and to give an Invitation to the lost Sheep of the house of Israel to come home; and was waiting to assume the Body which God had prepared, for the Spirit to dwell in.[24]

Note how "the wrath" remains karmic, impersonal, while the deity is personified as pneumatically inviting. Its Spirit at once *offers* "home" and *seeks* home–that is, "the Body." But now the Spirit assigns her a distinctive role indeed: "And then taking her leave of the family between the hour of nine & ten in the morning dropt the dying flesh & yielded up the Ghost. And according to the declaration of the Angels,–the spirit took full possession of the Body it now animates."[25] Upon recovery, the one who had been known as Jemima believed Jemima had died and been reanimated as the Spirit–the spirit of Christ or sent by Christ, but certainly the Holy Spirit.

As feminist theologian Sharon Betcher has demonstrated, this narrative recalls that of Guglielma of Milan, and at the same time exhibits the classic traits of " 'spirit sickness,' that interval of crisis, illness, even 'death' (accompanied by trance, visions and/or auditory callings), surrounding the transformation of a now spirit-filled person." This phenomenon "can be identified within numerous cultures where it serves the pneumatological function." That is, it "displaces communal expectations of the one who is ill," and thus "provides a clearing for the reformulation of the self, a self that now has divine authoritzation."[26]

Henceforth the girl would never again refer to herself as Jemima Wilkinson. Her new name was "the Universal Publick Friend." Indeed, the Friend could not be referred to as "her" any longer–no gendered pronouns or language now applied. The Friend preached and wandered, leading a processional of followers on horseback, flamboyant on a saddle of blue velvet and white leather, infamous for beautiful loose black curls in a time when all women bound and covered their hair, wearing black male clericals punctuated with flowing colored scarves. The Friend remained celibate, but did not require celibacy of followers, and preached mesmerizingly on biblical themes. Followers called themselves the Society of United Friends. Finally, over two hundred–many of whom were wealthy and educated, some married and in families, some single or widowed–settled to create a utopian community near Seneca Lake, New York. For a while much property was held in common, though this dimension of communitarianism did not sit well with the wealthier males. Respectful trade relations with Native Americans were carefully nurtured. ("Hath Not God Created Us All?" was the theme of the Friend's most famous sermon, at the gathering of the Council of the Six Nations to sign the Pickering Treaty in 1791.) Nonviolence was the rule, and a relative egalitarianism prevailed. Ritual was minimal besides daily Quaker-style sittings, where members, including the Friend, might spontaneously preach. The community's name was New Jersualem.

Again we see the transformation of apocalypse into the millennialist possibility. Betcher claims that millennialism "acted like a societal spirit sickness." Thus the spatiality of the western woodlands "even afforded a geographic 'clearing' in which to reconstitute not only the self, but the community."[27] As to gender, millennialism again affords, if in different terms, the opportunity to reverse the status of the sexes. As the detractor claims, this sense of the coming millennium afforded her "the belief that in some unlucky moment the order of nature had been reversed, that the empire of man was a mere assumption of power, obtained by force and fraud, and that under her happy auspices the fair sex were to be restored to those rights and dignities of which they had been thus despoiled."[28]

The Friend's preference of celibacy, like that of the Shakers, consisted less in a distaste for sex than in a revolution of power. Women were to "obey God rather than man," indeed, "ought not to intermarry with men, to give them pretext . . . for exacting obedience from us, who they acknowledge to be the better part of creation."[29] Does this "acknowledgment," itself rare, suggest a gap between theory and practice within the community? In any case, what the Shakers achieved by radically heightening the gender dyad, the Friend sought by just as radically deconstructing it.

Neither male nor female? Both male and female? Is this another instance of feminine self-abnegation, the denial of female identity in favor of some neutered androgyny? Gerda Lerner, for one, rather flatly predicates a feminine self-loss of the Friend in particular and of female mystics in general.[30] Betcher contends that, far from self-erasure, this was a radical act of self-construction:

> Though marked with sharp discontinuity, there is the reconstruction of the self with divine origins—a more powerful sense of self, deriving authority and inspiration directly from the divine. And this self with unbound hair worked with the authority and power to unbind society: the uneducated educating the elite; the farmer's daughter mixing with urban wealth; slaves were released and wealth was relinquished to the community; political 'sides' were ignored and racial animosities deflated. Can we talk about the 'loss' of self here or only different constructions of the self?[31]

Far from describing a life of internalized misogyny, the story of the Friend tells of a dramatic subversion of socially constructed gender categories. "Gender," writes Judith Butler, "ought not to be construed as a stable identity or locus of agency from which various acts follow; rather, gender is an identity tenuously constituted in time, instituted in an exterior space through a *stylized repetition of acts.*"[32] It seems to me the Friend lends credence to Butler's analysis. And vice versa. The possibility of dissent, according to Butler, locates itself not in a preconstructed feminine sex but in a playful parody of the inevitable repetition. Spirit-sickness seems to have purged the Friend (as earlier, less flagrantly, Hildegard and Theresa) of any delusion of original femininity or stable identity. Traumatic illness is grasped hold of as a bodily opportunity for liberation from the apparent biological continuity of gender: the psychosomatic interruption of the social construction is embraced as death and as resurrection.

Though not attentive to such spontaneous bodily conspiracy, Butler argues that gender is an effect, not the cause, of repetition. "The effect of gender is produced through the stylization of the body, and hence, must be understood as the mundane way in which bodily gestures, movements, and styles of various kinds constitute the illusion of an abiding gendered self."[33] To playfully decenter its elements, and thus dislocate masculine and heterosexist hegemony, is to make "gender trouble."

Through a costume that satirized male monopoly on ministry and scarves that mocked their grim masculinity, through flowing hair that dissidently mimicked an "original femininity" and unbound a woman's body, and through the bodily icon of powerful preaching and the stylized drama of riding processionals—picking and choosing with insouciant freedom among the elements of gender style—this Friend fashioned a persona unlike any before.

The revealed name of the Universal Publick Friend shatters by example the privacy of women. What of this "universal"? Is this the imperialist absolute that postmodernism cannot abide? Or would the relevant imperialism lie rather in our inability to honor such a dissident apocalypse, self-universalizing when it stands vulnerably against the absolute truths around it? "Universal" in this context means publicly accessible and unrestricted, opposed to the parochial absolutes that monopolize salvation and to the private properties of Calvinist elites. How literal was her apocalypse? There is no evidence the Society considered their New Jerusalem the only or the last, or even considered the question in finalizing terms. The Friend considered the epoch a "sifting time," but one with "room, room, room" for all.

The Friend moved from the community shortly before her death, expressing solidarity with the poor single women over against the increasing claims on property by the wealthy males. Disregarded by the world as an institutional failure, as were the Shakers, the community left few traces: embarrassed descendants of the community burned the remaining texts. Yet the Friend had momentarily healed apocalypse of its misogyny, its determinism, and its doom. Perhaps, given the rigid habituation required to maintain gender as we know it, the force of the apocalypse habit sometimes can be mobilized as therapy for the gender addiction. But only as it is itself transmuted. Counter-apocalyptically, the Universal Publick Friend made "gender trouble."

5

In 1848, in Seneca Falls, a few miles from the Friend's New Jerusalem, religious impulses of gender subversion erupted beyond the bounds of separatist communities, as the movement whose second wave was to break in the late twentieth century.

How does the grammar of apocalypse underwrite the discourse of gender equality? Only by setting the "Woman Movement" in the context of nineteenth-century North America can we discern its inherent apocalypse–or rather, discern the churning multivalency of the apocalypse script. Apocalypse at once habituates itself into a secular millennium of progress, into which women have inserted themselves in waves, and provides the retroapocalyptic material of backlash.

While mainstream Christianity continued to present itself as the conservator of male headship, the "union of progress with the symbols of the Apocalypse" that typified the Protestantism of the nineteenth century opened countervailing options. While a reading of John's Apocalypse provoked a few premillennialists to sell all and go wait upon a mountaintop, it "inspired many more in the mainstream denominations to promote revivals, missionary work, and other benevolent causes as a way of inaugurating the Kingdom of God on earth."[34] In these religious crusades, unlike the staid hierarchies of establishment congregations in which exclusion from ordination effectively silenced women and the laity, women such as Maggie Van Cott, Phoebe Palmer, and Amanda Berry played vocal, public roles.[35] "Spilling into the secular realm, millennialism sometimes motivated social reforms (as well as opposition to them) and provided a major way in which Americans defined their country as a Redeemer Nation."[36] The idea of our "manifest destiny," formulated in 1845, "cloaked imperialistic (and genocidal) motives while at the same time expressing a genuine sense of chosenness."[37]

The antislavery movement, and the political movement for women's rights to which it gave birth, represent the most dramatic overflow of the progress apocalypse. Sojourner Truth's skillful interweaving of women's rights, emancipation and biblical discourses represents a rather pure case of neoapocalypse: "I wanted to tell you a mite about Woman's Rights, and so I came out and said so. I am sittin' among you to watch; and every once and awhile I will come out and tell you what time of night it is."[38]

Such overtly religious millennialist moments rarely characterized early woman's rights oratory, however.[39] Yet the prophetic zeal of the movement laid claim to the conditional hope of an activist apocalypse for historical redemption. The Civil War, motivated by economic and race contradictions but inspired by the rhetoric of millennialism, "shattered the dream of infinite progress."[40] Routinely described by contemporaries as the American Armageddon, final victory could only be won at the price of a universal bloodbath: "He is trampling out the vintage," "His terrible swift sword." The "huge letdown"–for "the Apocalypse had not brought the millennium"–left the confidence of modernity wounded.[41] However, like the World Wars of the twentieth century, the Civil War opened new opportunities for urban middle-class women, employing them (for instance) in large numbers to run sanitary commissions.[42]

The Gilded Age of the 1870s and 80s, a period of "ruthless economic competition and consolidation" saw a professionalization of the middle class, arising in the growing gap between wealthy and poor. Attempting to "cast itself as the mediator able to diffuse potentially explosive class conflict," the middle class as a whole seemed to "sound more like women." The numbers of professional women rose dramatically during this period, and with their new economic independence many abandoned conventional family forms altogether. The National Woman Suffrage Association had been created in 1869, and its members branched out to address multiple, interrelated issues–"dress reform, women's suffrage, the liberalization of religion, aid for working class women and the opening of the professions to women, temperance, the rescue of prostitutes, and more open discussion of sexuality and birth control."[43]

This movement's activists attacked the ideologies of feminine purity, stressing from a scientific viewpoint the "importance of women's physiological self-awareness" in order to protect themselves against "hideous outrages on the mothers of the race" such as marital rape.[44] But then came a fierce backlash. Despite the Comstock Law (1872) making mailing or sale of contraceptive information illegal, a set of new laws restricting abortion, and the rolling back of the legal victories for women won in the late 1860s and the 1870s, the "Woman Movement" did not roll over and die. Indeed, it retained the appeal to a "scientific womanhood." However, it relinquished the turf of the female sexual body. A new strategy emerged. "Under the rhetoric of 'science,' many prominent activists reverted to the argument that woman's power resided in women's distance both from egotism and the body." However distasteful to those of us drawn to feminism for its body-positive potential, the new rhetoric of purity was a tour de force, forged in the teeth of the reversion of doctors, politicians, and clergy alike to the old identification of women with the bodily, the lustful, the base.

The resurgence of the movement in the face of the backlash depended upon a new infusion of millennialist energies: "By the 1880's there was a widespread belief that the politicization of selfless women would usher in a new golden age." Matilda Joslyn Gage wrote in 1881,

> The male element has thus far held high carnival, crushing out all the divine elements of human nature. . . . The recent disorganization of society warns us that in the disenfranchisement of woman we have let loose the reins of violence and ruin which she only has the power to avert. . . . *All writers recognize women as the great harmonizing elements of the 'new era.'*[45]

Frances Willard, a Methodist and perhaps the most visible woman leader of the period, taught the "coming reign of God and of woman."[46] The entrance of women into all realms of society would bring on the millennium itself: "She will come into government and purify it, into politics and cleanse [it] . . . for woman will make home-like every place she enters, and she will enter every place on this round earth."[47] More than a reaction to domesticity prevails in this discourse: it makes public what had been private and also oddly anticipates the ecological reclamation of earth as *oikos*, home to be cleansed of *man*made pollution, place of indwelling spirit and sustainable relations.

The "New Woman" would lead the way to a new age of spirit by conquering the age-old "bondage of the flesh"; she would master the "beast" within and without, and "eliminate the animal." Contemporary scientific triumphs, with their miraculous aura of the mental prevailing over the physical, inspired the rhetoric of an optimistic, scientific apocalypse, in which the androcentric heritage of both Christian apocalypse and scientific progress are dauntlessly reversed: "The clock of Time has struck the woman's hour." The price seems to be the radically dualistic identification of the Beast of Revelation with the animal body, now symbolically displaced from the Whore onto male economic and sexual greed.

During the period from 1880 to the First World War, the movements for peace, labor, temperance, and suffrage, intertwined with religious revivals and social anxiety, continued to grow despite the Victorian attempt to separate feminine purity from the New Woman's science and freedom. The terms "feminism" and "homosexuality" came into existence in the 1890s.[48] The economic and social forces of bourgeois progress, on top of the war, even more rapidly destabilized patterns of community and of both male and female roles. The millennium shook the social and spiritual integrity of those served by scientific progress as well as those it served up for exploitation.[49] New waves of immigrants, invariably known as "darker" whatever their color, like the Chinese or the Irish, lent added fodder to the anxiety and to a nostalgia for purity of both sex and race.

Amidst the crosscurrents of millennialist expectancy and disappointment, contradiction could be negotiated within the space of women's bodies—if they were sites of a unifying, secure purity. The Victorian family arose as the oasis of gendered stability in a time of inexorable social change, felt not least of all in the possibilities posed by early feminists. As historian Betty DeBerg writes, "Confused and unsure of themselves, men found a foil for their own ambiguous identities through the specific and stagnant qualities they ascribed to women. Men may not have known who they were or what characteristics they had, but by insisting that women had all the weak and inferior traits, they at least knew what they were not."[50] What Christopher Lasch called the "cult of the home" wrought of the bourgeoisie a stable class, ritually centered around the "household angel." Her "nature" fulfilled itself in the home, in private, nurturant, affective activities complementing the rational aggressions of the Victorian male. Here, in the ideology of "separate spheres," lies gender essentialism in earnest.

The New Women fought systematically against this domestic insulation, making inroads against the Victorian backlash again to the extent that they were able to turn the essentialist language against its sexist uses. "Born and reared within the limit set by the separate-spheres ideology of the Victorian middle class," the New Women "based their work and arguments on the assumptions of gender-specific spheres and character. Women's leadership in the public realm, from temperance to suffrage to church ministry, was desirable and necessary, they argued, because women were uniquely qualified to protect the home and all the virtues associated with it."[51] African American club women as well as white elite women appealed to the special powers of the women's sphere as a weapon against both race and gender conservatism.

The growing awareness of urban and industrial alienation and destitution finally gave birth to a prophetic theology of "the social gospel," intensely millennialist in its expectation of correcting the evils of social injustice within a century. But, on the other side of Christianity in the United States, an apocalypticism darkened by the Civil War developed. Articulated by Darby and rendered in Torrey, the vision of "the fundamentals" launched new premillennialist expectations of imminent and total calamity, the prelude to the Second Coming. Forms of biblical literalism, fiercely antiscientific though presupposing the Scottish commonsense philosophy and a kind of popular modern factualism, proliferated as never elsewhere or before. Emanating first from middle-class white urban culture in the East and Far Western regions of the country (contrary to the assumption of its southern and rural origins), fundamentalism became in the early twentieth century a major force in the United States. If scholars have renewed their interest in fundamentalism, it is because its restless antimodern apocalypse has never been defeated by the secular millennium of Progress. On the contrary, the apocalyptic monsters spawned by twentieth-century technology have provided rich illustrative material to the premillennialist faithful. But, as DeBerg has shown, scholars have ignored the foundational role of gender in the production of American fundamentalism: "What makes this oversight difficult to understand and harder to excuse is that issues of domestic relations, human sexual identity and behavior, and women's and men's spheres of activity dominated much of the rhetoric in the popular fundamentalist and proto-fundamentalist media."[52] In other words, a key to Christian fundamentalism's widespread popular appeal at the start of the twentieth century, vastly exceeding any concern to combat the twin foes of biblical and Darwinian science, lies in its defense of the quickly disintegrating Victorian doctrine of separate and complementary spheres.

At that moment we witness for the first time the potent and now so familiar pairing of conservative gender essentialism with apocalyptic biblicism. A popular fundamentalist magazine wrote that when woman assumes "the prerogative of power which belongs to the man and seeks to dominate the world or all of its activities, as she is doing today, she then possesses the spirit of the beast and is like an angel of light fallen from heaven."[53]

This rare acknowledgment of the dragon's female side seems to encode the response of the new backlash against the New Woman's answer to the last. DeBerg demonstrates that in many of the pamphlets and articles listing the signs of the end times–riots, violence, and crime were prominent–"most space was given to a discussion of the social behavior of the New Woman: the 'easy-going manner in which women of the highest rank and culture have allowed the old-fashioned rules and restraints which governed society to be relaxed.'" In these last and dreadful days, women "will be tempted to take part in this or that social reform, to give their sex the ballot and place them on political equality with men, for their own protection, and to reform society."[54] Political emancipation was a sure sign of the end. Women assuming leadership roles outside of the home but above all in religion embodied a foreboding sign of the approaching tribulations: "But the prominence of women in a sphere inconsistent with nature and with the meekness and quietness, which are the ornament of a Christian woman (I Pet. iii.4) is one of the signs of the times."[55] Quite logically, if the world is constituted of the proper harmony of the two spheres, then when "woman leaves her sphere" the world will fall apart.

The New Woman, that "Jezebel" threatening the family and the order of creation, was especially bold outside of evangelical Christianity. "[In] all the wicked and pernicious movements such as Spiritualism, Christian Science and Theosophy, women are in authority," writes one detractor. Another author, "disgusted" to find women preachers even among the Salvation Army and the Methodists, comes to terms with the unacceptable; "Oh well," he sighs, "it will only hasten the appearing of the antichrist. . . . As it was the first woman, so shall it be with the woman at the close of the age, listening to the tempter."[56]

Such a precise re-inversion of Sojourner Truth's famous inversion–"If the first woman God ever made was strong enough to turn the world upside down all alone, these women together ought to be able to turn it back, and get it right side up again!"–hardly seems coincidental.[57] The New Eve of the women's movement was riding the surge of the progressive millennium, provoking a retroapocalyptic backlash. Fundamentalism's bitter conservatism no more resembled the revolutionary if sexist anti-imperialism of John than did the hopeful apocalypse of the New Woman. These Christians vocalize the dread of a de-gendered world, the ultimate degeneracy. "More and more we are removing the old land-marks, and differences and distinctions are being rapidly obliterated." In the name of "difference," the voice of gender essentialism booms pro-phetically through the land–a history not to be forgotten when we ideal-ize an anti-essentialist "difference"! "O woman, stay a woman!" pleaded T. DeWitt Talmage, a nationally prominent preacher. "Do not try to cross over." At the high point of Western gender essentialism, the blurring of gender boundaries, the crossing of sexual identities, meant the end of the world. But fundamentalist logic at least comforted its adherents with the assurance that when the Antichrist comes with his feminist cortege, the Second Coming cannot be far behind.

In 1913, the journal *Our Hope* dubbed participants in the suffragist movement the "silly women of the last days."[58] The author did not con-sider the etymology of "silly," which first referred to defenseless crea-tures, especially women and children, deserving of compassion (a sphere forfeited by the New Woman), and which in its earliest form, "seely," meant "happy, blissful; fortunate, lucky, well-omened, auspi-cious," and also spiritually gifted, "enjoying the blessing of God."[59] Silly women. Through waves of backlash, through internalized apocalyptic loathing of ourselves as sexual bodies, swirling with liberation from a sexual body defined as whore by the beast, the oppressor–they would come again.

6

Seen from this perspective the Antichrist and the *Second Coming of women* are synonymous. This Second Coming is not a return of Christ but a new arrival of female presence, once strong and powerful, but en-chained since the dawn of patriarchy.[60]

With Mary Daly's blast of the trumpet in 1973, the second wave of feminism broke into theology. "Tour de force!" "Bull's eye!" rave fading pencil marks in the margins. The millennium of women was upon us. Deploying endtime tropes in reverse, she at once lays claim to the force of Apocalypse and disarms it with parody. Since the early church had enshrined Christ in its patriarchal renewal and stifled the bursting "fe-male presence" within its midst, Daly wonders what really loads the symbol of the evil Antichrist: "What if the idea has arisen out of the male's unconscious dread that women will rise up and assert the power robbed from us?" Given the Victorian fundamentalist association of the New Woman with the coming Antichrist, Daly's satiric association resounds with historic precision. Yet in proclaiming feminists the Antichrist indeed, she also invokes the eschatological tradition of feminism itself.

In a not coincidentally analogous move, I had realigned the Queen of Babylon, friend of Antichrist, with the dissociated dragon rage of the Queen of Heaven: parodic solicitation of the demonized female. If Daly perpetrates her own apocalypse, she thereby turns its power against the patriarchy of the genre. Moreover, at the point in her writing inscribed in *Beyond God The Father*, she partakes of neither apocalypse's absolutism nor its determinism. "Unlike the so-called 'First Coming' of Christian theology, which was an absolutizing of men, the women's revolution is not an absolutizing of women, precisely because it is the *overcoming* of dichotomous sex stereotyping, which is the source of the absolutizing process itself."[61] Still standing on the edge of institutional Christianity, she espoused the Tillichian metaphor of the boundary, an eschatological site of creative ambiguity.

The revelation of the unconditional vies, however, with the prophetic conditional: "This event, still on its way, *will mean the end* of phallic morality. Should it not occur, we may witness the end of the human species on this planet."[62] Given that "phallic morality" threatens not only women but all that lives, her prophecy in its *conditional* voice calls for responsibility. Yet the language of an inevitable and imminent revolution of history, in which the demonic forces are defeated and the good enshrined in radiant Presence, poses the only alternative to doom. Daly stands here within the heritage of apocalypse, summoning the force of Second Coming and Final Judgment to foreclose, if not on history, then certainly on "this age."

When, in 1978, Daly leaps beyond the boundaries (not that anyone noticed her fence-sitting) into the "new time/space" of *Gyn/Ecology*, she purges her writing of masculine marks of authority—including Tillich. What her right hand had granted male authors, the left now takes away. Though she had said "so what?" to Jesus' "feminism," she had contributed anyway to his feminist redemption. "Only the Second Coming of Women," she had argued, in *Beyond God the Father*, "can liberate the memory of Jesus from enchainment to the role of 'mankind's most illustrious scapegoat.' "[63]

She now relinquishes all positive appeal to Jesus, let alone Apocalypse. Yet she plunges all the more unconditionally into that latter rhetorical vortex. The qualitative shift of her prose medium, already pulsing between scholarship and incantation, propels her beyond the pale of *aletheia* into a poetry of *apokalypsis* studded with illumining engagements with the history of philosophy. Who more than Mary Daly writes feminist theory as apocalyptic oracle—if that means "elliptic, rhythmic and cryptogrammic" speech which "asserts itself as the premise of an impossible future and as a promise of explosion"?[64] Her inspired invective now engulfs all three "members" of the trinitarian "Men's Association": " 'The Processions of Divine Persons' is the most sensational one-act play of the centuries, the original *Love Story*, performed by the Supreme All Male Cast."[65]

To unbind feminist creativity from theological masochism (in which we embrace a *theos* who remains masculine no matter what pronouns we ingeniously apply), Daly unveils female "dismemberment by Christian and Postchristian myth." Noting the theologically unique status of Christ, she designates him "the Supreme Swinging Single, forever freed from challenge by Forceful Furious Females. . . . This christian demolition of the Goddess and mythic establishment of male divinity has paved the way for the technological elimination of women through the application of modern medicine, transsexualism, cloning, and other forms of genetic engineering." No wonder Daly (like all true apocalypticists) gets called paranoid. So she gleefully claims the attribute of "positive paranoia."[66] Having with satiric horror revealed the plot to cleanse the world of women, she dis/covers within "Postchristian myth" a cryptogram of Christ's apocalyptic Return: "This 'Word' is doublespeak . . . preparing the way for a phallotechnic Second Coming. It is the announcement of the ultimate Armageddon, where armies of cloned Jesus Freaks (christian and/or nonchristian) will range themselves against Hags/Crones, attempting the Final Solution to the 'problem' of Female Force."[67]

True to her goal of purification of language, the "Second Coming" is now confined to the androcentric lexicon, forbidden, along with all conventional Christian vocabulary, even a furlough for ironic inversion. Yet it is precisely at this high point in the writing of anti-apocalypse, where

Daly denounces the self-fulfilling prophecy of the end of the world, that an image provokes her to adapt a crucial piece of the apocalypse myth. This is, as we previously noted, the trope of the stripping and consuming of the Queen of Babylon:

> The ultimate contest was wrongly described in the Book of Revelation. . . . The author in his vision failed to note the Holy War waged by Wholly Haggard Whores casting off the bonds of whoredom. . . . The ultimately Holy War centers around the only genuine 'energy crisis.' Its focus is the wrenching free of female energy which has been captured and forced into prostitution by patriarchy, degraded into fuel for continuing its necrophilic processions.[68]

Declaring feminist holy war, Daly surrenders to the mesmerism of the book she debunks, indeed, to its most lethal fantasy. Speaking the "SUPREMELY REVOLTING WORD" of a millennial "female redeemer" about to open the scroll of her universal feminist martyrology, she bathes herself in the rhetorical blood of the Lamb and launches the final crusade. Of course, our weapons will not be boys' toys but "Female Force." More specifically, and certainly nonviolently, we will withdraw our energy, which *they* depend upon, from *their* war machines; and our victory is not imagined as the death of any men but as our passage into the feminist "Otherworld" of freedom and "Be-Longing."

To trace this pattern in Daly is to trace it in white feminism, in myself, and in the irresistible surges of Manichean energy which pump our progressive politics. "Unveiling" it I repeat it. Moreover, waves of backlash tend to corroborate Daly's positive paranoia. (History often validates the extremism of apocalypse.) It is not a question of proving Daly "wrong," but of rhetorical strategy–of what the effect of her "reversing the reversals" will be.

Although we cannot locate the pure "outside" of gender oppression– which Daly's "Otherworld" seems to promise–we can at least echo the deafening Word of the fathers in words of revolting hilarity. She poses, I would suggest, an eminent example of the satiric mimesis which Luce Irigaray and Judith Butler theorize as the only avenue of resistance– though they would likely not acknowledge her as such. To link Daly and Butler may seem tendentious, as Butler would likely find Daly guilty of the most obnoxious "cultural" or "radical" feminist gender essentialism, steeped in the myth of a pure feminine origin. With good reason, since Daly writes, "Avoiding their elimination we find our Original Being. Mending their imposed fragmentation we Spin our Original Integrity." We will return to the question of the essential(ist) Daly—or, rather, to the apocalyptic code inscribed in the question.

However nonviolent, the fantasy of a holy war, with its satisfying oppositionalism, demands militant unity if not uniformity among true believers. Thus Mary Daly has been endlessly criticized by other women (Most Likely to be Dissed Sis) who read in her a peculiarly purged and purist form of separatist sisterhood, very likely white, lesbian, and highly educated. Well before the anti-essentialist dismissal of "cultural feminism," she has been, with some justification, accused by other feminists of separatism, racism, elitism, Victorianism, puritanism, dualism, gnosticism, Manicheanism, and, indeed, apocalypticism. The problem is that these critiques themselves partake of the dualistic, virtuous, and purifying tone of apocalypse—minus, perhaps, Daly's genius for overstatement.

When I am not sucked, against my own initial resistance, into the vortex of her truth-rhythms, I regret an absence in her work of self-relativizing signals, of "perhaps" and "on the other hand" and "from this perspective." I regret the influence of her dissociative strategy on my generation. I regret her inability to engage the question of race in more than a peevish tone, like an apocalyptic warrior refusing to be shamed—that is, I read Daly's critique of "confessionalism" as her own defensive posture in relation to all other progressive critique. Not that any shame-based tactics, hers or those of her critics, are capable of interrupting the apocalyptic circle.

Daly's call to "Holy War" surely emits great if not "Original Integrity" from alpha to omega, culminating amidst cacophonous cackles in the "Rite of Unraveling."[69] High parody, burning a discursive free zone through ridicule and alliteration, fiery as Revelation but much funnier. Yet the parody directs itself relentlessly outward, predicated upon the labrys-swinging excellence of the feminist "Self." Does Daly laugh at her-Self?

7

Must a counter-apocalyptic feminism reject any model of the "woman warrior," of a women's war against the patriarchs? The militant apocalypse reveals itself in beauty in a text to which Daly appeals as she calls down holy war, citing Monique Wittig's *Les Guérillères*: " 'They say, put your legendary resistance to the test in battle. . . . They say, go spread over the entire surface of the earth. They say, does the weapon exist that can prevail against you?' "[70]

This 1969 cult classic, quoted often and ritually among American feminists, announced a purer vision of gender Apocalypse than ever Daly spun: we may call it Gynageddon. In the poetically compelling refusal of narrative linearity or subject in Wittig's novel, we again encounter a modernist version of rhythmic, cryptogrammic fantasy. Its utopia of amazons (though they throw off that name) recalls a time when they made war; then for the last two thirds of the novel they fight one. The book encapsulates a polemic against any romance with "the feminine," with goddesses, with those once-despised body parts—in other words, with *écriture féminine* in France and cultural feminism (such as that of Daly) in the United States.[71] In *Les Guérillères*, such early feminist knowledge is figured in texts called "the feminaries," which "the women" (*"elles,"* the virtually exclusive subject of the narration) decide may have "fulfilled their function": "They say that thoroughly indoctrinated as they are with ancient texts no longer to hand, these seem to them outdated. All they can do to avoid being encumbered with useless knowledge is to heap them up in the squares and set fire to them. That would be an excuse for celebrations."[72]

From bonfire of feminine vanities to bonfire of feminine texts. Frances Bartkowski interprets the shock value of this moment as a "narrative and political break from the inherited false continuity of history. Orthodoxy names heresy"; though the feminaries first seemed revolutionary, they have culled their knowledge from the "symbolic preserves of patriarchy."[73] But a thealogian suspects in any burning of books the triumph not of heretics but of heresy hunters—the moment when the revolution prefigures the violence of its own totalitarian dream. In the West the burning of books has not only represented, it has routinely anticipated, the burning of flesh.

The work's opening poem heaps up and glorifies icons of a modern messianic revolution: "GOLDEN SPACES LACUNAE/ . . . THE IMMOBILE BIRDS OF JET/THE WEAPONS PILED IN THE SUN/THE SOUND OF THE SINGING VOICES/THE DEAD WOMEN THE DEAD WOMEN/CONSPIRACIES REVOLUTIONS/FERVOR FOR THE STRUGGLE." For all its elliptical drama, the poem ends with a quite discursive slogan: "THE WOMEN AFFIRM IN TRIUMPH THAT/ALL ACTION IS OVERTHROW."[74] This is not precisely Marxism, for Wittig's revolution skirts class analysis, but rather a zealous transfer of the revolutionary paradigm still chic in the 1960s–along with its cult of warriors and worship of weapons–to the class of women, or rather to the vanguard of women prepared to die for the struggle. Unencumbered by economics, the revolutionary apocalypse returns in modernist purity: "The women say they have learned to rely on their own strength. They say they are aware of the *force of their unity.* They say, let those who call for a new language *first learn violence.* They say, let those who want to change the world first seize all the rifles. . . . They say that a *new world is beginning."*[75]

Familiar themes, these. Indeed, Wittig proceeds directly to the biblical imaginary. "He has invented your history. But the time approaches when you shall crush the serpent under your heel, the time approaches when you can cry, erect, filled with ardour and courage, Paradise exists in the shadow of the sword." In medieval iconography it was Mary, identified with the Queen of Heaven, who as the New Eve would crush her old "enemy," the serpent, under her heel. Wittig is evoking with approval the patriarchal archetype of the defeat of the snake–the bad earthy femininity–by the good mother, Mary. (Daly, trained as a theologian, would not have chosen these images except to reverse them: she knows the depth of their sexism.)

As the war proceeds, amidst much singing and bleeding, some famous sexists are captured. "For these there are got ready the racks the screw-plates the machines for twisting and grinding. The women stop their ears with wax so as not to hear their discordant cries."[76] And so this New Jerusalem, true to the original, also requires the hellish torture of its opponents. We are, I presume, to applaud our redemption from any lingering Victorian delicacy. Emboldened, the women march on: "They say, where shall we carry the flame, what land set ablaze, what murder perpetrate?" The enemy–"he"–will be totally destroyed, by fire and the sword–as ever, but now really. Wittig then turns to the earth. "They say, no, . . . I shall not rest my tired body before this earth to which I was so often compared, turned upside down from top to bottom, shall be incapable of bearing fruit. They light the pine-trees cedars . . . oaks olives. The fire spreads with great rapidity."[77] Far from sensing solidarity with the exploited, feminized earth, Wittig's women take vengeance on it: nature as scapegoat. The apocalyptic fire spreads, as it must, everywhere.

Wittig, who resists feminist gender dualism per se, indeed "gender" itself, does not demonize all the men. Many of them, the flowerlike ones, join the "she's," who lecture them thus:

> Now you understand that we have been fighting as much for you as for ourselves. . . . Today, together, let us repeat as our slogan that all trace of violence must disappear from this earth, then the sun will be honey-coloured and music good to hear. . . . *Let there be erased from human memory the longest most murderous war it has ever known, the last possible war in history.*[78]

The war to end all wars. How extraordinary to come across that messianic hype under the sign of the feminine pronoun. Wittig then literally inscribes a circle, to signify return to the nothing from which the new world will begin, as the master symbol of the text. With enough faith, violence, and unity, the old order will be so thoroughly expunged that we can start anew. After the orgy of violence, the blood we shed will itself—like the Lamb's—cleanse the world of future violence: a brave new world will be scrubbed clean of history and nature. One may remonstrate that this is not meant literally, these are tropes of radicalization. But one must answer that neither was the Book of Revelation meant literally; it likewise takes the form of nonlinear, collective mythopoeia. Wittig's warrior metaphors speak, they define, the terms of radicalism. And they choose to subject their readers once again to the redundancy of war.

Is this again a strategy of parody? Certainly Wittig's amazons mimic the man's game of war in a scene where they strew flowers, and her parody of gender itself, scuttling the familiar dyad and any possible "natures" (nature itself is torched) surely subverts all gender archetypes, even cherished feminist ones. There remains no original Woman. Butler writes, "The notion of gender parody . . . does not assume that there is an original which such parodic identities imitate. Indeed, the parody is *of* the very notion of an original."[79] Yet the militant seriousness of the war trope dominates the scenery in Wittig's novel, however often the women lift their heads together in the brave laughter of Homeric warriors.

While Wittig's constant repetition may rhythmically support a reiterative mimesis, I felt constricted by the breathless reiteration of the subject *"elles,"* "the women." Always the collective, anonymous *"elles dis-*

ent," "the women say." The collective feminine they–which speaks, sings, of one mind, unified, a Greek chorus of amazons. Such collectivity invites one into its mesmerism, yet it allows no dissent from its bold declaratives, no difference. In the final paragraph the narrative "they" breaks, for the first time, into a "we" which now includes the narrator: "Moved by a common impulse, we all stood to seek gropingly the even flow, the exultant unity of the Internationale. . . . The war is over, the war is over, said a young working woman next to me."[80] Ah, even as the first person singular is now glimpsed, it is legitimated by its politically correct comradeship (as though the status of the proletarian woman would be transparent after these years on the battlefield)–not unlike the "I" of John of Patmos, who refuses the authorial anonymity of the genre and yet evokes (in an equally breathless poetry of pulsing compression) the authoritative universality of its impersonal, collective vision.

But, some women say, we will not fight this "last possible war." Final solutions bear no daughters.

8

That the apocalypse habit operates among us in multiple contradictory forms is not surprising. The "positive paranoia" of the genre is as well warranted at the end of the twentieth century as the millennial hope for a new woman's era was at the end of the nineteenth. Backlash continues to threaten those women, particularly open lesbians, already exiled from the Eden of heterosexuality. As one journalist put it, "Ever since the Evil Empire turned out to be a collection of third-world countries, Americans aligned on the far right have tried to cast gay men and lesbians as the new enemy, calculating deviants seducing the nation's young, anti-Avon ladies selling sodomy door-to-door."[81] Sins against "compulsory heterosexuality" inscribe themselves at the top of the list of beastly abominations to be purged in the desired (but, remember, not necessarily coming) Armageddon of the new religious right. Within my own denomination, the term "feminist-womanist-lesbian" was recently invented as the new name of the beast daring to "re-imagine" Christianity. As I write, the renewed synergy of fundamentalist endism with nostalgia for the Victorian (or was it 1950s?) family builds: the potent imagery of the great feminist Whore retumesces across the world (partnered oddly with the Great Satan of America in certain biblical lands). As long as this is true, women's texts will intermittently mirror the threatening apocalypse. I do not propose to draw a "line in the sand" between feminist apocalypticism and feminist counter-apocalypse.

To recapitulate. Apocalypse always charges its batteries with sex/gender images, not originally as "essences" or "separate spheres" but as primal abhorrence: a male fantasy of a cosmic holocaust of other *males*, the oppressors, satisfyingly symbolized as Whore-queen and purged of female agency. In the lascivious sex of a powerful woman is inscribed the object of all endtime hatred–whether or not literal Jezebels were around to provoke a particular prophet. By faithfully guarding its purity, the virginal community could distill potency from powerlessness. Fundamentalist neo-Victorianism merely renders explicit what otherwise the social order sublimates and objectifies as its cryptoapocalypse.

But all along other communing dissidents were rereading the Apocalypse–Shaking it up, be-Friending it, converting it to Wisdom, re-riding its horses into liberated gender zones. If the women's movement has become entangled in a master code which emits, along with reaction, the terms of all Western progressivism, it has rarely simply reiterated the oppositional dualisms of the pattern. It has mimicked them, turning them against itself, absorbing the separatist hope and holy revolution but at the same time twisting the pattern into parodies of the paternal power. Though we will not achieve any lasting women's millennium or feminist New Jerusalem, and though we will trip into disappointment because we haven't, women's movements have pried open new spaces in history, perhaps unimaginable until the mid–nineteenth century. It is not clear that any other known endeavor has greater power to reconfigure the basic habits of planetary life–and thus to reawaken fear-of/hope-for the end of the world.

However, when we remain oblivious to our own apocalypticism we tend to continue its purifying pattern of unification against "the beast within and without." For instance, white feminists, though more enfranchised than most earthlings, have not easily relinquished the simplifying rhetoric of a once-for-all crusade righteously impatient with all diluting complexities among the ranks. "Patriarchy" as the cosmic ("structural") demon was revealed to us in numinous negativity, the extent, the wickedness, and the universality of its achievements provoking in us the horrified ecstasy of initiates of a new world. The careful distinction maintained in theory–even in Daly's–between "patriarchy" and "men" was difficult to sustain in second-wave feminist practice. Our casual rhetoric lurched into male-bashing snipes and a habit of brittle generalizing about *male* essence.

Most of us, of whatever sexual practice, avoided long-term separatism, respecting the complexity of our ties with men. Yet this respect was often accompanied by a vague self-abjection—the internalization of the image of the Babylonian Whore—as though we must have somehow sold out, intellectually or sexually. Uneasy with our own impurity, many feminists may in fact grant men tremendous private power over our inner lives just because we lack the categories for publicly discussing and so demystifying male influence—seeing it instead as messianic or demonic.

Demonizing the "other" serves the purpose of empowering a correspondingly vigilant self. But when that vigilance turns on the self (as it must within apocalyptic consciousness), demanding the inner purity of its participants, the dishonesty at least has a chance to show itself. The modern critique of identity politics and essentialism, by dispersing the chimera of simplistic commitments, seems to clear the way into a more honest pluralism. But only, I would suggest, if it avoids its anti-apocalyptic espousal of difference for the sake of difference can it keep counter-apocalyptic faith with its "different" sisters and brothers.

After all, it was women of color—the Combahee River Collective, "a group of black lesbian socialist-feminists from the Boston area in 1977"—who first articulated "identity as a political construct."[82] The bone of contention with white feminism that demanded such a boundary in the first place was our overextension of our own gender dualism, our white-women's feminine purity and innocence; women of color needed to assert their racial difference in solidarity with men of color over against white women's privileging of our *gender* difference. The double-edged sword/tongue cuts deep into the progressive rhetoric of our period.

9

This woman is Black
so her blood is shed into silence
this woman is Black
so her blood falls to earth
like the droppings of birds
to be washed away with silence and rain.[83]

It fell to women of color to expose the contradiction inherent in feminist unity, as Audre Lorde eloquently does in the lines quoted above. I want to argue, however, that white feminists are mistaken to account for the progressive rhetoric of unity–oneness of the movement and of the individuals within it–as essentialist. "Essence" in this context remains a misleading label. Whatever "identity" or "original integrity" accrues to it, such a subject belongs less to the classical tradition of hierarchical essences than to the prophetic tradition of protest. It is a collective subjectivity forged in the teeth of opposition, in which unity in struggle might make the difference between life and death. But once there is breathing room, once enough political space opens for women to compete with each other for leadership and resources within the movement, the purificatory habit seems inevitably to bare its teeth.

For example, this face of newly accrued power showed itself at the classic moment when Elizabeth Cady Stanton succumbed to the logic of racism for purposes of strategic unity. When the political system seemed to be moving to offer voting rights to (male) blacks rather than to (white) women, a fragile and fledgling movement born largely from the work of white women in the antislavery struggle reacted as the white male supremacist system intended them to: it retreated back into the race unity of white women. Key to the present thesis is the sudden proliferation of apocalyptic images ushering in the least glorious moment of Stanton's life as a writer: "Now, as the celestial gate to civil rights is slowly moving on its hinges, it becomes a serious question whether we had better stand aside and see 'Sambo' walk into the kingdom first."[84] She figures the still revolutionary Enlightenment ideal of individual rights, not surprisingly and of course not literally, as the New Jerusalem, a lure to women and blacks struggling to reform an ideal designed to exclude them. What she might have posed as a serious question about the divide-and-conquer tactics of white male politicians was thus disfigured into a reflex of Victorian racial and class elitism.[85]

African American women encountered another convulsion of the same reflex when, facing the sexism of the 1960s Black Power movement, they sought solidarity with white women. At that point any nonwhite woman would likely have her particular concerns subordinated to sisterhood. Yet any woman (a feminist mother among the childless feminists, Jewish among Christian, Christian among Goddess, pagan among socialist, working-class among academics) might find herself subject to a subliminal psychosocial static–a sense of exclusion from the queendom. Perhaps given the Armageddon charge of racial politics ever since the Civil War, infusing from the supremacist viewpoint "white" with all the radiance of Michael's legions and "black" with the revolting hues of the beast, it is not surprising that the women's movement displayed its lack of any original unity precisely along the color line. Or rather along *that* color line, because of course, as my Korean American students continually must remind the rest of us, there are several color lines, and each of them traces a history of women's differences. But the black/white social code of oppositional struggle had early lodged itself in the apocalyptic template of feminism itself. African American women did not seek out their painful privilege of shattering the illusion of women's solidarity. They merely found themselves repeatedly confronted by the unacknowledged self-contradictions of "sisterhood." When they tried to explain the complexity of their situation–in which they experience racism as no less oppressive than sexism, and white women as historically no more trustworthy than white or black men, and black men as more oppressed than white women–they met first with a quite unsisterly insistence on our common oppression. For white feminists, patriarchy was the true enemy, and belief in that credo determined true friends.

"Emphasis on 'common oppression,' " wrote bell hooks in 1984, "was less a strategy for politicization than an appropriation by conservative and liberal women of a radical political vocabulary that masked the extent to which they shaped the movement so that it addressed and promoted their class interests."[86] Given the first mass public success since suffrage of middle-class white women, bell hooks's early analysis got it right. But her point implies an important distinction: the claim of common oppression is not itself the problem. It counts as a credible "strategy for politicization" *until* coopted by a white women's elite, as it did for liberation theologians in the early Christian community *before* it was appropriated by the interests of a hierarchical elite. But of course, as between the original setting of the Apocalypse and its subsequent uses, or between Wall Street and White House assimilations of feminism and credibly "radical" politics, the boundary also wavers. Unless of course we are content with straight-line oppositionalism, that is, with fighting the fire of one apocalypse with that of another. Then we compete for victim status–who is the snowiest sacrificial lamb of all?–a game which white women, with the residual bourgeois passivity in which black women have rarely had the luxury to indulge, pursue all too cannily. Because that mythic tinge to moral righteousness does among liberals justify accruing to ourselves whatever financial and social power we can ("to the Lamb all honor and wealth and power and glory"), we do not stray far from hooks's point.

For white feminists the point remains that by overgeneralizing a particular narrative of gender oppression–indeed by mistaking a certain historical configuration as the truth for all women under the universal conditions of patriarchy (a virtual essence of feminine subjugation)[87]– we avoid the difficult struggle with difference. As we gleaned from Audre Lorde, difference is not valuable for its own sake but for the sake of the creative eros of connection. Difference *is* a relationship. Common oppression as rallying cry for a broad-based women's movement does not need to deemphasize difference. Defatalized, dehomogenized, the links between the oppression of the wives of the white elite and their (often black) serving women do not level difference but rather create a background against which differences can be seen in context. Pretense of sisterly communion will not mask the class, race, age, health differences; at the same time, it is dissociation from the hope that out of shared struggle we might someday congregate that drains political coalitions of their spirit.[88]

Radical feminism surrenders (like all apocalypticisms) to a double monism, a radical simplification of both the community of the saved and the mob of the damned. Because such homogenizing requires repression of contradictory and complicating evidence, provoking shame when one fails to fit the paradigm, the "multidimensional and bifocal" analysis required by the "womanist" method may free white folk to examine their own multidimensionalities with less guilt and more honesty.[89]

I remember listening one day to Delores Williams lecture on the difference between womanism and feminism,[90] trying not to brace myself against the revelation of my own racism, when suddenly an unexpected pleasure broke through: I had just inadvertently been given permission to acknowledge the complexity of my own relationships, even (paradoxically) my relationships to the white men from whom personally I have received so much nurture, friendship, and insight. An odd fringe benefit of hearing an uncompromising early womanist. Loosening up gender dualism in order to take adequate account of race, class, and other differences could mean not just more adequate politics but movement into the depth of our complex and continuous social formation, where apocalyptic dyads of victim and victimizer break into a richer narrative complex, where a "multidimensional and bifocal" view of our own intersubjective agency comes into focus.

10

A histrionic element entered white women's struggle with our own racism, however, something all too willing to redirect the dragon's rage against our own embattled century's worth of feminism–against ourselves. The almost ceremonial public confessions of feminist racism which ensued felt something like what John must have expected from Jezebel's chastened community. We had been eager to hear men denouncing other men as sexist; now white feminists got points from each other for denouncing other feminists as racist. By the same token I would glow with the pride of the elect when a black woman affirmed my antiracist efforts.

There is no getting around–or ahead–of the implication of white women's privilege in the Babylon of racism. But to criticize our own and our movement's implication in white supremacism need not imply dissociation from our heritage. The tendency exemplified in Susan Thistlethwaite's brave *Sex, Race, and God* becomes troubling, I believe, when it leads us to continue the tradition of (white, European, utopian) disconnection from the past–from, for instance, the past of white Victorian suffragists or even of Mary Daly's major works. Citing the usual charges of monism, dualism, and racism against Daly, as well as recycling Audre Lorde's critique, Thistlethwaite judges that "Daly should have attended to Harding's warning that feminists who are sensitized to gender issues in patriarchal theories they employ can be ideologically blind on issues of race and class."[91] Harding's point was well taken. But the Harding essay being cited appeared in 1988, the Daly pieces under fire were published in 1978 and 1984. The ahistoricism at play symptomatizes more than a trivial error. While the self-unveiling of white feminist racism requires work in and upon every epoch, the accompanying implication that *I* would have proved morally superior, that *I* would have transcended the same circumstances, neatly reinvests the very neo-Victorian politics of purity under criticism. Such rhetoric easily reconfigures a timeless sense of our own sinful-but-accepted virtue, guilty of its own version of the "ontological dualism" of which Thistlethwaite fairly enough charges Daly.

As to rhetorical tactics, and more importantly as to the *spirit* of the struggle, I suspect we will persist better in opposing both racism and sexism the more we take care to pay attention to our own cryptoapocalypse, our oppositional urge to purge and purify our feminism. Blaming other feminists for racism helps us to elude our own.

For instance, Lorde's "Open Letter to Mary Daly" in *Sister Outsider* raised important questions. She pointed out that as white feminists our collusion in race hierarchy could take the subtle form of forgetting to mention the icons of power of the subordinated race, that in our eagerness to construct a shared plateau of victimization we overlooked the fact that the playing field we leave is anything but level. Articulating this critique so clearly offered a "dark" gift to white feminism. Yet Lorde's tone is notably one of deep and pained respect, and her anger is explicitly aimed at dissolving a "real block to communication." Indeed, the substance of her plea is precisely and powerfully for "support and connection," asking that Daly "re-member what is dark and ancient and divine within yourself that aids your speaking."[92] Yet Thistlethwaite, in the vein (if not the richness) of white poststructuralism erases this side of Lorde's critique, propounding instead a surprisingly simplistic dualism of "the primacy of connection" over against the "temptation of connection."[93] She means to be righting the prior (and real) imbalance of white feminist romanticism about connection across differences, for which I would accept a certain responsibility. Indeed she confesses to "feeling it" in herself as she writes; and so, in the purifying tradition of apocalyptic self-sacrifice, overcomes her own "temptation." I would hope that counter-apocalypse would more consistently counter dualistic dialectics.

To make ourselves blameless and safe by confessing our racism and quickly moving on to denounce that of others seems to me a prime case of the dissociative strategy. True, it produces often enough a behavior-modifying shame, an institution-shifting conscience. So much the better. But while dissociation may correct, it never heals the systemic complex which provoked it. And so the transformations it effects within subjectivities and within societies will be shallow and short-lived, vulnerable to backlash; that is, they will be expecting the end of the world. Counter-apocalypse holds a collective sense of "sin," for which racism, like sexism, is a principality whose power permeates our somatic habits and our inadvertent privilege. If we wish to admit that *metanoia* reveals "our racism" we can only discuss structural dynamics and degrees; we cannot send another off into the desert as the guilt-offering for difference.

11

Where once the prime objects of academic feminist critique were the phallocentric narratives of our male-dominated disciplines, now feminist criticism has turned to its own narratives, finding them reductionist, totalizing, inadequately nuanced, volarizing of gender difference, unconsciously racist, and elitist.[94]

If for the second wave of feminism patriarchy was the opponent, if for African American women it was racism, sexism, and classism, then for poststructuralist feminists the enemy could be summarized as "essentialism." It doesn't rape, fire or lynch you, but essentialism has managed to draw to itself much of the apocalyptic indignation earlier reserved for injustice. This indignation has usually been directed against "essentialist feminists," and often indeed essentialism has been decried along with racism, elitism, and identity politics or cultural feminism. (All cryptograms for Mary Daly.) Elizabeth Spelman provides a typical example of anti-essentialist feminist discourse:

It would surely lighten the tasks of feminism tremendously if we could cut to the quick of women's lives by focusing on some essential 'womanness.' However, though all women are women, no woman is only a woman. Those of us who have engaged in it must give up the hunt for the generic woman—the one who is all and only woman, who by some miracle of abstraction has no particular identity in terms of race, class, ethnicity, sexual orientation, language, religion, nationality. . . . There are no short cuts through women's lives.[95]

Emancipatory movements caught in the exigencies of action do take shortcuts wherever possible–often perilous ones. Spelman writes from a context in which more leisurely strolls through the complex landscapes of women's lives become possible. Unfortunately, she constructs a straw feminist, a kind of neo-Victorian ideologue of Woman (Daly, predictably, is one of her primary targets).[96] And as we have seen, until the late nineteenth century, when pressure for the vote became the monofocal unifier, nineteenth-century New Women of both colors embraced a rich range of issues. And what feminist theory in recent decades has claimed that "a woman is only a woman"? Again one might suspect this now conventional white feminist scorn of prior feminisms as being a more sophisticated version of the zeal to purify ourselves–not of patriarchy but rather of feminist political vulgarity, of racism as a mark of monism, of utopian overstatement (thus we might become professionally invulnerable to all charges).

At its best the campaign against essentialism and its analogs questioned the simplifications and homogenizations to which any liberation discourse is prone; it thus dis/closed a space in which the nuanced particularities of women's differences may appear. But it may be helpful to decode the operative formula of poststructuralist anti-essentialism: apocalypse=essence=generic sameness, while anti-apocalypse=anti-essentialism=difference. These equations belie the radical philosophical difference between the classical eternalism of *aletheia* and the Near Eastern historicity of *apocalypse*. While both tropes partake of a general patriarchal purism, the terms of their "seeingness"–*aletheia and apokalypsis* (Kristeva)–diverge dramatically: the one the speculative gaze at an object, the other the abject and ecstatic vision of the future. So it is no surprise to sense beneath the surface of poststructuralism (despite its denial of any depth beneath text) its particular cryptoapocalypse–its own homogenizing gaze, camouflaged by its polemic against "the Same." Certainly it has freed up a space from coercive universals. But is there breathing room? Or does the interrogation of all positionality, the deferral of all decision, and the debunking of all presence close down the space for critical polyphony won by the emancipatory movements? Not to mention the space for a pneumatic feminism?

A relationist, which is to say in the present context, a counter-apocalyptic feminism does not defend "essence." The point is rather that much that we might not want to sacrifice to sophistication gets herded together under the misnomer of essence–gender, sex, nature, position, ground, horizon, project, social justice, end, purpose, identity, cosmology, and anything reminiscent of spirit. " 'Essence' itself becomes an abstraction that tissues over difference."[97]

True, however, to the counter-apocalypse operating constructively within feminist theory, certain feminists schooled in poststructuralism also resist the crusade to purge feminism of essence. For instance, there is something illumining in the way Naomi Schor, one of the editors of the collection *The Essential Difference*, carefully foregrounds her own affective tone of "sarcasm, cold fury, contempt" in response to "the policing of feminism by the shock troops of anti-essentialism." Schor submits that "what revisionism . . . was to Marxism-Leninism, essentialism is to feminism: the prime idiom of intellectual terrorism and the privileged instrument of political orthodoxy." While none of the anthologized authors would refer to anti-essentialism as a displaced apocalypse, Schor astutely intercepts the transference of a technical term from philosophy into the rhetoric of religio-political power and thus into the stream of effects we have followed thus far: "Borrowed from the time-honored vocabulary of philosophy, the word essentialism has been endowed . . . with the power to reduce to silence, to excommunicate, to consign to oblivion. Essentialism in modern-day feminism is anathema."[98]

Is Schor voicing just another final judgment against the prior final judgment? I think not. By opening with a meditation on tone, she interrupts the chain of apocalyptic effects. She neither masks nor sanctifies her anger: in this way she furthers conversation. In the same volume, Teresa de Lauretis argues that "essentialism" "covers a range of metacritical meanings and strategic uses that go the very short distance from convenient label to buzzword."[99] In other words, the anti-essentialism designed to respect difference, to release the multicolored complexity of women's realities, became another shortcut.

Noting that Mary Daly and Adrienne Rich are routinely cited both for their essentialism and their lesbian separatism, de Lauretis unmasks a hidden motive of anti-essentialism. She asks why these accusations happen to fall on those feminists who take "the risk of challenging directly the social-symbolic institution of heterosexuality." Noting that African American women are listed neither among essentialists nor anti-essentialists, she suspects among the latter "an unwillingness to confront and come to terms with the stakes, indeed the investments that feminism may have in the heterosexual institution. . . . But then again, the next question goes, without that confrontation, can we remain feminists?"[100]

De Lauretis' "outing" of this closet homophobia (practiced by some academic lesbians as well) does not mark a single cause of anti-essentialism. The mere shift from the prophetic rhetoric of the social movements which confront the aggregated powers of sexism, racism, heterosexism, and so on to the purely academic preoccupation with "essences" articulates a change in the status of feminism. In substantial numbers feminists now belong to the cultural establishment. We may wish to relish the pleasures of privilege undisturbed by the cruder rhetoric of praxis. Thus the "new skepticism about the use of gender as an analytical category," towards which anti-essentialism drifts, would well serve the attempt to incorporate into the professional elite.[101] And in that case the disciplining of lesbian "essentialists" may provide, as de Lauretis suggests, the lynchpin of assimilation today.

For if the apocalypse pattern indelibly subjugates woman as the bearers of sex, inscribing authority in a virginal masculinity which requires the strict maintenance of gender boundaries, and if, as Butler puts it, "the 'unity' of gender is the effect of a regulatory practice that seeks to render gender identity uniform through a compulsory heterosexuality,"[102] then the rabid dualism of the originative apocalypse pattern presupposes the strict sexual dualism of which heterosexism marks the edges. To decode that dense syllogism: the dualism of the apocalypse presupposes the hierarchy of one gender over the second, and the hierarchy of two genders presupposes the taboo against homosexuality. Virginity minimizes sex and thus the possibility of male slippage. But if sex, like the primordial serpent, can slither within and between the sacred sex/gender boundaries indiscriminately, the world falls down.

And yet the incapacity of Butler's work *Gender Trouble* to open up an interchange between the intellectual free play of endless cultural constructions of sex/gender and the bio-ecological co-constituents of the body suggests another entrée for our old "scientific" transcendence of the material. Once again, body is reduced to a "boundary" and culture is freed from "nature." Women's bodies and their cries–their *basanizo–*

again drop out of hearing. But these debates are only important to this analysis for their exemplification of an apocalyptic underbelly of the women's movement: has our anti-utopian, anti-essentialist "undecidability," so anti-apocalyptic in its self-understanding, fallen prey to the antisexual habit of the original New Jersualem? If so, it is not surprising that our unconscious replication of its pattern would tend toward a dissociative "transcendence" of feminism. Yet I cannot tell, nor can someone else tell me, where communal maturation of our discourse ends and self-immolating collusion with the apocalypse begins.

12

If the politics of identity veers by definition toward a single locus of accountability, and if more recent feminist theory has swerved toward a pluralism of undecidable incommensurabilities, a counter-apocalyptic feminism stretches identity into a fluid matrix of multiple mutualities. Women of color—and this means women of many colors—write from perhaps the sharpest experience of the relational complexity of resistance. Besides the burgeoning opus of African American women, examples proliferate in various genres, cultures, fields. Chung Hyun Kyung evoked the syncretism of an embodied multireligiosity as a Korean Christian woman at the shivering edge of a formidable multireligious patriarchy. Likewise, Rita Nakashima Brock's Japanese American heritage increasingly elaborates her affinity for a richly erotic political theology of healing rather than blaming relations. Cherríe Moraga as a Chicana lesbian writes of "making bold and political the love of the women of our race," yet refuses separatist lesbianism and single-issue feminism: "Any movement built on the fear and loathing of anyone is a failed movement," she concludes. A word well-aimed at the apocalypse in all of our movements![103]

Wedged into minority slots within a hegemonous culture where they must juggle gender, race, and class, women of color practice "multidimensional and bifocal" analysis for survival. What bell hooks writes in reference to the role of cultural studies in addressing a specific difference between Africans and African Americans speaks to the present project:

> It must be committed to a 'politics of difference' that recognizes the importance of making space where critical dialogues can take place between in-

dividuals who have not traditionally been compelled by politicized intellectual practice to speak with one another. Of course, we must enter this new discursive field recognizing from the onset that our speech will be 'troubled,' that there exists no ready-made 'common language.'... We are challenged to celebrate the polyphonic nature of critical discourse.[104]

What makes the difference between incommunicable differences and celebratory polyphonies? An already established "common language" would signify a blended "common oppression"; yet from the lack of a "ready-made" common discourse one may only infer the absence of any ready-made community, and for that matter, of any fixed underlying identity of the subject of oppression. If such a solid subject—"the oppressed" as such, the subject of subjection, the permanent apocalyptic victim—did already exist, what chance would there be of its own liberating self-empowerment? But such a gender- and race-troubling strategy for critical discourse breaks down the semblance of incommensurability, enabling communing moments. At such moments, precisely because we did *not already* share a language, we celebrate the new-found polyphony.

13

What then might keep the conversation of difference alive? When bell hooks pointed to a new "discursive field," her unabashedly spiritual sense of community may be imagined speaking its grammar. She considers her community challenged to "—as it happens in traditional African-American religious experience—*hear one another 'speak in tongues,' bear witness, and patiently wait for revelation.*"[105] No casual intertextuality here.

"Speaking in tongues" finds its textual origin in the Book of Acts account of the gathered group of the dead Jesus' friends (2:1–11). They burst, after weeks of meditative waiting, into a public disturbance on the Jewish Feast of Pentecost, an ecstasy of multi-ethnic communication in cosmopolitan Jerusalem. The multilayered wordplay of the text links a vision of "tongues" of flame lighting upon persons uttering the many "tongues." It was not that they all suddenly spoke a common language. Rather, amidst the cacophony of simultaneous foreign dialects, what stunned them was that they *understood* one another. Peter at that moment quotes Joel 2's ancient eschatological prophecy of gender and class egalitarianism.

Rethinking our relation to tradition after modernity may require of women's movements within and beyond theology a renewed attention to this sort of mystical multilingualism, kindled in a temporarily separated community and igniting among strangers. Of course the meaning of eschatology in the black church–which bears important resemblances to the pre-Constantinian tradition, both apocalypse and wisdom-based–cannot be lightly transferred to some generic feminist-womanist spirituality.

To bear witness one need not repeat the *martyrion* of apocalypse, but also one will not forget those suffering beneath the altar; to wait patiently for revelation will demand silent gaps, which theory will strain to fill. For a postmodern epistemology of polyphonic relation, revelation may erupt in a group's communication across disturbing difference or in the spirit of animal, vegetable, or mineral; in the heat of a double-edged tongue, or in the lull of your solitude. As in its musical form, polyphony does not require harmony; it only requires resonant relation.

14

We are female human beings poised on the edge of the new millennium.
> We are the majority of our species, yet we have dwelt in the shadows. We are the invisible, the illiterate, the laborers, the refugees, the poor.

And we vow: *No more.*

We are the women who hunger–for rice, home, freedom, each other, ourselves.

We are the women who thirst–for clean water and laughter, literacy, love.[106]

Glossalalia indeed: a multiplicity of women's voices gathered into the genre of a creed, neither as monolithic "woman" nor as mutually opaque "difference." The poetic statement quoted above, prepared for the global campaign of the Women's Environment and Development Organization, represents a set of voices readily and perhaps increasingly ignored within a white (feminist) academy as it distances itself from the "global," from "identity politics," and from the revolutionary hopes which first gave rise to such a political/spiritual rhetoric. Here a poetics of women's lives serves a global politics intent on gathering the global force of women into strategic coherence.

This is a coherence which contemporary theory may filter out on principle. "I think that all *global* problematics are archaic; that one should not formulate global problematics because that is part of a totalitarian and totalizing conception of history," Julia Kristeva stated in an interview.[107] Backing this altogether global gesture of disregard, Kristeva reiterates like a postmodern cliché the call to "local knowledges." These now turn out to reside in the work of "anthropologists, linguists" and other academic specialists. Is the true archaicism to be heard in the voice of the Western female academic enjoying the entitlements of bourgeois scholarship, impatient to screen out those voices who combine intensive local practices with their own global coalitions? One wonders how such a recoil to the supposed "local" from the delegitimized "global" accounts for its own privileged position within the aggressive globalism of late capitalism. (Not.)

I wonder if the Western feminist movement is at a crossroads, in which it can write itself as a decommunalized, depoliticized aggregate of iconoclastic, liberal women enjoying their privileges, or it can reach deeper into the flesh of the world, solidifying communal and ecological bonds locally and solidarities globally. I cannot sing quite the same song as the women of WEDO, but I find their spacetime intersecting, refiguring my own, their discourse tinged with a whimsy that allows me an opening. For they speak neither the traditional liberationist slogans of revolutionary apocalypse nor the deconstructive discourse of difference. Yet the "Women's Creed" quoted above contains key elements of both sensibilities. Its strong "we" situates itself within difference: "We are strengthened and blessed and relieved at not having to all be the same." Its tone, at once solemn and lyrical, also breaks recurrently into a playfulness absent from the old apocalypses of liberation.

After a forthrightly messianic allusion worthy of the woman clothed with the sun—"We are the mothers in labor to birth the politics of the 21st Century"—the creed quips, "We are the women men warned us about." But "men" do not appear here as the true enemy. Listing the tactics of a "they" which remains open, unnamed, never backed into the metanarrative of "patriarchy" or "capitalism," the statement continues, "They have tried to deny us, define us, defuse us, denounce us; to jail, enslave, exile, gas, rape, beat, burn, bury–and bore us." Certainly "they" carries an apocalyptic weight of "the enemy"–how not? Yet the irony of the last phrase (reminiscent of Daly's "chairmen of the Bored") disrupts with its grin not just the dignity of evil but the totalizing tendency of "they" and of the list itself.

Apocalypse in its counter-apocalyptic gesture: lightly mimicking more portentous manifestoes, these global voices of gathered women have nonetheless firmly claimed for themselves the metaphor of the millennium. Partly this is a calendrical convenience; at the same time they resort knowingly to an eschatological hope, the constructive affirmation of which counters the grim determinisms of The End. *"All this is political. And possible."* No guarantees or even probabilities are offered: wording a vast, self-organizing desire, not extrapolating its future from present trends, this hope does however situate the future in the "now." Yet a now not quite fixed, not quite–yet.

> Bread. A clean sky. Active peace. A woman's voice singing somewhere, melody drifting like smoke from the cookfires. The army disbanded, the harvest abundant. The wound healed, the child wanted, the prisoner freed, the body's integrity honored, the lover returned. The magical skill that reads marks into meaning. The labor equal, fair and valued. Delight in the challenge for consensus to solve problems. No hand raised in any gesture but greeting. Secure interiors–of heart, home, land–so firm as to make secure borders irrelevant at last. And everywhere laughter, care, celebration, dancing, contentment. A humble, earthly paradise, in the *now*.[108]

These images may seem like a rural pastorale to anyone for whom the realities of the third world seem "archaic." But they mark the meaning of habitat and history for a growing proportion of the population of postmodernity. That the "now" itself remains caught in its future raises disturbing parallels to apocalyptic endism and the old dream of a terrestrial paradise; the present slides towards its horizon, imminent but elusive, able neither to acquiesce in present horror nor to defer hope. Thus it speaks from and for a situation in which there is no escaping from the grief and deprivation, the *han* engulfing too much of the present. Yet the bold *"now"* precisely counters every species of apocalyptic postponement.

Perhaps only by its appeal to an indigenous sense of place does it relocate a fullness *already* accessible, in phrases like "indigenous to an utterly different dimension," or "we are whale-song and rainforest; the depth-wave rising huge to shatter glass power on the shore."[109] Eco-apocalypse does not yet preclude eco-*presence*. The counter-apocalyptic impulse within apocalypse enfleshes itself in its cosmos, remembering in its own body what *matters*. To materialize is to suffer–and, under siege, to suffer unjustly. In the situation in which the certainties of faith and of revolution have eroded for many of the people of the planet, these voices raised in a shaky confidence, refusing to wait patiently for either the supernatural or the free-market city of jewels to descend from on high, posit what is still *naturally* possible. In contrast to the status quo, their modest utopia would feel like heaven to many, like hell to some.

15

From the outset, feminist reconstructions of sex/gender have been divided and multiplied by the diverse strategies, affinities, and histories of actual women. On the one hand, the combatively crisscrossing and self-critical energies thus injected into feminism tend to dissolve the terms of any consensus; on the other, this difficult interplay of differences remains cause for hope. After all, it is an ecological rule that diversity nurtures resilience, and thus sustainability, while monocultures, purged by poisons and highly productive for a while, succumb first to drought and disease. To put the hope negatively: "they" who would make feminism their enemy might not be able to find and root out a force that is so multiply, ambiguously distributed throughout the topographies of human and nonhuman difference. In this way the political spatiality of difference resembles rural insurgency: the guerrillas melt maddeningly into the wilderness. Only what is "simply located"[110] can be simply eliminated. If place has shown itself within the topography of counter-apocalypse to be precisely the vital space of relations, a polyphonic relationalism guarantees a multidimensional movement. Or is it many movements? Who will count?

It was not just any difference, but sexual difference, metabolized by New Women and rightly recognized by the Victorian apocalypticists as threatening the end of the known world, which necessitated this chapter's discussion. And sexual difference now melts just as maddeningly into gender, and back with queer theory into sex–into two, three, many sex/genders. But I would not have us cease to resurrect the sexual bodies of gender. Judith Butler's feminist axiom holds good, that sex is to gender as nature is to culture. Yet it seems to me that the distinction between "nature" and "culture" is problematic, prone to dissolve toward one pole or the other. As there is no anatomical "sex" that we can access apart from our linguistic constructions, so there is at this point in history no "nature" free of human culture—as influence and construction.[111] So I am not sure the axiom does not still work. We have no access to the Edenic purity of a body in nature, free to make forays into sexist culture. But on the other hand neither need we fold the body and thus sex back into gender, into the seamless textualization of a totalizing cultural production with no cosmic remainder. Language itself, voiced in the countercultures in which we practice our heteroglossia, speaks from the semiotic, from the prelinguistic, from the silences of sensuality and the suffering of witness.

Therefore both the difference and the inseparability of me from my animal body register as the difference and the inseparability between the cultural construction of my gender and the biological base of my sex. Gender and sex, like, or indeed *as* self and body, plead for a communing relationship of their own. Mimetically transfiguring the site of oppression by inhabiting the place not of the pure body but a body of wounded wisdom, women and men of whatever affectional persuasions live as bodies already, in spite of all pretty well communing with themselves and with the circumambient universe. Not "in control" of my body but neither merely identical to "it," "I" am something like its facilitator, even the chairperson, of my body. Elected by aeons of evolution, millennia of culture, and decades of self-signifying acts. "I" am part of this body, accountable to it and making major decisions for it, for good or for ill. In the spacetime of this personal *topos*, I am also enmeshed in public friendships with the social body of my voluntary communities and inescapable publics. There, in the transient loop where body, society, and earth overlap, I—at moments when I "get wisdom"—am patiently and indirectly re-engendering myself. Through a lifetime.

Perhaps sex *is* to gender as body is to self; so body is to self, then, as ecology is to community. I have shared my meditations on the importance, after all, of grounding, even solidifying our movement as women, the women's movement, *in* the body—bodies of our inward, complex sociality as individuals; bodies of our communing and confronting social diversity; bodies of our most literal of all ground, the earth. But we need not–indeed, short of some sort of neoprimitive revival on a purged planet, cannot–get fixed there.

The "earth came to her rescue"–but the Sun Woman was not herself limited to the terrestrial element. Earth and air, then–the ground and the horizon, at which latter edge the interpretive elsewhere of a collective female has begun to imagine itself again as holy. She had always snuck into patriarchal theology as the divine Sophia.

An epistemology of wisdom–listening to the silences before the tongues ignite, then patiently translating, interpreting, the polyphony–leads us not finally to plurality for its own sake. The many are there and will continue to increase. They are a given. Rather, plurality tucked into the relationship of complexity–"folded together"–serves the endlessness of counter-apocalypse. Not a pluralism of indifference but a coordinate multiplicity, a polyvocal mutuality, will keep us living graciously. To learn the practice of paradox, the difficult discipline of waiting until undecidability lifts enough to decide in the face of ambiguities which remain, requires "a head of wisdom." But then, as Wisdom herself once said, "Happy is the one who listens to me, watching daily at my gates . . . ; but those who miss me injure themselves" (Prov. 8:34ff).

Women before feminism have communed at the edge of time. Feminism has pushed the celebration and its attendant traumas into the world at large, and now it is for us to ease out of our less productive dualisms, our more stale apocalypses, into something neither lost nor found. Sisterhood, with its gender foundations, remains unsteady–so perhaps we can shake together more rhythmically. Dancing out demons, dislocating sexual fates, unblocking spirits. Perhaps we might become public friends. If not universal, all the more global. In the meantime the calendrical millennium will pass, and some will drop, disappointed, from the shaky "we." Jezebel, never a literalist, has her task cut out for her.

The gate where they waited glowed pearly in the predawn moonlight. The moment had arrived. Breathe. Babs, yawning, hugged her. "Sophie," hissed young Jeri, eyes sparkling preternaturally in the dark, "I got a message from your son an hour ago. Everything's cool." Relieved, she felt the familiar tang of pride, hurt, detachment–flushed by gratitude at the shift from long alienation to friendship. Without his work, this mission . . . "Listen!" Jezebel pointed. Thunder in the distance: the desert horsepeople. The red dragon growled disdainfully. Jealous of those silky skins? she chuckled. They all fell silent. Breathing together. They tensed as they heard the alarms go off on the other side of the city. Suddenly the unmistakable cadence of the four, and shouts, and her son leaping off the enormous white one, handing her the reins while his friends slid off the others. "Those drunk old jockeys didn't know what hit 'em," he snorted. The horses seemed disoriented, defiant, but oddly acquiescent. Quickly they discarded the saddles and reassuringly stroked the spirited beasts, whose colors seemed magically to brighten and glow. The women mounted swiftly, Jezebel whistling the leitmotif of the Valkyries; Babs however required a boost from the boys. As the throng of furious soldiers, executives, politicians, priests began to flood through the gate, the women's dragons swooped off with the young men, the desert people thundered up just in time, creating a duststorm of distraction, and the four galloped eastward. The dawn covered them in glory.

7. Spirit

Counter-Apocalyptic
In/conclusion

How could we tire of hope?
—so much is in bud.

How can desire fail?
—we have only begun

to imagine justice and mercy,
only begun to envision

how it might be
to live as siblings with beast and flower,
not as oppressors....

So much is unfolding that must
complete its gesture,

so much is in bud.

Denise Levertov, "Beginners"

1

In the interest of un-ending time, we have dug up here and there an apoc-alypse template embedded in Western histories of hope. The dirt has seemed to pile into a sort of spiral mound. But who knows whether it is the digging of the site or the site itself that accounts for this dimly recog-nizable design? Amidst what Julia Kristeva might call this "topology of catastrophe," archaeology has at each point cast up its own construction. A counter-apocalypse, if it could not tinker with the remains, would be buried in its own ambivalence. So I have not just reconstructed a particular religious history; I have built little altars along the way, incongruous montages, parodies perhaps, of the original piety, but not lacking in reverence. Each configural zone, as it dis/closes its present possibility, has given cause for celebrations. "So much is in bud."

The tutelary spirit of the five rhetorical zones encrypted in the last four chapters now itself appears as the sixth. This one wants at once to unseal the apocalypse and re-seal it, healing the agony, recognizing itself amidst the kaleidoscope of eyes, animating a certain Wisdom. She insists on both and neither, but makes her own demands: "watch daily at my gates" (Wisdom of Solomon). Now, at the silence of the last seal—again, still, never again—that spirit threatens to appear "in person." But perhaps only to reveal its polynymity: it has been appearing in so many guises all along, usually content to remain anonymous. This last chapter produces a version of what in theology is called pneumatology—the study of the doctrine of the Spirit. It is my hope that the *pneuma* will dis/close criteria by which to affirm finitude while averting finality. Finitude without end.

2

In the current endeavor, then, every twist of the rhetorical spiral has reconfigured a traditional zone of history, critique, and construction. The dynamism of each has depended, admittedly, upon a (possibly apocalyptic) binary of apocalypse and anti-apocalypse. But anti-apocalypse showed itself repeatedly as cryptoapocalypse, and so these meditations on the effects of the text of Revelation have served as pre-text for the development of a counter-apocalypse—itself not immune from occasional alternation between outsized ideas and skeptical deflations. A chiastic structure has emerged in each chapter's thematic movement from apocalypse, via anti-apocalypse, to counter-apocalypse. Contradiction is not solved but can be transformed into contrast, according to Whitehead's cosmology.[1] Perhaps here, then, structure, as in that of John's text, can prove retrospectively revealing.

First of all, after getting oriented within the pre-text of contemporary apocalypse, we reread the last book of the Book of Books. Imprinting its unchangeable finality upon any remaining future, that book's opposite could only be its erasure—and so the End of the Book. But then an unclosable text began instead to read itself into the margins of Revelation, a midrash that enabled us to converse with the spirits of the Last Word, to coax, to invert, to convert them to some more congregative conversation.

Next we considered our second rhetorical zone–time. Threatened millennia ago with its end, time yielded up what is considered "history"–stretched toward The End as a posthistory to be at once dreaded and desired. But reminding ourselves of Apocalypse's own nonlinear medium may allow us to ease history back into a *helical timefulness*, a rhythm akin to the spiral nebula, the shifting seasons, the entrainment of relations. If our third dimension, apocalyptic space as cosmic displacement by an end-driven time, deposited us as pilgrims within a trivialized topography, counter-apocalypse relocated us in the *topical place* of our overlapping habitats. Regarding the fourth: while the apocalypses of community have provoked a late modern anti-utopianism that seeks locality but eschews community, counter-apocalypse resisted the binary of utopia and individualism, configuring instead the complexity of a *communing polyphony.*

And then a fifth zone–gender–appeared, feeling still self-conscious among those other, less sexually charged, more classically ennobled ideas. Beyond exclaiming at the crudities of good virgin-mothers and bad prophet-whores constellated by a deadlocked masculine fixation on mostly male enemies, feminist theology has been maturing intellectually. We may yet outlast the opposition of an "essentialist" feminist identity, which tends to reify sex, versus an "anti-essentialist" feminist cultural constructivism that tends to disembody sex. Something like Judith Butler's "parodic performance" of gender may be reread to avoid an undecidable postgender/postfeminism–to inscribe instead its proliferating politics upon our eco-cultural bodies. The open ends of a *dis/closive gender* do not imply either indecision or anti-nature. Neither reifying nor erasing the traumatic injustice by which the dualism of male and female has been written in the flesh, the pneumatic play of spirit at the boundaries of the sexual binary opens options for what is biblically speaking both male and female and neither male nor female. Or in the odd grammar of Paul's Galatians, "neither male and female."[2]

3

Does this "both/and neither/nor" require the articulation of a third way, a third aeon? Or would that third already subdivide and proliferate?

Amidst the multiple intersections of apocalypse and its internal oppositions, a certain dialectic of counter-apocalypse has after all "unveiled"
itself. The movement here may be likened (hopefully without the pon-
derous weight of his binary architecture and certainly without his infinite confidence in the Infinite) to Hegel's revision of God as Spirit: "not
something quiescent, something abiding in empty identicalness but as
something which necessarily enters into the process of distinguishing
itself from itself, of positing its other, and which comes to itself only
through this other, and by positively overcoming it—not by abandoning
it."[3]

So I do not abandon apocalypse. I have argued that our history cannot
delete it without committing it. At the same time, I have undeniably been
hoping that its oppositions might generate a "third" space, open but not
empty, in which the presuppositions of endism may be positively overcome—"sublated," at once preserved and transcended. In another rhetoric, spirit "lures" the contradictory energy toward the third, the con-
trastive option.[4] Or rather we are ourselves lured along that path of
multiple yet mutual contrast, a way which is neither apocalypse nor anti-
apocalypse. A way never known in advance, no matter how many names
we give it. A way that appears only as we walk there.

I suggest that counter-apocalypse entails a sublation of eschatology
into pneumatology, into the dis/closive play of hope as a shifting luminosity at the edge of the present. Thus the contribution theology might
make lies where the other disciplines that we draw upon are largely forbidden to walk—in the liminal cross-overs, in the spiralling strands of relation *between* dimensions such as those considered above.

Yet these configured zones are themselves matrices of relationship.
Might we then speak of a *relation of relations*? Perhaps thus defined the
discourse of Spirit has its purpose here—not as the Hegelian super-
subject of History, not as the Third Person of a trinitarian patriarchy, not
as the abject of a tired modernism. Spirit as this infra-relation appears
rather as *intersubject* of our crisscrossing stories, twining together like
the code of the genetic double helix. Still, spirit-language only matters if
it *matters*—if its spiral materializes in the muddy interstices of struggle
and ambivalence. If it can be read without being reduced to the tropes of
humanism or launched into a literalism of transcendence.

So I will tell a story in and about the spirit of counter-apocalypse—a
type (not a prototype) of the end of modernity, another kind of recapitu-

lation, at once narrative and practical. For if the Book of Revelation has been a habit-forming text, then only a theoretical construction which gets off the stage of the academy and into *practice*–which *performs* its counterpoint–can make any difference.

4

I first visited El Salvador a year after the signing of the peace accords which ended that country's civil war. One could still taste the mysterious and renowned hope of "the struggle." The peace process was less than promising, but even in a situation of diminishing optimism, the commitment to which so many had given their lives still gave off a kind of luminosity; the stunning revolutionary hope that for over a decade had been saving North American pilgrims from cynicism was everywhere still visible. One still felt the presence of Archbishop Romero, who prophesied his own resurrection in the life of the people–in the dignity and persistence of the people; as in antiquity, the "blood of the martyrs" seemed to promise the fruit of a new and globalizing resistance to death. While our particular Salvadoran companions, like their mentor Romero, had never surrendered to the full victory-or-death apocalypse of the revolution and would not bear arms, they had repeatedly risked their lives for the struggle.

Here had taken place the best of revolutionary neoapocalypse: an armed insurgency shaped in respectful collaboration with the Christian left.[5] The guerrillas had largely excluded civilian targets and had treated their "enemy" captives with relative decency; unlike most insurgencies, this one did not imitate the terror and torture tactics of the national security state. A revolutionary community that recognizes its biblical debt and so acts with some accountability to that text apparently differs from those revolutions which deny their own religious prehistory and so suck from it a fanatical spirit. Also, the distinct space of the Salvadoran revolution cannot be understood apart from its global web of spiritual witness– hence the indispensable role of all the international peace and justice groups, largely Roman Catholic but including many Protestants and nontheists as well, in bringing about a negotiated settlement. The very ideal of negotiation belies the winner-take-all posture of the apocalypse script. In the Salvadoran resistance grew the seeds of a possible counter-apocalypse.

While this unique history had not lost its meaning, at the point of my second visit, two years later (with some of the same travelers), I felt myself to be attending an anticlimax. After all the blood and fire, the insurgency appeared defeated not in war but by elections and the economy. "During the war," spokespeople for progressive religious and political communities often told us, "we were united, we knew the enemy, and whether as part of the armed struggle or working to alleviate its effects, we knew what to do. We thought peacetime would make the task easier. This is not so. Now we have peace without justice. We have democracy without liberation."

It was as though all the tensions repressed for the sake of solidarity had burst out, sundering the left; the revolution's leaders were accusing each other of corruption as people withdrew energy from politics to tend to private lives ravaged by twelve years of terror. In other words, we were visiting a post-apocalyptic moment. The relative certainty of a militant, self-purging unity within a strictly polarized situation had persisted through unbearable tribulations; it had maintained a hope not for utopia but for a society where the victims of the murderers, the torturers, the rapists, the oppressors would be vindicated—where "all who thirst may drink of the waters"—no mean metaphor in this parched and contaminated landscape.

By 1995, the revolutionary apocalypse had evaporated, leaving the effects of its tribulations without fulfilling the promises of its victory. The "base communities" and liberation Christians who had so heroically aligned their faith with the insurgency continued (and continue) to remember their martyrs and to minister to the cultural and physical needs of their society. But along with a larger communal cohesiveness, the certainty of good and evil, of pro or con, had crumbled. One sensed a disciplined intent not to surrender to the disappointment, not to fade into despair. Not that the leaders in the work of justice had "tired of hope."[6] Rather, that hope's apocalyptic clarity—the vision of an equitable and sustainable society born from the blood of martyrs—had dissipated. People talked of the present as a time of uncertainty and transition, with the political left lacking either the skills of democracy or the vision of the future and the right (fortunately) also divided. The heady, distinctive mix of revolutionary and Christian eschatology had given way to ambiguity. If pre-modern and modern apocalypses converged creatively in "the struggle," suddenly a postmodern situation prevailed, a time of multiple undecidabilities and shards of ambiguous possibilities. The received modern horizon of social justice seemed willy-nilly to have dispersed.

In the meantime, one witnesses the new cryptoapocalypse of transnational capital, its huge tin *maquiladoras* mushrooming across the good land of an ecologically devastated country.[7] While the apocalypses of war come and go, economic, ethnic, and ecological dooms gallop steadily on (unleashed in this very geography by Columbus), relentlessly devouring the "*otro mundo*" in the name of the Same—wealth and progress, modernization and development.

To return to the above question: there are those in (for instance) El Salvador who persist—not merely resisting, as though the reflex of opposition sufficed. What sets them apart from the sense of confused vision and political exhaustion? Let me suggest that this is precisely a matter of spirit. In El Salvador one particular team, facilitated by Marta Benevides with virtually no institutional support or economic back-up, has consistently criticized the "instrumentalization" of Christianity by Marxism as well as the institutionalization of religion to pacify the poor and ennoble the rich. They speak now of a "spirituality of relation" which demands that before I argue or seek to convert you to my party line, I enter into a relation which might change me as well. Edgar Nunez suggests that this is "a time of ideas," and though in his daily life he carries burdens barely comprehensible to Northern bourgeois academics, he is curious, inspired, excited at the potentialities for the transition.

These activist thinkers, the ones who are not dispirited, work on the transformation of social relations within the context of ecological relations, and therefore have a special involvement with the indigenous minority, the poorest among Salvador's poor, people who still show the signs of an earth-centered spirituality. As such a facilitator, Marta Benevides works in the countryside with a few indigenous cooperatives in five communities to save their land, which remains their sole possible livelihood if these communities are to survive. She says now that she eschews the language of "the struggle." After nearly two decades of struggling at home and in exile, she declares she "does not want to be a redeemer" and "does not want to be crucified." She describes her commitment (a matter of almost around-the-clock effort, demanding sometimes quixotic, sometimes risky "work on behalf of their common good") as not struggling but "being." She will "live the way," not fight for it. After much soul-searching and grief, she has stepped beyond the apocalyptic cycle of dualism and disappointment, of messianism and martyrdom—out of the oppositionalism of the struggle. Yet she has not removed herself from responsibility to and for those endangered people she considers her true *pueblo*.

Ekstasis–to "step beyond." But what has she stepped into? It must be said that a new relationship founds her work: a relation to what she alternately calls the "I Am," the "deep self," and the "spirit." It now communicates with her in startling dialogic clarity; it has a voice. It has already healed her of a crippling physical illness. And quite tangibly, however frustrated, disappointed, or lonely she finds herself in her present work against the odds, she is not dispirited. *Al contrario!*

It was the third day of our second visit. The dust rising from the path choked but did not stop us. We then climbed as a group of gringos and mostly indigenous Salvadorans up a mountain peak worked (like most verdant places) as a coffee plantation. Marta led us to a site once sacred to the Nahuats, where several small waterfalls spill into a pool. Popular as a local recreation site, its dramatic beauty was marred by the ubiquitous garbage. One had to soften one's focus to see through the veil of refuse. We changed into our bathing suits, splashed happily about, picnicked. We placed our compostable waste as ever in appropriate holes, then got out the bags brought by people from the cultural center in the adjacent town. (In a country beset by growing cholera rates there is nothing innocent about garbage.) Marta had even invited a couple of engineers who work with the pistons driven by the waterfalls and continuously clogged by garbage. In less than an hour a group of fifteen or so had performed a little miracle, and we stared around, along with a monkey staring down at us, at our pristine new creation. The great semitropical trees, the hot pink of flowering wild impatiens, the sparkling waters blinked paradisiacally back at us. We had picked up all the garbage.

With arms looped and hands held, through Marta's guidance everyone, including two children and the engineers, spoke into the circle, articulating surprise, gratitude, synergy, joy, resolve, the redemption of garbage, and the aptness of this sign/act for us North Americans, from whom the garbage culture comes. Variously addressing Spirit, God, the spirits, the earth, each other. Not esoteric like glossolalia, but many-tongued spirit-speech nonetheless.

We then carried the garbage out, and those from the town center later displayed it with a banner saying "Let us not violate our sacred *tierra madre*"–hoping to stir a community action to make the site an ecological zone (or at least to raise a consciousness of the degrading habits developed amidst the war's apocalyptic waste of humans and nature, now accelerated by "the market." However Marta and her team might later recycle that symbolic gesture, our own group had experienced, after several days of living together, our first communing moment. Not that it could be wrought into a stable community. In a holy place dis/closed by a woman, lush with universe and with ethnic, racial, class, and gender edges temporarily fluid, heightening the translucency of difference.

Why call the moment "spiritual," and jeopardize its carnality, vibrant with splashing, working, eating, laughing, thoughtful bodies? Within the experience itself and within its present narration, I would suggest that spirit language mediates the awkward, enlivening play of intentional relation. The traditional rhetoric of relation *to* spirit, as if to a literal "other," threatens to reify the event. Yet perhaps it allows certain self-vocalizations which could not be addressed to others or to selves.

But how would I *place* such an episode? Does it not illustrate a typical first-world pilgrimage into the exotic, a kind of social justice romance? Of course. I might list out the intensive preparation, the pedagogical deliberations, the curricular transformations, and the variety of long-term conversions, relationships, and accountabilities that seem to have resulted from both trips. But I have been avoiding the social justice credentialing scripted by my generation's own apocalyptic virtue.

Spirit is the point. In the mediations embodied in an emotional new set of relationships, a certain sensual power of dis/closure was released. Eyes opened. What is important is that such an opening was not a once-for-all conversion but an iconic moment, able to indigenize itself into our futures, able to discharge global energies into our local lives, nourishing our own deeper roots in North America. Standing outside of the numbing haze of our own displaced spaces, we could *see*–not just re-analyze–our own implication in the five hundred years, its genocidal climax, its ongoing economics. And we could foresee the third-world conditions toward which our own culture lurches. So we could prepare to persist within our own imminent future. But deeply, with a new permission and taste for laughter and wisdom. Mediating between self and other—between ancestors and futures, languages and bodies, between North and South, garbage and beauty, between apocalypse and its aftermath—"spirit" inflects a grammar of possibilities inarticulable in any single voice, simply located.

5

But which spirit? Surely "not the *Holy* Spirit, the one from my First Baptist Church growing up in Kentucky!" comments a friend in mock horror. So secular progressives need "spirit discernment" as much as conservative Christians. *Which* spirit? Many spirits or One? Human spirit? Nature spirit? Capitalized Spirit? *Holy* Spirit? But what if spirit cannot answer to the definitionalism of these questions?

Progressive Christians, perhaps even more deliberately than other progressives, habitually denigrate anything "spiritual"—characterized as inward, mystical, nonrational—as though it will distract from their ethical commitments. "Social justice Protestants" in particular are prone to play out another little drama of apocalyptic virtue. In this move they coincide with their opponents, the Christian conservatives, who have been equally suspicious of the Spirit. For in the history of orthodoxy, the "Holy Spirit" has played the role of spook, dissident, odd one out, required in order to make the Father and Son work but never granted their authority—the ghostly Third without whom the First and the Second Persons do not add up to the Trinity. Simultaneously with its derevolutionizing of apocalypse, Christian orthodoxy carefully sealed the Spirit into dogmatic isolation, purging it of human, cosmic, or plural content. Even in liberal Christian communities, if Spirit-language is used without frequent prophylactic repetitions of "Father" or "Son," someone will call for "the discernment of spirits."

The First Epistle of John (not John of Patmos) offered the original criterion for "discerning spirits": any which do not acknowledge "that Jesus was incarnate" are unholy. Not that "Jesus was Lord"—this point was not triumphalist, but rather suggested that a discarnate spiritualism would undermine the community's distinctive construction, forefigured in the flesh of Jesus, of a new holiness of *embodiment*. Spirit, as the immanence of the holy in the material world, must be expected to con-spire with the radically immanent project of the incarnation. An innumerable host of spirits could pass John's test: he still thinks in the pneumatic plural. But the First Epistle of John is routinely misread as separating the one true Holy Spirit from all others.[8] So Christian spirit discernment normally turns out to be a Christian identity-defense against the specificities and multiplicities of spirit. To save Spirit from its own plurality, the mono-spirit of the West has to abstract it from the multitude of bodies and zones which it otherwise inhabits.

Christian nervousness about the Holy Spirit early encrypted itself within the Western church by tacking the *filioque* ("and the Son") clause onto the Nicene Creed: the Spirit proceeds not just from the Father but also from the Son. A strange new subordination of a One at the same time declared equal to the other Two was thus sealed into orthodoxy. This arcane fragment of theological grammar may not be as trivial as it seems. Jürgen Moltmann has for the sake of both trinitarian sociality and of cosmic-ecological salvation advanced a twentieth-century crusade to delete the *filioque* clause.[9] Ante-Nicene creeds had the Spirit proceeding direct from the Father; for Tertullian the Son and the Spirit were two hands of the Creator. Spirit did tend to collapse into the spirit *of* the Father and the Son, forfeiting a primal integrity still evident in Hebrew scriptures and to some extent in Christian. But the double processionalism formally rendered the gender-elusive Spirit ontologically derivative from the first two Personnae of the Trinity. The more sacramental-pneumatic Eastern Christianity took permanent umbrage at this insult.

The gender imaginary at work in the *filioque* has less frequently been noted. Proceeding from the Father "and the Son," the gender-elusive Holy Spirit became an epiphenomenon of the ultimate man-to-man interaction. An odd mediator, more like a divine tool than a divine person, the presence of God in the world but not ever quite God: the Spirit does the work of the trinity without the prestige. It would not seem coincidental, then, that the Spirit carries all manner of feminine grammatical and metaphoric associations. Normally, but for troublesome outbreaks such as we first noted in Guglielma, orthodoxy successfully suppresses them. But these gender-bending pneumatic possibilities have been accumulating again. For instance, liberation theologian José Comblin, who has no difficulty soliciting the radical apocalyptic solidarity of the Holy Spirit with the poor, also tries to affirm the traditional femininity of the spirit-symbol. He draws an admirable analogy to the Peruvian and Bolivian "Pachamamma": "Instead of purely and simply rejecting this cult, so important to the religion and culture of the indigenous peoples, we could see it as a providential preparation for experience of the Holy Spirit." But his subsequent nod to the patriarchs is disappointing: "Maternal divinities provided a prefiguration, *though confused and erroneous,* of the Holy Spirit."[10] Even to grant the Trinity a mere one-third feminine power threatens to import disturbing indigenous and maternal elements. One senses the abjection such a refiguration would arouse amidst the all-male hierarchies.[11]

The woman behind the throne, a cosmic mom mediating family relations, the anonymous housewife of the universe–the ultimate case of responsibility without authority? In these pages we have seen the Spirit as the break-away power of the apocalypse: John of Patmos wrote "in the spirit"; the Joachite Age of the Free Spirit underwrote all Western revolutions and progressivisms. If Hegel rationalized *Geist* as the dynamic self-consciousness of modernity–the "New Age" itself–the left wing of his followers forged an almost invincible materialism out of his pneumatology. They discipline spirit into revolutionary monoliths forged "over and against," finally brooking no uncertainty, no multiplicity among those true believers who called themselves "orthodox" Marxists.

So this is what I wonder: If orthodox Christendom had not so successfully moved to subdue the Spirit, repressing the multiple fire-tongues of heteroglossia at about the same time it capitulated to the (Holy) Roman Empire, might Spirit have found less violently apocalyptic self-expression? And what if those female-identified messianisms that have intermittently burst nonviolently upon the scene signify Spirit trying to compensate for the perverse hegemony of masculine tropes by incarnating itself–as Guglielma, Ann Lee, the Universal Publick Friend?

6

"What might have been and what has been point to one end, which is always present."[12] Does the counter-apocalyptic possibility hidden in the apocalypse suggest a present path? I think we need to track back, to discern what might have been implicit all along–the pneumatic dimension already at work within the prior five configural zones, now demanding its moment of re-cognition. Still hoping to escape Final Judgment for such ambiguous moves, I move to what in music is called a reprise. But we must listen to its unresolved tensions, to its caesurae–as in that silent interval which followed the opening of the seventh seal–for echoes of spirit.

Text and Spirit

The text of Revelation proves nothing. So I have evoked it neither as proof-text nor as anti-text for my own postulates. But it communicates much. In some sense I have let it funnel a vast stream of feminist ambivalence toward all biblical religion; but though in its peculiar position it postures as *the* book of the Book of Books, I have tried to signal that it does not and cannot stand *pars pro toto* for the Bible. Like all theologians, I assess one part of the Bible in the light of my favorite parts, letting internal criteria pass judgment. But I have not distilled one biblical "idea"–such as love, justice, or hope–as the fixed center of a "canon within the canon," in the way of some feminist theology. Nevertheless, the operative relationalism does discern a normative equilibrium circulating through that prophetic/wisdom complex constituted by just those ancient values–a complex by contrast to which John's Apocalypse, enmeshed within it, appears to suffer from disequilibrium.

Counter-apocalyptic writing, therefore, as a species of open and thus dis/closive text, at once rereads Apocalypse and rewrites its present effects. Neither affirming its self-closure as a book of the final disclosure nor colluding in its erasure from the history with which it is indelibly entwined, I have sought openings into and out from that text. It is the thesis of this concluding chapter that a force I call spirit–as a name for the sustaining power of life and for our anthropomorphic apprehension of it–inhabits that opening. In other words, spirit sticks a theological foot in the door of world-closure.

In mainstream theology, the trope of the Holy Spirit has encoded the communing and communicative capacities both of the Trinity and of the church. As Third Person, mediating within and for God, it softened the harsher dualism of the Father-Son orthodoxy. "In a way that is difficult to specify, the Holy Spirit completes the intradivine process of communication," writes Roman Catholic theologian Avery Dulles. "The Holy Spirit is frequently called Subsistent Love, the sigh, breath, or kiss by which the mutual union of the Father and the Son is sealed."[13] I cannot here speculate on the power of such homoerotic metaphors within the charged context of a male celibate community (often cloistered if not closetted). Theological leadership thus distilled itself from a heterosexist culture in which biological fathers remain emotionally distant from sons; a distance that doubtless found healing intimacy in the performative symbols of transcendent male union. The trinitarian *opening* into relation is thus, however, immediately "sealed" into a *fusion*.

Credited with the continuing work of the church, the inspiration of its hierarchy and the instruction of its theologians, the Spirit has always operated within the temporal space of the deferred End. Vatican II opened the gates to ecumenical and liberation theologies when, in the name of the Holy Spirit, it criticized biblicism and emphasized an ancient tradition whereby scripture is insufficient without the ongoing interpretive work of "tradition." "This tradition which comes from the apostles progresses in the Church under the assistance of the Holy Spirit. . . . Thus, as the centuries advance, the Church constantly tends toward the fullness of divine truth, until the words of God reach their consummation in the Church."[14] Despite the still exclusivist teleology of this rhetoric, conservatives hated its implication that something might be missing in the canonized and apostolic origins. So again this spirit provokes a certain historical evolution–but under such ecclesiocentric terms that Spirit ends up as the guarantor of triumphalist "progress." Garbed in pontifical splendor as the Holy Ghost, *pneuma* stiffly haunts its own openings.

In both Catholic and Protestant theology, text and pneuma intersect at the point of reading. Within the Catholic tradition of "spiritual exegesis"[15] the reader performs a kind of *lectio divino*, a "spiritual reading,"[16] sinking imaginatively into the text as means to an altered, meditative state. Then spirit is experienced as wisdom-instructor. Indeed, Anthony Thistleton gives us as his example of the hermeneutics of "spiritual reading" a meditative account of "the power of the eschatological symbols in the Apocalypse. . . . They function as both communicative and productive texts."[17] Karl Barth's "pneumatic exegesis" similarly invoked a vital relationship to "the Spirit" as the presupposition of the "hearing of the Word." Such reading strategies suggest counter-literalist, counter-authoritarian and for our purposes possibly counter-apocalyptic moves accessing a potentially live zone of extratextual relations.

Yet these reading strategies still seek to authorize knowledge as

Christocentric and thus the exegete as authoritative theologian. Thus appointed "primary author,"[18] "the spirit" does not promote contextual and critical readings of scripture, readings that might expose *dispiriting* points of injustice–of sexual and ethnic chauvinism, for instance–within the text itself. Though these strategies do wedge a pneumatic opening between the scriptural context and the present reading–deploying a "cultural linguistic" approach, which frees the text from modern literalisms and universals–at the same time they lock it into parochial purity: it is not to be interpreted, let alone criticized, by extrabiblical criteria.

The pneumatic reading I have undertaken of Revelation's text and of its extrabiblical effects assumes, however, that the Bible never has been and never can be insulated from its surrounding lifeworlds. The textualism of counter-apocalypse has sought to check its pneumatological flight with an entire set of historicist habitats, tracing the production and reproduction of apocalyptic contexts in history, and at the same time nesting within the ephemeral present of the reader.

If, as I will argue, the spirit–in Christian rhetorical contexts the Holy Spirit–names the very logic of internal relationality, then of course I may consider myself in relation to *it* when a reading stimulates a heightened *sense* of relation. That is, when text takes on a "life of its own" that lifts me into critical mutuality not just with the text but with life. The Syriac tradition identified the Holy Spirit with Life itself–"And from that [life] is the Spirit which is within me. / And it cannot die because it is life"–and all Christian traditions confess it as the giver and gift of life, the sustainer of life.[19] If it motivates practices we would today recognize as ecologically and communally sustainable, the *pneuma* becomes the eminent counter-apocalyptic agent. Hardly anti-apocalyptic, since John of Patmos, like all his heirs, was "in the spirit." But in the present pneumatic imaginary, spirit was busy countering the binary means and cataclysmic effects of apocalypse, working for sustainable community, communication, creation, deferring The End. Such a textual hermeneutic, undertaking a politics of spirit in finite format, by definition takes *time*.

Time and Spirit

The apocalypse has shown itself indelibly time-full. Classical theology re-verticalized the cosmos into an eternal hell and heaven, between which was wedged the transient classroom of time: how you test out in history mattered only as prep for your finals. In the Joachite revision of apocalypse in the eleventh century, we witnessed arising the great millennialist challenges to the triumphalist anti-utopia of the church. Literally in/spired by the name of the "Free Spirit," the "Third Status" of the Third Person marked pneumatology as indelibly insurgent. Modernity would capitalize on this renewed utopianism. It would present itself as the New Age, offering Europe its New World. Spirit, translated ever more into the indubitably masculine grammar of *Geist*, fueled the rationality of progress.

And postmodern times? They seem to vibrate between an ultramodern extinction of all species of spirit, and a recognition of their own pneumatological postrationality. Ihab Hassan's multiply reprinted juxtaposition of modern and postmodern traits whimsically but significantly contrasts the modern "father-son" to the postmodern "Holy Spirit."[20] Is his one more identification of *this* age as finally the Joachite "third aeon" just one more modernist manipulation, ever unaccountable to its textual antecedents, of the hope for the age of free, ecstatic distribution of the Spirit? No doubt. At the same time, given the potent antiliteralism of every deconstructive gesture, the subtext of such an allusion to the premodern trinitarian hope may be worth surfacing.

If postmodernity has learned anything, it must be that the facile modern embrace of the New has gotten old; that if it deconstructs the roots of its futurism, it would find–as in John, Joachim, or even Hegel–no linear movement from past to future. It would find in those arcane visions a complex pattern of overlapping epochs, each helically recapitulating the prior. The simpler apocalypse of polarity, enabling the great revolutionary or counterrevolutionary simplifications by mass sacrifice, has dominated the social formation of modernity.

In order therefore to release the radically democratic, plurivocal, and sustainable potencies of the present, we may need to retrieve a relation to select premodern traditions of spirit. Not just for the sake of historical continuity but for that of the very time, the temporal rhythm, of spirit. This is why I have been making more visible certain spirit-centered counter-traditions of apocalypse that thread their way through modernity's denial of all tradition.

In the context of a postmodernist discussion of postcolonial feminist filmmaking, a woman artist lends us a timely clue:

> One type of reality that continues to be widely discussed and challenged in Third World contexts is the one characterized by a transition between tradition and modernism. What is at stake, on the one hand, is the recycling of these concepts within the framework of dualistic thinking and vertical ranking (East/West; North/South; Developed/Underdeveloped; Regress/Progress; Instinct/Reason; Nature/Culture; Heart/Mind; Woman (guardian of Tradition) /Man (advocate of Modernity)–hence the impasse that results from such perceptual stagnation; on the other hand [we have] the . . . blindness to the collapse of the modern project and our confidence in its enlightening and emancipatory potential. . . . Postmodernism therefore does not come *after*, but *with* modernism.[21]

An interesting pass, where women, and in particular women of the two-thirds world, provide through links with their own place and past a way to revalorize "tradition." Brave new worlds of the West show themselves as hegemonic missionary movements. Blind faith in modernity's ability to replace the old with the new does not contradict the reactionary push to center the present in premodern fundamentals. Rather, apocalypse has worked subliminally within the millennialist-progressive impulse and with bitter explicitness within premillennialist fundamentalism to generate its purged future-perfect, free of the complexity of present places and past times.

But the point of dis/closing apocalypse is precisely not to unleash apocalypse: rather, the counter-apocalypse emerging amidst the disarray of late modernity suggests–shades of Joachim–a postmodernity of *spirit*. Spirituality can no longer be left either to calcified traditionalism or to New Age commodification. But then neither can tradition be left in the past, nor the new age in the future. The timefulness of spirit dis/closes a crowded present, thronged by contradictory impulses from the past and contested possibilities for the future. It resists the urge to purge. The discerning of the spirit is then not a strategy of dissociation from others but rather one of "mutualist associations." As John Cobb has taught, theology can reinterpret divinity as that lure which invites disparate multiplicities into the immediate future of a new "togetherness."[22] The helical character of time requires the complex process of subjects constituted of their mutual relations with each other. And vice versa. Spirit-time in this view evinces the properties of social democracy.

We who are heirs of the "great religions" and of the great atheisms hardly know yet what a spirituality would be like which does not seek to transcend time and control its matter, to end history, to flee the clutter of relations and the fear of death. A spirituality which instead makes its way within and through the subtle pulseways of now and then. As finality softens into an open end, eschatology becomes pneumatology. This transition recalls that of another time: from John the Baptist's apocalypticism to that of Jesus' counter-apocalyptic *basileia*. After, or perhaps next to, the fire and the wormwood: the yeast rising and the seed germinating and the lost coin found. The garbage recycled. In place.

Place and Spirit

Such a spirit would indigenize us. Its temporality at any given moment dissolves into place. Yet christendom has inspired a civilization of furious displacement. A counter-apocalyptic discipline might gain insight from Moltmann's recent reform of eschatology by pneumatology. He has defined spirit as *vitality*: the spirit of God is none other than the *spirit of life*, not known in an amoral "élan vital" so much as in the "love of life." He makes the link to spatiality explicit:

> When the heart expands and we can stretch our limbs, and feel the new vitality everywhere, then life unfolds in us. But it needs a living space in which it can develop. Life in the Spirit is life in the "broad place where there is no cramping" (Job 36, 16). . . . But how else could "life in the Spirit" be understood, if the Spirit were not the space "in" which this life can grow and unfurl?[23]

The spirit no longer lifts us beyond space and its troubling chains of material association, but embraces us in place, indeed *is* that space. Does such a reformation of Christianity bode well for a planet rent by our crusading, colonizing spatiality? In the same passage, Moltman writes, "So in the new life we experience the Spirit as a 'broad place'—as the free space for our freedom, as the living space for our lives, as the horizon inviting us to discover life." Unfortunately this expansiveness can still too well resonate to a colon/ialist's imagery of hope, the Blochian (and early Moltmannian) privilege of the ever-receding horizon, energizing us to "discovery" of more New Worlds.

Nonetheless, this rhetoric may at the same time divert some Christian adventure from its missionary outwardness. "We explore the depths of this space through the trust of the heart. We search out the length of this space through extravagant hope. We discover the breadth of this space through the torrents of love which we receive and give."[24] Is this language "spiritual" in the insidious sense of replacing the "external," material world with an immaterial one? Or still troublingly expansive, coming from its European social location, rather than, for instance, that of Vítor Westhelle's Latin American "vital space?"[25] Moltmann remains vulnerable to such interrogation. But one can just as well read his pneumatological place-sense as a theological corrective to the Western apportionment of our subjectivities into separate spatialities.

When relationships crowd, or seem to, when breathing room–the room of *ruach*–feels choked and we are tempted to reclaim that heroic independence, we say instead: "I need some space." The late twentieth-century trope of "space" maintains a certain materiality of reference while functioning as the metaphor for an opening of subjectivity *within* a circumstance that would otherwise suffocate. As in, "to converse with the maternal in an unsticky tone, where there is space for tonal shifts and distancing."[26] The "sticky," abject maternality/materiality has guaranteed denizens of an oedipal civilization perpetual flight from and to "home" and therefore to and from place itself. Perhaps only when the maternal implanted as our origins comes into its spiritual dignity can we find the space we need, in place. Only then, perhaps, do the cartographies of colonization, the conquest of women "out there" and the return to mom "in house," come unglued.

Postcolonial place cannot be visited apart from mindfulness of our own bodily symbiosis within it–the mystery of the incarnation. Our own. That sense of what Glen Mazis calls "earthbodies"[27] conversely only comes to light within a subjectivity which attends its own mind's symbiosis with the bodily space. There the most limited habitat tucks within its recesses an inexhaustible–because cosmological–spatiality. This is not a matter of contentment with some given "nature" but of contructing "enabling environments" in and through which material circumstances can be altered.[28] Something like this can be attributed to the primitive Christian metaphor of the *basileia*: the kingdom of God, better translated as the divine commonwealth, imagined a spatiality constituted by the creaturely plenum of finite, spirit-filled mutualities locally congregating.

The tropical mountain, my favorite coffee shop downtown, the street with homeless mendicants, my desk in the sun—these become "my place" only through what Bachelard had called a "poetics of space." Kinds of relationship, of timing and communing, come to life in the place and in the memory of the place. "Love" names the self-affirming power of the relation of relations at that moment when it *places* me, makes me at home in its in-dwelling complexity.[29]

I cannot know the spirits of place as do those people who have never lost their place-bound traditions. I do know that to name spirit spatially and space spiritually wedges a foot in the closing door of modern time. In the midst of the uncanny closures of planetary habitat for the third millennium, in the midst of the extinctions peoples and species crammed into unlivable proximities, access to "a broad place where there is no cramping," to the breathing room of *ruach*, may dis/close clues for survival within the crowding. If uncramped, spirit-space materializes "vital space." Pneumatic space, enfolded within our actual habitat as its "implicate order," loves an opening.[30]

Community and Spirit

Spirit, closed into its traditional timeless, spaceless, and private subjectivity, has been successfully domesticated. When it overstepped the bounds of this pious interiority, it was duly disciplined, hereticized, persecuted. Mostly its status in the Christian Trinity kept it in line. Yet despite the droning numerology of trinitarian logic, the Third Person nonetheless enshrined the essence of sociality. In Augustine's trinitarian analogy, the Father is the Lover, the Son the Beloved, and the Spirit is Love itself; that is, the Third Person is the relation between the first two. "And yet here are two things that are one, he [*sic*] that loves and love; or if you like so to put it, that which is loved and love. And these two, indeed, are *mutually* said *relatively*."[31] Within a rare use of relational ontology within the syntax of a substance metaphysics, the Trinity evoked not the logic of independent essences but of interdependent personae—the Spirit encodes the mutuality of mutual relations. But within the grammar of substance, the exceptional relationalism of this trinity just proves the rule—the earthly rule of separate entities arrayed in hierarchies of dominance.

Moltmann has brought this submerged potential to a promising fruition. Arguing that the New Testament phrase "the fellowship of the Holy Spirit" "has to be understood in trinitarian terms as a *community of per-*

sons, and not in a unitarian sense as a *community of essence*,"[32] he goes on to do what two thousand years of Christian orthodoxy assiduously avoided: he opens the model of mutual participation symbolized by the interaction of the three-in-one into relations in the world.

> *The creation of community* is evidently the goal of God's life-giving Spirit in the world of nature and human beings. . . . *Bios*–life–is always symbiosis, and symbiosis–*conviviality* in the literal sense–is the clearly detectable goal whenever more complex, open systems are built up in the world of the living. . . . The trinitarian fellowship of the Holy Spirit is the full community of the Creator, Reconciler and Redeemer with all created being, in the network of all their relationships.[33]

In his mix of traditional with biological language, Moltmann has made a convivial move. The radicalism of Moltmann's designation of the Holy Spirit as "the Spirit of Life" may not be audible outside of theological circles, yet anyone disturbed by the pacifying power of a privatizing spirituality and by the conquest of nature sanctioned by a "transcendence" of *bios* can perhaps appreciate the gesture. This "conviviality" of "all created being" dis/closes the metaphysical cage which had kept the Spirit confined to the Father and Son. Moreover, the gender implications are not altogether lost on Moltmann. As long as God the Spirit could only proceed from the dyad of Father & Son, the rhetorical sanction for a church hierarchy of dominant males and their spiritual sons remained intact.

Representing the next generation of German Protestant progressivism, Michael Welker's systematic pneumatology shows the spirit implicated in the emergence, the ambiguities, and the transformations of the biblical "justice and mercy traditions." His avoidance of the Apocalypse– a telling if typically liberal omission–suggests discomfort with its merciless justice. Welker traces the spirit to its point of reemergence in the experience of the *basileia*. Contemporary movements provide his point of departure: congenially, he designates the movements of liberation and feminist theologies as new "works of the Spirit."[34]

While Welker centers the Holy Spirit in "the Spirit of Christ" too tightly for my taste, he recognizes that such rhetoric might

> admittedly degenerate into an indeterminately held correctness that justifies diverse relations of domination and forms of structural violence. . . .

All sorts of theologies and forms of piety have made their peace with a numinous and opaque "Spirit of Christ," nationalistic, chauvinistic, patriarchal, sexist, and racist, scornful of the old and the sick, hostile to children, justifying and stabilizing exploitative and unmerciful relations, and in all cases de facto hostile to the Spirit.[35]

Indeed, such a christomonism has repeatedly eclipsed the pluralism of spirit, manifest in and beyond every religion.[36] Welker's criteria ultimately conduce to the penance of Christianity in "the Spirit of deliverance from human distress and sin, and the Spirit of the restoration of both solidarity and the capacity for communal action." As *public person*," spirit stands against the "Spirit of the Western World," the progress-Geist of global exploitation and planetary destruction. If under the postmodern conditions of what Welker calls "the moral market" we are to make normative decisions of "justice and mercy," the pneumatological rhetoric of transformation offers a tradition-charged resource. Its neoapocalyptic character becomes most evident in Welker's political contextualization:

> In an international situation in which whole countries are politically and judicially neglected . . . and in which the struggle to prevail economically is the order of the day, this "Comforter" may appear to be an illusion. Yet in truth the Spirit acts in such an international situation as the revealer of "judgment" on the powers that rule this world.[37]

Is this another triumphalist guarantee of final closure and a happy ending? "From the perspective of structural patterns of life plunged into misery, the Spirit bears witness that *this* international situation has no staying power, no validity, that contrary to all self-righteousness of both the 'pious' and the 'impious,' it is marked by unbelief, . . . and nothingness, and is dependent on the delivering power of the Spirit."[38] Welker thus skillfully maneuvers final judgment toward a counter-apocalyptic critical pneumatology. Moreover, his understanding of the "personhood" of the Holy Spirit (in terms of Niklas Luhmann's definition of personality as a "domain of resonance") begins to translate the publicness of spirit into a "web of resonance that we help to shape as much as we are marked by them."[39] One hopes that his multidimensional attunement to the ambiguities of scripture and the multivalencies of culture will lead him beyond neoorthodox and narrative models toward a thoroughgoing polyglossia of spirit.

If the trinitarian model implies a "consubstantiality" of multiple persons who are both same and different, it must also, *pars pro toto*, allow us to perceive the multiplicity inherent in each member. For all its arcane chauvinisms, the Christian Trinity arguably functions as the formative pattern in the West for the possibility of co-constitutive relations between subjects. Thus its persons each holographically share each other's functions, but differently. They do not become the same. Yet this trinitarian prefiguration of a radical democracy of relations, held captive to theological supernaturalism, never issued into the exploration of the *constitutive* difference–the difference of the other as I refract it in myself; the difference which co-constitutes me, disrupting my self-sameness, proliferating possibilities.[40]

In Western theological history this trans-subjective multiplicity suggests itself virtually everywhere as the multitude of spirit(s). Neither strictly one nor merely many, the spirits of place, of ancestors, of elements and directions, of animal species, angels and saints, pervade indigenous communities. And biblical texts also brim with pneumatic multiplicity: Revelation fairly bursts with the panoply of strange angels, of animal and ancestral spirits, of elemental powers caught up in catastrophe and new creation. Its polymorphic perversity was subdued along with its revolutionary potencies.

Invoking such a pluralism, James Hillman launched a post-Jungian polemic against "spirit" on behalf of "soul."[41] The former he singled out as the monolithic, rationalizing, and egocentering agency of monotheism, deadening to soul. Soul, by contrast, expresses the "polytheistic psychology" of a deliteralizing, suffering, animating imagination. Soul is not a substance, a given, an essence, but a perspective and a production: it must be "made." He exposes the monolithic and masculinizing spirit, distinguished from the affective, somatic "psyche" already present in the letters of Paul. Yet he does not recognize that such spirit has been only gradually and incompletely purified as "Geist." So his own reading mirrors the spirit-monolith, homogenizing rather than releasing the plurality of spirits. Despite his preoccupation with "depth" he does not look "beneath the altar" to note the irrepressible spirit spectrum of ghosts and utopias, tongues and totems. For Hillman "soul-making" belongs to the death-realm of the underworld, to be distinguished from the apocalyptic hell.

Surely spirit, as life-force, moves in and around the psychological and biological spirals of death and dying–unless it is imagined to deny death, to stifle its internal communities, to press its own singular infinity. Counter-apocalypse "makes soul" in the spirit of an ecologically and communally sustaining vitality. Here the grandiose polarities of Christian and non-, of *spiritus* and *anima*, male and female, spirit and matter, one and many, individual and community, beginning and end, seem beside the point. Here what *matters* is the work of materializing the possibilities of spirit, wherever, whenever we are. In its soulful ambience we can keep the polyphonic conversation *living*. Which is to say, not fleeing death and its painful materialities. Community formed in the folds of this finitude distinguishes painstakingly between the suffering which can only be comforted and the suffering whose cause can be eradicated. But that sociality presupposes the release of its spirit from either its single-minded masculine front or its private double, its compensatory femininity.

Gender and Spirit

As public vitality has privately been fueled by women, so the Spirit has mystically energized the Father and Son. Thus women haunt devitalized facsimiles of themselves–(holy) ghosts of women? So much anonymous labor, immanent to the point of existential stagnation. So many rebellions stifled, subdued, returning them to the thankless tasks of survival, the little humiliations of love. Preoccupied with the means of existence, the ends elude her: "those / who age after age, perversely, / with no extraordinary power, / reconstitute the world."[42] Women? Their spirits? The Spirit herself?

The irritation of "inclusive language" for the deity, an issue still threatening to sink theological feminism back to Sunday School levels, won't go away. But aside from provoking religious conservatives to spray their manhood on our public work, what does the rhetoric of a female Spirit–of, or *as* "God"–mark? A *gynomorphic* projection of our wishes onto the universe? Back to Feuerbach. Mere metaphors of female, and therefore of an immense swathe of human desire, as tropes both of the politics and of the mystery exceeding the reaches of any particular experience? Better. But at any rate, if the spirit now steps into the theological limelight as Public Person, it is very difficult not to figure it as another

"Him." Never mind the feminine grammar of *pneuma* or *ruach*. Never mind that in pre-orthodox Christianity the Syriac fathers sang of the Holy Spirit as a mother engaging in intriguing cross-gender behavior with "the Father": "The Son is the cup, / And the Father is He who was milked. / And the Holy spirit is She who milked Him." Moreover, "The Holy Spirit opened Her bosom, / And mixed the milk of the two breasts of the Father." The milky trinitarian gender play which here sprang a pneumatological leak within the father religion was quickly and quietly suppressed.[43]

In a historic retort, Mary Daly notes that when feminists first ask to be mirrored in the image of God, "the classic answer has been: 'You're included under the Holy Spirit. He's feminine.'"[44] So Daly relegates him/her as another Drag Queen to the All-Male Actus Purus of the Trinity. But I have been less prone to purge out patriarchal residues. I am less willing to relinquish his/her/its power to resist Power, to dis/close what has been sealed, to "make gender trouble" at high levels—of high modern feminism as well as high church patriarchy.

In the revisionist feminist Catholicism of Elizabeth Johnson, the Holy Spirit reveals Herself straightforwardly as the new First Person of the Trinity, proceeding neither from Father nor from Son.[45] Sister Johnson, C. S. J., thinks in sisterhood with the rigorously post-Catholic Daly, who analyzed the classical "procession" of the Third Person from the Father and Son as a case of Virginia Woolf's "processions of the sons of men." But Johnson's reading strategy seems truer to Daly's methodological "re-reversals" than Daly's own dismissal of the Holy Spirit. Drawing on the inter-testamental hints in the wisdom literature of a "subtle, all-pervasive spirit"[46] who is the divine Wisdom herself, Johnson wryly names the first person of the revised trinity "Spirit Sophia." Under Johnson's systematically sisterly gaze "She" is seen proceeding in interpersonal unity with "Jesus Sophia" and "Mother Sophia." While scolding Aquinas for his bald misogyny, she generously mimics his definition of the Holy Spirit as *mutuus amor*, a "mutual love" exemplifying the love of equals, a reciprocity barely conceivable in the predemocratic ambience of superiors and inferiors.

> Speaking of the Spirit as the power of mutual love proceeding has strong affinities with the model of relationship most prized by feminist thought. Love is the moving power of life, that which drives everything that is toward everything else that is. . . . Spoken of in terms of mutual love pro-

ceeding, God who is Spirit cannot be used to legitimize patriarchal structures but signals a migration toward reciprocity in community as the highest good.[47]

God the Spirit, however, even as "mutuality," certainly *can* and has been used to legitimize patriarchal structures. The trinitarian mutuality, precisely articulated as an exception to human hierarchy, has only proved the rule of hierarchical relations. But when Spirit joins the movements of women, do we not discern its self-symbolization of resistance to "patriarchal structures"—as in the Shakers, the Friends' New Jerusalem, the Salvadoran team? Then, perhaps, "as the creative dynamic of mutual love, the Spirit vitally moves, attracts, impels, connects, and sets up a solidarity of reciprocal, freeing relation throughout the whole world as well as between herself and creation."[48]

But by what mechanism might it pervade and prevail "throughout the whole world"? Johnson's "thealogy" suffers from the enthusiastic overreach of most theological discourse (no doubt including my own), which invariably mistakes its hopeful eschato-logic for the immediacy of a transcendent presence: the possible feels so radiantly real in the pneumatic dis/closure that it is mistaken for the already real. (This is the spiritual version of what Whitehead called the "fallacy of misplaced concreteness.") Moreover, the trinitarian system, even gently parodied as Sophialogy, tends to lift spirit out of the zones of finite incarnation.[49] Nonetheless, the normative appeal of such feminist thealogy, stubbornly and effectively continues to put its hope into practice.

Patriarchal Christianity has been unveiled *as such*. It can no longer exist except as antifeminism, shamed into defining itself publicly in terms of women: what better example of successful symbolic delegitimation? Within the negation of its negation, the icons and iconoclasms of women of spirit test the tradition's capacity to heal its own crippled hope for mutuality. The woman clothed in the sun, the serpent, *Shekinah*, Sophia, Roma-Babylon, the New Jerusalem, Jezebel their prophet— might these figures revealed "in the spirit," edited by the "iron rod," reengender spirit itself?

7

There is a spirit that pervades everything, that is capable of powerful song and radiant movement, and that moves in and out of the mind. The colors of this spirit are multitudinous, a glowing, pulsing rainbow. Old Spider Woman is one name for this quintessential spirit, and Serpent Woman is another, and what they together have made is called Creation, Earth, creatures, plants and light.[50]

Beyond symbolic strategies, the question of the ontology of spirit still lurks: whatever the pronoun, does this spirit who sometimes accepts the modifier "holy" exist *pervasively*? Is it something more than a signifier signifying other signifiers? Is it really *out there*?

Gender analysis may provide a nicely decentering clue to a discussion which otherwise replicates the monotonous binaries of secular and sacred, nature and supernature, female and male. Theologically, feminists are to choose immanence, patriarchs prefer transcendence. For of course it is precisely the facile distinction between transcendence and immanence which is at stake; the practice of defining the holy as the separate, of walling it off as the Transcendent Other, alien to the point of Apocalypse. If the divine in any of its "coinhering" personae can be publicly imagined as female, maternal associations kick in. The rabid antifeminism of the Protestant right clarifies the consequences: if God is a mother, then God can be conceived of as giving birth, therefore as having bodily continuity with the begotten creation; that would collapse the Transcendent Creator into the Creation—and then He would have no power to save us from ourselves. "The mother goddess is uniquely appropriate to represent the worldview of continuity, but [this] is fraught with immense danger for the biblical view of transcendence."[51]

Instead of arguing with this undignified literalism, let us reconsider how every self constitutes itself out of its dizzying subliminal haze of relations at this moment. Most of that self-construction takes place unconsciously, beneath the range of deliberate choice. The subject can neither separate from all the others nor fuse with them. When they are still rhetorically vital, symbols of spirit "throw together" (*sym-bolon*) the largely unconscious matrix of influencing relations, drawing them into a spontaneous meaningfulness the ego cannot master. When it pretends to mastery, the symbol has become, in the classic Tillichian distinction, a sign, a social tool.[52] Such an instrumentalized image can also be used for the opposite purpose, the work of *dia-bolein*—the "throwing-apart," the separation into diabolical simplicities.

One way or another, spirit-language, including "God," addresses that sublinguistic matrix of complexity in which we by definition cannot fix a borderline between the self and all the creaturely others. It may be handy, healthy, even life-saving to draw boundaries—until, that is, we deny how relative, how fluid, how permeable the borders remain. A pneumatic feminist relationalism blows along these borders even as the signifiers of "the Father's Law" (Lacan) patrol them. But if we no longer honor the binary of a subject dominating its object—as supremely codified in Karl Barth's "wholly other," the subject in relation to whom we are all objects—then neither can any smug distinction of immanent spirits and transcendent Spirit be maintained. At least not in *good* faith.

Yet both those who claim the "secular" and those who claim the "sacred" require precisely the division between them: the former wish to keep the boundaries opaque, to exclude from existence anything beyond the multiple but controllable and arbitrary signifiers of its own discourse; the latter want to mystify that "beyond" into a delusional transparency, which authorizes its discourse of control over the immanent spirits. In the theocratic premodernity of that latter gesture, theology worked to simplify and repress spirit—with apocalyptically explosive consequences. Instead, Christianity might develop the style of what Moltmann calls "immanent transcendence."[53] If transcendence is within "all experiences, not just experience of the self," this conceptualization might help to rediscover the spirit both in-dwelling and transcending the webbed present of our interdependencies. If this transcendence is not the same old flight from the mother-matrix, it lets go of the past only because the past has already become part of this present. (Spider Grandmother returns, perhaps perched on a web-site on the Internet as this third millenium opens.)

Lending space where relationships suffocate, resistance where they oppress, respect where they sustain, and mutuality where they are capable of love, spirit arises again as the *relation of relations*. Much more than we can ever grasp or control influences the decision of any moment. So the old doctrine of "grace" or its lack—grace both "prevenient" and "sanctifying"—may address an irreducible spontaneity of freedom itself. But it would not share the Augustinian or Reformation opinion that a transcendent "God" is choosing in and for us through an omnipotent providence. Rather, "God" (among other symbols) encodes at once, and paradoxically, the abysmal plenitude of relations and the rightness of *some* relations. Such rightness breaks into view when within freedom love takes place; when within nature evolution occurs; when within justice mercy prevails; when within chaos beauty appears. To implicate spirit is not to replace but to complicate human agency. We may then consider spirit at work in its unbounded intersubjectivity, neither instead of us or instrumentally through us but *with, among, in* and *as* us–working the multiple prepositions of the basileia zone. Some of the fiercest early battles of pneumatology in the trinitarian formula were fought over the propriety of "with," "in," "through," or "and" the Holy Spirit. Indeed, Basil in the fourth century pled unsuccessfully for a prepositional multiplicity of spirit-invocations.[54]

Again, *whose* spirit? What is the status of the substantive? Perhaps when spirit expresses *mutuus amor* "she passes into holy souls and makes them friends of God, and prophets" (Wisdom of Solomon 7:27). This "she" is meant at once as the spirit of these "holy souls" and the linguistic reference of the symbol "God." Human wisdom partakes of divine. If we reclaim this tradition, for example, do we surrender to the "Transcendental Signified"–the fruit forbidden by structuralism and poststructuralism?

As to the capacity of religious (or any) language to refer to Something beyond language, perhaps in one sense we "sin boldly" (Luther) and in another not at all. "She" functions in the verse from the Wisdom of Solomon not so much as the "Transcendental Signified" but as a signifying trope, *immanently* signified: that to which the trope refers, its "signified," does not lie outside of the maze of signifying processes, but is revealingly and chaotically part of it. I am here presupposing a certain cosmology according to which everything to which language could conceivably refer, that is, anything which exists and most of which is nonhuman and "natural," is ipso facto a hermeneutical event, an "interpretive process." Anything to which language points is actively interpreting itself and therefore that which stands in relation to it. Transcendence is a process of transformation immanent within the relationships constituting the discursive field. Within what is biblically referred to as "the deep."

The spirit, on the face of it, dances "over" the deep: but in the genesis zone, where the end of the world is inconceivable, there is after all no up and down, no over and under, and the primordial wind-breath can only be heard whistling *through* the prevenient complexity, the *tehom* of relations neither monstrous nor angelic and much of both. This deep, the matrix of relations, always precedes and follows our acts of self-constitution, exceeding "cultural-linguistic" boundaries, animating "nature" and as such, ourselves. In us talking mammals the matrix craves conscious reciprocity. This entails rightness of relation: justice toward each other and toward the ecosphere function as *necessary* conditions of this communing complexity. But *insufficient*: feminism has in various vocabularies made the case that "justice" will justify public apocalypse unless gender justice works its way into the integral complexity. Otherwise mercy and love get left to the mother-worlds of private relations and soft moments.

Complexity will no doubt continue to frighten our culture into end-time dualisms, numbly commodified or religiously signified. I have therefore experimented with an edge of theological discourse, which divests itself of finalities without doubting the powers of closure. It therefore must not now reinvest some revisionist binary of "God" and "world," "male" and "female," "spirit" and "flesh" with stabilized definitions, with fixed presences or permanent absences. If Spirit at present prefers to perform female symbols of herself, it is only mockingly, with playful, wounded transience. What Judith Butler says of sex, we may at the same time (with a perversity no doubt offensive to theorists both theist and atheist) say of the sex of Spirit: "No longer believable as an interior 'truth' of dispositions and identity, sex [God] will be shown to be a performatively enacted signification (and hence not 'to be'), one that . . . can occasion the parodic proliferation and subversive play of gendered meanings."[55]

8

Apocalips

To play with mimesis is thus, for a woman, to try to recover the place of her exploitation by discourse, without allowing herself to be simply reduced to it. . . . It also means to 'unveil' the fact, if women are such good mimics, it is because they are not simply re[ab]sorbed in this function. *They also remain elsewhere . . .*[56]

Thus Luce Irigaray plays with apocalypse: "unveiling" the subversive mimicry of women's language, of our speaking, for example, the *lo-*

goi of philosophy, of theology. Somehow in this mime dance we bi-locate, hovering dialectically, not necessarily "grace"-fully between the place where language prefabricates our inarticulate hope and ... "Elsewhere"? Where else? Not quite, I think, Daly's utopic "Otherworld," though it may lie just on the other side of Irigaray's self-reservation. We take a clue from Irigaray's early trope, for which she earned herself the "essentialist" title: "Woman 'touches herself' all the time . . . for her genitals are formed of *two lips* in continuous contact."[57] *There*? Read literally, Irigaray seems to have inflated a minor autoerotic sensation (I may feel more contact with the treetops through my skylight on any given day) into the prediscursive ground of feminine identity. But why read such a writer univocally? "Within herself," she continues, "she is two–but not divisible into one(s)–that caress each other." But really, "woman is neither one nor two but many." So Irigaray offered of women's embodiment a parable of the uncountable, unaccountable, difference between what we could once just call the sexes. Between, therefore, the gender that is imposed and the sex that is enjoyed. Our self-related, complex sexual subjectivity became a fleshed-out trope not of a future "nowhere" but of a present "elsewhere."

But how does such a place of incarnation communalize, how does it politicize its sensuous gesture? How do the two lips speak, beyond lovemaking, in counter-apocalyptic solidarity with other women, other men? After all, in Revelation 12 two lips parted in birth, only to be met by the opening lips of the beast: red anguish stains the romance of feminist self-carnation, and the only way to decolonize the site of our "exploitation by discourse" and the politics behind it may lie through the open mouth of the dragon. In other words, back through our split from the living, material universe. "I think that we must not merely instigate a return to the *cosmic*," muses Irigaray at a later stage of her own discourse, "but also ask ourselves why we have been held back from becoming *divine women*."[58] (Thanks for asking, sniggers the erstwhile woman clothed with the sun.) Indeed, if we have already ascertained the need for feminist counter-apocalyptic cosmology, Irigaray's question is as welcome as it is surprising, coming as it does out of a Lacanian-Derridian discourse whose U.S. effects include a foundational anti-cosmology and anti-theology.

Irigaray discloses a yearning rare among feminist philosophers–a yearning not for "siren goddesses" conspiring against the gods, but for some *imago* of female self-visualization that might link us at once to the wider universe and to each other. Something more, I presume, than the rewarmed leftovers of the psychoanalytic Mother. This is familiar territory for feminist theology, with its established tradition of deducing women's right to mirror ourselves in "the image of God" from a biblical syntax, of constructing female or gender-neutral metaphors of the divine. But as dissident metaphors turn to systematic signs, their signifying power, like manna from heaven, seems to evaporate. Perhaps for this reason I scavenge among hints left by presumed nontheists for theological clues.

If "women lack a God they cannot communicate or commune with one another," Irigaray continues. "If I can't relate to some sort of horizon for the realization of my genre, I cannot share while protecting my being." In this feminist theological gesture she suggests that a female image of God will strengthen for women the psychic boundaries which allow us intimacy without self-loss. Without such a female God, "sharing implies fusion-confusion."[59] Whatever the male signocracy does with "Him" they at least have always the option to firm up their self-esteem in the mirrors of the male God. With the word "horizon," Irigaray invokes the width of an interpretive framework holding open a space wide enough to facilitate communication across nettlesome differences. And prophylactic enough to inhibit narcissistic fusion with each other, with any others, with a private self-image.

In other words, the horizon or boundary written at the *eschaton* of our sensory field as the symbolizing of female sacrality at once contains, enlarges, and interprets the bottomless "deep" of our relations. Performing something like the dis/closive function of spirit discussed above, this permeable horizon at once opens and gathers the self within its field of others. Within the possibility of its space, we may fluidly mirror, mime each other, ourselves, in (after all) something like the ancient mimesis of God–yet, unlike the ancient icons of eternal form, this is a nonrepresentational *imitatio dei*, fluidly gathering and releasing its symbolic forms within a zone that chaos theory also begins to insinuate.

If the image to imitate has been almost exclusively male–but for the haunting interventions of the Spirit and her odd panoply of martyrs, saints, seers, and lunatics–it preserved the cosmic "mirror phase" for a heroic ego predicated on female submission; in other words, for an ego that in its normative masculine autonomy could never tolerate the immanence of the divine, the mirroring to itself of a labyrinth of relations from which perhaps even death would provide no escape. The feminist struggle over God's unacknowledged sex, for all its barbarisms, thus carries an iconic power of self-disclosure unmatched in the West. But if such revelation is not to imitate the perennial masculine idolatry, if indeed it is open beyond the self to mediate relation to a thick material universe, it needs to perform its theological narratives in the mode of an *ironic* sacrality. Thus the opening, at this moment received back through Irigaray's "lips," needs still the slash–finger, phallus, or double-edged tongue–of dis/closure wedged into it.

What if those flesh-to-flesh relations do occupy the space of cosmology? Could new tales be spun of a relation of relations, kaleidoscoping the Spirit? What if theology could tell its old tales without twisting itself into Jamesian "overbelief"? Even as a willing seminarian, I could never imagine a *credible* God, Goddess, or Higher Power who would want a credo, need to get credit, get named, get worshipped. Creedal beliefs are a dry substitute for the practices of wisdom. But might she/we still tell the stories–for instance, of the spirit of the creation still breathing itself into "all flesh"? Of Wisdom, Hochma-Sophia, permeating the creation?[60]

Wisdom among the Jews and Christians seems to have lost her irony, however, well before she herself was lost. But not altogether. In her commentaries on the Hebrew personification of Wisdom as a woman, Claudia Camp has exposed her mirror-interplay with her shadow-opposite, "the Strange Woman," in the Book of Proverbs. While Proverbs sets the binary up according to the familiar misogyny, presenting a whore-adulteress bad woman as the foil for the good and wise one, Camp argues that what appears to be a split presents such precise parallels (e.g., they are both "embraced," for good or ill, and always "in the street" and "in the marketplace") that the two in fact function as "a single paradoxical entity," that of a classic trickster figure. While in indigenous religious traditions the trickster tends to encompass both sides, the virtuous and the vagrant, the wise and the foolish, the biblical patriarchy had to split her in two precisely in order to preserve her–the price for absorbing such a dangerously and uniquely female icon of the divine? Above all her sexuality had to be driven out: no "biblical knowing" for Woman Wisdom! Thus her own split mirrors that of the women of John's Apocalypse: whores on the one side, virgins on the other. Indeed, Camp performs a trickster's reading strategy as well: "This subtle underlying unity of personified Wisdom and the Strange Woman provides a counterweight to the more polemical overtones of ancient instruction ('Understand, my son, that there are two distinct groups of women in the world . . .') and modern critique ('Look, my daughter, how men have divided us into virgins and whores . . .')."[61]

Perhaps we may stretch Camp's own conclusions into the present one. "The trickster paradigm opens yet a third possibility: a positive valuation of women's power as anti-structural, regenerative because of its liminality." Somewhere between neo- and counter-apocalypse, perhaps, Camp hopes that "a new world is possible." As to her statement that the "energy for change will come in women's seizing the paradox of our existence, drawing on the power of our liminality for ourselves, reading the Bible as tricksters ourselves,"[62] this liminal wisdom, not stagnating in contradiction but inviting through paradox, eventuates also in something like Kristeva's "women's time." Recognizing the "potentialities of victim/executioner which characterize each identity," we face in ourselves the paradox of good and evil at every level: the "interiorization of the founding separation of the sociosymbolic contract, as an introduction of its cutting edge into the very interior of every identity, whether subjective, sexual, ideological."[63]

As we invite Wisdom to heal again, we find she has been more and less together than we thought, inscribing here and there a spirit of mimicry and metamorphosis, of laughter and survival. Silly women, daring the hegemonic One to show its—lips.

9

If spirit does not *pre*form the choices we find ourselves making, perhaps we may *per*form spirit. Lacking a static other upon whom to fix our hopes or against whom to direct our apocalypses, we may be released into a widening gyre of relations. But through its very embrace of relations spirit can always be materially overwhelmed by the death-march. Then "it"—whether as "God" or history, fate, or nature—cannot intervene to save us from the consequences of our actions, even if they include species suicide. In answer to the anguished question of theodicy—the "where is God?" in the face of the holocaust—God as spirit is right *there*, in the midst of apocalypse. And neither unwilling nor impotent to intervene, but simply not the sort of entity who could. Divine force cannot, after the close of the twentieth century and the re-riding of the four horsemen, be imagined as an agency subsiding in an omnipotent transcendence. To abstract "its" agency from our own is to refuse responsibility for ourselves. The spirit left to its own devices is an inefficient cause.[64]

But if the "spirit of life" can in any particular place, time, or community be defeated by the material forces of systemic dysrelation, it also always resists its own subjugation. Spirit masses its own bodily force: not in wretched rag-tag crusades but in the form of contagious materialization. (The resurrected Body prefigured such a counterforce, but got endlessly deferred by members awaiting its Second Coming.) Indeed, while any master narrative of progress merely reflects the captivity of the apocalypse, nonetheless the cumulative and helical movement of relation in time does permit glimpses of social evolution and collective democratization. However transient, such congregations of possibility leave spirit's traces in our margins and in our mainlines, available as "potentiality for the becoming" of the future. A counter-apocalyptic momentum builds in the body of the apocalypse habit.

Apocalypticizing his own age—which he was the one to name "modernity"—in such a way that nonetheless has counter-apocalyptic reverberations, Hegel inadvertently summons up the birth (*basano*) of Revelation 12: "Spirit has broken with the world it has hitherto inhabited and imagined, and is of a mind to submerge it in the past, and in the labour of its own transformation."[65]

There is, for instance, no escaping the following logic: as long as I admit that I consider the gains of feminism to be real and indeed "world historical," and that I would not prefer to have lived in any prior age, I am acknowledging that at times the spirit *has* made evolutionary leaps. Or that at times our species has organized enough spatial and temporal and social vitality to labor in "its own transformation." In this zone of zones, which the Nazarene had signified as the realm of God, do the transfiguring configurations of Spirit not accumulate as potential for "the next step"?

We hope and labor for a critical mass of spirit in history, for the mass "conversion of the mind to the earth" (Ruether). Our time mobilizes both collective death-pathologies and social protest movements on behalf of a sustainable and just life for all. We know now with a certain electronically unavoidable collectivity that if we as a species do not convert to practices of "peace, justice and the integrity of creation" we as a species wreak disaster upon our immediate future. Or we may just surrender to the habitual oscillation between infantile optimism and indifferent despair. The dispirited readily turn to apocalypse, seeking vitality amidst the violence; the complex demands of the present flee before the single, deafening word; smoke and fire fill the screen, and beasts strip the great whore. Wherever overtly apocalyptic hope has been literalized it has been proved literally *wrong*; the normative hope, however, cannot be falsified. It can be named: hope for mutual respect in proximate and in political relations, for justice and mercy upon the land and within the city, for transnational, trans-species healing and renewal. The hope that the spider-spirit of wisdom might subvert the "world-wide web" of power/knowledge. This hope can only be verified, however, by being *made true*: spirit practiced, materialized, spun, performed.

If we can hold this wisdom-spirit close, healing her dissociation, tickling the trickster back to life, letting the lips of her universe murmur in our flesh, might she speak her difference as our own?

10

For I am the first and the last.
I am the honored one and the scorned one.
I am the whore and the holy one.
I am the wife and the virgin.
I am the mother and the daughter. . . .
I am the barren one and many are her sons.
I am she whose wedding is great,
and I have not taken a husband. . . .
I am the silence that is incomprehensible
and the idea whose remembrance is frequent.
I am the voice whose sound is manifold
and the word whose appearance is multiple.[66]

A biblical genre of wisdom writing manifested itself historically at the same time as apocalypse, overlapping with it, authored by scribes and yet speaking a different language. Its word of multiplicity roots the subject of its voice in the paradox and practice of a spacious present tense. At the limits of what can be said, this wisdom does not seal the book shut but plays to the silence. The "I" of the "I am," the revealer-voice of this mysterious little text, "The Thunder, Perfect Mind," unearthed with dozens of "lost gospels" at Nag Hammadi, finding its first popular audience nearly two millennia later by way of African American women artists,[67] is considered that of a cosmic wisdom-figure. She who is the First and the Last: yes, another ancient apo/calypse. I will not set "Thunder" into opposition with John's Revelation, which wrote the Western judgment against socioeconomic oppression and its blueprint of hope. But as though rebutting the misogynist stereotypes of the warrior apocalypse, "Thunder" metrically undermines any dualistic hierarchy of holiness over fleshliness, of virginity over sexual maturity, of maternity over barreness, of son over daughter, etc.

The apocalyptic syntax of hardened opposition melts into the cadence of paradoxical antitheses. "I am the abiding and I am the dissolving." Neither a terminal world nor an essential identity? "I am the one below, and they come up to me." Thus the up-down reference of dominative transcendence is neither privileged nor reversed but overcome, sublated. And on for several hundred verses. Both terms of each pair lose their binary, moralist significance by being simultaneously referred to the "I am."

This "I Am" refuses objectification even as deity or non-deity. She "is" not the spirit: one might consider her more precisely a textual performance of pneumatic wisdom. A female revealer-figure claims the voice of thunder—the seven thunders John of Patmos heard coming with voices from the throne room? Yet if his thunders can be seen to prefigure Christian bombs, hers crack with *koan*-like self-disclosure. Her "I Am" seems to have healed the split between the Good and the Strange Woman, releasing the trickster who loves to tease the either/or logic of apocalypse toward a more sustainable Wisdom. At the same time the "I Am" recasts the female characters of the Apocalypse. The scorned whore, the single mother of the son, and the honored virgin con-spire—sisterly "co-spiriting" at the level of metaphor. They resist mutual contradiction. No longer divided and conquered, they rescript the genders of the possible. I fantasize their waiting these millennia for a catalyzing social moment. "So much is in bud."

Wisdom seems to inscribe its own spirit-strategy: to deconstruct mere contradiction, both social and psychic, by maneuvering, tricking, luring it into polyphonic contrasts. Sometimes, however, the oppositions lock into systemic injustices and will not give. Then no counter-apocalypse can prevent the tears. Some suffering, and some causes of suffering, remain irredeemable: that's hell. "So much has been destroyed."[68] Toxic to the spirit of life, too late for justice, tragic waste can only be recycled as grief. But grief congregates with a productive rage and even a primal laughter. "Elemental passions," after all.[69] The relation of relations solves nothing. But in its time, in its place, it composts almost everything. As my Greenpeace T-shirt puts it, "no time to waste." Still, in the end as in the beginning, what you have is the time of your life.

———

"How long, oh Lord?" the martyrs beneath the altar rasp again, hoarsely. "How about now?" she answers. The seven horn combo breaks into a jazz improvisation to "On That Great Gittin Up Morning" and the four horses outside in the meadow start prancing. Thumping his tail to the downbeat, the red dragon lazily chomps on the garbage. Jezebel, hair still wet from her dip, leans against him to write a letter to her congregation. "Have you seen my son? Or Jeri?" Sophie, serving refreshments, asks Jezebel. But the latter merely winks and with a flourish of her double-edged pen returns to her writing. Babs, crowned in flowers, taps her shoulder and they break into a shimmy. That does it; finally some of the ghosts step out, looking sharp in white linen. Hesitant at first, they soon start shaking to the music. The earth opens wide to sing.

Notes

Preface

1. Julia Kristeva, "Women's Time," trans. Alice Jardice and Harry Blake, *Signs: Journal of Women in Culture and Society* 7, no. 11 (1981): 34.

1. Opening

1. Bill McKibben, *The End of Nature* (New York: Random House, 1989).
2. John Coffin, "Bible Predicts Worst-Ever Weather," *Sun*, 8 August 1995, 12–13.
3. Sonny Fontaine, "Here's a Place Where Elvis Is God," *Sun*, 8 August 1995, 7.
4. Ronald Smuthers, "A Sighting of Elvis? No, But Quite a Studying," *New York Times*, 5 August 1995, 6.
5. Robert Booth Fowler, *The Greening of Protestant Thought* (Chapel Hill: University of North Carolina Press, 1995), 47.
6. Much of the evidence for the apocalyptic nature of Reagan's faith, and that of other right-wing activists, is gathered by Grace Halsell in *Prophecy and Politics: Militant Evangelists on the Road to Nuclear War* (Westport, Conn.: Lawrence Hill & Co., 1986), 40ff.
7. *Time*, 1 August 1994, cover text.
8. Thanks to Rosemary Ruether for sharing information and photographs from the Philippines.
9. Thomas J. Altizer, *Genesis and Apocalypse* (Louisville, Ky.: Westminster/John Knox, 1990), 9.
10. Ibid.
11. Ibid., 10.
12. Charles B. Strozier, *Apocalypse: On the Psychology of Fundamentalism in America* (Boston: Beacon, 1994), 2.
13. Julia Kristeva, *Powers of Horror: An Essay on Abjection* (New York: Columbia University Press, 1982).

14. James C. Scott, *Domination and the Arts of Resistance: Hidden Transcripts* (New Haven: Yale University Press, 1990).

15. Ibid., 5.

16. Richard A. Horsley, *Jesus and the Spiral of Violence: Popular Jewish Resistance in Roman Palestine* (San Francisco: Harper & Row, 1987).

17. See Dietmar Kamper and Christoph Wulf, eds., *Looking Back on the End of the World*, trans. David Antal (New York: Semiotext(e), 1989).

18. Ibid., 34.

19. Jacques Derrida, *D'un ton apocalyptique adopté naguère en philosophie* (Paris: Éditions Galilée, 1982).

20. Lee Quinby, *Anti-Apocalypse* (Minneapolis: University of Minnesota Press, 1994), 33.

21. Ibid., xii.

22. Stephen D. O'Leary, *Arguing the Apocalypse: A Theory of Millennial Rhetoric* (New York and Oxford: Oxford University Press, 1994), 73, 75.

23. Augustine, Letter 199, "To Hesichius," in *Writings of Saint Augustine*, trans. Sister Wilfrid Parsons (New York: Fathers of the Church, Inc., 1955), vol. 2, 384.

24. See Chapter 2 of this work.

25. Jürgen Moltmann, *Theology of Hope* (New York: Harper & Row, 1967), 16.

26. Ibid. "Present and future, experience and hope, stand in contradiction to each other in Christian eschatology" (18).

27. Jürgen Moltmann, *The Way of Jesus Christ* (New York: HarperCollins, 1990), 316.

28. Jürgen Moltmann, *God in Creation* (San Francisco: Harper & Row, 1985).

29. Moltmann, *Way*, 262.

30. Ibid., 258f.

31. Ibid., 317.

32. Anne Primavesi, *From Apocalypse to Genesis: Ecology, Feminism, and Christianity* (Minneapolis: Fortress, 1991), 2.

33. Norman Cohn, *Cosmos, Chaos, and the World to Come: The Ancient Roots of Apocalyptic Faith* (New Haven and London: Yale University Press, 1993), 77ff.

34. Ibid., 114f.

35. Martin Buber, *Paths in Utopia* (New York: Collier/Macmillan, 1949), 10.

36. Paul Hanson, *The Dawn of the Apocalyptic* (Philadelphia: Fortress, 1979; rev. ed.), 11.

37. Ibid., 11.

38. Ibid., 12.

39. Elisabeth Schüssler Fiorenza, *The Book of Revelation: Justice and Judgment* (Philadelphia: Fortress, 1985), 6.

40. Ibid., 4.

41. Ibid., 6.

42. Kristeva, *Powers*, 11.

43. Kristeva, *Powers*, 154f.

44. Ibid., *Powers*, 203.

45. Sandra Harding calls feminist theory to a "robust and principled" ambivalence in the choice between modernism and postmodernism in "Feminism, Science, and the Anti-Enlightenment Critiques," in *Feminism/Postmodernism*, ed. Linda J. Nicholson (New York: Routledge, 1990), 86.

46. Jung Young Lee, *Marginality: The Key to Multicultural Theology* (Minneapolis: Fortress, 1995).

47. Ibid., 67.

48. Kristeva, *Powers*, 154.

49. Frances Fiorenza, *Foundational Theology: Jesus and the Church* (New York: Crossroad/Continuum, 1984), 301–21.

50. Judith Plaskow, *Standing Again at Sinai* (San Francisco: Harper & Row, 1990).

51. Rita Nakashima Brock, *Journeys by Heart* (New York: Crossroad, 1988; rev. 1993).

52. Rosemary Radford Ruether, *Sexism and God-Talk* (Boston: Beacon, 1983).

53. Paul Ricoeur, *Figuring the Sacred* (Minneapolis: Augsburg Fortress, 1995), 236.

54. See George Linbeck, *The Nature of Doctrine* (Minneapolis: Fortress, 1984), and Hans Frei, *The Eclipse of the Biblical Narrative* (New Haven: Yale University Press, 1974).

55. Lindbeck, quoted in Anthony Thiselton, *New Horizons in Hermeneutics* (Grand Rapids: Zondervan, 1992), 557.

56. Lindbeck, quoted ibid., 557.

57. Ricoeur, *Figuring the Sacred*, 237.

58. Ibid., 238.

59. Ibid., 238.

60. bell hooks, *Feminist Theory from Center to Margin* (Boston: South End Press, 1984).

61. See Chapter 3 of this work.

62. See the discussion of Kristeva above.

63. Lynne Segal, *Is the Future Female?* (New York: Peter Bedrick Books, 1987), ix (emphasis mine).

64. Ibid., 246.

65. Jürgen Moltmann, *The Spirit of Life* (Minneapolis: Fortress, 1992).

66. Schüssler Fiorenza, *Revelation: Vision of a Just World* (Minneapolis: Fortress, 1991), 36.

67. Daniel Boyarin, *Intertextuality and the Reading of Midrash* (Blooming-ton: Indiana University Press, 1990), viii.

68. For example, Daniel Boyarin, James Kugel, Gerald Bruns, David Blumenthal.

69. David Blumenthal, *Facing the Abusing God: A Theology of Protest* (Louis-ville: Westminster/John Knox, 1993), 60.

70. Thanks for comments from my colleague Peter Ochs, who meant by "phil-onic" a more interiorized plurivocality than the literal communality of rabbinic midrash; and to elaboration by V. Burrus. See also David Daw-son, whose "book describes how some ancient pagan, Jewish, and Chris-tian interpreters used allegory to endorse, revise, and subvert competing world views and forms of life"—in distinction from a merely textual inter-pretation (David Dawson, *Allegorical Readers and Cultural Revision in Ancient Alexandria* [Berkeley: University of California Press, 1992], 1).

71. Hans-Georg Gadamer, *Truth and Method* (New York: Seabury, 1975). On "effective historical consciousness" see 267–74; on the event horizon and the character of truth, 446. For a receptive critique of Gadamer's approach from the perspective of a "political cultural theology," see Mark L. Taylor, *Remembering Esperanza* (Maryknoll, N.Y.: Orbis, 1990), 46–75.

72. Michel Foucault, *The Foucault Reader*, ed. Paul Rabinow (New York: Pan-theon, 1984), 88.

73. Ibid., 87 (emphasis mine).

74. Ibid., 86.

2. Text

1. Allan A. Boesak, *Comfort and Protest: The Apocalypse from a South Afri-can Perspective* (Philadelphia: Westminster, 1987), 38.

2. Ibid., 34.

3. Ibid.

4. A key text in all reformed, amillennialist theology, according to Steve Young (private conversation).

5. Boesak, *Comfort and Protest*, 38.

6. The *kairos* metaphor caught fire, and has leapt through the two-thirds world as a political eschatology of great urgency, an apocalypse not of unconditional doom, but of the dramatic prophetic conditional—that if you change the ways of injustice, then we may all flourish together. The eschatological victory illustrated in the election of Mandela, which fol-lowed upon the heels of these documents, surely prefigures, but does not guarantee, such a global future.

7. Pablo Richard, *Apocalypse: A People's Commentary on the Book of Revela-tion* (Maryknoll, N.Y.: Orbis, 1995), 3.

8. Richard Horsley, *Jesus and the Spiral of Violence: Popular Jewish Resistance in Roman Palestine* (San Francisco: Harper & Row, 1987), 143.

9. Adela Yarbro Collins, *Crisis and Catharsis: The Power of the Apocalypse* (Philadelphia: Westminster, 1984); "Early Christian Apocalypticism: Genre and Social Setting," *Semeia* 36 (1986); John J. Collins, *The Apocalyptic Imagination: An Introduction to the Jewish Matrix of Christianity* (New York: Crossroad, 1987). Also see Leonard Thompson, "A Sociological Analysis of Tribulation in the Apocalypse of John," *Semeia* 36 (1986): 147–74. Thompson's historical research tends to deflate the "crisis theory," or at least the common assumption that there is a direct correspondence between the intensity of objective persecution and the intensity of apocalyptic passion; it would also question the analogy of John's situation to that of Boesak, who wrote the commentary from a prison cell and thus found himself all too well situated to identify with John.

10. Oberey Hendricks, "Guerilla Exegesis: 'Struggle' As a Scholarly Vocation–A Postmodern Approach to Biblical Hermeneutics," *Semeia*, forthcoming (Fall 1996).

11. Jonathan Z. Smith, in *Map Is Not Territory* (Leiden: Brill, 1978), argues that in the ancient Near East, "wisdom and apocalyptic are related in that they are both essentially scribal phenomena," but that "full-blown apocalypse" dissociates itself, unlike wisdom traditions, from a specific king. He positions apocalypticism as *"wisdom lacking a royal patron"* (74f.).

12. Mary Daly, *Gyn/Ecology* (Boston: Beacon, 1978), 102f.

13. *I, Rigoberta Menchú: An Indian Woman in Guatemala*, ed. Elizabeth Burgos-Debray, trans. Ann Wright (London and New York: Verso, 1984), 233.

14. See Adela Yarbro Collins, "The Origin of the Designation of Jesus as 'Son of Man,' " *Harvard Theological Review* 80 (October 1987): 391–407.

15. Thorleif Boman, *Hebrew Thought Compared with Greek* (New York: W. W. Norton, 1960). There are exceptions of course (cf. Isaiah 6).

16. "For the Hebrews who have their existence in the temporal, the content of time plays the same role as the content of space plays for the Greeks. As the Greeks gave attention to the peculiarity of things, so the Hebrews minded the peculiarity of events" (Boman, 139). Also note here Ernst von Dobschutz, who made the classic and overdrawn distinction, "Zeit und Raum im Denken des Urchristentums," *Journal of Biblical Literature* 41 (1922): 103–25. Also Henri Bergson, who in *Time and Existence* exposed the Western spatialization of time–which I will later argue is not problematic because of space and its reputed reifications, but because of the sort of arrhythmic, linear temporality which dominates in its own spatialization.

17. See, for example, Elizabeth Schüssler Fiorenza, *Revelation: Vision of a Just World* (Minneapolis: Fortress, 1991), 47.

18. Apart from the introduction and conclusion, Revelation is remarkably devoid of overt Christological references. This absence may suggest a still unresolved tension here between Hebrew monotheism and the primitive Christology, thus John is impelled at once to identify the risen Jesus as the Lord of Isaiah, and yet repelled to reify such an identification; or, suggests J. Massyngberde Ford in *Revelation* (New York: Anchor Bible/Doubleday, 1975), the frame represents a Christian editorial job on a Jewish vision—which suggests the same tension (12f).

19. See also Habakkuk 2:2f: "Write the vision: make it plain on tablets, so that a runner may read it. / For there is still a vision for the appointed time; / it speaks of the end, and does not lie."

20. The warrior will reappear for the final battle, and be named "The Word of God." Hence the Christological translation of Christ into Word parallels darkly the creation theology of the Gospel of John ("In the beginning was the Word"). The famous Johannine prologue had borrowed from Proverbs 8 a divine creative principle known in Greek as Sophia, translated her into Logos, and identified her/it with the Christ; the resurrected Christ is the *principium* by which the creation would be renewed. Certainly the John of the Apocalypse intends world renewal as well, indeed, more cosmically, more totally, more concretely, than the fourth Gospel. It is John of Patmos's specific Christological formula for renewal—the s/word of omnicide—which will concern us.

21. Mark C. Taylor, *Erring: A Postmodern A/theology* (Chicago: University of Chicago Press, 1984), 76ff. "The text" reveals itself as an interminable, illimitable process, mysteriously demystifying all "ends," expanded endlessly by the intertextuality of the text in its fertile relations with prior texts and future readings; moreover, the term "text" is preferred to "book" on the assumption that "book" still carries within itself the phonocentric bias, that is, the privilege of the ancient oral traditions and therefore the authority of a monolithic Word.

22. History, which is the history of civilization, which is history of the written word and thus of writing, is, by the way, the his/tory of patriarchy. Or, in Gertrude Stein's words, "Patriarchal Poetry their origin and their history their history patriarchal poetry their origin patriarchal poetry their history their origin . . ." (*The Yale Gertrude Stein* [New Haven, Conn.: Yale, 1980], 115). But even feminist hermeneutics cannot, paradoxically, write itself out of the very hermeneutical circle which has tried to eject women "write out of history" (Judy Chicago). We remain accountable for our

uses of the Book and for its uses of us, for it has already been mediating our relationships to each other.

23. See Frederick Jameson, *The Political Unconscious: Narrative as a Socially Symbolic Act* (Ithaca: Cornell University Press, 1981).

24. Schüssler Fiorenza, *Revelation*, 45ff.

25. Erich Neumann's *The Great Mother* traces all "archetypal feminine" imagery from a clay pot; as to the iron rod, say no more!

26. Certainly the "conquering" in 2:26 pertains to the survival of the Christian community as a distinct force, thus to maintaining its identity and ethics over and against "the nations." One can even interpret such boundary maintenance as protest against the Empire and its colonial clients among the prospering middle classes, for whom the shared meal of sacrificed animals was part of guild activity. However, such a political reading may also obscure the fact that these *eidolon* include all the many images of the sacred of non-Jewish peoples and nations, subject to endlessly varying forms, uses, meanings within their local communities. Thus one can just as well read in John's indignation an intolerant and self-righteous rejection of everything pagan as "idolatrous."

27. Antoinette Clark Wire, *The Corinthian Women Prophets: A Reconstruction through Paul's Rhetoric* (Minneapolis: Fortress, 1990). For a critical evaluation of the arguments, methodology, and conclusions of this controversial book, see Jeffrey S. Siker and Margaret M. Mitchell, "Review Essay" of op. cit., *Religious Studies Review* 19, no. 4 (October 1993): 305–11.

28. Elisabeth Schüssler Fiorenza, *The Book of Revelation: Justice and Judgment* (Philadelphia: Fortress, 1985).

29. Ibid.

30. Sigmund Freud, "On Dreams," *The Freud Reader*, ed. Peter Gay (New York: Norton, 1989), 151.

31. Contrast in context Ezekiel's understanding of the purpose of prophecy: "Man," says God to the prophet, "I have made you a watchman for the Israelites; you will take messages from me and carry my warnings to them. It may be that I pronounce sentence of death on a wicked man: if you do not warn him to give up his wicked ways and so save his life the guilt is his" (Ezek. 3:16f.).

32. John Dominic Crossan, *The Dark Interval* (Sonoma, Calif.: Polebridge Press, 1988).

33. The phrase is Owen Barfield's, *Romanticism Comes of Age* (Middletown, Conn.: Wesleyan University Press, 1967).

34. Julia Kristeva, *Powers of Horror: An Essay on Abjection* (New York: Columbia University Press, 1982), 207.

35. Allen Callahan, "The Language of Apocalypse," Society for Biblical Literature presentation, 1994, manuscript pp. 19–20 (subsequently published in *Harvard Theological Review*, Winter 1995/6).

36. Just a wink to Jacques Derrida's own little apocalypse of the Book, in "The End of the Book and the Beginning of Writing," *Of Grammatology*, trans. G. C. Spivak (Baltimore: Johns Hopkins University Press, 1974), 6ff.

37. D. H. Lawrence, *Apocalypse* (New York: Viking, 1980), 51.

38. Nietzsche also cites Tertullian's apocalyptic polemic against the Roman games at length, where that church father promises Christians far more sensational sights at the End—of, for instance, the torment of the damned. See *The Birth of Tragedy and The Genealogy of Morals* (New York: Anchor/Doubleday, 1956), 182ff, 185.

39. Schüssler Fiorenza, *Revelation*, 60.

40. "He was led like a lamb to the slaughter" (Is. 53:7).

41. For another South African liberation perspective, more counter-apocalyptic in tone, stressing the parables and beatitudes of "the kingdom," see Albert Nolan, *Jesus Before Christianity* (Maryknoll: Orbis, 1976), 58: "To say 'Thy kingdom come' is the same as saying 'Thy will be done *on earth* as it is in heaven.'"

42. Crossan "argued that John the Baptist was an apocalyptic prophet preparing his followers for the imminent advent of God the Coming One but that Jesus, after originally accepting that vision, eventually changed his response some time after the execution of John. He then emphatically contrasted a follower of John and a member of the Kingdom" (John Dominic Crossan, *The Historical Jesus: The Life of a Mediterranean Jewish Peasant* [San Francisco: Harper, 1991], 227, 259).

43. New Testament scholar Ron Farmer develops an apocalyptic hermeneutic of persuasive versus coercive power, based on his use of process theology. See his Society for Biblical Literature seminar paper (1993), forthcoming in "Divine Power in the Apocalypse to John: Rev. 4–5 in Process Hermeneutics," ed. by Eugene H. Lovering, Jr. (Atlanta: Scholar's Press). Also, Carl G. Jung reread the Book of Revelation as a compensation of the one-sided gospel of love with a gospel of power (see Jung's *Answer to Job*, trans. R. F. C. Hull [Princeton, N.J.: Princeton University Press, 1973]). I suspect rather that the compensation is moving in both directions.

44. Elizabeth Janeway, *Powers of the Weak* (New York: Alfred A. Knopf, 1980).

45. Kristeva, *Powers*, 52f.

46. John himself seems to have here reworked a five-hundred-year-old vision of Zechariah, another prophetic ancestor of true apocalypticism. In Zechariah, four different colored horses, one ridden by an angel, had

been "sent to range through the world" (Zech. 1:8ff), but these horses have returned bearing news of world peace, and the angel (*angelos*, messenger) announces compassion for a Jerusalem destroyed seventy years earlier for the first time–so the horse-angel has been reversed in John.

47. François Lyotard, *The Postmodern Condition: A Report on Knowledge* (Minneapolis: University of Minnesota Press, 1984), xxiv, 82.

48. Rudolf Otto, *The Idea of the Holy* (New York: Oxford University Press, 1926).

49. Lawrence, *Apocalypse*, 52.

50. Ibid., 54.

51. Ibid.

52. Chapter 6 will explore this fundamentalist apocalypse of the New Woman.

53. Lawrence, *Apocalypse*, 82.

54. Ford, *Revelation*, 105.

55. Schüssler Fiorenza, *Revelation*, 63.

56. Some among traditional Christian commentators consider him demonic, possibly Gog, the last enemy (Ezek. 38:3) or even the Antichrist, parodying the later messiah of Armageddon, who will also appear as a warrior on a white horse (but with a sword), "a terrible imitation of Christ, a Christ of hell" (M. Rissi, *Interpretation* 18 (1964): 407–18).

57. Boesak, *Comfort and Protest*, 67.

58. Ernest R. Sandeen, *The Roots of Fundamentalism: British and American Millennialism, 1800–1930* (Chicago: University of Chicago Press, 1970).

59. Its apocalyptic component grows out of the early nineteenth-century movement of Darby and the Scofield Bible, called dispensationalism, a Scottish transplant to North American soil. Teeming with the optimistic millennialist expectancy of the original American apocalypticism, this soil was no longer so well able, after the Civil War (our own red horse), to sustain its progressive approach to the Christianization of the world. Contrary to the nineteenth-century vision of eras of cultural progress marching toward the kingdom of God, fundamentalism chronographs the decay of human history. Creation moves through seven dispensations, the sixth (always) ending "now." The seventh will be the millennial rule of the saints from Jerusalem after the Second Coming.

60. Thus the scenario for war was elaborately laid out in the terms that worked so well with the rise of Regan-era anticommunism–"Russia is a Gog" (one continually chokes on the junk rhetoric)–has the Soviet Union, via Daniel, coming down from the North to invade the Middle East, taking advantage of an "Arab-African confederacy headed by Egypt (King of

the South)" which has already begun the "Armageddon campaign" against Israel.

61. In the commentaries lining the shelves of "Christian" bookstores careful statistics may accompany the horses. The red horse of war is accompanied by reference to the nuclear physicists' doomsday clock and citations of military expenditure levels; the black horse of famine arrives in a context set by pages of responsible ecological statistics, accompanied even by a brief admonishment to be our "brother's keeper," sharing scarce resources until the Lord returns. This moderation is even more in evidence in Billy Graham's *Approaching Hoofbeats* (New York: Avon, 1983). In late twentieth-century form, a conservative hermeneutic has at least faced up to the imminent threats of nuclear war and other modern cycles of self-destruction.

62. 1 Thessalonians 4:17 is the sole biblical reference for the dispensationalist doctrine of the "rapture" (from the Greek *harazo*, "to carry off" into the clouds). The only similar reference in Revelation is at 11:12, were the two dead witnesses—and no one else—ascend to a cloud. Endless exegetical gymnastics have been required to incorporate this singular Pauline passage into the overall framework of John's Revelation, resulting in pre-tribulationist (the rapture comes before the tribulation), mid-tribulationist (the rapture comes midway through seven years of tribulation), and post-tribulationist (the rapture comes at the end of the tribulation) perspectives. See John F. Walvoord, *The Rapture Question* (Findlay, Ohio: Dunham, 1957).

63. Hal Lindsy, *The Late Great Planet Earth* (New York: Bantam, 1973), 142.

64. Ibid., 158.

65. Texe Marrs, *America Shattered: Unmasking the Plot to Destroy Our Families and Our Country* (Austin, Tex.: Living Truth, 1991).

66. Ibid., 45. Note also Marrs's book charging Hillary Clinton's "conspiracy" to promote Mary Daly's agenda, *Big Sister Is Watching You* (Austin Tex.: Living Truth, 1993).

67. Marrs, *America Shattered*, 97.

68. Quoted in Timothy P. Weber, *Living in the Shadow of the Second Coming: American Premillennialism, 1875–1982* (Chicago: University of Chicago Press, 1987), 53.

69. Charles Strozier, *Apocalypse: On the Psychology of Fundamentalism in America* (Boston: Beacon, 1994). Strozier found many fundamentalists saddened by the prospect, if uninterested in social change.

70. Elisabeth Schüssler Fiorenza, *Invitation to the Book of Revelation* (New York: Image/Doubleday, 1981), 84.

71. Ibid., 85.

72. *"Han* is a deep feeling that rises out of the unjust experiences of the people. 'Just indignation' may be a close translation. . . . *Han* is the suppressed, amassed, and condensed experience of oppression caused by mischief or misfortune so that it forms a kind of 'lump' in one's spirit" (Suh Nam-dong, "Towards a Theology of Han," in *Minjung Theology: People as Subjects of History,* ed. the Commission on Theological Concerns of the Christian Conference of Asia [Maryknoll, N.Y.: Orbis, 1981], cited in Young-Chan Ro, "Symbol, Myth, and Ritual: The Method of the *Minjung,*" in *Lift Every Voice: Constructing Christian Theologies from the Underside,* ed. Susan Brooks Thistlethwaite and Mary Potter Engel [San Francisco: Harper & Row, 1990], 47).

73. Kristeva, *Powers,* 47.

74. Ibid., 47.

75. "The old heroic ego loses its stuffing and returns to a two-dimensional shade." Thus writes James Hillman on the unconscious work of the underworld to build an "imaginal ego" (*Dream and the Underworld* [New York: Harper & Row, 1979], 102).

76. Leslie Marmon Silko, *Almanac of the Dead* (New York: Penguin, 1991), 722–23.

77. A multiple of twelve–pertaining to the tribes, possibly the disciples, and certainly the horoscope.

78. Elaine Pagels, *Adam, Eve, and the Serpent* (New York: Random House, 1988).

79. Deferral, as the alternative to immediacy, demands the endless mediating play of the text with itself. See Jacques Derrida, "Différance," in *Speech and Phenomena and Other Essays on Husserl's Theory of Signs,* trans. David B. Allison (Evanston, Ill.: Northwestern University Press, 1973), 142–43.

80. Concoctions of Christian, New Age and indigenous prophecies speak of Mama Earth, too long taken for granted and exploited, literally shrugging off Western civilization. "Throughout the Book of Rev are mentioned great earthquakes that would strike . . . when the Earth needs cleansing. Spirit says . . . the reason it's necessary is that humans are not willing to make the necessary changes without being forced into them. They are too selfish and greedy to give the Earth a rest where it is needed" (Sun Bear with Wabun Wind, *Black Dawn, Bright Day* [New York: Fireside/Simon & Schuster, 1992], 48).

81. See Mark L. Taylor on "the exchange abstraction" and symbolic matricide, *Remembering Esperanza: A Cultural-Political Theology for North American Praxis* (Minneapolis: Fortress, 1990), 127ff.

82. Smith, *Map Is Not Territory,* 146.

83. Here the rolling up of the sky is accompanied by every mountain and island being "removed from its place"–no minor shake-up, but complete terrestrial dislocation. Structurally, this imagery anticipates the final moment, the moment of ultimate upheaval, immediately prior to the new creation, after all the battles have been won, just prior to the resurrection of all the dead for the final judgment.

84. Schüssler Fiorenza, *The Book of Revelation*, 172.

85. Schüssler Fiorenza, *Revelation*, 33.

86. The Iliad and the Odyssey, for instance, sustain a far more "historical" sense of time.

87. Boman, *Hebrew Thought*, 134.

88. Jack Miles, *God: A Biography* (New York: Alfred Knopf, 1995), 17.

89. See Graham, *Approaching Hoofbeats*, 219ff. "Affirming the efforts of ecology," he writes, "we cannot act as though we are helpless to work for the world's renewal. We must do what we can, even though we know that God's ultimate plan is the making of a new earth and a new heaven . . . it may be several generations from now" (221).

90. The one world government consists mainly of the World Council of Churches and the United Nations. Fundamentalists would not find an alliance between H. W. Armstrong and the "world government movement" surprising, for in fundamentalist eyes the Worldwide Church of God is a cult organization.

91. Not even in the Psalms.

92. Marina Warner, *Alone of All Her Sex* (New York: Alfred Knopf, 1976), 246f.

93. Lawrence, *Apocalypse*, 74.

94. Despite textual proscriptions, there was widespread fascination with the zodiacal signs among Jews, as evinced by synagogue mosaics and other archeological data, and also by the texts of Qumran, a nearly contemporaneous apocalyptic community, not to mention the appearance of three Chaldean astrologers in Jesus' birth narrative.

95. Lawrence, *Apocalypse*, 75.

96. Ford, *Revelation*, 188.

97. Ibid.

98. See Demaris S. Wehr, *Jung and Feminism: Liberating Archetypes* (Boston: Beacon, 1987); and Catherine Keller, *From a Broken Web* (Boston: Beacon, 1986), chap. 3.

99. Quoted in Frederick C. Grant, *Hellenistic Religion* (Indianapolis: Bobbs-Merrill, 1953), 132.

100. Ibid.

101. Sigmund Freud, "Notes on a Case of Paranoia," *Standard Edition of the*

Complete Psychological Works of Sigmund Freud, trans. James Strachey (London: Hogarth Press, 1958). "A world-catastrophe of this kind is not infrequent during the agitated stage [the third phase, that of the return of the repressed] in other cases of paranoia" (68f).

102. Page du Bois, *Torture and Truth* (New York: Routledge, 1991), 152. "The slave on the rack waits like the metal, pure or alloyed, to be tested. . . . *Basanos* assumes first that the slave always lies, then that torture makes him or her always tell the truth, then that the truth produced through torture will always expose the truth or falsehood of the free man's evidence" (35–36).

103. Virginia Burrus, "Torture and Travail: The Production of Truth in the *Letter of the Churches of Lyons and Vienne,*" American Academy of Religion presentation, November 1994.

104. The term is *krazo* (Ford, *Revelation*, 198). It occurs four times in the Gospel of John.

105. Ford, *Revelation*, 200.

106. Kristeva, *Powers*, 10.

107. The verb *harpazo* is that term which, when translated (from 1 Thessalonians 4:17, where those alive on earth are "caught up" to meet Christ in the air) as "to rapture," is so favored by fundamentalists.

108. See, for example, Dorothy Dinnerstein, *The Mermaid and the Minotaur* (New York: Harper & Row, 1976); Nancy Chodorow, *The Reproduction of Mothering* (Berkeley: University of California Press, 1978); and my analyses of these works in my book *From a Broken Web* (Boston: Beacon, 1986).

109. However, in God's hands, the rod is for vindication of the oppressed (cf. Psalm 2:9 and Exodus 4 and 7). God also breaks the rod of the oppressor (Isa. 9:4).

110. Jung, *Answer to Job*.

111. Adela Yarbro Collins, *The Combat Myth in the Book of Revelation* (Missoula, Mont.: Scholars Press, 1976), 65.

112. See Keller, *From a Broken Web*, 71ff.

113. Cf. Jung's still indispensable theory of "the shadow," the unconscious symbolization of the traits repressed in oneself as undesirable and so tending to develop a certain ferocity unless recognized and integrated. Carl Gustav Jung, *The Archetypes of the Collective Unconscious*, vol. 9, 1 (Princeton: Princeton University Press, 1959/1969), 20f.

114. Morris Berman, *Coming to Our Senses* (New York: Simon & Schuster, 1989), 85.

115. Luce Irigaray, "The Mechanics of Fluids," in *This Sex Which Is Not One,*

trans. Catherine Porter with Catherine Burke (Ithaca: Cornell University Press, 1985).

116. Susan Bordo, *Unbearable Weight: Feminism, Western Culture, and the Body* (Berkeley: University of California Press, 1993).

117. Pharaoh is characterized by Ezekiel as "the great dragon sprawling in the midst of its channels" (29:4).

118. Michael E. Lodahl, *Shekhinah/Spirit: Divine Presence in Jewish and Christian Religion* (Mahwah, N.J.: Stimulus/Paulist), 51.

119. Luce Irigaray, "Place, Interval," in *An Ethics of Sexual Difference*, trans. C. Burke and G. Gill (Ithaca: Cornell University Press, 1993), 39f.

120. Warner, *Alone of All Her Sex*, 247.

121. Nelle Morton, *The Journey Is Home* (Boston: Beacon, 1985), 174f.

122. The Sophia debacle broke in relation to the conservative uproar over a 1993 ecumenical conference called "Re-Imagining," celebrating the World Council of Church's Decade of the Churches in Solidarity of Women. See Catherine Keller, "Inventing the Goddess: A Study in Ecclesiastical Backlash," *Christian Century* 3 (6 April 1994): 340–42; and Heather Elkins, *Worshiping Women: Re-forming God's People for Praise* (Nashville: Abingdon, 1994), 167, n.44.

123. A feminist organization called "Woman in the Wilderness" combines vigorous adventure into the wilds with a spiritual and political practice of female bonding. This group derived its name from a seventeenth-century Pennsylvania millennialist utopian experiment, the Order of the Woman in the Wilderness (China Galland, *Longing for Darkness* [New York: Penguin, 1990], 12). It does not require political separatism to demand places of our own, for a time, and times, and half a time.

124. Tiamat or Leviathan, the consort or the manifestation of goddess, the seducer or the image of Eve.

125. Schüssler Fiorenza, *Revelation*, 13. Supposedly her own reading strategy, which focuses on the agency of the reader rather than "the androcentric linguistic medium," allows a deliteralized interpretation. Arguing that "such misogyny" appears nowhere else in the book of Revelation, and that its language "does not function as a cipher with a one-to-one meaning," she infers that Revelation 14:4–5 should not be read "literally," and that therefore a properly "metaphorical" reading refers the phrase to "the idolatry of the imperial cult" (188), since, presumably, Babylon/Rome is a "mother of harlots."

   Surely the number 144,000 is not meant literally, and androcentric or grammatically masculine language does not necessarily "intend" to exclude women, but when a text goes to the length of adding a perfectly prosaic explication of the exclusive sexuality envisioned (as I cannot but read the phrase "these who have not defiled themselves with women" to do), the excuse of metaphor no longer applies. Moreover, as we have seen, the book is charged with multilayered sexisms, and even if there are no other deliberate assaults on the general worth of women, it is impossible to deny the misogynist tenor of the work. That women do not through the ages find themselves generally alienated on the basis of gender from Revelation and other such texts is only an argument for a reading which honors the tensions and possibilities dwelling in the margins. Schüssler Fiorenza rightly wants to save–for women–the liberationist reading of the text from feminist dismissal. This goal may be achieved more credibly by acknowledging and struggling with the sexism of most ancient and contemporary prophetic voices for justice (as she routinely does in the rest of her work). Of course the sexual imagery of 14:4 correlates with the symbolization of Rome as Whore of Babylon, but, as will become all too clear, that hardly solves the problem of sexism!

126. *Village Voice*, vol. 37, issue 19 (May 12, 1992).

127. The inversion play of opposites, typical for the apocalyptic genre, is ubiquitous (for instance, the mirroring of the wound of the lamb in the wound of the beast, and the harpers in heaven and on earth).

128. "When that writing stops voyeurism becomes a perversion" (Kristeva, *Powers*, 46).

129. Daly, *Gyn/Ecology*, 104.

130. Ibid., 111.

131. Saddam Hussein gets credit for the phrase.

132. Ford, *Revelation*, 319f. Archeologists surmise that Qumran served as an armed camp as well as a religious retreat; it was crushed by a Roman battalion.

133. Howard Eilberg-Schwartz, *God's Phallus and Other Problems for Men and Monotheism* (Boston: Beacon, 1994), 88.

134. Ford, *Revelation*, 329.

135. Hence the Pentagon's "nightmare scenario" in the Gulf War: if Hussein had decided to conform to UN dictates and *negotiate* a solution.

136. Augustine, *City of God*, trans. Henry Bettenson (New York: Penguin, 1972, 1984), 965 (1.22.3).

137. Thomas Hardy, *Jude the Obscure.*

138. The phrase quoted is from "Aquarius" in the rock musical *Hair!*

139. Burrus, "Torture and Travail."

140. This tradition designs entire cities, building into them certain eschatological values consciously and responsibly.

141. Doris Lessing, *The Four-Gated City* (New York: Alfred Knopf, 1969).

142. Ford, *Revelation*, 326.

3. Time

1. Francis Fukuyama, "The End of History?" *The National Interest* 16 (Summer 1989): 3f.

2. Paul Ricoeur, *Time and Narrative*, trans. David Pellauer (Chicago: University of Chicago Press, 1984–1988).

3. Jack Miles, *God: A Biography* (New York: Alfred Knopf, 1995), chap. 1.

4. Thorlief Boman, *Hebrew Thought Compared with Greek* (New York: W. W. Norton 1960), 134.

5. Michael Foucault, *The Foucault Reader*, ed. Paul Rabinow (New York: Pantheon, 1984), 87.

6. Roland Barthes, "Introduction to the Structural Analysis of Narratives," *Image, Music, Text*, trans. Stephen Heath (New York: Routledge, 1979), 2.

7. Barthes, "Introduction," 1.

8. Ibid., 35.

9. John Dominic Crossan, *The Historical Jesus: The Life of a Mediterranean Jewish Peasant* (San Francisco: Harper, 1991), 258.

10. See Crossan, 246, on "to see."

11. Martin Werner, cited in Bernard McGinn, *Apocalyptic Spirituality* (New York: Paulist Press, 1979), 16.

12. Melanie Klein, "The Emotional Life of the Infant," in *Envy and Gratitude and Other Works, 1946–1963* (New York: Delacorte, 1975), 73.

13. Albert Schweitzer, *The Quest of the Historical Jesus*, trans. W. Montgomery, 2nd ed. (New York: Macmillan, 1948).

14. McGinn, *Apocalyptic Spirituality*, 15ff.

15. Ibid., 16.

16. Stephen D. O'Leary, *Arguing the Apocalypse: A Theory of Millennial Rhetoric* (New York and Oxford: Oxford University Press, 1994).

17. Ibid., 17.

18. J. Daniélou finds in this "Millenarianism . . . the form in which Jewish Christianity expressed the doctrine of the Parousia." *The Theology of Jewish Christianity* (Chicago: Reguery, 1964), 384.

19. This division only crystallized in the sixth century and was put into widespread usage in the eighth. See Robert Markus, *The End of Ancient Christianity* (Cambridge: Cambridge University Press, 1990), 88.

20. Markus, *The End*, 89.

21. Lactantius, quoted in McGinn, *Apocalyptic Spirituality*, 76 (my emphasis).

22. He even questioned the authorship of the text.

23. Eusebius, *Vita Constantini* 3.15, cited in Crossan, *Historical Jesus*, 424.

24. McGinn, *Apocalyptic Spirituality*, 26.

25. Augustine, *The City of God*, trans. Henry Bettenson (New York: Penguin, 1972, 1984), 593 (2.14.26).

26. Ibid., 877 (2.19.17).

27. Ibid., 907f (2.20.7).

28. Ibid., 916 (2.20.9).

29. Ibid., 940 (2.20.21).

30. Ibid., 963 (2.20.30).

31. The themes of Elijah's return, the Jews' conversion, the name "Antichrist," and the conflagration of the earth, do not occur in Revelation.

32. "Then why should not God have power to make the bodies of the dead rise again, and the bodies of the damned to suffer torment in the everlasting fire, since he made the world so full of innumerable marvels?" (Augustine, *City of God*, 976 [2.21.7]).

33. To which Augustine answers, "A slave is very justly punished by a term of years in fetters when he has attacked his master with a passing word" (*City of God*, 987 [2.21.11]). Ergo, how much more deserving are all descendents of Adam of hell.

34. Augustine, *City of God*, 486 (2.12.13).

35. Augustine, *Serm.* 81, 8, trans. Peter Brown, *Augustine of Hippo* (London: Faber, 1967), 298.

36. Marjorie Reeves, *Joachim of Fiore and the Prophetic Future* (London: SPCK, 1976), 2.

37. McGinn, *Apocalyptic Spirituality*, 26.

38. Markus, *The End*, 107.

39. Reeves, *Joachim of Fiore*, 22f.

40. John M. Wallace-Hadrill, *The Barbarian West: A.D. 400–1000* (New York: Oxford University Press, 1962).

41. Norman Cohn, *The Pursuit of the Millennium* (New York: Oxford University Press, 1957; 1970), 68ff, 70.

42. Quoted in Frederick Turner, *Beyond Geography: The Western Spirit Against the Wilderness* (New Brunswick: Rutgers University Press, 1980), 79.

43. Ibid., 79.

44. Turner, *Beyond Geography*, 80.

45. Cohn, *Pursuit*, 121.

46. Ernst Bloch, *The Principle of Hope* (Cambridge, Mass.: MIT Press, 1986; German ed., 1959) vol. 2, 515.

47. Martin Bloomfield, "Recent Scholarship on Joachim of Fiore and His Influence," in *Prophecy and Millenarianism*, ed. A. Williams (Harlow, 1980), 23.

48. Reeves, *Joachim of Fiore*, 1.

49. Ibid., 8.

50. Quoted ibid., 14.

51. Especially via the imagery of Isaiah and the wisdom teachings of Jesus.

52. Reeves, *Joachim of Fiore*, 8.

53. Reeves, 36. Cf., for example, John of Parma and the more zealous Gerard of Borgo San Donninno.

54. The pope was John XXII. For a full discussion of the "counterfeit holiness" of the papal Antichrist from 1200 to 1335, see Bernard McGinn, *Antichrist: Two Thousand Years of Fascination with Evil* (San Francisco: Harper San Francisco, 1994), 143ff.

55. Reeves, *Joachim of Fiore*, 40, n. 34.

56. On the concept of the closed Europe which supersedes the twelfth-century awakening, see Frederich Heer, *The Medieval World: Europe 1100–1350*, trans. Janet Sondheimer (New York: Mentor, 1963), 27ff, 101ff.

57. Reeves, *Joachim of Fiore*, 50.

58. See Chapter 6 of this work.

59. Reeves lamely infers that the women had been given "insufficient outlets" in the preceding two centuries, implying that before that there had been adequate vocational opportunities, and that it is really just a matter of the paternal leadership "giving" women a bit more space within the preestablished structures–failing to recognize that these structures were predicated on minimizing the role of women "within the historical process" (see Reeves, *Joachim of Fiore*, 51).

60. Mary Daly, *Beyond God the Father* (New York: Harper & Row, 1967), 95ff.

61. Cohn, *Pursuit*, 162.

62. Ibid., 161.

63. Bernard McGinn, ed., *Meister Eckhart and the Beguine Mystics* (New York: Continuum, 1994), 6.

64. Marguerite Porete, *A Mirror for Simple Souls*, trans. Charles Crawford (New York: Crossroad, 1990), 132.

65. Cf. Mechthild of Magdeburg and Hadewijch of Antwerp; this is true also of other medieval mystics such as Angelina and Beatrice. See Emilie Zum Brunn and Georgette Epiney-Burgard, eds., *Women Mystics in Medieval Eurpoe*, trans. Sheila Hughes (New York: Paragon House, 1989).

66. Reminiscent of the better-known Meister Eckhart, who most likely listened to her sermons in Paris. See Crawford's introduction to the *Mirror*,

12; also Maria Lichtmann, "Marguerite Porete and Meister Eckhart: *The Mirror for Simple Souls* Mirrored," in McGinn, *Meister Eckhart*, 65–86.

67. Porete, *Mirror* 35.

68. Ibid., 10.

69. Heinrich Kramer and James Sprenger, *The Malleus Maleficarum*, trans. Montague Summers (New York: Dover, 1971), 171.

70. Hildegard of Bingen, *Scivias*, trans. Columba Hart and Jane Bishop (New York: Paulist Press, 1990), 351, 366.

71. Gerda Lerner, *The Creation of Feminist Consciousness: From the Middle Ages to 1870* (New York: Oxford University Press, 1993), 49ff.

72. Turner, *Beyond Geography*, 65.

73. Though I would disagree with Turner's characterization of the lost integrity as "the timeless cycle of myth and nature," which stems from his over-reliance on Jung and Eliade, I concur with the sense that Jesus and the apocalyptic writers attempt to address the devastations wrought by the ancient colonizations of tribal life. And we will return later to the naturalist Christology implied below: "The Messiah was betrayed, not in his person as by Judas, but in his message by the Fathers of the Church. For that message seems to be of the divinity that dwells within and that is present in all creation, and of how to live in accordance with this. Yet in the historical interpretation of Jesus in the vast industry of Christology, the emphasis shifted from the message to the historical figure, who was now presented as having once intervened in the history of this world only to show it as the contemptible thing it truly was" (Turner, *Beyond Geography*, 63).

74. James H. Moorhead, *American Apocalypse: Yankee Protestants and the Civil War, 1860–1869*, (New Haven: Yale University Press, 1978), 42–81.

75. Sandra Harding, *Whose Science? Whose Knowledge?* (Ithaca: Cornell University Press, 1991).

76. Joseph Camilleri and Jim Falk, *The End of Sovereignty?: The Politics of a Shrinking and Fragmenting World* (Brookfield, Vt.: Edward Elgar, 1992), 223.

77. Lewis Mumford, *Technics and Civilization* (New York: Burlingame, 1963).

78. Camilleri and Falk, *Sovereignty*, 223–24.

79. Paula Gunn Allen, *The Sacred Hoop: Recovering the Feminine in American Indian Traditions* (Boston: Beacon, 1986), 149, 51.

80. Charles S. Maier, "The Politics of Time: Changing Paradigms of Collective Time and Private Time in the Modern Era," in Charles E. Maier, *Changing Boundaries of the Political* (Cambridge: Cambridge University Press, 1987), 155.

81. Mary Daly, *Pure Lust: Elemental Feminist Philosophy* (Boston: Beacon, 1984), 289.

82. Sven Birkerts, *The Gutenberg Elegies: The Fate of Reading in an Electronic Age* (Boston: Faber & Faber, 1994), 129.

83. Ibid., 130.

84. Peggy Korneger, "Hope," in *A Feminist Dictionary*, ed. Cheris Kramarae and Paula A. Treichler (Boston: Pandora Press, 1985), 196.

85. Bloch, *Hope*, 3:1372 (his emphasis).

86. Ibid., 3:1373 (his emphasis).

87. Camilleri and Falk, *Sovereignty*, 224.

88. Ibid.

89. Christina Thürmer-Rohr, *Vagabonding: Feminist Thinking Cut Loose*, trans. Lise Weil (Boston: Beacon, 1991).

90. Karen Fields, "Power and Eschatology: Time in the Colonial Context," (unpublished essay), 2.

91. Quoted in and translated by Mary de Shazer, *A Poetics of Resistance* (Ann Arbor: University of Michigan Press, 1994), 77.

92. Ibid., 77f.

93. Camilleri and Falk, *Sovereignty*, 225.

94. Jürgen Moltmann, *Theology of Hope* (New York: Harper & Row, 1967), 16.

95. Karl Barth, *Church Dogmatics IV*, 3 (Edinburgh: T & T Clark, 1962), 938f.

96. May Sarton, "Now I Become Myself," *Collected Poems 1930–1993* (New York: W. W. Norton, 1974; 1980; 1984; 1988; 1993).

97. Sandra Lee Bartky, *Femininity and Domination* (New York: Routledge, 1990), 72.

98. Edith Wharton, *The House of Mirth* (New York: Vintage, 1990; first published 1905), 29.

99. Luce Irigaray, "Place, Interval," in *An Ethics of Sexual Difference*, trans. C. Burke and G. Gill (Ithaca: Cornell University Press, 1993), 35.

100. Julia Kristeva, "Women's Time," trans. Alice Jardine and Harry Blake, *Signs: Journal of Women in Culture and Society* 7, no. 1 (1981): 13–35.

101. Ibid., 17.

102. Ibid., 20.

103. Ibid.

104. Judith Butler, *Gender Trouble: Feminism and the Subversion of Identity* (New York: Routledge, 1990).

105. Karl Friedrick von Weiszacker, *Die Geschichte der Natur* (München: Carl Hauser Verlag, 1948).

106. *Koyaaniqatsi*, Godfrey Reggio, PBS/CPB, score by Philip Glass, 1982.

107. Martin Heidegger, *Being and Time*, trans. John Macquarrie and Edward Robinson (New York: Harper and Row, 1962), 416.

108. Alfred North Whitehead, *Science and the Modern World* (New York: Free Press/MacMillan, 1925; 1967), 127.

109. Kathleen Sands, *Escape from Paradise* (Minneapolis: Fortress Press, 1994), 168–69.

110. Stephen Hawking, *A Brief History of Time* (New York: Bantam, 1988), 152.

111. Rebecca S. Chopp, *The Power to Speak: Feminism, Language, God* (New York: Crossroad, 1989), 50f.

112. Whitehead, *Science and the Modern World*.

113. Gunn Allen, *The Sacred Hoop*, 154.

114. Ibid., 149.

115. Elkins, *Worshiping Women*, 17ff.

116. See especially Arthur Waskow's ecological reconstruction of Judiasm, ceremonialized in practices such as a "green Sabbath," which builds on the Jewish laws against labor, animal exploitation, and the use of technology for one day every week ("The Greening of Judaism," *Moment*, June 1992, 45–47).

117. Leslie Marmon Silko, *Almanac of the Dead* (New York: Penguin, 1991), 629.

4. Place

1. Doreen Massey, *Space, Place, and Gender* (Minneapolis: University of Minnesota Press, 1994), 180.

2. "That Mountain Far Away," Tewa, in *In the Trail of the Wind: American Indian Poems and Ritual Orations*, ed. John Bierhorst (New York: Farrar, Straus & Giroux 1971; 1990), 47. Originally printed in *Songs of the Tewa*, trans. Herbert Joseph Spinden, N.Y.: The Exposition of Indian Tribal Arts, 1952.

3. Glen Mazis, *Earthbodies*, forthcoming.

4. Rosemary Radford Ruether, *Gaia and God* (San Francisco: Harper San Francisco, 1992), 85.

5. See Edward Casey, *Getting Back into Place: Toward a Renewed Understanding of the Place-World* (Bloomington: Indiana University Press, 1993).

6. Massey, *Space*, 168.

7. Manuel Castells, *The City and the Grass roots: A Crosscultural Theory of Urban Social Movements* (Berkeley: University of California Press, 1983), 311f.

8. Vandana Shiva, *Staying Alive* (London: Zed Books, 1988), 37.

9. David Harvey, *The Condition of Postmodernity* (Cambridge, Mass.: Blackwell, 1989), 117; also Massey, *Space*, 133.

10. James A. Swan, *Sacred Places* (Santa Fe: Bear & Co., 1990), 44.

11. Marcus Schneck, *Your Backyard Wildlife Garden* (Emmaus, Pa.: Rodale, 1992), 18.

12. Felicitas Goodman, *Ecstacy, Ritual, and Alternate Reality* (Bloomington: Indiana University Press, 1988), 17.

13. Peggy Reeves Sanday, *Female Power and Male Dominance: The Origins of Sexual Inequality* (New York: Cambridge University Press, 1981).

14. Goodman, *Ecstacy*, 18 (emphasis hers).

15. Ibid.

16. Ibid., 19.

17. Swan, *Sacred Places*, 174.

18. Gerda Lerner, *The Creation of Patriarchy* (New York: Oxford University Press, 1986).

19. Goodman, *Ecstacy*, 25.

20. Ibid., 25, 27.

21. Ibid., 29.

22. Ibid., 29ff.

23. Norman Cohn, *The Pursuit of the Millennium* (New York: Oxford University Press, 1957; 1970), 53ff.

24. John B. Cobb, Jr., *Christ in a Pluralistic Age* (Philadelphia: Westminster, 1975), 195ff.

25. Elaine Orr, "In this Motherless Geography," originally appeared in *Journal of Feminist Studies in Religion*, vol. 3, no. 2 (fall, 1987).

26. Kirkpatrick Sale, *The Conquest of Paradise: Christopher Columbus and the Columbian Legacy* (New York: Plume/Penguin, 1990), 4.

27. Noam Chomsky, *Year 501: The Conquest Continues* (Boston: South End Press, 1993), 5.

28. Contrary to population orthodoxy, the ecological crisis is not caused by impinging hordes of (dark-skinned) fertile humans, though certainly population in the two-thirds world exhausts its own habitats and those of other species. See Catherine Keller, "Chosen Persons and the Green Ecumenacy: A Possible Christian Response to the Population Apocalypse," in *Ecotheology: Voices from South and North*, ed. David G. Hallman (Maryknoll, N.Y.: Orbis, 1994), 300ff.

29. Sale, *Conquest*, 12.

30. Samuel Eliot Morison, quoted ibid., 95.

31. Ibid., 95.

32. *Journals and Other Documents on the Life and Voyages of Christopher Columbus*, trans. Samuel Eliot Morison (New York: Heritage Press, 1963), 64–67 (journal entries for October 12 and 13).

33. Frank E. Manuel and Fritzie P. Manuel, *Utopian Thought in the Western World* (Cambridge: Belknap/Harvard University Press, 1979), 33ff.

34. Conversation with Sharon V. Betcher.

35. Letter to Santangel, *Journals*, 182.

36. Journal entry for October 12, ibid., 65.

37. Julia Kristeva, *The Kristeva Reader*, ed. Toril Moi (New York: Columbia University Press, 1986), 62ff.

38. Coma, a member of the second journey, gives the most likely explanation: "Bad feeling arose and broke out into warfare because of the licentious conduct of our men towards the Indian women, for each Spaniard had five women to minister to his pleasure" and "the husbands and relatives of the women, unable to take this, banded together to avenge this insult and elminate this outrage . . . and attacked the Christians in great force" (Sale, *Conquest*, 139).

39. DeCuneo letter on the Second Voyage, *Journals*, 212.

40. Sale, *Conquest*, 140.

41. Tainos over fourteen had to supply the rulers with a hawk's bell of gold every three months, for which they received a copper token; any found without the token around their necks would have their hands cut off and bleed to death. Then the horrors of the mines: normally a third of the men died within their required yearly time. In the meantime, the women were dying at home. (Source: Howard Zinn, *A People's History of the United States* [New York: Harper & Row, 1980], 4, 6–7.)

42. Ibid., 4–5.

43. He was told not to return to Hispaniola, where he had left his brother in charge.

44. Manuel and Manuel, *Utopian Thought*, 60.

45. Quoted in Sale, *Conquest*, 175.

46. Quoted ibid., 176. Cf. *Journals*, 286: "But as for this other hemisphere I maintain that it is like a half of a very round pear which had a long stem, as I have said, or like a woman's teat on a round ball."

47. Johan Huizinga, *The Waning of the Middle Ages* (New York: Anchor/Doubleday, 1954), 138.

48. Julia Kristeva, *Powers of Horror: An Essay on Abjection* (New York: Columbia University Press, 1990), 1.

49. Ibid., 8.

50. Ibid., 54.

51. Naomi Goldenberg has done especially fine work making Melanie Klein's metaphors available for feminist theory today. See Goldenberg, *Returning Words to Flesh* (Boston: Beacon, 1990), 156–71.

52. Harvey, *Postmodernity*, 253.

53. M. de Certeau, *The Practice of Everyday Life* (Berkeley: University of California Press, 1984).

54. Letter to Torres, *Journals*, 291.
55. Harvey, *Postmodernity*, 249.
56. Huizinga, *Waning*.
57. Christopher Columbus, *The "Libro de las profecías" of Christopher Columbus* trans. D. C. West and A. King (Gainesville, Fla.: University of Florida Press, 1991).
58. Quoted in Sale, *Conquest*, 190.
59. Ibid., 191.
60. Quoted ibid., 197.
61. Jack Weatherford, *Indian Givers: How the Indians of the Americas Transformed the World* (New York: Fawcett Columbine, 1988), chap. 1.
62. "Spiritual" in the sense meant by the conquering Europeans, understood by Hegel as infinitely superior to the "aborigines" whose degenerate culture was so weak that it "must expire as soon as Spirit approached it." "A mild and passionless disposition, want of spirit, and a crouching submissiveness . . . are the chief characteristics of the native Americans," so "slothful" that, under the kind "authority of the Friars," "at midnight a bell had to remind them even of their matrimonial duties"; only slavery enabled the "Negroes," like the Indians, to become "participant in a higher morality and the culture connected with it" (Hegel, quoted in Chomsky, *Year 501*, 4f).
63. Carolyn Merchant, *The Death of Nature: Women, Ecology, and the Scientific Revolution* (San Francisco: Harper & Row, 1980), 132.
64. Rita Nakashima Brock and Susan Thistlethwaite, *Throwing Stones: The Sex Industry in Asia and America*, forthcoming.
65. Christina Thürmer-Rohr, *Vagabonding: Feminist Thinking Cut Loose*, trans. Lise Weil (Boston: Beacon, 1991), 24.
66. Quoted in Manuel and Manuel, *Utopian Thought*, 260.
67. "For the founding fathers of modern science, the reliance on the language of gender was explicit: they sought a philosophy that deserved to be called 'masculine,' that could be distinguished from its ineffective predecessors by its 'virile' power, its capacity to bind Nature to man's service and make her his slave" (Evelyn Fox Keller, *Reflections on Gender and Science* [New Haven: Yale University Press, 1985], 7).
68. Quoted in Manuel and Manuel, *Utopian Thought*, 517.
69. Condorcet, speech of acceptance to the Academy of Sciences, ibid.
70. Frederic Jameson, *Postmodernism, or, The Cultural Logic of Late Capitalism* (Durham, N.C.: Duke University Press, 1991), 154.
71. Henri Lefebvre, *The Production of Space* (Oxford: Blackwell, 1991), 302.
72. Camilleri and Falk, *Sovereignty*, 307.

73. The geography of GATT, NAFTA, and other instruments of the "free market" has so globalized the mobility of capital and so enforced the dislocation of peoples that it operates–at near instantaneous, nearly timeless rates of speed–in a deceptive aura of all-inclusive, boundless freedom. This transgression of all boundaries achieves Harvey's "annihilation of space by time." Its freedom is in fact a freedom from any local communal or ecological sensibilities, one by which accelerating proportions of the earth and its peoples are rendered down-and-out, landless, homeless, dislocated. It is not that the traditional dualisms of social space have been overcome in the name of the "freedom" and "reform" the World Bank touts; rather, the dualism has become universal and thus truly apocalyptic.

74. Camilleri and Falk, *Sovereignty,* 308. This is a more spatially conscious and integrative version of Iris Marion Young's proposal for "coalitions" as the basis for a sustainable "politics of difference."

75. Vítor Westhelle, "Creation Motifs in the Search for a Vital Space: A Latin American Perspective," in *Lift Every Voice: Constructing Christian Theologies from the Underside,* ed. Susan Brooks Thistlethwaite and Mary Potter Engel (San Francisco: Harper San Francisco, 1990), 129–30 (emphasis mine).

76. Ibid., 130.

77. For further discussion, see my essay "Powerlines," *Theology Today* 52, July 1995.

78. Westhelle, "Creation Motifs," 129f.

79. Ibid., 132.

80. Ibid., 134.

81. If *Endzeit gleicht Urzeit,* this is not because God can replace a world destroyed by human injustice; rather it is because of what Westhelle beautifully calls the "metabolism" of *creatio continua.* "Metabolism" is what "throws together"–in the random and purposeful interlinkages of life. The metabolic interdependence of people with each other and the land constitutes an ongoing activity of production and reproduction which counts as the perpetual origination of new life not loosed from but *out of the matrix of* the old. Because that matrix has become–again, in Westhelle's terms–dominated by "diabolism" ("what throws apart"), being bound together (re-ligio) *again* becomes necessary.

82. Alfred North Whitehead, *Process and Reality* (New York: Free Press, 1929; 1978), 40, 46, 59.

83. Sallie McFague, *The Body of God: An Ecological Theology* (Minneapolis: Fortress, 1993).

84. Pablo Santos, Filipino activist, citing another tribal Filipino, a Lumad,

Datu Mandagese. Quoted in Pablo Piacentini, ed., *Story Earth: Native Voices on the Environment* (San Francisco: Mercury House, 1993), 103.

85. Pablo Santos writes that "all the indigenous people of the Philippines believe they are the sons and daughters of the Earth. . . . For the Aeta people, land cannot be bought or sold, it cannot be owned by just one person–the Earth is for everybody so that everyone can live. . . . The Earth is sacred" (ibid.).

86. "Ecofeminist images of women . . . retain the patriarchal stereotypes of what men expect women to be. These stereotypes freeze women as merely caring and nurturing beings, instead of expanding the full range of women's human potentialities and abilities" (Janet Biehl, *Rethinking Eco-Feminist Politics* [Boston: South End Press, 1991], 15).

87. Piacentini, *Story Earth*, 102.

88. Kirkpatrick Sale, *Dwellers in the Land: The Bioregional Vision* (Philadelphia: New Society Publishers, 1991), 42.

89. Massey, *Space*, 19.

90. The churches participate in this maturation inasmuch as they engage and join the social movements, such as in the World Council of Churches.

91. Camilleri and Falk, *Sovereignty*, 312.

92. Adrienne Rich, "Notes Toward a Politics of Location," in *Women, Feminist Identity, and Society in the 1980's*, ed. Miriam Diaz-Diocaretz (Philadelphia: John Benjamin, 1985), 9.

93. McFague, *The Body of God*, 99.

94. Judith Butler, *Gender Trouble: Feminism and the Subversion of Identity* (New York: Routledge, 1990).

95. Judith Butler, *Bodies That Matter: On the Discursive Limits of Sex* (New York: Routledge, 1993).

96. *Oxford English Dictionary.*

97. Glen A. Mazis, *The Trickster, Magician, and Grieving Man: Reconnecting Men with Earth* (Santa Fe: Bear Publishers, 1993), 11. For a more rigorous, less gender-focused analysis, see Mazis, *Emotion and Embodiment: Fragile Ontology* (New York: Peter Lang, 1993).

5. Community

1. Michel Foucault, "Is It Useless to Revolt?" trans. James Bernauer, *Philosophy and Social Criticism* 8 (1981): 6.

2. Martin Buber, *Paths in Utopia* (New York: Collier/Macmillan, 1949), 7.

3. Ernst Bloch, *The Principle of Hope*, trans. Neville Plaice, Stephen Plaice, and Paul Knight (Cambridge: MIT Press, 1986), vol. 2, 515. We discussed earlier the historicizing of hope, the medieval consequences of which we

registered among Beguines, radical Franciscans, Guglielmites, and adepts of the Free Spirit, but also among the Pauper's and People's Crusades.

4. Ibid.
5. Norman Cohn, *The Pursuit of the Millennium* (New York: Oxford University Press, 1957; 1970), 210.
6. Ibid., 214.
7. Ibid., 215.
8. Ibid., 213.
9. Thomas Münzer, *The Letters of Thomas Münzer*, ed. P. Matheson (Edinburgh: T. & T. Clark, 1988), 140.
10. Ibid., 67.
11. Ibid., 22.
12. Ibid., 136.
13. Quoted in Bloch, "Vindication," in *Principle of Hope*, vol. 1, 335.
14. Münzer, *Letters*, 144.
15. Cohn, *Pursuit*, 239.
16. Bloch, *Principle of Hope*, vol. 3, 1357.
17. Münzer, *Letters*, 134.
18. Münzer, quoted in Bloch, vol. 3, 1301.
19. Münzer, quoted in Bloch, vol. 3, 1195.
20. Frank E. Manuel and Fritzie P. Manuel, *Utopian Thought in the Western World* (Cambridge: Belknap/Harvard University Press, 1979), 195.
21. Quoted ibid., 199.
22. Cohn, *Pursuit*, 262.
23. Ibid., 266.
24. Ibid., 275.
25. Ibid., 267.
26. Christopher Hill, *The World Turned Upside Down* (New York: Viking, 1972), 12.
27. Quoted ibid., 107.
28. Quoted ibid., 224f.
29. Quoted ibid., 104.
30. Quoted ibid., 106.
31. Quoted ibid.
32. Quoted ibid., 113.
33. Quoted ibid., 111.
34. Ibid., 257.
35. Joel W. Martin, *Sacred Revolt: The Muskogee's Struggle for a New World* (Boston: Beacon, 1991).

36. Ibid., 8.

37. Ibid., 127ff.

38. Ibid., 144.

39. Ibid., 146.

40. Wilson writes that "the catalytic impulse of millennialism has not, however, wholly failed." "However briefly and however misguidedly, millennialism represents a type of social consciousness which transcends the personal and the local, the bodily ailment and the neighboring witch. . . . The vision of a transformed social order has at least lifted the consciousness of men [*sic*] to some measure of awareness about the conditions for the maintenance of a separate and different way of life" (Bryan R. Wilson, *Magic and the Millennium: A Sociological Study of Religious Movements of Protest Among Tribal and Third World Peoples* [New York: Harper & Row, 1973], 7). This rendition, approving of the degree of universalism and abstract disembodiment introduced by the millennial vision, not surprisingly underplays the suffering wrought by imperialism.

41. Martin, *Sacred Revolt*, 74.

42. James H. Cone, *The Spirituals and the Blues: An Interpretation* (New York: Seabury, 1972), 87.

43. Martin, *Sacred Revolt*, 74.

44. Ibid., 76.

45. Charles Lippy, "Waiting for the End: The Social Context of American Apocalyptic Religion," in Lois P. Zamora, ed., *The Apocalyptic Vision in America* (Bowling Green, Ohio: Bowling Green University Popular Press, 1982), 51.

46. Cone, *The Spirituals*, 99.

47. Theophus H. Smith, *Conjuring Culture: Biblical Formations of Black America* (New York: Oxford University Press, 1994).

48. Cone, *The Spirituals*, 90.

49. Ibid., 92.

50. Delores Williams, *Sisters in the Wilderness* (Maryknoll, N.Y.: Orbis, 1993).

51. Buber, *Paths*, 9.

52. Herman E. Daly and John B. Cobb, Jr., *For the Common Good* (Boston: Beacon, 1989).

53. Buber, *Paths*, 10.

54. Manuel and Manuel, *Utopian Thought*, 566.

55. Quoted ibid., 576.

56. Quoted ibid., 572.

57. Ibid., 574.

58. Ibid., 671.

59. Quoted ibid., 618.
60. Quoted ibid., 637.
61. Ibid., 675.
62. Quoted ibid., 589.
63. Quoted in Buber, *Paths*, 12.
64. Quoted ibid., 31.
65. Ibid.
66. Ibid., 129.
67. Ibid., 134.
68. Thomas Hood, quoted in Steven Goldsmith, *Unbuilding Jerusalem: Apocalypse and Romantic Representation* (Ithaca, N.Y.: Cornell University Press, 1993), 265.
69. Ibid., 266.
70. "The matter is, alas, profound, as Mann well knew" (Harold Bloom, *The Anxiety of Influence*, quoted ibid., 265f).
71. And though it was Mary Shelley who wrote the novel *The Last Man*, she seems mimetically to reenact, in the masculinity of the narrator's voice, the patriarchy of the genre of apocalypse: "The silencing of the feminine voice, the silencing of the very possibility of linguistic heterogeneity, becomes the preliminary symbolic act necessary for language to transcend history, for words to enter the immaterial and universal condition of the New Jerusalem" (Goldsmith, *Unbuilding Jerusalem*, 311).
72. In theology at the end of the nineteenth century these poles express themselves as God-relations–Kierkegaardian solitude of the "knight of faith" and Schleiermachian "feeling of absolute dependence"–whose reference to John's Apocalypse is if anything more sublimated than that of the secular romantics.
73. Iris Marion Young, *Justice and the Politics of Difference* (Princeton: Princeton University Press, 1990), 229.
74. Ibid., 234.
75. Communitarianism tries at its best, as in the Green Party platform, to appeal constructively to such backward yearnings for the golden age of village life; but it may too readily get sucked into the postliberal vortex of exclusionary localism.
76. Young, *Justice*, 234.
77. Young, 234.
78. Young, 321.
79. Judith V. Jordan, "Empathy and Self Boundaries," in *Women's Growth in Connection: Writings from the Stone Center*, edited by Judith V. Jordan et al. (New York: Guilford Press, 1991), 73.

80. Seyla Benhabib, *Situating the Self: Gender, Community, and Postmodernism in Contemporary Ethics* (New York: Routledge, 1992), 197f.
81. On the debate over "essentialism," see Naomi Schor and Elizabeth Weed, eds., *The Essential Difference* (Bloomington: Indiana University Press, 1994).
82. Audre Lorde, *Sister Outsider* (Trumansburg, N.Y.: Crossing Press, 1984), 123.
83. Ibid., 115.
84. Ibid., 122.
85. Ibid., 123.
86. bell hooks and Cornel West, *Breaking Bread: Insurgent Black Intellectual Life* (Boston: South End Press, 1991), 18.
87. Ibid.
88. Ibid., 82, 83.
89. Buber, *Paths*, 134.
90. Lorde, *Sister Outsider*, 54ff.
91. Young, *Justice*, 229.
92. Mary Daly, *Pure Lust: Elemental Feminist Philosophy* (Boston: Beacon, 1984).
93. Cf. chapter 4.
94. Michael Welker, *God the Spirit*, trans. John F. Hoffmeyer (Minneapolis: Fortress, 1994), 308.

6. Gender

1. Tina Pippin, *Death and Desire: The Rhetoric of Gender in the Apocalypse of John* (Louisville: Westminster/John Knox, 1992), 107.
2. Mary Daly, *Pure Lust: Elemental Feminist Philosophy* (Boston: Beacon, 1984), 223.
3. Beryl E. Satter, "New Thought and the Era of Women: 1825–1895," (Ph.D. diss., Yale University, 1992).
4. Charlotte Perkins Gilman, *Herland* (New York: Pantheon, 1979), 60.
5. Identity politics can be seen as countering essentialism, or tempering it at least–in that identity politics can be shifting, fluid, contingent.
6. Diane Elam, *Feminism and Deconstruction* (New York: Routledge, 1994), 120.
7. Ibid.
8. Jane Leade, *The Revelation of Revelations* (London: A. Sowle, 1683), 65. See also Catherine F. Smith, "Jane Leade: The Feminist Mind and Art of a Seventeenth-Century Protestant Mystic," in *Women of Spirit*, ed. R. R. Ruether and E. McLaughlin (New York: Touchstone/Simon & Schuster, 1979), 183–202.

9. Quoted in Leslie Wahl Rabine, "Essentialism and Its Context: Saint-Simonian and Poststructuralist Feminists," in Naomi Schor and Elizabeth Weed, eds., *The Essential Difference* (Bloomington: Indiana University Press, 1994), 135.

10. Quoted ibid. The original text is capitalized as shown.

11. Ibid., 133.

12. Ibid.

13. Ibid., 134.

14. Antoinette Doolittle, *The Shaker* 2 (June 1872), quoted in Linda A. Mercadante, *Gender Doctrine and God: The Shakers and Contemporary Theology* (Nashville: Abingdon, 1990), 13.

15. Gerda Lerner, *The Creation of Feminist Consciousness* (New York: Oxford University Press, 1993), 102.

16. Mercadante, *Gender Doctrine*, 42.

17. Quoted ibid., 71.

18. Ibid., 53f.

19. Quoted ibid., 86.

20. Ibid., 117.

21. Ibid., 123.

22. Ibid., 137.

23. Jemima Wilkinson, Document 14 in Rosemary Radford Ruether and Catherine M. Prelinger, "Women in Sectarian and Utopian Groups," in *The Colonial and Revolutionary Periods: A Documentary History*, vol. 2 of *Women and Religion in America*, ed. R. R. Ruether and R. S. Keller (San Francisco: Harper & Row, 1983), 312.

24. Wilkinson, Doc. 14, ibid., 313.

25. Ibid.

26. Sharon V. Betcher, "The Second Descent of the Spirit of Life from God: The Assumption of Jemima Wilkinson," unpublished paper, 1993.

27. Ibid.

28. David Hudson, *The History of Jemima Wilkinson, Preacheress of the Eighteenth Century* (Geneva, N.Y.: Hull, 1821), 286.

29. Ibid., 164.

30. Gerda Lerner, *Feminist Consciousness*, 102–3.

31. Betcher, "The Second Descent," 25.

32. Judith Butler, *Gender Trouble: Feminism and the Subversion of Identity* (New York: Routledge, 1990), 140f.

33. Ibid.

34. James H. Moorhead, "Between Progress and Apocalypse: A Reassessment of Millennialism in American Religious Thought, *Journal of American History* 71 (1984): 524–42.

35. Martha Tomhave Blauvelt and Rosemary Skinner Keller contrast the role of women in the nineteenth-century revivals to the eighteenth: "Eighteenth-century female evangelism was so limited largely because of ideological restraints. Women lacked a 'Cult of True Womanhood' to give them confidence in female moral superiority and to unite them in a holy sisterhood. Further, they were not yet able to appropriate the implications of the Declaration of Independence–that they too had been endowed by their Creator with certain unalienable rights through the birthright of equality. . . . A study of nineteenth-century evangelicalism indicates that the Wesleyan movement proved the most liberating religious tradition for women in all areas of religious expression–preaching, missionary and missionary society organizations, deaconess societies, and social reform. Yet one must not minimize the struggles with established authorities that accompanied women's entrance into these fields. (See "Women and Revivalism," in *Women and Religion in America*, vol. 2, 326f.

36. Moorhead, *Progress and Apocalypse*, 524f.

37. Charles Strozier, *Apocalypse: The Psychology of Fundamentalism* (Boston: Beacon, 1994), 171.

38. Sojourner Truth, "What Time of Night It Is," in Miriam Schneir, ed., *Feminism: The Essential Historical Writings* (New York: Vintage, 1972; 1994), 98.

39. They made their theological case for equality from Genesis 1 and natural theology, and otherwise stuck to legal and ethical argumentation.

40. Strozier, *Apocalypse*, 171: "The antislavery movement, from the moment of its active beginnings in the 1830's, drew its entire inspiration from biblical images of moral reform, and when it turned toward an accommodation with violence in the 1850's generated apocalyptic . . . leaders like John Brown, while even its moderates, like William Lloyd Garrison, thundered with Mosaic certainty: 'Ardently as my soul yearns for universal peace, and greatly shocking to it as are the horrors of war, I deem this a time when the friends of peace will best subserve their holy cause to wait until the whirlwind, the fire and the earthquake are past.' "

41. Ibid., 182.

42. Satter, "New Thought," 190.

43. Ibid., 92.

44. Elizabeth Cady Stanton, quoted ibid., 94.

45. Matilda Joslyn Gage, quoted in Satter, 122 (my emphasis).

46. Nancy Hardesty, Lucille Sider Dayton, and Donald W. Dayton, "Woman in the Holiness Movement," in Ruether and McLaughlin, *Women of Spirit*, 226ff.

47. Quoted in Satter, "New Thought," 123.

48. Elaine Showalter reads in the period a cultural insecurity "expressed in fears of regression and degeneration, and the longing for strict border controls around the definition of gender, as well as race, class, and nationality" (quoted in Strozier, *Apocalypse*, 182, n. 65).

49. Henry Ward Beecher's "The Tendencies Of American Progress" explores in eschatological nuance the temptations and dangers for the nation of unfettered corporate growth: "Organized wealth is one great danger which lies ahead, looming up gigantically. . . . The community will have to find ways to protect itself." Yet the millennialist optimism often breaks through unambiguously, to extol the nation's goodness as "almoner of employment, family, independence": "On the whole, the general tendency of wealth is such as to lead me today to thank God for the increasing wealth of America" (Washington Gladden's "The Nation and The Kingdom"). Source for these quotes is Conrad Cherry, *God's New Israel* (Englewood Cliffs, N.J.: Prentiss Hall, 1971), 237, 256.

50. Betty A. DeBerg, *Ungodly Women: Gender and the First Wave of American Fundamentalism* (Minneapolis: Fortress, 1990), 17.

51. Ibid., 28.

52. Ibid., 7.

53. Quoted ibid., 58.

54. Ibid., 126.

55. Ibid., 124.

56. Ibid.

57. Sojourner Truth, "Ain't I a Woman," in Schneir, *Feminism*, 95.

58. DeBerg, *Ungodly Women*, 76, 57. A reference to 2 Tim 3:6.

59. *Oxford English Dictionary.*

60. Mary Daly, *Beyond God the Father* (Boston: Beacon, 1973), 96f.

61. Ibid., 97.

62. Ibid.

63. Ibid., 96.

64. Kristeva.

65. Mary Daly, *Gyn/Ecology* (Boston: Beacon, 1978), 38.

66. And like any canny prophet, she expected that epithet, defiantly claiming it for herself as "positive paranoia" (*Gyn/Ecology*, 125). At the same time the advance in biological engineering since she wrote does not reassure one that her paranoia *or* her persecution fully accounts for the prophecy.

67. Daly, *Gyn/Ecology*, 88f.

68. Ibid., 105.

69. Ibid., 422.

70. Ibid., 105.

71. Frances Bartkowski, *Feminist Utopias* (Lincoln: University of Nebraska Press, 1989). "We can think of Gilman's *Herland* as the 'mother-text' and Wittig's novel as the first of the contemporary Amazon-texts" (23).

72. Monique Wittig, *Les Guérillères*, trans. David Le Vay (Boston: Beacon, 1969/1985), 49.

73. Bartkowski, *Feminist Utopias*, 38.

74. Wittig, *Les Guérillères*, 5.

75. Ibid., 85.

76. Ibid., 110.

77. Ibid., 126.

78. Wittig, Ibid., 127.

79. Butler, *Gender Trouble*, 138.

80. Wittig, *Les Guérillères*, 144.

81. Anna Quindlen, editorial, *New York Times*, 25 June 1994.

82. Mary DeShazer, *A Poetics of Resistance* (Ann Arbor: University of Michigan Press, 1994), 34.

83. Audre Lorde, *Sister Outsider* (Trumansburg, N.Y.: Crossing Press, 1994), 89.

84. Elizabeth Cady Stanton, quoted in Susan Thistlethwaite, *Sex, Race, and God* (New York: Crossroad, 1989), 37 (my emphasis).

85. As so many male heroes among the heritage of recognized geniuses had had their misogynist posteriors exposed in our public, now we began to hear the racist expediency of the white women who led the nineteenth- and early twentieth-century struggle for suffrage. They would not jeopardize solidarity with the white women of the American South. For instance, the National American Woman Suffrage Association held to their states' rights position in the face of criticism (by a white male liberal) in 1903 of their abandonment of any quest for suffrage for black women–promoted by Susan B. Anthony, Carrie Catt, Anna Howard Shaw, and others–which "was tantamount to an endorsement of white supremacy in most states, particularly in the south." White women perennially cite Sojourner Truth as evidence of black women's contribution to the early women's movement. But every time she spoke at women's rights conventions, groups of white women protested. For this example and an altogether excellent analysis of the problem, see bell hooks, "Racism and Feminism," in *Ain't I a Woman: Black Women and Feminism* (Boston: South End Press, 1981), 119–58.

86. bell hooks, *Feminist Theory: From Margin to Center* (Boston: South End Press, 1984), 5–6.

87. Still not truly an essence, which is timeless; and by definition no feminist metanarratives construe patriarchy as timeless, though some few have strayed into Jungian archetypes of essential complementarity.

88. Sharon Betcher in conversation connected the common oppression motif to the tension of false empathy from the able-bodied to the disabled and awareness that without some compassion, nothing is changed; she related the dilemma to Elaine Scarry's sense in pain or torture of the complete isolation of the sufferer, and yet also to the transformation experienced when one's own pain is placed in the context of the daily oceans of pain—thus somehow finding relief in being shared.

89. Kelly Brown Douglas, *The Black Christ* (Maryknoll, N.Y.: Orbis, 1994), 98.

90. Delores Williams, the 1986 Nelle Morton Lecture at Drew University.

91. Thistlethwaite, *Sex, Race, and God*, 16. Given Elisabeth Schüssler Fiorenza's virtually unmitigated enthusiasm for the Book of Revelation, it is perhaps not surprising that in her critique of feminist Christologies, she has adopted Thistlethwaite's dismissive position on feminist relationalism. So intent is she to equate a liberation rhetorical hermeneutic with an anti-relationalist posture that she identifies leading Asian American theologian Rita Nakashima Brock's *Journeys By Heart* as a leading perpetrator of main "white lady" theology! Such are the apocalyptic perils of "black-white" thinking. Cf. *Jesus: Miriam's Child, Sophia's Prophet* (New York: Continuum, 1994), 57.

92. Lorde, *Sister Outsider*, 69.

93. Thistlethwaite, *Sex, Race, and God*, 86.

94. Susan Bordo, "Feminism, Postmodernism, and Gender-Scepticism," in *Feminism/Postmodernism*, ed. Linda J. Nicholson (New York: Routledge, 1990), 134f.

95. Elizabeth V. Spelman, *Inessential Woman: Problems of Exclusion in Feminist Thought* (Boston: Beacon, 1988), 187.

96. Ibid., 123–25.

97. Steve Young, in conversation.

98. Naomi Schor, in Schor and Weed, *Essential Difference*, vii.

99. Teresa de Lauretis, "The Essence of the Triangle, or, Taking the Risk of Essentialism Seriously: Feminist Theory in Italy, the J.S., and Britain," in Schor and Weed, *Essential Difference*, 1.

100. De Lauretis, "The Essence," 33.

101. Susan Bordo, "Feminism," 134f.

102. Butler, *Gender Trouble*, 31.

103. Chung Hyun Kyung, *Struggle to Be the Sun Again* (Maryknoll, N.Y.: Orbis, 1990); Rita Nakashima Brock, *Journeys by Heart* (New York: Crossroad, 1988); Cherríe Moraga, "From a Long Line of Vendidas: Chicanas and Feminism," 189–90, in *Feminist Studies/Critical Studies*, edited by Teresa de Lauretis (Bloomington: Indiana University Press, 1986).

104. bell hooks, *Yearning: Race, Gender, and Cultural Politics* (Boston: South End Press, 1990) 133.

105. Ibid., 133 (my emphasis).

106. "A Women's Creed," Beijing Preparatory Documents, Women's Global Strategies meeting *Working Group Reports* (2 December 1994), 1–2. Prepared in relation to the UN Summit on Social Development, this "creed" was written by a white North American poet, Robin Morgan, in collaboration with several third world women at a meeting at Glen Cove, N.Y., sponsored by the Women's Environment and Development Organization, 29 November–2 December 1994.

107. Alice Jardine, "Julia Kristeva [Interview]," in Russell Ferguson, William Olander, Marcia Tucker, and Karen Fisk, eds. *Discourses: Conversations in Postmodern Art and Culture* (Cambridge: MIT Press, 1990), 84.

108. "Women's Creed."

109. Ibid.

110. Alfred North Whitehead, *Process and Reality* (New York: Free Press, 1929), 137; Whitehead, *Science and the Modern World* (New York: Free Press/MacMillan, 1925; 1967), chap. 3.

111. See Bill McKibben, *The End of Nature* (New York: Random House, 1989).

7. Spirit

1. Alfred North Whitehead, *Process and Reality* (New York: Free Press, 1929), 348.

2. Dennis R. MacDonald, "There Is No Male and Female," *Harvard Dissertations in Religion*, no. 20 (Philadelphia: Fortress, 1987).

3. G.W.F. Hegel, *Encyclopedia of the Philosophical Science* no. 381 Zusatz, cited in P. C. Hodgson, *God in History* (Nashville: Abingdon, 1989), 112.

4. Process theology conceives of "the divine element in the universe" as a lure to feeling and thus to a realization of novel possibilities, actualized through the resolutions of contradictions into contrasts. See Whitehead, *Process and Reality.*

5. Lecture by Otto Maduro at Drew University, February 1995.

6. From Denise Levertov, "Beginners."

7. Presuming upon the remaining natural resources of a tiny land whose earth, water, and air already suffer worse degradation than any Latin American country but Haiti.

8. See comment on 1 John 4:1–2 in Herbert G. May and Bruce Metzger, *The New Oxford Annotated Bible, Revised Standard Version* (New York: Oxford, University Press, 1977): "Note the contrast between *spirits* (supernatural powers claimed by *false prophets*) and the Holy *Spirit.*"

9. Jürgen Moltmann, *The Spirit of Life* (Minneapolis: Fortress, 1992), 306ff; see also José Comblin, *The Holy Spirit and Liberation* (Maryknoll, N.Y.: Orbis, 1989), 164–75.

10. Comblin, *Holy Spirit,* 50 (my emphasis).

11. Sharon Betcher, without whom I might not be pneumatologizing at all, writes of the Spirit in its female-associated Western history in terms of the Kristevan abject. See her forthcoming Ph.D. dissertation, "Getting Grounded: Spirit Incarnate and the Kindling of Livelihood," Drew University, 1997.

12. T. S. Eliot, "Burnt Norton," *Four Quartets* (New York: Harcourt, Brace & World), 13.

13. Avery Dulles, *The Craft of Theology: From Symbol to System* (New York: Crossroad, 1992), 38.

14. Ibid., 8, 95.

15. Ibid., 73.

16. Anthony C. Thistelton, *New Horizons in Hermeneutics* (Grand Rapids: Zondervan, 1992), 578.

17. "The meaning of Scripture must be communicated by the Spirit of God in a revelatory action whose fruit in us is Christian knowledge, 'gnosis' " (Yves Congar, quoted in Dulles, *Craft,* 74).

18. Dulles, *Craft,* 38.

19. Ode 28:8, *The Odes of Solomon,* ed. and trans. J. H. Charlesworth (Oxford: Clarendon Press, 1973), 109.

20. Reproduced in David Harvey, *The Condition of Postmodernity* (Cambridge, Mass.: Blackwell, 1989), 43.

21. Laleen Jayamanne, Leslie Thornton, and Trinh T. Minh-ha, "If upon Leaving What We Have to Say We Speak: A Conversation Piece," in *Discourses: Conversations in Postmodern Art and Culture,* ed. Russell Ferguson, William Olander, Marcia Tucker, and Karen Fisk (Cambridge: MIT Press, 1990), 55.

22. "Togetherness" was a term coined by Whitehead as a way of expressing the constitutive character of relations, as collected in the form of "actual occasions," i.e., the momentary individuals which are the subjects of the process cosmos (see Whitehead, *Process and Reality*).

23. Moltmann, *Spirit,* 178f.

24. Ibid.

25. Vítor Westhelle, "Creation Motifs in the Search for a Vital Space," in *Lift Every Voice: Constructing Christian Theologies from the Underside,* ed. Susan Brooks Thistlethwaite and Mary Potter Engel (San Francisco: Harper & Row, 1990), 128–140.

26. Jayamanne et al., "If upon leaving," 49.

27. Glen Mazis, *Earthbodies*, forthcoming.

28. Women's Environment and Development Organization.

29. See the Gospel of Thomas: "Split a piece of wood and I am there. Lift up the stone, and you will find me there" (Logion 77), in *The Nag Hammadi Library*, ed. James Robinson (San Francisco: Harper & Row, 1977), 126.

30. David Bohm, *Wholeness and the Implicate Order* (London: Ark/Routledge, 1980).

31. See Augustine, "On the Trinity," *The Works of St. Augustine* (Peabody: Hendrickson, 1994), 126.

32. Moltmann, *Spirit*, 219.

33. Ibid., 219; 221.

34. Michael Welker, *God the Spirit* (Minneapolis: Fortress, 1994).

35. Ibid., 220.

36. Welker seems rather to be attempting to pneumatologize Christ (like Moltmann) and (less like Moltmann) to thereby emphasize the "multipresence" of the Spirit. Yet as long as the plurality of spirit manifestations remains identifiable with "the Spirit's diverse acts of making Christ present," the drive to either baptize or demonize any extra-Christian spirit phenomenon will tend to overpower the incipient christo-pluralism.

37. Welker, *God the Spirit*, 227.

38. Ibid.

39. Ibid., 315.

40. Catherine Keller, *From a Broken Web* (Boston: Beacon, 1986), 167ff.

41. James Hillman, *Dream and the Underworld* (New York: Harper & Row, 1979), 41.

42. Adrienne Rich, "Natural Resources," in *The Fact of a Doorframe: Poems Selected and New, 1950–1984* (New York: Norton, 1975, 1978), 264.

43. Ode 19, *The Odes of Solomon*, 82.

44. Mary Daly, *Gyn/Ecology* (Boston: Beacon, 1978), 38.

45. Elizabeth A. Johnson, *She Who Is* (New York: Crossroad, 1992).

46. See n. 60, below.

47. Johnson, *She Who Is*, 143.

48. Ibid.

49. Sharon V. Betcher has sharpened for me the importance of distinguishing Spirit from Wisdom, contrary to a feminist trend exemplified by Elizabeth Johnson, both to keep Spirit "grounded" in the finite flesh and to guard it from absorption as an attribute of "God."

50. Paula Gunn Allen, *The Sacred Hoop* (Boston: Beacon, 1992), 13; Johnson, *She Who Is*, 132, n. 20.

51. "In profound ways a mother and her child are continuous. For nine months they are physically one in ways which are impossible for the male to imitate. If the desire is to represent a transcendent God, the male terms are the only alternative" (John N. Oswalt, "Why We Don't Call God Mother," in *Good News*, January/February 1995, 16).

52. Paul Tillich, *Dynamics of Faith* (New York: Harper Bros.: 1958).

53. Moltmann, *Spirit*, 34.

54. After diligently exposing "the origin of the way heretics closely observe the use of prepositions," Basil had to settle for a compromised "*and* the Holy Spirit" (St. Basil the Great, *On the Holy Spirit* [Crestwood, N. Y.: St. Vladimir's Seminary Press, 1980], 18ff).

55. Judith Butler, *Gender Trouble* (New York: Routledge, 1990), 33.

56. Luce Irigaray, *This Sex Which Is Not One* (Ithaca: Cornell University Press, 1985), 28.

57. Ibid., 76.

58. Luce Irigaray, "Divine Women," in *Sexes and Genealogies*, trans. G. Gill (New York: Columbia, 1993), 60.

59. Ibid., 62.

60. "For in her there is a spirit that is intelligent, holy, unique, manifold, subtle, mobile, clear, unpolluted. . . . For wisdom is more mobile than any motion; because of her pureness she pervades and penetrates all things" (Wisdom of Solomon, *The New Oxford Bible with the Apocrypha*, Revised Standard Version, 7:22).

61. Claudia V. Camp, "Wise and Strange: An Interpretation of the Female Imagery In Proverbs In Light of Trickster Mythology," *Semeia* 42 (1988): 18f.

62. Ibid., 33.

63. Ibid., 34.

64. Charles Hartshorne, *Omnipotence and Other Theological Mistakes* (Albany: State University of New York Press, 1984); David Ray Griffin, *God, Power, and Evil* (Philadelphia: Westminster, 1976).

65. G. W. F. Hegel, *The Phenomenology of Spirit*, trans. A. V. Miller (New York: Oxford University Press, 1977), 6–7.

66. "The Thunder, Perfect Mind" (6:2), in *Nag Hammadi*, 271–277.

67. Quoted as an epigraph to Toni Morrison's *Jazz* and to Julie Dash's film *Daughters of the Dust*.

68. Rich, "Natural Resources," 67.

69. Mary Daly, *Pure Lust* (Boston: Beacon, 1984), 227; see also Luce Irigaray, *Elemental Passions*, trans. Joanne Collie, (New York: Routledge, 1982).

Index

der, 264; and individualism, 201,
210–12, 213, 215; and mutuality,
207, 209, 213, 215, 217–19, 222; and
premillennialism, 56; and radical feminism, 257; and revolu-
tion, 277, 278, 292–96; and
socialism, 183, 202, 206–8, 213;
and spirit, 292–96
Comstock Law, 239
Comte, Auguste, 117
Condorcet, Marquis de, 165, 166, 204
Cone, James, 200–201
Confessions (Augustine), 101–2, 135
Constantine, 19, 96, 97, 142, 232
Constitution (United States), 203
consumerism, 169
Contract Social, Le (Rousseau), 203
contradiction, 67
convivencia, 222
Corinthians, 45, 94, 209, 221
Cornell, Drucilla, 224
corpus christi, 221
Cortés, Hernando, 158
Cosmas of Praque, 185
Council of Nicaea, 97
counter-apocalypse, 19–32, 34, 51, 63,
83, 273–310; and Daly, 248–49;
and de/colon/izing spaces, 145–
46, 168–72, 174–75; and dis/clo-
sure, 19–20, 23–25, 27–32, 34; and
gender, 227, 248–49, 259–60, 262,
268; and time, experience of, 86,
98–99, 112, 114–15, 121, 124–25, 127,
130–31, 133, 135–36, 138; and the
Universal Publick Friend, 237;
and visions of community, 182,
196, 201, 212, 215–19, 221–22
countercultures, 110–11
creatio ex nihilo, doctrine of, 172
Cromwell, Oliver, 193
Crossan, John Dominic, 48, 51, 91,
318*n42*
Crusades, 162

cryptoapocalypse, 8–9, 29, 57, 84,
261; and de/colon/izing spaces,
166, 148; and gender, 225, 253,
259; and visions of community,
209, 219
Cuba, 158

D'Ailly, Pierre, 160
Dallas school, 56
Daly, Mary, 40–41, 67, 227, 260–61,
268; the Antichrist in, 112, 244–
45; chairman of the Bored in,
103, 268; dismissal of the Holy
Spirit by, 297; distinction
between patriarchy and men in,
253; and essentialism and separatism, 262; on gender and the
image of God, 297; *Gyn/Ecology*,
245; Otherworld in, 247, 303;
revolting hag in, 229; and the second wave of feminism, 244–48,
253; and Thistlethwaite, 258, 259;
and time, conceptualization of,
103, 119; use of allegory by, 77;
and Wittig, 249–50
Darby, 242
Darwinism, 242
Day of Judgment, 18, 51
Dead Sea Scrolls, 78
death, 42, 71, 81, 143, 277; fight to the,
xiii; in Heidegger, 85, 133; and
spirit, 234, 296, 306; and time,
experience of, 84–85, 90, 101, 133,
137
DeBerg, Betty, 240, 242–43
De Bonald, 166
deep, the, 301–2, 304
deferral, 59, 169; desire and, dualism
of, 106; and time, experience of,
91, 95, 106, 116, 135
Delaunay, Sonia, 31
De Lauretis, Teresa, 262–63
Demar, Claire, 228–29